Kings Cross Station
St Pancras International Station

CORAM'S FIELDS
page 132

FINSBURY

SHOREDITCH

BETHNAL GREEN

HOXTON

OLD STREET

CLERKENWELL

page 132

Farringdon Station

...ish ...um

...OMSBURY

Smithfield Market

page 136

page 100

City (Thameslink) Station

St Paul's Cathedral

THE CITY

...ne Market

WHITECHAPEL

Fenchurch St Station

COVENT GARDEN

Covent Garden Market

Somerset House

Blackfriars Station

Cannon Street Station

Charing Cross Station

Thames

Shakespeare's Globe Theatre

Tower of London

Royal Festival Hall

National Theatre

Tate Modern

HMS Belfast

Tower Bridge

page 160

SOUTHWARK

GLA City Hall

...TEHALL

London Eye

Southbank Centre

County Hall

Waterloo East Station

Waterloo Station

Borough Market

London Bridge Station

Palace of Westminster
...inster ...ey

page 184-5

BERMONDSEY

...ST...ER

Lambeth Palace

Imperial War Museum

ELEPHANT AND CASTLE

THE BOROUGH

Wealdstone

M1

Kenwood House

Highgate Cemetery

Haringey

Wembley

Hampstead

Haskney

Olympic Site

Ifford

Wembley Stadium ★

Camden

Islington

Brent

REGENT'S PARK

Madame Tussauds ★

Newnham

Beckton

Ealing

Notting Hill

St Paul's Cathedral ★

Tower of London ★

Blackwall Tunnel

London (City)

Vauxhall Station

Kensington Palace ★

HYDE PARK

Buckingham Palace ★

Big Ben ★

Docklands

The O2 (North Greenwich Arena) ★

Woolwich Ferry

Thames Barrier

VAUXHALL

Hammersmith and Fulham

London Wetlands Centre ★

BATTERSEA PARK

Westminster Abbey ★

Lambeth

Woolwich

...te ...in

Kew Gardens ★

Richmond upon Thames

Putney

Greenwich

Lewisham

BUSHY PARK

RICHMOND PARK

Wimbledon Common

Wandsworth

Clapham

Horniman Museum ★

Twickenham

Kingston upon Thames

Wimbledon

Streatham

Sydenham

Crystal Palace ★

Hampton Court Palace ★

Merton

Mitcham

0        2 miles
0      2 km

**Greater London**

D1111194

# INSIGHT GUIDES
# LONDON

APA PUBLICATIONS L

Part of the Langenscheidt Publishing Group

## ✷ INSIGHT GUIDES

# LONDON

*Series Editor*
**Rachel Lawrence**
*Project Editor*
**Catherine Dreghorn**
*Picture Researcher*
**Tom Smyth**
*Cartography Manager*
**Zoë Goodwin**
*Publishing Manager*
**Rachel Fox**

---

### Distribution

*UK & Ireland*
**Dorling Kindersley Ltd, a Penguin Group company**
80 Strand, London WC2R 0RL, UK
customerservice@dk.com

*United States*
**Ingram Publisher Services**
One Ingram Blvd, PO Box 3006
La Vergne, TN 37086-1986
customer.service@ingrampublisher services.com

*Australia*
**Universal Publishers**
PO Box 307
St Leonards, NSW 1590
sales@universalpublishers.com.au

*Worldwide*
**Apa Publications GmbH & Co. Verlag KG (Singapore branch)**
7030 Ang Mo Kio Ave 5,
08-65 Northstar @ AMK,
Singapore 569880
apasin@singnet.com.sg

---

### Printing

**CTPS - China**

---

©2012 Apa Publications (UK) Ltd
*All Rights Reserved*

*First Edition 1989*
*Thirteenth Edition 2012*

**www.insightguides.com**

# ABOUT THIS BOOK

What makes an Insight Guide different? Since our first book pioneered the use of creative full-colour photography in travel guides in 1970, we have aimed to provide not only reliable information but also the key to a real understanding of a destination and its people.

Now, when the internet can supply inexhaustible (but not always reliable) facts, our books marry text and pictures to pro-vide that more elusive quality: knowledge. To achieve this, they rely on the authority of locally based writers and photographers.

This book turns the spotlight on a city that continues to change dramatically. Construction has begun on the Crossrail railway, a considerable addition to the city's transport network, The Savoy hotel has reopened after a three year and £100million refurbish-ment, Southwark and the South Bank have been transformed, and the regeneration of the long-neglected East End, the main focus for the 2012 Olympics, continues. *Insight Guide London* covers all this, and much more.

---

## CONTACTING THE EDITORS

*We would appreciate it if readers would alert us to errors or outdated information by writing to:*

**Insight Guides, P.O. Box 7910, London SE1 1WE, England.**
insight@apaguide.co.uk

## THE CONTRIBUTORS

This fully updated edition of *Insight Guide London* was commissioned and edited by **Catherine Dreghorn**, Assistant Editor in Insight's London editorial office.

London's rate of change continues apace, helped in no small part by recent events: the continuing economic reces-sion occasioned by the "credit crunch", the wedding of Prince William to Kate Middleton at Westminster Abbey, the build-up to the 2012 Olympics and the Queen's Diamond Jubilee.

The entire book has therefore been comprehensively updated by **Rebecca Ford**, an award-winning travel journalist who lives in London and who writes extensively about Britain. She writes for various national newspapers, magazines and guidebooks, on everything from rail-way journeys and wildlife to food, drink and spas. As well as updating the text, she penned the new feature on the royal wedding.

The thirteenth edition of this book builds on previous editions produced by **Rachel Lawrence, Dorothy Stannard, Brian Bell, Roger Williams** and **Andrew Eames.** Past contributors whose work is still evident here include **Roland Collins** (history), **Srinvasa Rao** (Who Lives in London?), **Allison Lobbett** and **Tim Grimwade**. The design was created by **Klaus Geisler** and the principal photographer was London-based **Ming Tang-Evans**, a regular contributor to Insight Guides. **Glyn Genin** also contributed images. **James Macdonald** was the cartography editor for this guide.

The book was proof-read by **Catherine Jackson** and the index compiled by **Liz Cook**.

**4**

# THE GUIDE AT A GLANCE

The book is carefully structured both to convey an understanding of the city and its culture and to guide readers through its attractions and activities:

◆ The Best Of section at the front of the book helps you to prioritise. The first spread contains the Top Sights, while Editor's Choice details unique experiences, the best buys or other recommendations.

◆ To understand London, you need to know something of its past. The city's history and culture are described in authoritative essays written by specialists in their fields who have lived in and documented the city for many years.

◆ The Places section details all the attractions worth seeing. The main places of interest are coordinated by number with the maps.

◆ A list of recommended restaurants, bars and cafés is printed at the end of each chapter.

◆ Photographs throughout the book are chosen not only to illustrate geography and buildings, but also to convey the moods of the city and the life of its people.

◆ The Travel Tips section includes all the practical information you will need, divided into five key sections: transport, accommodation, shopping, activities (including nightlife, events, sports and tours) and an A–Z of practical tips. Information may be located quickly by using the index on the back cover flap of the book.

◆ A detailed street atlas is included at the back of the book, complete with a full index. You will find all the restaurants and hotels plotted for your convenience.

## PLACES & SIGHTS

**Colour-coding** at the top of every page makes it easy to find each area in the book. The colours correspond with those on the orientation map on pages 66–7.

**A locator map** pinpoints the specific area covered in each chapter. The page reference at the top indicates where to find a detailed map of the area highlighted in red.

**Margin tips** provide extra little snippets of information, whether it's a practical tip, a whimsical quote, an historical fact or advice on shopping and eating or things to do with children.

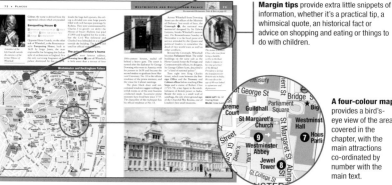

**A four-colour map** provides a bird's-eye view of the area covered in the chapter, with the main attractions co-ordinated by number with the main text.

## PHOTO FEATURES

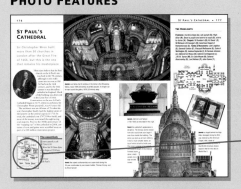

**Photo Features** offer visual coverage of London's major sights. The map shows the sight's location, while "The essentials" panel conveys practical information: address, contact details, website, opening times, and whether there's a charge.

## RESTAURANT LISTINGS

**Restaurant listings** feature the best establishments within each area, giving the address, phone number, opening times and price category followed by a review. The grid reference refers to the atlas at the back of the book.

### Sarastro
126 Drury Lane, WC2
☎ 7836 0101; www.
sarastro-restaurant.com
⏰ L & D daily. ££–£££
[p319, E2]
"The show after the show" is this restaurant's slogan. The flam-

## TRAVEL TIPS

**Advice-packed Travel Tips** provide all the practical knowledge you'll need before and during your trip: how to get there, getting around, where to stay and what to do. The A–Z section is a handy summary of practical information, arranged alphabetically.

## Contents

### Best of London

**Top Sights**        **8**

The British Museum . . . . . . . . **144**
Buckingham Palace . . . . . . . . **80**
The Houses of Parliament . . . . **75**
The London Eye . . . . . . . . . **186**
Piccadilly Circus . . . . . . . . . . **89**
St Paul's Cathedral . . . . . . **176**
Tate Modern . . . . . . . . . . . **198**
Tower Bridge . . . . . . . . . . . **195**
The Tower of London . . . . . . **178**
Trafalgar Square and the
   National Gallery . . . . . . . . **99**

**Editor's Choice**        **10**

### Introduction

Guide at a Glance . . . . . . . . . . . . . . . . . . . . **4**
London's Allure . . . . . . . . . . . . . . . . . . . . **19**
Who Lives in London? . . . . . . . . . . . . . **21**

### History

The Making of London . . . . . . . . . . . . . . **27**
Decisive Dates . . . . . . . . . . . . . . . . . . . . . . **36**

### Features

Theatreland . . . . . . . . . . . . . . . . . . . . . . . . **42**
Eating Out . . . . . . . . . . . . . . . . . . . . . . . . . **46**
Retail Therapy . . . . . . . . . . . . . . . . . . . . . **52**
Markets . . . . . . . . . . . . . . . . . . . . . . . . . . **54**
The Architectural Legacy . . . . . . . . . . **56**

### Insights

**Mini Features:**
How Parliament Works . . . . . . . . . . . . . **74**
The Royal Wedding . . . . . . . . . . . . . . . . . . **92**
Blue Plaques . . . . . . . . . . . . . . . . . . . . . . **138**
The 2012 Olympics . . . . . . . . . . . . . . . . **252**
**Photo Features:**
Westminster Abbey . . . . . . . . . . . . . . . . . **86**
National Gallery . . . . . . . . . . . . . . . . . . . **108**
National Portrait Gallery . . . . . . . . . **110**
London's Parks . . . . . . . . . . . . . . . . . . . . **122**
Madame Tussauds . . . . . . . . . . . . . . . . **132**
The British Museum . . . . . . . . . . . . . . **144**
St Paul's Cathedral . . . . . . . . . . . . . . **176**
The Tower of London . . . . . . . . . . . . . . **178**
Tate Modern . . . . . . . . . . . . . . . . . . . . . . **198**
The Imperial War Museum . . . . . . **200**
The Science Museum . . . . . . . . . . . . **214**
Victoria and Albert Museum . . . **216**
The Natural History Museum . . **218**

## Places

Orientation .............................. **65**
■ Westminster and
    Buckingham Palace ...... **71**
■ Soho and Chinatown .......... **89**
■ Trafalgar Square
    and Covent Garden ........ **99**
■ Mayfair to Oxford Street .... **113**
■ Marylebone and Fitzrovia **125**
  Bloomsbury ..................... **135**
■ Holborn and the
    Inns of Court .............. **150**
■ St Paul's and the City ...... **159**
■ Southwark and
    the South Bank ............ **183**
■ Knightsbridge, Kensington
    & Notting Hill ................ **203**
  Chelsea ........................ **221**
  Village London
  West London ................... **234**
■ North London ................. **242**
■ East London .................... **250**
■ South London ................. **256**
■ Day Trips ........................ **267**

## Restaurants & Bars

Westminster ........................... **85**
Soho and Chinatown ................ **95**
Trafalgar Square and
  Covent Garden ................. **106**
Mayfair to Oxford Street .......... **120**
Marylebone and Fitzrovia ...... **130**
Bloomsbury and King's Cross **142**
Holborn and the Inns of Court **157**
St Paul's and the City ........... **174**
Southwark and South Bank .... **196**
Knightsbridge & Kensington .... **212**
Chelsea .............................. **228**
West London ........................ **241**
North London ........................ **248**
East London ........................ **255**
South London ....................... **263**
Day Trips .............................. **273**

## Travel Tips

### TRANSPORT
Getting There **276**
Getting Around **278**
Trips Out of London **280**

### ACCOMMODATION
Choosing a Hotel **281**
Westminster and Victoria **283**
Soho and Covent Garden **284**
St James's and Mayfair **285**
Marylebone, Bloomsbury and
  Holborn **287**
The City and Canary Wharf **288**
Southwark and South Bank **288**
Knightsbridge, Kensington and
  Chelsea **289**
Outside the Centre **290**
Excursions **291**

### SHOPPING
Antiques **292**
Art **293**
Books **293**
China and Glass **293**
Clothing and Footwear **294**
Men's Clothes **295**
Department Stores **295**
Food and Drink **296**
Gifts and Souvenirs **296**
Jewellery **297**
Specialist Shops **297**
Markets **297**

### ACTIVITIES
The Arts **298**
Nightlife **300**
Calendar of Events **302**
Sport **305**
Tours **306**

### A–Z of PRACTICAL INFORMATION
**308**

### Maps
Map Legend **317**
Street Atlas **318**
Street Atlas Index **336**
London **inside front cover**
Central London **68–9**
Westminster and
  Buckingham Palace **72**
Soho and Chinatown **90**
Trafalgar Square and
  Covent Garden **100**
Mayfair to Oxford Street **114**
Marylebone and Fitzrovia **126**
Bloomsbury and King's Cross
  **136**
Holborn and the
  Inns of Court **152**
St Paul's and the City **160**
Southwark and South Bank
  **184–5**
Knightsbridge, Kensington
  and Notting Hill **204**
Chelsea **222**
Village London
  **230–1**
East London **251**
Day Trips **268**
Tube map
  **back cover**

# THE BEST OF LONDON: TOP SIGHTS

At a glance, everything you won't want to miss, from long-established icons like Tower Bridge and Big Ben to exciting newer landmarks such as Tate Modern and the London Eye

▽ **Big Ben and the Houses of Parliament**
The clock tower of this flamboyant Gothic-style building is a symbol of London. Guided tours of the Houses of Parliament can be arranged during the summer recess in August and September.
*See page 75*

△ **Buckingham Palace**
The best time to see the palace is during the Changing of the Guard. If you would like to see inside, then you must time your visit to coincide with the Queen's annual trip to Balmoral (late July–Sept) when some of the State Rooms of the palace open for guided tours.
*See page 80*

◁ **The London Eye**
For the best views in London take a trip on the London Eye on the South Bank. The stately wheel takes 30 minutes to rotate, allowing plenty of time for picking out London's sights. On a fine day you will be able to see for 25 miles (40km).
*See page 186*

◁ **Trafalgar Square**
London's best-loved square has shooting fountains and Nelson's Column and is over-looked by the National Gallery. *See page 99*

▷ **Piccadilly Circus**
Presiding over this gateway to the West End and Theatreland is the famous statue of Eros. *See page 89*

▽ **Tate Modern**
For modern art in an inspired setting, visit this power station-turned-art-gallery on the South Bank. *See page 198*

◁ **St Paul's Cathedral**
Built after the Great Fire of London of 1666, St Paul's is Christopher Wren's greatest work. *See page 176*

▷ **The British Museum**
This immense museum contains some of the world's most important treasures from antiquity. *See page 144*

▽ **Tower Bridge**
The famous bascule bridge is a triumph of Victorian engineering. *See page 195*

▷ **Tower of London**
Established by William the Conqueror, the Tower has a long and bloody history. *See page 178*

# THE BEST OF LONDON: EDITOR'S CHOICE

Here are our ideas on what to do once you've seen London's top sights, plus some tips and tricks even Londoners won't always know

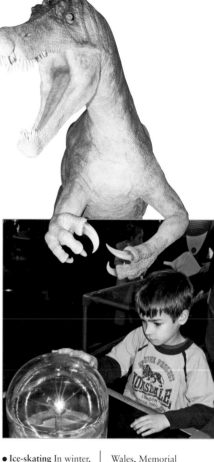

## BEST FOR CHILDREN

● **Look and learn** The **Darwin Centre**, in the **Natural History Museum**, allows children to examine specimens and watch scientists at work. Next door, the **Science Museum** has **Who Am I?**, a great hands-on section. *See pages 218 and 214.*

● **Museum of Childhood** This outpost of the V&A appeals to adults and children alike. *See page 251.*

● **On the Wild Side** London Zoo in Regent's Park is one of the world's top zoos. *See page 128.*

● **The London Aquarium** Sharks, seahorses, touch pools and much more. *See page 185.*

● **The River Thames** Moored on

the Thames, **HMS** *Belfast*, a World War II battleship, is suitable for older children *(see page 194).* Younger ones will enjoy the piratical-looking *Golden Hinde*, a replica of Sir Francis Drake's ship *(see page 192).* Or take a tour on a **Duck**, an amphibious vessel used in WWII. *See page 315.*

● **Madame Tussauds** Teenagers love spotting their favourite celebrities, even if they are made of wax. *See pages 132–3.*

● **London Dungeon** Scary fun ideal for 10–14-year-olds. *See page 194.*

● **London Transport Museum** A huge hit with younger children. *See page 105.*

● **Ice-skating** In winter, ice rinks spring up outside the Natural History Museum and Somerset House. *See pages 206 and 150.*

● **Playgrounds** Best is the Diana, Princess of

Wales, Memorial Playground with its pirate ship and teepees. *See page 211.*

● **Toy shops** Visit **Hamleys** in Regent Street or **Harrods**. *See pages 119 and 204.*

**ABOVE:** animatronic dinosaur in the Natural History Museum and hands-on fun at the Science Museum. **LEFT:** Hamleys' bears.

## BEST VIEWS

- **The London Eye**
Unbeatable vistas
whichever way you
look. *See page 186.*
- **Monument** Climb the
311 steps for views
over the City. *See
page 172.*
- **Waterloo Bridge**
Panoramas day and
night. *See page 187.*
- **Westminster Cathedral**
Take the lift to the top
of the 330ft (100 me-
tre) tower. *See page 79.*
- **One New Change**
The sixth floor of this
new shopping centre
offers stunning views
of St Paul's Cathedral.
*See page 172.*

- **Richmond Hill**
The view from here is
protected by an act of
Parliament.
*See page 238.*
- **Parliament Hill**
Far-reaching views
across London.
*See page 245.*
- **Restaurants and bars
with views** include
the Tate Modern
**Restaurant** *(see page
197)*, the **Oxo Tower
Restaurant** *(see above
picture and page
196)*, **La Pont de la
Tour** *(see page 197)*,
**Babylon** *(see page
213)* and **Vertigo 42**
*(see page 175).*

## BEST WALKS

- **Old and new London**
An introductory
walk, starting from
Westminster Abbey,
crossing Westminster
Bridge, strolling
along the South Bank
past the London Eye,
Tate Modern and
Shakespeare's Globe,
and then crossing
the Millennium
Bridge to St Paul's
Cathedral.
*See pages 77–8,
186–191 and 159.*
- **Hampstead Heath**
Meadows, woods,
lakes and ponds,
with great views
over London.
*See page 245.*

- **Hyde Park and
Kensington Gardens**
Sculptures, foun-
tains, gardens and
playgrounds in the
centre of the city. *See
pages 210–11.*
- **Regent's Canal**
Walk all or part of
the 14km (8½ miles)
from Paddington to
Limehouse, taking in
Camden Lock and
Little Venice. *See
page 244.*
- **Richmond**
Offers fabulous
views, a deer park,
interesting pubs and
17th-century Ham
House. *See pages
238–9.*

**RIGHT:** one of the city's "green lungs".
**BELOW:** the famous Harrods department
store has seven floors of luxury products.

## ONLY IN LONDON

- **Harrods** The store
that has everything.
*See page 204.*
- **Shakespeare's Globe**
The play's the thing,
as in Elizabethan
days. *See page 190.*
- **Royal Pageantry**
The Changing the
Guard ceremony at
Buckingham Palace
takes place daily at
11.30am May–July

(alternate days rest of
year). *See page 82.*
- **Pearly Kings and
Queens** You'll spot
these colourful
characters at East
End festivals and
markets. *See page 22.*
- **The V&A**
The world's largest
collection of decora-
tive arts. *See pages
206 and 216–7.*

## HISTORIC PUBS

- **The George** This pub off Borough High Street, rebuilt in 1676, is London's only galleried coaching inn. *See page 197.*
- **Black Friar** Built in 1875 on the site of the Black Friars Monastery, this is London's only Arts and Crafts pub. The marble interior carries bronze friezes depicting the activities of monks. *See page 156.*
- **Lamb and Flag** Traditional pub tucked down a tiny alleyway in the heart of Covent Garden. *See page 107.*
- **The Grenadier** Hidden away in a quiet cobbled mews, this pub used to be the mess of the Duke of Wellington's officers. *See page 229.*
- **Jerusalem Tavern** Once an 18th-century coffee shop, this is now an intimate pub with cubicles, Georgian-style furniture and ales from Suffolk's St Peter's Brewery. *See page 175.*
- **The Mayflower** It was by this waterside pub in Rotherhithe that the Pilgrim Fathers moored their ship before setting off for Plymouth and thence the New World in 1620. *See page 195.*
- **Ye Old Cheshire Cheese** Famous olde-worlde pub off Fleet Street, rebuilt after the Great Fire but retaining a medieval crypt. Frequented by many well-known literary figures in the past, including Charles Dickens and Dr Samuel Johnson. *See page 155.*

## DISTINCTIVE HOTELS

- **The Savoy** Grand riverside hotel near Covent Garden, re-opened after a £100 million refurbishment. *See page 284.*
- **Brown's** Intimate luxury in the heart of Mayfair. *See page 285.*
- **The Goring** Where Kate Middleton spent the night before THAT wedding. *See page 283.*
- **Hazlitt's** An 18th-century property in Soho. *See page 284.*

## SUMMER IN THE CITY

- **River Cruises** Cruise down to Greenwich or the Thames Barrier, or up to Hampton Court Palace. *See page 307.*
- **Open-air drama** Watch Shakespeare at the Globe Theatre on the South Bank or in Regent's Park. *See pages 190 and 128.*
- **The City in Bloom** See whole gardens recreated at the **Chelsea Flower Show** held in late May in Chelsea or visit the lovely **Rose Garden** (June through to late autumn) in Regent's Park. *See pages 225 and 127.*
- **Sporting Greats** See tennis played at Wimbledon and cricket played at Lord's. *See page 305.*
- **Cool off** Swim in the bathing ponds on Hampstead Heath, in the Serpentine in Hyde Park, or in the Oasis, a heated outdoor pool, in Holborn. *See page 306.*
- **Picnic in the Park** London's parks, such as Green Park or St James's Park, are great for lunching al fresco. *See page 80.*

**ABOVE:** enjoying a drink in The George's cobbled courtyard.
**FAR RIGHT:** dancer at Notting Hill Carnival, held on the last weekend in August; the Trooping the Colour ceremony celebrating the Queen's official birthday in June.

● **Lord Mayor's Show** The Lord Mayor rides out in his gilded coach from the Guildhall to the Law Courts. Second Saturday in November.
● **Last Night of the Proms** Exuberant finale to the annual

BBC-sponsored Henry Wood Promenade Concerts in the Albert Hall and Hyde Park. Held on a Saturday night in mid-September.

*For a full listing of festivals see pages 302–5.*

## BEST FESTIVALS

● **Notting Hill Carnival** This is Europe's biggest street festival, with Caribbean bands, extravagant costumes and floats. Held over the last weekend in August.
● **Chinese New Year** Dancing dragons and exotic food in

Soho's Chinatown. Late January/early February.
● **Trooping the Colour** The Queen rides out on Horse Guards Parade, with the Household Cavalry in red tunics and bearskin hats. The Saturday closest to 10 June.

## MONEY-SAVING TIPS

**Half-price Theatre Tickets** The tkts booth in Leicester Square sells same-day tickets for West End shows at up to 50 percent off, plus a £3 service fee (Mon–Sat 10am–7pm, Sun 11am–4pm). There is another branch in the Brent Cross shopping centre in north London (Mon–Fri 10am–1.30pm, 2–4.30pm, Sat 10am–7pm, Sun noon–1.30pm, 2–4.30pm; www.tkts.co.uk). Tickets for some plays at the National Theatre can be purchased for £12 through the Travelex scheme *(see page 44 for details)*.

**Museums and Attractions** The national museums and galleries (including Tate Modern, Tate Britain, the National Gallery, National Portrait Gallery, British Museum, Science Museum, Natural History Museum, the Victoria and Albert Museum, Imperial War Museum and National Maritime Museum) are free. Most other museums and attractions have entrance charges. The London Pass allows free entry to some 55 attractions. At press time, prices for an adult pass ranged from £52 for a one-day pass (including travel on Tube and bus) to £135.50 for a six-day pass including travel (children under 15 £32/

£86.20). Details: tel: 0870 242 9988; www.londonpass.com.
**Public Transport** The Underground (Tube) is expensive compared with most European metro sytems, but money-saving Travelcards and Oyster cards are available. Children under the age of 11 can travel free on the network (as well as the Docklands Light Railway and buses), providing they are accompanied by an adult *(see page 278)*. Buses are quite a bit cheaper than the Tube and offer a sightseeing tour along the way. Alternatively walk – many places, especially in the West End, are closer than you might think.

# LONDON'S ALLURE

What attracts millions of visitors is a potent
mixture of continuity and tradition plus the
excitement of never knowing what they're
going to find round the next corner

Henry James described the capital as a "giant animated encyclopaedia
with people for pages". With all its variety and history, it's hard to
know where to start as a tourist, but James's emphasis is a good one.
Even though the immensity of London makes it hard to embrace as a whole
and you don't find long-time residents proclaiming their feelings through
"I ❤ London" stickers, the people and the culture matter as much as the
buildings. To most residents, the city is a collection of communities or villages, once independent but long since swallowed up, along with much
of the surrounding countryside, by the expanding metropolis.

At the centre of this patchwork city is a common area of shared London,
a London of work and play. This book deals primarily with shared London, the essential London of the West End, the City and South Bank, but it
also covers some of the interesting local "villages" such as Hampstead,
Islington, Greenwich and Brixton.

London, it is sometimes said, is as unrepresentative of the United Kingdom as New York is of the United States. There's some truth in this. Both
cities have astonishingly cosmopolitan populations, their restaurants are
almost as diverse as their immigrants, they are important centres of international finance, they pioneer the latest fashions, and their range of shops
and theatres is absurdly disproportionate to their size.

But London is umbilically linked to the rest of Britain in some crucial
respects. Unlike New York, it is a capital city, spawning governmental institutions. It is also an ancient city, dating back to Roman times. Foreign forces
have not occupied it since the Normans arrived in 1066 and, although it
was bombed during World War II, most of its iconic buildings survived.

As a result, it exudes a palpable sense of the nation's history. You can
walk in the footsteps of Shakespeare, or Dickens, or Churchill. You can
journey along the Thames, as Henry VIII did. You can visit the room in
the Tower of London where Sir Francis Drake lived out his last days. You
can drink in the pubs where Dr Samuel Johnson drank in the 18th century.
You can sit in the reading room where Karl Marx studied. This book will
show you how to do all these things, and more.                            ❑

---

**PRECEDING PAGES:** St Martin-in-the-Fields with Trafalgar Square in the foreground; Tate
Modern from the Millennium Bridge. **LEFT:** street in Shad Thames, southeast London.

# WHO LIVES IN LONDON?

**There have been racial tensions, even riots. But the city has absorbed many waves of immigrants and, with more than a quarter of central London's population born outside the UK, is a truly international metropolis**

**C**elts, Romans, Saxons, Angles, Jutes, Danes and Normans were the first to tumble into London's melting pot. The first Far Eastern immigrants arrived in 1579, followed by Indians, Huguenots, Irish and the dispossessed of eastern Europe. And always there was the tide of new blood from the rest of Britain, drawn to London by hopes of fame, fortune, anonymity, or simply a new start. Today, nearly one in three of London's 7½ million residents is from a minority ethnic group, and around 300 languages are spoken.

## The Cockney

Is there, then, any such thing as a "true" Londoner? Cockneys would seem to qualify, but being a cockney is as much a state of mind as it is a turn of phrase, and it is not exclusively

*The original definition of a cockney – someone born within the sound of Bow bells, the clarion of St Mary-le-Bow in Cheapside in the City – would today exclude most Londoners.*

genetic. Cockneys no longer need to be white and Anglo-Saxon; there are Italian, West Indian, Jewish and Pakistani cockneys. Nor do they necessarily have to be Londoners; the high cost of living has driven many out, and neigh-

**LEFT:** one of the many "faces" of London.
**RIGHT:** an excellent way to navigate London as mopeds are not subject to the congestion charge.

bouring towns such as Stevenage have large cockney populations. So what then makes a cockney? Certain traditions, being a member of an identifiable urban group, a distinctive language – and a quick sense of humour.

Cockney is a London accent with no use of the aspirant "h", the "t" in the middle of words such as "butter", or the final "g" in words ending "ing". Cockneys traditionally spoke in a rhyming slang said to have originated among barrow boys who didn't want their customers to understand their conversations. A "whistle" is a suit, short for whistle and flute, "trouble and strife" means wife; new slang terms are continually being invented. News vendors and market

## Century of immigration

In the 19th century the port of London was the largest in the world, and clippers such as the *Cutty Sark* had races to bring the year's first tea crops home from China. The Chinese community was in Limehouse, where Sherlock Holmes went to mull over his latest conundrums in the relaxing atmosphere of the opium dens. Ming Street, Peking Street and Mandarin Street are the sole legacy of the community that was heavily bombed in World War II. Today, Chinatown is around Gerrard Street in Soho. Here resident Chinese opened restaurants after the end of WWII to cater for British and US forces. Although the streets and annual New Year's festivities mark this out as the centre of London's Chinese population of 80,000, they live in all parts of the capital.

traders are often cockneys – they are shrewd, street-wise people, who prefer to work for themselves and who value freedom more than wealth. The aristocracy of the cockneys are the pearly kings and queens, whose suits are embroidered with mother-of-pearl buttons – a marketing gimmick in the 19th century and now worn at festivals (see www.pearlysociety.co.uk for events).

The traumas of 19th-century Europe led to the mass exodus of Jews, and east London

---

## THE LONDON CABBIE

Perhaps the closest most visitors get to meeting a true Londoner is when they catch a cab. Taxi drivers, or cabbies, are experts on the city, and are essential to its life, coursing through its veins in their black cells (not that all the cabs are black any more: advertising has turned some of them into perambulating billboards).

Cabbies take pride in their job, knowing that nowhere else in the world does a taxi driver need to know so much in order to qualify for a licence to work. Would-be drivers must spend up to four years learning London in minute detail (called "doing the Knowledge"). They do this by travelling the streets of the metropo-

lis on a moped, working out a multitude of routes from a clipboard mounted on the handlebars. Having acquired "the Knowledge", a driver must then pass a special driving test.

About 25,000 drivers work in London, of whom half are owner-drivers. The others either hire vehicles from the big fleets or work night shifts in someone else's cab. In all, there are more than 15,000 vehicles. The classic cab, known as the FX4, was launched in 1959 and some models are still going strong. The newer Metrocab, although more spacious, has taken a while to find the same place in customers' – and cabbies' – affections.

Only a small proportion of drivers are women, though the number is increasing. It is also very much a white, working-class occupation, and traditionally a large percentage of drivers are Jewish. Whatever their origins, most London taxi drivers, particularly the older ones, have a reputation for being garrulous.

became England's Staten Island, with half a dozen refugee ships arriving every day. The Jews settled around the East End, giving it a dominant character. Since then the community, once around 250,000, has dispersed – to Stamford Hill, Golders Green and Finchley.

The Irish had been coming to Britain since the Anglo-Norman invasion of Ireland in the late 12th century. Mainly Catholic, they suffered for their faith in the Gordon riots of 1780, a dozen years before St Patrick's Catholic Church, which today holds services in Spanish, Portuguese and Cantonese, was built in Soho.

Irish immigration during the 19th century was brought about largely through the great famine of 1846–52. The Irish were a significant force in the 19th century's building boom, especially on the railways, and many settled in Camden and Kilburn. Today's population, around three percent of Londoners, is scattered across north and west London.

**FAR LEFT:** Ghanaian fan before a friendly football match with England. Ghanaian communities are concentrated in north and east London. **ABOVE LEFT:** London has many Asian communities. **ABOVE:** Brick Lane is the centre of the Bangladeshi community.

> *Londoners frequently complain about overcrowding. But the population was higher in 1931 when it reached over 8 million, half a million more than today.*

## European settlers

Following the German invasion of Poland in 1939, the 33,000-strong Polish military in exile settled as a state-within-a-state in Mayfair and Kensington. Their pilots shot down one in seven German planes in the 1940 Battle of Britain. At the end of the war 150,000 were settled in London. While that number later dropped, a new wave of Polish immigrants from the EU in the 21st century meant 123,000 Poles were resident in London in 2010.

The Italians first settled around the church of St Peter's in Clerkenwell, in an area known to the residents as The Hill and to Londoners as Little Italy. The population was at its height from 1900 to 1930 but, when Italians living in Britain were interned during World War II, their role as restaurateurs began to be eroded

by Greek Cypriots, who had been filtering into Britain since the 1920s. Disruptions on Cyprus caused further immigration in the 1950s and 1960s, with Greek and Turkish Cypriots amicably settling side by side in north London. The densest Greek community is around Green Lanes in Haringey, north London, where traditions are maintained in male-only cafés.

## Seasonal Arabs

In summer, when Middle East temperatures become too hot for comfort, London has traditionally attracted many Gulf Arabs, who spend much of their time enjoying the coolness of the parks and the shopping opportunities. First coming in the wake of the oil price hikes of the 1970s, they funded a mosque in Regent's Park, which can hold 1,800.

Seasonal Arabs are less common since the war in Iraq, but there are resident communities from Egypt, Iraq and Morocco. Most live in Kensington and Bayswater, and they congregate in Edgware Road, north of Marble Arch, where their restaurants, cafés and shops shine into the night. London is still one of the largest Arab media centres.

## Commonwealth immigrants

The 20th century saw immigration mostly from the Commonwealth, and the resulting ethnic influence extends as far as Heathrow. The airport itself was largely built by construction workers from India's Punjab. After the Sikhs came the Caribbeans, who found work on London's buses, Underground railway network and in the health service.

But while London likes to think of itself as a multicultural society, it has few black or Asian top administrators or civil servants. You can pass through the City or the Inns of Court or Docklands without meeting many business tycoons, leading lawyers or top editors from the settlers' communities. Until the general election of 1987, there were no ethnic-minority members of Parliament; that situation has since changed and there are now around 27.

## Why there's a welcome

Partly because London's vast number of hotels, bars and restaurants have a great need for cheap but hard-working labour, immigration has been a less contentious issue in the capital than elsewhere in the country. Many caterers welcomed the expansion of the European Union in 2004 because it gave them legitimate access to affordable help from eastern Europe. But even in London there are worries about the pressures migrants place on public services.

Generally, though, London welcomes every type of visitor. Karl Marx, Mahatma Gandhi and Indira Gandhi all studied here. Charles de Gaulle lived in exile here. Writers Paul Theroux, Salman Rushdie and V.S. Naipaul chose to work here. Even Harrods, the quintessentially English store, was owned by an Egyptian, Mohamed Al-Fayed, from 1985 to 2010 and is currently owned by Quatar Holdings. It sells 40 percent of its merchandise to tourists. ❏

**LEFT:** buskers entertain the crowds at Columbia Road flower market. **TOP:** a favourite pastime.
**ABOVE:** Brick Lane in east London.
**ABOVE RIGHT:** socialising in Soho.

### HOT PROPERTY

Over the past decade or so the dream of living in London has become unattainable for many young people unless they are prepared to rent with friends or strangers, or live with family.

London's long overheated property market pushed the average price of a London home to over £446,000, with properties in the posher areas, such as Kensington and Chelsea, averaging £1.3 million and seeing rises of up to £600,000 a year. The property crash caused prices to drop by up to 16 percent, but a return to bonuses in the City and very wealthy international buyers (Russian, Arab and American) looking for a London base continue to keep it afloat.

Es nouuelles Dalbion
Si vous en plaist escou
on frere z mon conpaing
Achez qua mon retor
Ay este deca la mer
Et ceu a loye ise chier

# THE MAKING OF LONDON

*Fire, plague, population explosions, aerial bombing, economic recessions, urban blight, terrorism... London has survived everything history could throw at it, yet it has remained one of the world's most seductive cities*

In AD 43 the invading Roman army chose gravel banks between what is now Southwark and the City as the site of a strategically important bridge. Roman London, the Celtic "Llyn-din", the fort by the lake, quickly took shape, but suffered a setback 17 years later when British guerrillas led by Queen Boudicca attacked and burned areas around Lombard Street, Gracechurch Street and Walbrook so completely that archaeologists have identified a change in the colour of the earth.

A rebuilt Londinium, as the Romans called it, had by AD 100 supplanted Colchester as the capital as well as the trading centre of Britain. But in 410, Rome itself was threatened by the

> Roman Londinium had a timber bridge, quays, warehouses, a governor's palace, baths and amphitheatre. Roads radiated to Colchester, York, Chester, Exeter, Bath and Canterbury.

Germanic races from the north and recalled its garrison from England. Culture withered and Londinium crumbled as the Anglo-Saxons allowed the Roman buildings to become derelict.

## Recovery and expansion

The city's position made it a natural trading centre and gradually it recovered its impor-

**LEFT:** view of London from the poems of Charles, Duke of Orleans, 1394–1465. **RIGHT:** aerial view of Roman Londinium from the northwest, *c.* 2nd century AD.

tance. In the 8th century the literary monk, the Venerable Bede, called it "A market for many peoples coming by land and sea". South of London Bridge, a residential area developed, later known as the Borough.

Two miles (3km) upriver on Thorney Island, the Monastery of St Peter was established, later the great West Minster. Following his accession in 1042, Edward the Confessor moved his court from the City to Westminster, creating the division of royal and mercantile power still in place today. In lieu of making the usual pilgrimage to Rome, he rebuilt the abbey, where most succeeding kings were crowned, married and, until George II (d.1760), buried.

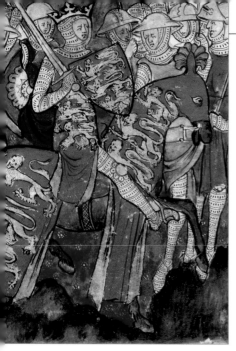

## City landmarks

In 1066 William the Conqueror brought the laws of Normandy to England, and gave London privileges that are still honoured today. Self-direction in local affairs was satisfied by the election of a first Mayor (later Lord Mayor) in 1189, with aldermen and a court. A new St Paul's Cathedral was started and the great keep of the White Tower completed in 1097. Westminster Hall was designed as a banqueting hall but, although the largest building of its kind in Europe, fell short of William's dreams – he said it was "a mere bedchamber" compared to what he had expected. By 1176 work had begun on a stone London Bridge, and the suburb on the south bank was growing.

## Union and plague

The city had grown to 50,000 by the time of Geoffrey Chaucer, the "father of English poetry" – this in spite of the "Black Death" of 1348, when some 200 bodies a day were taken outside the city and buried in mass graves. This virulent bubonic plague, carried by rats and fleas, ravaged much of Europe but had a particularly devastating effect on London because of the city's narrow streets and insanitary housing.

London stopped growing in the 14th century. The City (now with a capital C) quite simply had no ambitions to get any bigger. Had it wanted to expand, it would have had to change its character, perhaps endangering in the process its hard-won privileges and sacrificing its unique position as a major European market and port. Whatever was happening outside the walls (not completely demolished until the 18th century), the City maintained a blinkered detachment that was not disturbed until Queen Victoria's reign.

## The Golden Age

The much married and celebrated divorcé Henry VIII (1491–1547) almost qualifies as the "father" of modern London, though the changes he brought about were the outcome of a bid for

personal freedom from the Church. In 1534, after the Pope refused to annul his marriage to Catherine of Aragon so that he could marry Anne Boleyn, Henry cut all ties with Roman Catholicism. He had already pronounced himself head of the Church of England and persuaded Parliament to authorise the dissolution of the monasteries, their property and revenues being granted to the Crown. Cardinal Wolsey's house was added to an expanding palace in Whitehall. Hyde Park and St James's were enclosed as deer parks.

Convent (now Covent) Garden and Clerkenwell, Stepney and Shoreditch, Kennington and Lambeth all expanded during this time, taking London's population to 200,000. A lasting monument to the era is Henry VIII's Hampton Court Palace, southwest of London *(see page 239)*.

Henry's daughter, Elizabeth I, whose mother, Anne Boleyn, had been beheaded for supposed adultery, came to the throne in 1558. She was truly London's queen and the "Golden Age" began, in commerce, education and the arts. William Shakespeare, a Londoner by adoption, was far from adulated by the authorities. When the Lord Mayor banned the-

atrical performances from London, he and his fellow playwright Ben Jonson moved outside the Mayor's jurisdiction to new sites on the

> *Little survives of Tudor London's wood-framed houses with their oversailing upper storeys, but a flavour can be found in the Old Curiosity Shop near Lincoln's Inn (see page 154).*

south bank of the Thames, an area notorious for bear pits, brothels and prisons.

## Revolution and style

Being childless, the "Virgin Queen" Elizabeth chose James VI of Scotland to succeed her as James I of England, thus launching the Stuart dynasty. Religious conflict continued, and a Catholic faction attempted to blow up Parliament in the infamous "Gunpowder Plot". On 5 November 1605, Guy (Guido) Fawkes was caught about to ignite barrels of gunpowder in the cellars. Fawkes was executed, but 5 November, Guy Fawkes Day, is still marked with fireworks and the burning of an effigy.

Against a background of conflict between the king and Parliament, London responded to a new influence: the Italian architecture of Palladio as seen through the work of Inigo Jones. The purity of Jones's style is best seen in the

---

**TOP LEFT:** William the Conqueror accompanied by knights and soldiers, by an unknown artist (14th century). **LEFT:** Westminster Hall, *c.*1460.
**ABOVE:** detail, *London from Southwark, c.*1630 by an unknown artist. **ABOVE RIGHT:** *Queen Elizabeth I,* attributed to George Gower.

Queen's House at Greenwich, begun in 1616. Three years later came the Banqueting House in Whitehall.

## Water, pestilence and fire

Great tragedies lay ahead for London. In 1665 the inadequate water supply and lack of sanitation brought the dreaded plague to the overcrowded city, and before it ran its course 100,000 inhabitants died. The Great Fire, less than a year later, came as if to cleanse the stricken city. From a baker's shop on Pudding Lane, Eastcheap, the flames raged for five days, watched and recorded by the great 17th-century diarist Samuel Pepys. Miraculously, only half a dozen people were recorded as dead, although the number may well have been higher.

After the fire, 13,000 houses and 87 parish churches lay in ruins, but rebuilding was immediately planned.

## Wren's dream

Christopher Wren, Surveyor General to the Crown, was inspired by Paris. London, too, he thought, should have *rond-points*, vistas and streets laid out in a grid pattern. But Wren's best ideas were never realised. Expediency dictated that the new should rise quickly on the sites of the old, with one prudent difference: new buildings were made of brick, not wood.

Wren turned his inventive powers to rebuilding 51 of the City's damaged churches. His achievements lie in the individuality of their soaring towers and steeples which rise above the rooftops. In 1675 work began on his masterpiece, a new St Paul's Cathedral.

### BUNHILL FIELDS

Many victims of the Great Plague of 1665 were buried in plague pits in Bunhill Fields on City Road *(see page 164)*, where these days city workers eat their lunches. The cemetery was specially built for plague victims, though the site had previously operated as a deposit for old bones from St Paul's churchyard where space was at a premium. The burial ground was not consecrated and was later associated with Nonconformists, including many notable ones such as Daniel Defoe, John Bunyan, author of *Pilgrim's Progress,* and the poet and artist William Blake.

House building spread through the green fields beyond Soho towards Hyde Park and across the Tyburn road. As the ripple of this 18th-century building ring moved outwards, the older centre was coming to the end of its useful life. The need for better communications brought demands for another river crossing. Westminster Bridge was completed in 1750, but nearly 20 years passed before the City had its own second bridge, at Blackfriars. White-hall was beginning to take on its 20th-century character, the palace of kings being replaced by the palaces of government.

## Splendour and sweatshops

By 1800 London was poised on the brink of a population explosion. In the next 35 years it was to double in size – and the railways were yet to come. While Britain was at war with Napoleonic France, work on public buildings withered, but housing swelled with the increasing numbers of civil servants. Paddington and Marylebone, Camberwell and Kensington, Knightsbridge and Chelsea forged their identities.

Unlike the West End, the East End suffered ribbon building along the roads to Essex. Whitechapel High Street was "pestered with cottages", and Wapping with mean tenements. It was an area vulnerable to the impact of new

developments in commerce following the Industrial Revolution. Canals had already linked the Thames with the industrial Midlands. Docks cruelly dismembered the riverside parishes. In 1825, 1,250 houses were swept away for St Katharine's Dock alone. The inhabitants were compressed, sardine-style,

> London became increasingly affluent in the early 19th century. Visiting in 1814, the Emperor of Russia asked, "Where are your poor?" Clearly he had not been east of the Tower of London.

into accommodation nearby. The character of the modern East End was in the making. "Sweatshops" and the labour to go with them multiplied in this fertile soil of ruthless competition, poverty and immigration.

By the 1830s the Industrial Revolution was making its impact on the Thames below Wapping. The marshy pools of the Isle of Dogs, long used for duck shooting and hunting, were deepened to make the West and East India

---

**TOP LEFT:** *The Great Fire of London 1666*, by an anonymous artist, *c.*1675. **LEFT:** tomb in Bunhill Fields. **ABOVE:** portrait of Samuel Pepys by John Riley. **RIGHT:** *Gin Lane*, an engraving by William Hogarth, whose works vividly depict 18th-century London life.

Docks. Wharves and shipyards lined the banks of the river itself in Blackwall, Deptford and Greenwich. With all this activity, London's air was dense with smog – smoke mixed with fog – although this word had not yet been coined.

## Congestion and crime

By the early 19th century London was becoming impossibly congested, so bridges were built at Waterloo (1811–17) and Hammersmith (1824–27). London Bridge was rebuilt (1823–31) and foot passengers given a tunnel under the Thames at Wapping.

Courts of law and prisons responded to rising crime, while gentlemen's clubs met the Regency passion for gambling. In Bloomsbury's Gower Street, London University was born, and a fruit and vegetable market came to Covent Garden. Great collections were housed in the British Museum and National Gallery.

Londoners were on the move. In 1829 Mr Shillibeer introduced them to the omnibus, and the first steam train arrived with the London & Greenwich Railway of 1836. Terminal stations followed at Euston, King's Cross and Paddington by 1853, and at Blackfriars, Charing Cross and St Pancras by 1871.

## Cleaning up the Thames

At Westminster, the Houses of Parliament burnt down in 1834 when a furnace overheated, but soon Charles Barry and Augustus Pugin's Gothic extravaganza rose phoenix-like from the ashes: the House of Lords by 1847, the Commons and clock tower by 1858 and the Victoria Tower by 1860.

By this time, the "sights" of London had dropped into place. The British Museum gave a home to the Elgin Marbles in 1816, and Trafalgar Square gave a hero's welcome to Nelson's column in 1843. The City Corporation, meanwhile, made efforts to unlock the congested streets, cutting swathes through Holborn's houses and cemeteries for the viaduct to bridge the Fleet valley. Fleet Street, the Strand and Whitehall were by-passed by the grand boulevard of the Victoria Embankment. Tower Bridge opened in 1894, steel dressed up in stone to make it look historic.

### THE GREAT EXHIBITION OF 1851

In 1851 Queen Victoria opened the Great Exhibition of the Works of all Nations in Hyde Park, its magnificent glass building – dubbed "the Crystal Palace" – displaying Britain's skills and achievements to the world and attracting some 6 million visitors. With the profits of £186,000, Prince Albert, Queen Victoria's German-born husband, realised his great ambition: a centre of learning.

Temples to the arts and sciences blossomed in Kensington's gardens, nicknamed "Albertopolis". What was later named the Victoria and Albert Museum opened in 1852, moving to its present site in 1857, followed by the Royal Albert Hall in 1871, the Albert Memorial in 1872, and the Natural History Museum in 1881.

By 1859 another problem had arisen, serious enough to cause the adjournment of the House of Commons: the unbearable stench from the Thames. Londoners still depended largely on the river for drinking water, and at the same time disposed of their sewage in it. Cholera was common until the City Engineer, Joseph Bazalgette, devised a scheme to take the sewage well downstream to Barking in Essex and release it into the river after treatment. His scheme is still the basis of the modern drainage system.

> By the end of the 19th century, London was throbbing with life and unloading the British Empire's fortunes across its wharves. Its docklands were called the warehouse of the world.

### Dickens and social reforms

But London had become polarised. In the east, there was poverty and overcrowding, and in the west affluence and spacious living. The novelist Charles Dickens described the refuge of down-and-outs and penny-a-nighters in novels such as *Bleak House* (1853). Public conscience was aroused by his writings and those of the social reformer Henry Mayhew. This encouraged both political action and private philanthrophy.

The railways and new roads did some of the reformers' work for them, sweeping away many insanitary dwellings. Soon London's city's edge opened up due to the first suburban railway, the Metropolitan, in 1863.

### World War II and the Blitz

Britain's capital has evolved piece-meal over centuries, without any overall plans. Twice in its history, however, it has had to be rebuilt. On the first occasion, after the Great Fire of 1666, and on the second, after World War II and the Blitz, which killed 29,000 London civilians.

World War II left Britain impoverished and without the empire that had provided so much of its wealth. Utilitarian buildings, often of charmless concrete, replaced those destroyed in the

**ABOVE FAR LEFT:** *Covent Garden*, by Phoebus Leven, 1864. **ABOVE LEFT:** detail from *A Street Scene with Two Omnibuses*, by James Pollard, 1845.
**ABOVE:** firefighting during the Blitz, World War II.
**RIGHT:** many thousands of London children were evacuated to the countryside during the Blitz.

Blitz and were condemned by Prince Charles, who said that modern town planners and architects did more damage than the Luftwaffe.

## Swinging London

The 1950s were a time of post-war austerity with rationing still in place and efforts concentrated on regeneration in the face of a rapidly disintegrating empire. But there was also a massive baby boom and by the mid-1960s, as the post-war babies became teenagers, times were a-changing. While Paris became the centre of serious political action, London was the place to have fun, where old notions of deference, responsibility and hierarchy were swept away, cultural and sexual attitudes were liberated, and fashion and pop music prevailed. Swinging London centred on Soho's Carnaby Street, the King's Road in Chelsea, where Mary Quant's shop Bazaar epitomised the new fashions, and Barbara Hulanicki's store Biba in Kensington.

Meanwhile, many of the East End's pre-war slums were replaced by new housing estates and tower blocks to meet the growing demand for decent public housing. The deep social problems created by the estates had yet to make an impact.

## The roaring eighties

In the 1970s the pendulum swung the other way. Traditional industries collapsed all over Britain. Container ships made London's old wharves and warehouses redundant and the port that had once welcomed 14,000 vessels a year crumbled into dereliction.

### LONDON'S MAYOR

In 1997 the UK elected a new Labour government led by Tony Blair, ending 17 years of Conservative rule under which the Greater London Council, which had administered London, had been abolished. The new Labour government decided to restore a measure of self-government to the capital by creating a new post for the city: an elected mayor (distinct from the ceremonial post of Lord Mayor, whose role is confined to the financial "square mile" of the City of London). The first election was won by Ken Livingstone, who had controversially led the Greater London Council (abolished by Margaret Thatcher (and by no means loved by Blair's New Labour). He was succeeded by the exuberant Boris Johnson (left) in 2008, a former editor of *The Spectator*, distinguished by his unruly thatch of blond hair. He introduced a city cycle hire scheme, which quickly became known as the Boris Bike.

By the time the economic boom of the 1980s created a demand for taller office buildings, there was somewhere convenient to put them: the former docklands. The area around Canary Wharf, with its 800ft (244-metre) -high One Canada Square tower, was dubbed Chicago-on-Thames. Meanwhile, for home buyers, the dream of living in London itself faded as the strong economy pushed London house prices and rents well beyond the pockets of the lower paid.

## The South Bank soars

The next area to be revived was Bankside, the south bank of the Thames where Shakespeare first staged his greatest plays and Dickens mined the material for many of his novels. Riders on the London Eye, the giant observation wheel erected to mark the millennium (see page 186), looked down on a hive of building activity. This activity has now moved east and includes the building of The Shard near London Bridge.

The area regenerated itself as the entertainments centre it had been 400 years previously. Near where a replica of Shakespeare's Globe Theatre was completed in 1997, a disused power station was transformed into Tate Modern, a modern art museum. The Millennium Bridge, the first new river crossing in central London for more than a century, enabled pedestrians to walk from St Paul's Cathedral to Tate Modern in seven minutes.

**ABOVE LEFT:** male models pose in 1966. Second from left is clothes designer Ossie Clark, a leading figure in 1960s London. **ABOVE:** Eurostar platform at St Pancras International station. **RIGHT:** middle distance Olympic medallists Kelly Holmes and Steve Cram celebrate London's winning bid to host the 2012 Olympic Games.

## An eye to the future

In July 2005, London surprised itself by winning its bid to host the 2012 Olympic Games. On the very next day terrorist bombs killed more than 50 people on three Tube trains and a bus, raising the question of how to make such a sprawling cosmopolitan city more secure.

> The 2012 Olympics has been the catalyst for improvements to London's transport system and the development of East End brown field sites.

Preparations for the Olympics led long neglected parts of east London to be transformed to house the main stadia and Olympic Village. At the same time, the hitherto bleak area around King's Cross and St Pancras stations has been turned into a fitting setting for the new Eurostar terminal. The restoration and re-opening of the 5-star St Pancras Hotel, designed in the 1860s by Sir George Gilbert Scott, seems to symbolise London's capacity for re-invention and renewal.  ❑

# DECISIVE DATES

IVLIVS CÆSAR

## Early times

### 55 BC
Julius Caesar *(above)* discovers Britain. He launches an invasion and defeats Cassivel-launus, a British chieftain. However, Roman forces do not stay.

### AD 43
Londinium settled during second Roman invasion; a bridge is built over the Thames.

### AD 61
Boudicca *(below),* Queen of the Iceni tribe in East

Anglia, sacks the city before being defeated.

### c.200
Three mile (5km) -long city wall built.

### 410
Troops are withdrawn to defend Rome.

### 449–527
Jutes, Angles and Saxons arrive in Britain, dividing it into separate kingdoms.

### 604
The first St Paul's Cathedral founded by King Ethelbert.

### c.750
Monastery of St Peter is founded on Thorney Island, later to become Westminster Abbey.

### 8th century
Shipping and manufacturing flourish on the river bank near today's Strand.

### 884
London becomes the capital of Britain under Alfred the Great.

### 1042
Edward the Confessor moves his court from the city to Westminster and rebuilds the abbey.

## After the Conquest
### 1066
William I, Duke of Normandy and descendant of the Vikings, conquers Britain. He introduces

French and the feudal system.

### 1078
Tower of London's White Tower built.

### 1154
The Plantagenets, descen-dants of the French House of Anjou, take over throne.

### 1176
A new London Bridge is built of stone.

### 1189
City's first mayor is elected.

### 1240
First parliament sits in Westminster.

### 1290
Jews are expelled from the city – a ban not lifted until the 17th century.

### 1300
St Paul's Cathedral, now rebuilt in stone after a fire in 1087, is consecrated.

**1381**
Much of London is laid waste by the Peasants' Revolt led by Wat Tyler.

**1485**
The Tudor Age begins. Of Welsh descent, the Tudors preside over the English Renaissance, under Queen Elizabeth I (reigned 1558–1603).

**1514**
Building of Hampton Court Palace begins.

**1532**
Henry VIII builds Palace of Whitehall, the largest in Europe. It catches fire in 1698.

**1534**
Henry VIII *(above)* declares himself head of the Church of England and dissolves the monasteries.

**1536**
St James's Palace is built.

**1588**
William Shakespeare (1568–1616) begins his

dramatic career in London.

**1605**
Guy Fawkes *(above)* tries to blow up Parliament.

**1620**
The Pilgrim Fathers set sail for America.

**1642–9**
Civil war between the Cavalier Royalists and the Republican Roundheads. Royalists are defeated. Charles I is executed.

**1660**
After 11 years, monarchy is restored under Charles II.

**1660–9**
Samuel Pepys writes his famous diary.

**1664–6**
The Great Plague kills one-fifth of the population.

**1666**
The Great Fire destroys 80 percent of London's buildings.

**1675**
Sir Christopher Wren (1632–1723) begins work on St Paul's Cathedral.

**1694**
The Bank of England is established.

**1714**
The House of Hanover is ushered in by George I. The architectural style prevalent for the next 20 years is known as Georgian.

**1735**
George II makes 10 Downing Street available to Sir Robert Walpole, Britain's first prime minister.

**1764**
The Literary Club is founded by Samuel Johnson, compiler of the first English dictionary.

**1783**
Last public execution held at Tyburn (Marble Arch).

**1811–20**
The Prince Regent, later George IV, gives his name to the Regency style.

**1820**
Regent's Canal completed.

**1824**
The National Gallery is established.

**1829**
Prime Minister Robert Peel establishes a police force (nicknamed "peelers" and later "bobbies").

**1834**
Rebuilding of the current Houses of Parliament, after the old palace of Westminster is destroyed by fire.

**The Age of Empire**

**1837**
Queen Victoria *(below)*

comes to the throne at 18.

**1840s**
Trafalgar Square *(above)* laid out on the site of royal stables to commemorate Nelson's victory.

**1849**
Tea merchant Henry Charles Harrod takes over a small grocer's shop in Knightsbridge.

**1851**
The Great Exhibition is held in Hyde Park.

**1857**
The Victoria and Albert Museum opens.

**1859**
A 13.5-tonne bell, nick-named Big Ben, is hung in the clock tower of the Houses of Parliament.

**1863**
The first section of the Underground railway is built between Paddington and Farringdon Street.

**1888**
Jack the Ripper strikes in Whitechapel.

**1890**
First electric railway is built in deep-level tunnels, between the City and Stockwell.

**1894**
Tower Bridge is built.

**1903**
Westminster Cathedral is built. Marks & Spencer's first penny bazaar opens in Brixton.

**1904**
The first London motor taxi is licensed.

**1914**
World War I begins.

**1915**
Zeppelins and, later, Gotha airplanes begin dropping incendiary and explosive bombs on the city.

**1922**
British Broadcasting Company transmits its first programmes from Savoy Hill *(below)*.

**1923**
The first Football

Association cup final is held at Wembley Stadium.

### 1939–45
World War II. Children are evacuated, and London is heavily bombed.

## Modern London

### 1951
Festival of Britain *(below)*; new concert halls built on South Bank near Waterloo.

### 1956
The Clean Air Act, introducing smokeless fuel, ends the asphyxiating smogs.

### 1976
National Theatre opens.

### 1982
Flood-preventing Thames Barrier *(above right)* is finished. Built after hundreds of people were killed when a storm caused a tidal surge in 1953.

### 1986
The Greater London Council is abolished.

### 1991
The first Canary Wharf tower is completed in Docklands.

### 1994
The first trains run through the Channel Tunnel to Paris and Brussels.

### 1997
Shakespeare's Globe opens on Bankside.

### 2000
Tate Modern opens on Bankside. The London Eye opens at County Hall.

### 2001
Greater London Authority is set up under mayor Ken Livingstone. Major museums drop entrance charge.

### 2002
The Millennium Bridge opens again after its unsettling wobble is cured.

### 2003
A £5 congestion charge is imposed on cars entering central areas.

### 2004
Planning permission is granted for "The Shard", which will be London's tallest building at 1,016ft (310 metres) when completed.

### 2005
On 6 July London is chosen to stage 2012 Olympic Games *(below)*. The following day bombs explode on three Tube trains and a bus, killing 52 people.

### 2007
The new Wembley Stadium opens. Eurostar terminal opens at St Pancras.

### 2008
The "credit crunch" – house prices crash and Northern Rock bank is nationalised.

### 2009
MPs' expenses scandal rocks Parliament.

### 2011
Phone hacking scandal – the *News of the World* closes after 168 years, and senior Metropolitan policemen resign.

### 2012
London Olympics are held. Queen Elizabeth II's Diamond Jubilee is celebrated.

# THEATRELAND

**Shakespeare, Sondheim, ABBA and a host of stars – the best (and the worst) of plays and musicals turn up in the West End. And theatre-lovers with a sense of adventure will find all kinds of innovative shows in fringe venues scattered around the city**

The opening of Shakespeare's Globe on Bankside in 1997 was seen by some as a triumph of culture over commercialism. Here, for the price of a ticket, you can sit on rock-hard benches, squint through the sun streaming in through the large opening in the thatch roof, peer around pillars to try to catch lines from the acoustically challenged stage, and even, if the directors are to be taken at their word, cat-call and lob the occasional tomato if a performance is not to your liking.

This is theatre heritage to appeal to the tourist and even the purist, an Elizabethan playhouse risen from the rubble of time; many make for its doors simply to savour the experi-

ence. The brainchild of American actor-director Sam Wanamaker, who didn't live to see it completed, the theatre is a replica of the 1599 auditorium in which William Shakespeare staged many of his plays. Like many theatres over the years, the original Globe was destroyed by fire.

## That's show business

London's theatrical history goes back to a playhouse opened at Shoreditch in 1576 by James Burbage, the son of a carpenter and travelling player, and its development encompasses a strong tradition of taking sideswipes at social issues. In the *Roaring Girl* of 1611, for example, playwright Thomas Dekker dwelt at some length on London's traffic jams.

In modern times, live theatre was supposed to succumb first to films, then to TV, yet it is still one of those essential attractions every vis-

> *In spite of reports to the contrary, London's theatre scene is not declining. Theatres have broken their attendance records for several years running.*

itor to London is supposed to experience, even if most opt for a blockbuster musical rather than anything more adventurous.

In the days when *South Pacific* and *Camelot* dominated musical theatre no-one would have guessed the West End would hijack the genre from Broadway. Yet in the 1970s, Tim Rice and Andrew Lloyd Webber first demonstrated the

possibilities of rock-musicals with *Jesus Christ Superstar* and *Evita*, before Lloyd Webber moved on to dominate the stage musical with *Cats* (a collaboration with the late T.S. Eliot) and *Phantom of the Opera*.

Critics might scoff, but shrewd theatre brains saw that income from musicals could underwrite other work. Trevor Nunn masterminded the Royal Shakespeare Company's 1985 production of *Les Misérables*, which went on to conquer the world.

Musicals dominate the modern West End and are its biggest money-spinners – even though Lloyd Webber himself seems to have lost the urge to produce much new work and has been more prominent as the promoter of the Bollywood-based *Bombay Dreams* and a revival of *The Sound of Music* for which the starring role of Maria was cast via a reality TV show.

Broadway has reasserted its clout, whether in revivals of musical classics like *Guys and Dolls* and *Chicago* or recent successes such as *The Producers*, *Wicked* and *Monty Python's Spamalot*. The trend that gets critics tearing their hair out, though, is for the pop-music musical, reprising the song catalogue of favourite artists. Begun by ABBA-based *Mamma Mia!*, this has continued with *Dancing in the Streets* (Motown), *We Will Rock You* (Queen) and even *Daddy Cool* (Boney M). The plots weaved around the songs are wafer-thin, but the crowds keep coming in.

## WHERE TO SIT

It's useful to know the terminology of English theatre layout. What in America is called the "Orchestra" (the seats at the lowest level) is in England called the "Stalls"; then, in ascending order, come the "Dress Circle" (or "Royal Circle"), and the "Upper Circle" (or "Grand Circle" or "Balcony"). The very top balconies, once known as "The Gods", are not recommended to anyone with vertigo or a hearing impediment.

If in a party, consider asking for a box, which can sometimes work out cheaper than seats in the stalls. You can doze off more privately, too.

**PRECEDING PAGES:** Hackney Empire Theatre, which opened in 1901 as a music hall. **LEFT:** the London Palladium theatre. **ABOVE:** a revival of the classic *Guys and Dolls*. **TOP RIGHT:** theatre in the round at Shakespeare's Globe. **ABOVE RIGHT:** a Royal Shakespeare Company production of *Hecuba*.

Some claim musical-mania has squeezed out new drama, but the theatre pages in *Time Out* don't really bear this out. New productions of classics still appear each year, new writing still gets aired in fringe and mainstream venues, and writers such as Tom Stoppard, Alan Bennett or Mark Ravenhill do not lack audiences.

### Hollywood-on-Thames

As well as locally grown stars such as Michael Gambon, Ian McKellen, Maggie Smith, Diana Rigg and Judi Dench, American actors have never been strangers to the West End – Dustin Hoffman played Shylock in *The Merchant of Venice* here in 1989 – but lately this flow has become a flood, as nearly every Hollywood name has seemed to feel a need to add a London stage appearance to their resumé.

Nicole Kidman caused a great stir when she appeared naked in David Hare's *The Blue Room* in 1998, and Val Kilmer, Woody Harrelson, Glenn Close and Christian Slater are among other famous faces seen on London stages, to varying reviews. Kathleen Turner won huge praise in a production of *Who's Afraid of Virginia Woolf*, but London's favourite American actor is Kevin Spacey. After scoring a massive hit in *The Iceman Cometh* in 1998, he accepted the job of part-time artistic director of the venerable Old Vic theatre, helping to raise funds to repair its leaky roof and promising to appear in two plays a year. His programmes as director have been sometimes eccentric, but seldom predictable.

### National companies

London has two major state-subsidised companies: the National Theatre and the Royal Shakespeare Company. The National has the advantage of its own huge building

---

### WAYS TO BUY YOUR TICKETS

Despite the popular notion that everything in London is so successful that it sells out fast, most shows have some seats, especially early in the week. It's the more expensive tickets – generally for musicals – that are usually hardest to obtain.

The best way to get tickets is from the theatre itself, either by calling at the box office or online. This cuts out the sometimes extortionate fees of ticket agencies. Agencies and hotels are most handy for obtaining hard-to-get tickets.

Many theatres offer unsold tickets for performances the same day at reduced "standby" prices, although some are only available to students. Tickets for same-day performances are also available at around half-price from

the tkts ticket booths in Leicester Square (Mon–Sat 10am–7pm, Sun 11am–4pm). Matinees can be cheaper, but understudies may replace the stars. The National Theatre puts some same-day tickets on sale at 9.30am at its box office on the South Bank.

Tickets are offered outside theatres by touts for anything up to 10 times their face value. This isn't illegal, but check the ticket's face value and the position of the seat before purchasing.

on the South Bank, with three auditoria. Its concrete exterior isn't to everyone's taste, but its technology is impressive – revolving stages are only the start of it. By contrast, the RSC gave up its London home at the unloved Barbican Centre in 2001 (its main base is in Shakespeare's home town, Stratford-upon-Avon), and only recently returned to presenting a regular London season, at the Duke of York's Theatre on St Martin's Lane.

Criticisms levelled at the National have been its comparative lack of modern European plays and the prominence given during Trevor Nunn's directorship to big musicals such as *Oklahoma!* and *My Fair Lady* – felt by many to be more the concern of the commercial West End (to which these productions profitably transferred). The current director, Nicholas Hytner, has introduced more variety and innovation, and aided by business sponsorship has made many seats available for just £12. *War Horse*, with its stunning life-sized puppets, is just one example of the National's work.

---

**FAR LEFT:** Dame Judi Dench in a production of Coward's *Hay Fever* at the Theatre Royal Haymarket.
**ABOVE LEFT:** Kevin Spacey, artistic director of the Old Vic. **ABOVE:** *War Horse* at the National Theatre.

## Off-West End to the fringe

There are many smaller or "fringe" venues around London, from substantial theatres to tiny rooms above pubs. Their productions range from low-budget Shakespeare to political shows and international theatre. Much of new young British writing is dark, funny and well-observed.

The Royal Court, the Donmar Warehouse, the Young Vic, the Almeida in Islington and the Tricycle in Kilburn are the main outlets for

> Val Kilmer, Matt Damon and Madonna failed to impress on the London stage, but Kathleen Turner, Juliette Lewis and Jude Law have been acclaimed.

new writing, which between them have pioneered many of London's most exciting recent productions. Lively pub theatres include the Bush (in Shepherd's Bush), the King's Head (Islington) and the Gate at Notting Hill Gate.

Every summer there is a very enjoyable open-air theatre season in Regent's Park, focusing on Shakespeare's comedies. ❑

# EATING OUT

**London's thousands of restaurants and cafés offer some of the world's best culinary experiences – some even at a decent price. New eateries open as frequently as new movies, and are just as subject to the whims of fashion. So how do you find the good and avoid the bad?**

London, once derided for mediocre cuisine, is today straining under a bombardment of Michelin stars. You can eat nachos and noodles, tapas and tempura, balti and bhajis; you can try pizza with Japanese toppings, choose from nearly 200 Thai restaurants or even eat English, a privilege reserved until a few years ago for diners at greasy-spoon cafés or, more tastefully, the traditional Rules or Simpson's in the Strand.

This revolution began in the 1980s, when the restructuring of London's financial world produced a legion of footloose brokers and traders looking for places to spend skyrocketing salaries. Innovative restaurants, like designer labels, were avidly sought out. At around the same time, the British discovered food. Cookery programmes proliferated on TV, book shops filled up with lavishly illustrated cookbooks and newspapers covered new restaurant openings with ever more excitement. The phenomenon of the "celebrity chef" was born.

Until then it had been *de rigueur* for chefs to be French, and the country's best-known were Albert and Michel Roux of Le Gavroche. Now local stars emerged: the late Rose Gray, and Ruth Rogers, wife of the architect Sir Richard Rogers, opened their River Café alongside the architect's offices in Fulham, West London, presenting Tuscan cooking with a metropolitan twist. At the same time Terence Conran, the

> The Conran empire marked a shift of emphasis away from chefs and towards restaurateurs. Famous chefs took to running their restaurant chains rather than doing much cooking.

style-maker whose Habitat stores had brought the earthy kitchenware of Provence to Britain, opened Bibendum restaurant in the splendid Art Deco Michelin tyre company building in Fulham Road, the first of a string of Conran venues in striking locations with emphatically stylish decor. The epitome of the style is Quaglino's, near Green Park, with a look that deliberately recalls a 1930s ocean liner. This was food as entertainment, out-to-impress dining that sym-

bolised the early 1990s, but – though some have maintained high standards – these are not restaurants where you can generally expect much individuality or charm.

## Current movers and shakers

Nowadays, London's food scene has settled down a little: it's still devoted to fads – Moroccan one year, Argentinian the next – but alongside them there's also a more consistent idea of quality, as the city has got used to the idea of being one of the world's dining capitals. Some stalwarts have absorbed new trends while sticking to what they know their clients want: the River Café remains inviolate, The Ivy and Le Caprice are ever-popular with the rich and famous, the Savoy Grill with businessmen, and Le Gavroche with traditionalist gourmands. The fashion for "mega-restaurants" has faded, as was indicated in 2007 when Terence Conran himself gave up control of his restaurant chain, passing it over to his former managers under a new name: the D&D Group.

Attention has shifted back from restaurant entrepreneurs to cooks, although London's

best-known chef, Gordon Ramsay, manages to be both. A former footballer whose cooking skills won Michelin recognition and whose short temper made him a TV star, Ramsay still

### FIRST, FIND YOUR TABLE

The downsides of London's top restaurants include terrifying prices, a growing air of exclusivity, and arrogance when it comes to dealing with anyone trying to make a reservation. Tables for dinner at Gordon Ramsay's main restaurant must be booked two months in advance, at The Ivy several weeks ahead; phone lines are often busy for hours, and when you do get through staff may be abrupt. One way to get around this is to go for lunch.

Instead of booking, turn up early just after noon. Tom Aikens, The Wolseley, Le Gavroche and The Ivy are among the prestigious venues that often have lunch time tables free.

**LEFT:** Mexican taco café Taqueria, on Westbourne Grove. **ABOVE:** St John in Clerkenwell, the location of several notable new restaurants. **ABOVE RIGHT:** Terence Conran's Bibendum occupies the former Michelin tyre company HQ on Fulham Road.

Ramsay, most combine classical, French-based training with an eclectic, adventurous approach. Other stars of the moment include Chris Galvin, now in charge of the top-floor restaurant at the Hilton on Park Lane (as Galvin at Windows), and Tom Aikens, with his eponymous restaurant in Kensington.

cooks himself (sometimes), instals talented young chefs in his restaurant stable and is an inescapable media face. London's grand hotels, traditional bastions of good cookery, have spruced up their restaurants to keep up with the dining boom, and Ramsay has taken astute advantage of this, taking over Claridge's restaurant. His protégée Angela Hartnett now has her own restaurant, Murano. There are many other inventive young British chefs around town, notably Heston Blumenthal. Like

## Around the world, and back again

Many fans of eating out in London, however, say that what they enjoy most is the incredible variety of cuisines on offer. Its status as an international city attracts fine cooks from every

## THE FACTS ABOUT FISH AND CHIPS

A classic British dish, fish and chips originated in the 1850s. Today, under 10,000 fish and chip shops remain in Britain, compared with over 30,000 in the 1930s. Many of the best were started by immigrants, especially Italians (Rock & Sole Plaice in Covent Garden, and the Fryer's Delight in Theobalds Road, Holborn) and Greek Cypriots (the Golden Hind, in Marylebone Lane since 1914, and Costas in Notting Hill). Nautilus in Fortune Green Road, West Hampstead, is Jewish and coats its fish in matzo flour. You will also find fish and chip shops run by Chinese, Turkish Cypriots or central Europeans.

Other notable fish and chip establishments are the long-standing favourites the Sea Shell in Lisson Grove, and Geales in Notting Hill. Fish Central is a blessing to concert- and theatre-goers near the Barbican Centre, Seafresh in Wilton Road is handy for Victoria Station, and Masters Super Fish is convenient for Waterloo. Recently, too, there has even been a trendy newcomer in the old-fashioned world of fish and chips, with the opening of the stylish Fish Club in Clapham.

You generally get better value in a real fish and chip restaurant (attached to a takeaway shop) than in pubs or restaurants that offer fish and chips on their menus. One test, apart from truly fresh, sustainably sourced fish and crisp batter, is that they offer fresh lemon instead of just malt vinegar.

part of the world to work here. French chefs are still prominent, such as Hélène Darroze (The Connaught) or Morgan Meunier (Morgan M), and even France's grandest current chef has a London operation, L'Atelier de Joël Robuchon. Far Eastern or South Asian restaurants are no longer just cheap options either: London has some of the finest Indian (Amaya, Café Spice Namaste), Japanese (Nobu) and Chinese (Bar Shu) restaurants in the world outside their countries of origin, and you can find regional variations, such as the superb south Indian vegetarian food of Rasa Samudra.

There has also been a re-evaluation of traditional British dishes, long dismissed as dreary. Pioneer of this new British style was Alastair Little in his Soho restaurant, but it was extended with still more zest by Fergus Henderson at St John. He has been hugely influential in showing that British favourites such as oxtail, smoked herrings and farm-reared pork, can be delicacies if prepared with care and flair.

## The middle ground

The ever-rising standard of fine dining in London may grab the headlines, but it has to be said that for most people who do not have limitless wallets or full mastery of the strategems used to get a table in restaurants such as Gordon Ramsay's, these are places that are only visited for a special occasion. Among more regularly accessible eating places, London's fad-chasing can be

a source of disappointment, as time and again restaurant promoters have placed "concept" – decor, style, general trendiness – above quality of food, or value for money. This being so, it's pleasing to report that one of the best current trends has been for the new culinary flair at last to filter down into a wider range of restaurants at mid-range prices. Many "new-British" restaurants, especially, are decently priced: even

### WHERE TO EAT

The biggest concentration of restaurants is in the West End, with Soho providing the most interesting choice. Chinatown, north of Leicester Square, has a bewildering array of Asian eateries, and Covent Garden good-value pre-theatre suppers. Kensington and Chelsea, with their abundance of wealthy residents, contain many expensive restaurants but also a good sprinkling of reasonably priced bistros.

Islington and Notting Hill also offer a good choice, and Clerkenwell and Shoreditch house some of the most interesting new restaurants. The City, whose oyster bars and restaurants cater to business lunchers, tends to be a ghost town in the evenings and at weekends.

the prestigious St John is not expensive, particularly for lunch, and places such as Shoreditch's Canteen or Roast in Borough Market similarly offer flavour-rich, modern food in stylish settings. Eating out in London may still be more expensive than in many cities, but at least the difference is getting a little less.

The trend for big institutions to re-examine their food has thrown up attractive novelties too: major museums such as the National Gallery, Tate Britain and Tate Modern all now

> *The local gastropub has started to become London's equivalent of the Parisian street-corner bistro.*

have imaginative, good-value restaurants, and even the Royal Institute of British Architects has opened up its elegant Art Deco "canteen" as a smart modern brasserie, the RIBA Café.

### The great pub renaissance

Another vital element in making good food more accessible – as well as the unstoppable growth of "ethnic" restaurants – has been the revolution in pub food. Realising there was more money to be made from food and wine than just beer and crisps, pub after pub has become a "gastropub", throwing out the limp sandwiches and plastic "ploughman's lunches" of old-style pub fare in favour of chalkboard menus that mix traditional British favourites with French, Italian or Oriental influences.

Old standards like sausage and mash have been given new life by the use of Toulouse sausages and mustard sauces, and imaginative salads have become a hallmark. This combination of good food and a relaxed feel that preserves a fair bit of the atmosphere of a London pub, typified by The Eagle (159 Farringdon Road, EC1), The Cow (89 Westbourne Park Road, W2) or trendier variants like the Lot's Road Pub & Dining Rooms (114 Lots Road, SW10), or the Princess Victoria (217 Uxbridge

Road, W12), has been a real winner with both Londoners and visitors. The London gastropub can sometimes seem to have become a new cliché – every one has to have stripped floorboards and stressed furniture – but they're ideal for anyone looking for good-value interesting food in an informal setting.

## The chain gang

As in every part of the world, in London plenty of restaurants, cafés, bars and pubs belong to chains. These can be an advantage when you're in unfamiliar territory and in search of something reliable; they're a disadvantage when a formula is replicated ad nauseam, and standards are low.

Some local London chains, though, are worth looking out for, especially if you're travelling with a family. Giraffes (South Bank and many more areas) are bright modern brasseries with "global fusion food" (Mexico to Australia and more) that appeal equally to adults and

children. For Italian standbys (pasta, pizza) Carluccio's Caffè, ASK and Strada are good bets, while Sofra branches provide enjoyable Turkish fare. The many Wagamama outlets are excellent Japanese-style noodle houses, while in a higher price slot the six Royal Chinas in London are comfortable Chinese restaurants. ❏

---

**FAR LEFT:** Marylebone's stylish RIBA Café, at the Royal Institute of British Architects. **LEFT:** open kitchen at The Eagle, a gastropub on Farringdon Road. **ABOVE:** The Cow in Notting Hill, one of many good gastropubs scattered around west London.

---

### AFTERNOON TEA, AS IT SHOULD BE

Throughout the world there are people still convinced that everyone in England sits down for "afternoon tea" around 4pm every day, using best-quality porcelain. Sadly, this is a myth, and a full-scale, formal tea – with thin-cut sandwiches, a variety of cakes and a choice of fine teas – is nowadays a luxury. The venues that really keep up the tradition are the grand hotels, most typically Brown's, The Ritz, the Langham and the Dorchester, all of which offer tea with all the trimmings (reservations and smart dress are required).

Recently, too, there has been a bit of a tea revival, and several upscale restaurants now offer set afternoon teas, such as The Wolseley, as do smart stores like Fortnum & Mason.

# RETAIL THERAPY

**London's innovative department stores are redesigning the one-stop shopping experience**

The past decade has seen dramatic changes in that most traditional of London shops, the department store. The stuffy image has gone and stores are now imaginatively designed spaces stocking everything from freshly cut flowers and organic food to cutting-edge designer clothes and bespoke jewellery. Their hairdressers have become on-site spas, and they offer a host of bars and restaurants.

Oxford Street has the greatest concentration of department stores, headed by Selfridges. Marks & Spencer and John Lewis provide a more traditional shopping experience, while round the corner on Regent Street, Liberty is both eccentric and chic. Head to Knightsbridge for Harvey Nichols, the fashionista's choice, and Harrods.
*For a comprehensive listing of London's department stores, see page 295 of Travel Tips.*

**ABOVE:** Liberty was started by Arthur Liberty in 1875 and was originally known for its homewares and fabrics, both of which are still going strong today. Past collaborations with British designer Luella Bartley and Ronnie Wood of the Rolling Stones have made this Regent Street institution more fashionable.

**BELOW:** Liberty's eye-catching 1920s mock-Tudor building was created using the timbers of two ships, HMS *Impregnable* and HMS *Hindustan*. The home interiors floor feels more like an exhibition of contemporary furniture. In the accessories department, the iconic William Morris Liberty print adorns everything from notebooks to bikinis.

**ABOVE:** opened as a grocer's shop in 1849, today Harrods is a tourist destination in its own right. Harrods sells pretty much everything you can think of in surroundings that range from the sublime to the ridiculous. But whatever you think of Harrods, no trip to London would be complete without a visit to its wonderfully extravagant food halls.

**LEFT:** Selfridges has become the ultimate London department store. Combining luxury brands with high-street concessions, it manages to be both accessible and cool. The store has a changing programme of themed events to keep things interesting, as well as services ranging from leather repairs to ear piercing.

**BELOW:** for a department store specialising in fine food and beverages visit Fortnum & Mason at 181 Piccadilly.

## BRITISH DESIGNERS

Creativity and eccentricity mark out British designers from the international fashion pack.

Stella McCartney's designs mix strong tailoring with feminine fabrics. Her popularity has sparked collaborations with Adidas and high street chain H&M.

Vivienne Westwood's theatrical clothes never fail to cause a stir. She has shops at 430 King's Road, SW10, and in Conduit Street, W1.

Paul Smith is known for his tailoring and retro-inspired designs. Look out for his best-selling silk ties and signature striped accessories.

Philip Treacy's sculptural headgear can be found in the top department stores, including Harrods.

Mulberry is famous for its leather accessories – from personal organisers to weekend bags, all embossed with the classic tree logo.

Cath Kidston's distinctive floral and polka dot designs are used for everything from gifts, clothes and accessories to tents.

# MARKETS

**There are few better introductions to London's rich mix of cultures and tastes than a visit to one of its markets**

Many of the capital's markets have been in operation for centuries and a visit can conjure up images of an old London now largely lost to supermarket chains and developers. At the same time, London's markets are experiencing a revival, and alongside the traditional stalls selling fruit and veg you'll find organic meat and fish and specialist produce from all round the world.

The revival of markets has encouraged the renovation of surrounding areas and all kinds of independent shops and restaurants are popping up. For some this has gone a step too far – for example, there is little doubt that the creation of a restaurant and boutique precinct at Spitalfields has damaged something of its original haphazard appeal – and the high prices charged for goods have taken the edge off bargain-hunting.

Despite this, a wander around places like Borough Market, Broadway Market and Spitalfields continues to be a treat for all the senses – you just have to be prepared to brave the crowds.

**ABOVE:** on Sunday mornings Londoners flood to Columbia Road Market in Hoxton *(see page 250)* for cut flowers, bulbs, shrubs, trees and garden ornaments. The old-fashioned streets around the market offer funky shops and cafés too.

**BELOW:** the variety and quality of fresh produce at Borough Market is unrivalled in London, and some of the prices certainly reflect this. If you're happy to brave the lunchtime crowds, many of the stalls offer takeaway snacks – a firm market favourite are the hot chorizo and rocket rolls from Spanish supplier Brindisa's stand.

**ABOVE:** markets are a great place for finding all manner of unusual handmade items, such as these hand-knitted covers for mobile phones.

## MARKET TREASURES

A wide range of clothing, crafts and trinkets are available at Camden's various markets.

The covered market at Greenwich is the place for handmade jewellery and accessories. Quality varies and it's very crowded, but if it gets too much adjourn to the calmer antiques market a short walk away.

**ABOVE:** the Sunday UpMarket at Ely's Yard (Brick Lane) is a treasure-trove of second-hand clothing and one-off designs.

**BELOW:** Leadenhall Market *(see page 171)* is a fine example of one of London's great 19th-century covered markets. It was used as a setting for Diagon Alley in the film *Harry Potter and the Philosopher's Stone.*

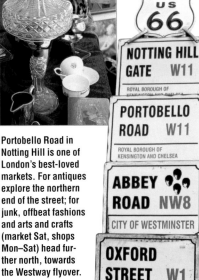

Portobello Road in Notting Hill is one of London's best-loved markets. For antiques explore the northern end of the street; for junk, offbeat fashions and arts and crafts (market Sat, shops Mon–Sat) head further north, towards the Westway flyover.

# THE ARCHITECTURAL LEGACY

Central planning played no part in London's haphazard development, and the city's organic growth, together with the contribution of men of genius such as Christopher Wren, John Nash and Inigo Jones, has given the capital its principal allure: infinite variety

John's Chapel, with the squat pillars and round arches of Norman Romanesque architecture.

Medieval London grew out of the Gothic style, imported from France in the 13th century and in vogue until the 1550s. Far more delicate than Norman, it made outer walls thinner by supporting them with exterior buttresses, allowing larger windows. Southwark Cathedral is a fine example of simple, unadorned early English Gothic; Westminster Abbey, begun in 1245, was enhanced by royal mason Henry Yevele (1320–1400), London's first known architect. He also built the Jewel Tower and Westminster Hall in the Houses of Parliament, a vauntingly ambitious space with a timber roof by carpenter Hugh Herland.

L ittle remains of Roman Londinium, and even less of Saxon Lundenwic. Glimpses of the Roman city wall can be had at Tower Hill, and foundations of a Temple of Mithras have been exposed in Queen Victoria Street. The Saxons built mostly in timber, but were grateful for Roman stones. All Hallows-by-the-Tower has a Saxon arch, built with Roman tiles. Otherwise, they left little trace.

## Norman to Gothic

The Norman Conquest of 1066 brought firmer resolution to the city, in the White Tower in the Tower of London, a sturdy box that showed the natives who was in control. Within it is St

> *The Tudor monarchs were great builders and brought the first real touches of grandeur and extravagance to London's buildings.*

## Tudor London

The finest work of Gothic architecture in London is the lavish Henry VII's Chapel in Westminster Abbey, completed by his son, Henry VIII. The Tudor monarchs oversaw constant expansion and building in London. A hallmark of Tudor buildings – also called "Elizabethan", after Queen Elizabeth I – is the use of half-timbering and red brick. Staple Inn in High Holborn is the sole survivor from this time, but the era also saw the building of London's first theatres such as Shakespeare's Globe, now reconstructed near its original Southwark site.

Brickwork was confined to the rich, used to produce octagonal towers, fancy chimneys and patterns of colours and shapes. Royal palaces were built like this at Greenwich, Hampton Court, St James's, Lambeth and Westminster. London has only one example of the Jacobean style (from King James I): Prince Henry's Room (1610–11) above 17 Fleet Street. Its original ceiling, with geometric patterns, is still in place.

## Inigo Jones and the Italian style

James I and his son Charles I brought a new elegance to London in the work of Inigo Jones (1573–1652). The court architect had studied in Italy, and brought Italian Renaissance ideas. He introduced classical proportions in his Banqueting Hall in Whitehall and the Queen's House in Greenwich, and his original Palladian layout for Covent Garden, set out, with the neoclassical St Paul's church, London's first true square.

## Wren and the Great Fire

Sir Christopher Wren (1632–1723) is undoubtedly London's greatest architect, but if there had been no Great Fire in 1666 his name would not be so well known. In three days 80 percent of London's buildings were destroyed: among the losses were the Guildhall and Old St Paul's, as well as 87 churches.

Wren was a scientist and self-taught architect. His plans for the rebuilding of London were rejected, but he managed 53 churches in

---

**FAR LEFT:** Tudor building on Fleet Street. **LEFT:** Temple, one of the four Inns of Court. **ABOVE:** John Nash's Park Crescent, off Portland Place. **ABOVE RIGHT:** St Paul's Cathedral. **RIGHT:** the "Gherkin" (the 30 St Mary Axe tower in the City) is open to the public once a year.

### OPEN HOUSE

During London Open House weekends more than 600 buildings of architectural and historical interest that are usually closed to the public open their doors, free of charge. The main weekend is usually in mid-September, but more limited Open House tours are run all year. See www.londonopenhouse.org for details. At some venues you will need to book.

the City and Westminster (26 remain) as well as St Paul's. These very English classical-baroque monuments eschewed earlier styles, their windows bathing white and gold interiors with light. His mastery of design is also displayed in the superb Greenwich and Chelsea hospitals, and several royal palaces.

## John Nash and Georgian London

John Nash (1752–1835) is the man who gave the West End style. He gained his reputation designing country houses, and in 1811 was commissioned by the Prince Regent, later George IV, to turn his "Marylebone Farm" into Regent's Park, ringed by elegant neoclassical villas. Nash added theatrical terraces, colonnades and sculpted pediments, and his master plan included connecting the park with the Prince's residence – Carlton House Terrace, by The Mall – via Portland Place and Regent Street, London's first refined boulevards.

Nash's supremely elegant Regency style was

### THE SKY'S THE LIMIT

Until the 1950s no new building in London was allowed to exceed the height of St Paul's Cathedral (355ft/108 metres). However, over the past few years London's skyline has been changed by a wave of giant-scale building, in Canary Wharf and the City of London in particular.

Until 2010, the tallest tower in London was Canary Wharf's One Canada Square at 800ft (244 metres), but a new benchmark has now been set by the controversial London Bridge Tower, known as "The Shard", a 1,016ft (310m) spire which is scheduled to be completed by May 2012. When finished it will be the tallest building in Western Europe.

The City competes with Heron Tower, Bishopsgate at 755ft (230m) with its mast, which will soon be dwarfed by the Bishopsgate Tower at 945ft (288m) due for completion

in 2013. The most distinctive structure, though, must be Norman Foster's building at 30 St Mary Axe (dubbed "The Gherkin") in the City.

the summit of Georgian architecture. The houses of Bedford Square are typically Georgian, with brick facades, sash windows and elaborate porticoes. As Italian influence waned, all things Greek became the vogue: Sir Robert Smirke (1780–1867) accordingly built the British Museum as a giant temple, to house Lord Elgin's plunder from the Parthenon.

## Victorian revivals

Against this pagan Greek influence, Augustus Pugin (1812–52) contended it was time to return to "true Christian architecture", the Gothic. His chance to lead the revival came on 16 October 1834, when the old Palace of Westminster burnt down. His design for the new Houses of Parliament, carried out with Charles Barry (1795–1860), took as inspiration the Henry VII chapel in Westminster Abbey.

Gothic Revival was the cornerstone of Victorian architecture. It produced a distinctive Tower Bridge, while Sir George Gilbert Scott

(1811–78) built St Pancras Station as a romantic castle. Victorian eclecticism even allowed a Tudor Revival, as in New Hall at Lincoln's Inn.

## Modern architecture

Britain was virtually bankrupted by World War II, which accounts for the number of utilitarian blocks that had to be built quickly and cheaply in the 1950s and '60s, which have not worn well. Buildings from the 1951 Festival of Britain such as the Royal Festival Hall, though, stand out beside more brutalist Modernist projects such as the all-concrete National Theatre (1967–77).

London's economic boom in the 1980s and the redevelopment of vast areas like Docklands have launched a whole new wave of construction, begun by Richard Rogers' futuristic Lloyds building in 1986. A city that resisted tall buildings has acquired skyscrapers, led by the mammoth Canary Wharf (since 1987).

The latest focus for new building is the Olympic Park in east London, site of the 2012 Games. London's new architecture is a mix of provocative styles – a playful giant wheel, Norman Foster's tapering City tower the "Gherkin" – reflecting a new openness and a readiness to add still more to London's endless variety. ❏

**ABOVE LEFT:** St Pancras Station *(far left)* and the Natural History Museum *(above and below)* typify Gothic Revival, a favourite of Victorian architects.
**ABOVE:** the "Gherkin" close up.

# ORIENTATION

The Places section details all the attractions worth
seeing, arranged by area. The areas are shown on a
colour-coordinated map on pages 66–7. Main sights
are cross-referenced by number to individual maps

For a cosmopolitan city of 7.7 million people, London is quite parochial. Each neighbourhood, each street corner, is proud of its own identity. Central London is the shared London of all these groups and of nearly 20 million visitors a year as well. Symbols of London – the Beefeaters, the bobbies, the cabbies, the red buses, the pageantry, the Royal Family, the Houses of Parliament – all are here, along with the stock market, motorcycle messengers, dirty air and crawling traffic.

After an initial tour by boat or on an open-top bus to orientate yourself, the best way to see Central London is on foot. Although Greater London sprawls for 610 sq miles (1,580 sq km), the central area is surprisingly compact. Walkers have time to appreciate the infinite variety of architectural detail that traces the city's long development. What's more, they will be treading in the footsteps of some of history's most celebrated citizens – to aid the imagination, blue plaques *(see page 138)* show where the great, the good and the notorious lived.

We begin the Places section by focusing on the royal and ruling heart of the city, Parliament and Buckingham Palace. The ensuing chapters cover the remainder of the central area, from Piccadilly to Chelsea, and cross the river to explore the vibrancy of Southwark and the South Bank. Village London *(pages 233–263)* tours some of the most interesting local communities outside the central area, usually reached by bus or Underground. Day Trips *(pages 267–273)* suggests a range of convenient excursions from London.

All the sites of special interest are numbered on specially drawn maps to help you find your way around, and a street atlas begins on page 317.

As a visitor, you may be one of the 72 percent who visit the Tower of London, or the 92 percent who make their way to Piccadilly Circus. But you will probably also be one of the millions who find some small, distinctive corner of this remarkable city to be enthusiastic about. ❏

---

**PRECEDING PAGES:** Oxford Circus at Christmas; St Paul's Cathedral.
**LEFT:** the River Thames as seen from Victoria Tower, Palace of Westminster.

British Museum
pages 144–49

Piccadilly Circus
page 89

Trafalgar Square
page 99

Buckingham Palace
page 80

Big Ben
page 76

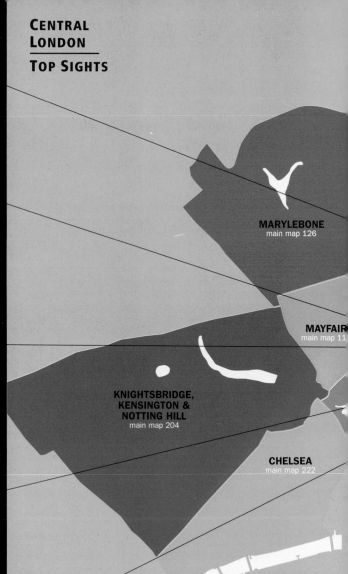

# CENTRAL LONDON

## TOP SIGHTS

MARYLEBONE
main map 126

MAYFAIR
main map 11

KNIGHTSBRIDGE,
KENSINGTON &
NOTTING HILL
main map 204

CHELSEA
main map 222

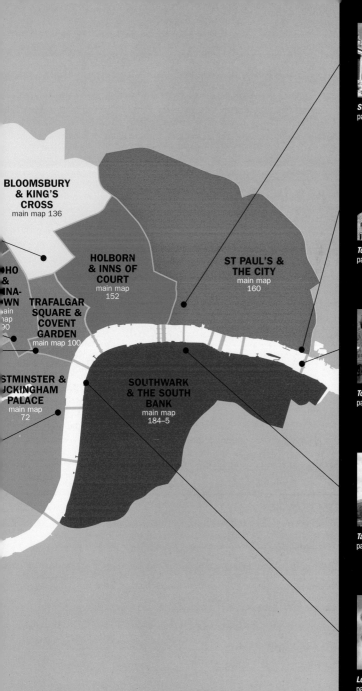

**BLOOMSBURY & KING'S CROSS**
main map 136

**HOLBORN & INNS OF COURT**
main map 152

**ST PAUL'S & THE CITY**
main map 160

**HO & NA-WN**
main map 90

**TRAFALGAR SQUARE & COVENT GARDEN**
main map 100

**STMINSTER & UCKINGHAM PALACE**
main map 72

**SOUTHWARK & THE SOUTH BANK**
main map 184–5

*St. Paul's Cathedral*
pages 159, 176–7

*Tower of London*
pages 173, 178–81

*Tower Bridge*
page 195

*Tate Modern*
pages 189, 198–9

*London Eye*
page 186

# Central London

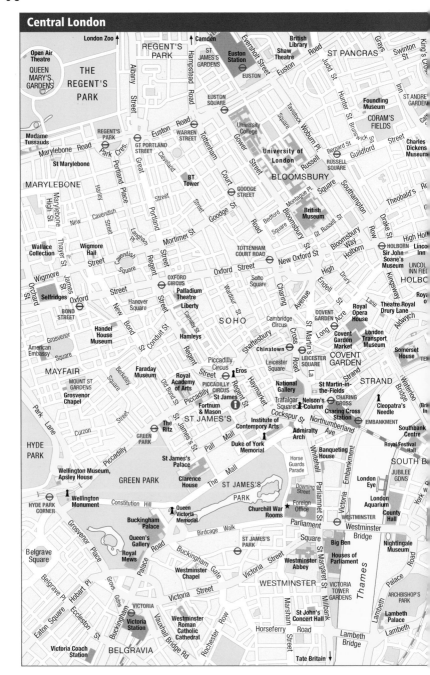

London Zoo ↑
↑ Camden
REGENT'S PARK
Hampstead Road
Eversholt Street
British Library
St Pancras
Grays Inn
Swinton St
King's Cro...

Open Air Theatre
QUEEN MARY'S GARDENS

THE REGENT'S PARK

ST JAMES'S GARDENS

Euston Station

Shaw Theatre

Euston

Judd St

Hunter St

ST ANDRE GARDEN Cale...

Albany Street

EUSTON

Euston Street

EUSTON SQUARE

Tavistock Square

Woburn Pl

Foundling Museum

CORAM'S FIELDS

Charles Dickens Museum

Madame Tussauds

Marylebone Road

Euston Road

REGENT'S PARK

WARREN STREET

University College

Gower Street

Bernard St

Brunswick Sq

Guildford St

St Marylebone

Park Cres.

GT PORTLAND STREET

Cleveland Street

University of London

RUSSELL SQUARE

Southampton Row

Theobald's Ro...

MARYLEBONE

Marylebone High St

Portland Place

Great Portland Street

BT Tower

GOODGE STREET

BLOOMSBURY

Montague Pl

Russell Square

Drake St

High Hol...

Wallace Collection

Harley Street

Cavendish Street

New

Thayer St

Wigmore Hall

Wigmore Street

Mortimer St

Goodge Street

Bedford Square

Bloomsbury

Gt Russell St

Bloomsbury Way

Holborn

HOLBORN

Sir John Soane's Museum

LINCOLN INN FIEL

Lincol Inn

James St

Orchard St

Selfridges

Oxford Street

Cavendish Square

Regent Street

Wardour Street

TOTTENHAM COURT ROAD

New Oxford St

Soho Square

High

Drury

Endell St

HOLBO

Roya

Bond Street

Langham St

OXFORD CIRCUS

Palladium Theatre

Liberty

Charing Cross Road

Shaftesbury Avenue

COVENT GARDEN

Long Acre

Royal Opera House

Theatre Royal Drury Lane

Aldwych

Handel House Museum

Hanover Square

Camaby St

SOHO

Cambridge Circus

St Martin's Lane

Covent Garden Market

London Transport Museum

Somerset House

TE...

American Embassy

Grosvenor Square

Conduit St

Hamleys

Chinatown

Leicester Square

LEICESTER SQUARE

COVENT GARDEN

Strand

STRAND

MAYFAIR

Berkeley Square

Faraday Museum

Royal Academy of Arts

Piccadilly Circus

Eros

PICCADILLY CIRCUS

Haymarket

National Gallery

St Martin-in-the-Fields

Waterloo Bridge

MOUNT ST GARDENS

Old Bond St

Regent St

St James

Trafalgar Square

Nelson's Column

CHARING CROSS

Cleopatra's Needle

Grosvenor Chapel

Piccadilly

Fortnum & Mason

Institute of Contemporary Arts

Cockspur St

Charing Cross Station

EMBANKMENT

Bri In

Park Lane

Curzon Street

The Ritz

GREEN PARK

St James's St

Pall Mall

Admiralty Arch

Northumberland Ave

Southbank Centre

HYDE PARK

Piccadilly

Duke of York Memorial

Horse Guards Parade

Banqueting House

Whitehall

Royal Festival Hall

SOUTH B

Wellington Museum, Apsley House

St James's Palace

The Mall

ST JAMES'S PARK

Downing Street

JUBILEE GDNS

London Eye

HYDE PARK CORNER

Wellington Monument

Constitution Hill

Clarence House

Queen Victoria Memorial

Birdcage Walk

Foreign Office

Churchill War Rooms

London Aquarium

County Hall

York W

Buckingham Palace

GREEN PARK

Parliament Street

Westminster

WESTMINSTER

Nightingale Museum

Belgrave Square

Grosvenor Place

Queen's Gallery

Royal Mews

Palace Road

Buckingham Gate

ST JAMES'S PARK

Victoria Street

Parliament Square

Westminster Abbey

Big Ben

Houses of Parliament

Westminster Bridge

Thames

Belgrave Pl

Hobart Pl

Grosvs Gdns

Westminster Chapel

Buckingham Palace Road

Victoria Street

WESTMINSTER

VICTORIA TOWER GARDENS

ARCHBISHOP'S PARK

Lambeth Palace

Eaton Square

Eccleston St

VICTORIA

Victoria Station

Vauxhall Bridge Rd

Westminster Roman Catholic Cathedral

Rochester Row

St John's Concert Hall

Marsham Street

Horseferry Road

Millbank

Lambeth Bridge

Palace Road

Lambeth

Victoria Coach Station

BELGRAVIA

Victoria Street

Tate Britain ↓

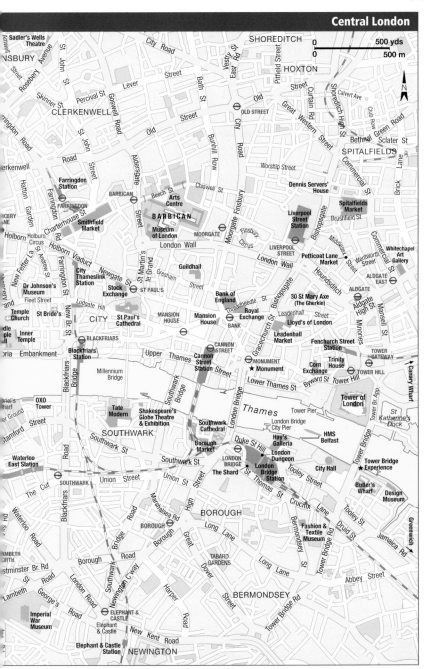

0          500 yds
0          500 m

Sadler's Wells Theatre
SHOREDITCH
HOXTON
NSBURY
St John St
Roseberry Avenue
Skinner St
Percival St
CLERKENWELL
St John St
erkenwell
Road
Street
Farringdon Station
FARRINGDON
ICERY NE
Smithfield Market
rkenwell
Hatton Garden
Holborn
Holborn Circus
Dr Johnson's Museum
Fleet Street
New Fetter La
St Andrew's St
Farringdon St
and
Temple Church
St Bride's
ple ll
Inner Temple
oria
Embankment
City Road
Lever Street
Goswell Road
Old Street
OLD STREET
Bath St
City Road
Bunhill Row
Worship Street
Great Eastern Street
Curtain Rd
Shoreditch High St
Calvert Ave
Club Row
Bethnal Green Road
Sclater St
SPITALFIELDS
Brick Lane
Commercial St
BARBICAN
Arts Centre
Beech St
Chiswell St
Aldersgate Street
Moorgate
Charterhouse St
BARBICAN
Museum of London
MOORGATE
London Wall
Finsbury Circus
Dennis Servers' House
Liverpool Street Station
LIVERPOOL STREET
Spitalfields Market
Brushfield St
Bishopsgate
Middlesex St
Wentworth Street
Commercial St
Whitechapel Art Gallery
Petticoat Lane Market
ALDGATE EAST
City Thameslink Station
St Martin's le Grand
Newgate Street
Gresham Street
Guildhall
London Wall
Houndsditch
ALDGATE
Aldgate High St
Mansell St
Stock Exchange
Holborn Viaduct
Ludgate Hill
Fleet Street
ST PAUL'S
Bank of England
Threadneedle St
Bishopsgate
30 St Mary Axe (The Gherkin)
Leadenhall Street
Minories
St Paul's Cathedral
CITY
New Br St
MANSION HOUSE
Mansion House
BANK
Royal Exchange
Gracechurch St
Leadenhall Market
Lloyd's of London
Fenchurch Street Station
TOWER GATEWAY
BLACKFRIARS
Upper Thames Street
CANNON STREET
Cannon Street Station
MONUMENT
★ Monument
Lower Thames St
Corn Exchange
Byward St
Trinity House
TOWER HILL
Tower Hill
Canary Wharf
Blackfriars Station
Blackfriars Bridge
Millennium Bridge
Southwark Bridge
London Bridge
Thames
Tower Pier
Tower of London
Tower Br. App.
St Katherine's Dock
ariel's harf
er Ground
OXO Tower
amford
Street
Tate Modern
SOUTHWARK
Shakespeare's Globe Theatre & Exhibition
Southwark Cathedral
London Bridge City Pier
Hay's Galleria
HMS Belfast
Tower Bridge
Tower Bridge Experience ★
Waterloo East Station
SOUTHWARK
Southwark St
Union Street
Borough Market
Duke St Hill
London Dungeon
London Bridge Station
City Hall
Butler's Wharf
Design Museum
The Cur
Blackfriars Bridge Road
Union St
The Shard
St Thomas St
Tooley Street
Tooley St
Druid St
Greenwich Rd
Waterloo Road
Marshalsea Rd
High Street
LONDON BRIDGE
Crucifix Lane
Jamaica Rd
AMBETH ORTH
Road
stminster Br Rd
George's Road
Borough Road
Borough High St
BOROUGH
Great Dover Street
Long Lane
Fashion & Textile Museum
Bermondsey St
Tower Bridge Rd
Abbey Street
Lambeth
George's Road
London Road
Southwark Bridge Road
Newington C'way
TABARD GARDENS
Harper Road
Long Lane
BERMONDSEY
Tower Bridge Rd
Imperial War Museum
ELEPHANT & CASTLE
Elephant & Castle
New Kent Road
Dover Road
Elephant & Castle Station
NEWINGTON

# WESTMINSTER AND BUCKINGHAM PALACE

Westminster is the centre of official London. Parliament meets here, the Queen and the prime minister have their London homes here, and state funerals are conducted in Westminster Abbey

**A**s the focus of government and the monarchy, Westminster contains within its ancient and easily walked boundaries the headquarters of the nation's policy-making civil servants, the prime minister and the Cabinet, and the Royal Family. Many kings and queens are buried in Westminster Abbey, founded by the last Saxon ruler, Edward the Confessor (1042–66).

## WHITEHALL

Official London begins immediately south of **Trafalgar Square** *(see page 99)*, where the broad and unmistakably official thoroughfare of **Whitehall ❶** stretches imperiously southwards towards the Houses of Parliament. Most buildings along here are government offices, built from Portland stone in an imposing classical style.

On the right, beyond the Trafalgar Studios, are the former offices of the Admiralty (for centuries the headquarters of the Royal Navy until the Ministry of Defence took over in 1964), and the offices of the Household Cavalry's headquarters, known as the **Horse Guards ❷**. Outside this colonnaded building are two mounted Life Guards in fancy uni-

forms, white gloves, plumes and helmets, rigidly oblivious to the throng of camera-toting tourists. Changed every hour from 10am to 4pm, they guard the site of the main gateway to what was the Palace of Whitehall, used by King Henry VIII in the 16th century and burnt to the ground in 1698. Through the archway of Horse Guards and opening out on to St James's Park is the huge **Horse Guards Parade**. Here in June the Queen's birthday is honoured by a splendid pageant called **Trooping the**

Map on page 72

**Main attractions**
HORSE GUARDS
BANQUETING HOUSE
CHURCHILL WAR ROOMS
HOUSES OF PARLIAMENT
WESTMINSTER ABBEY
TATE BRITAIN
WESTMINSTER CATHEDRAL
ST JAMES'S PARK
BUCKINGHAM PALACE
THE MALL

**LEFT:** Westminster Abbey.
**RIGHT:** Buckingham Palace.

*A member of the Life Guards outside the entrance of the former Palace of Whitehall.*

Colour; the name is derived from the regimental colours which are paraded.

## Banqueting House ❸

✉ Whitehall; www.hrp.ork.uk 📞 0844 482 7777 🕐 Mon–Sat 10am–5pm 💷 charge 🚇 Embankment

Opposite Horse Guards, on the other side of Whitehall, is the Renaissance-style **Banqueting House**, built in 1620 by Inigo Jones, the man responsible for bringing this Italian style of architecture to England. It is the only surviving fragment of the palace destroyed by fire in 1698.

Inside the huge hall upstairs, the ceiling is divided into nine large panels filled with rich baroque paintings by Rubens. They were commissioned by Charles I to glorify (or deify) the House of Stuart (Rubens was paid £3,000 and knighted for his work), but the Civil War followed and Charles I was beheaded on a scaffold outside the building. The hall is still used for official state banquets.

## The prime minister's home

London's most famous address, **Downing Street** ❹, just off Whitehall, is little more than a terrace of four

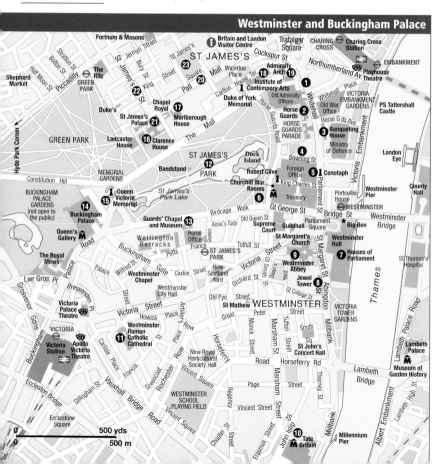

### Westminster and Buckingham Palace

*Recommended Restaurants, Pubs & Bars on page 85*

18th-century houses, sealed off behind a heavy gate. The street is named after the diplomat Sir George Downing who went to America with his parents in 1638 and became the second student to graduate from Harvard University. No. 10 is the official residence of the prime minister, and the venue for Cabinet meetings.

The plain black door and net-curtained windows suggest nothing of stylish rooms or of the state business conducted inside. Successive prime ministers have lived here since 1735. The chancellor of the exchequer has his official residence at No. 11.

Across Whitehall from Downing Street are the offices of the Ministry of Defence. Just south of here, the **Cenotaph** ❺, the national war memorial designed by Sir Edwin Lutyens, breaks Whitehall's monotony. On Remembrance Sunday in November it is the focal point of a service attended by the Queen and political leaders to remember the dead of two world wars as well as other conflicts.

Beyond the Cenotaph, Whitehall becomes **Parliament Street**. The stolid buildings on the same side as the Horse Guards house the Foreign and Commonwealth offices; its designer, Sir George Gilbert Scott, described it as "a kind of national palace".

Turn right into King Charles Street, which runs between the **Foreign Office** and the **Treasury** and **Cabinet offices** before reaching **Clive Steps** and a statue of Robert Clive (1725–74), a key figure in the establishment of British power in India. Beside the steps is a small wall of sandbags, the only above-ground sign of the Churchill War Rooms, one of London's best small museums.

*The statue of Robert Clive, who rose from being a humble scribe in the East India Company to become governor of the Bengal Presidency, laying the foundations for British rule in India. His suicide at the age of 49 was linked to opium use and depression.*

**ABOVE LEFT:** No. 10 Downing Street.
**BELOW:** Horse Guards.

## How Parliament Works

England is known as the mother of
parliaments, and the Westminster
Parliament has been a model for
democracies all over the world

The Houses of Parliament consist of the
House of Commons and the House of
Lords. The Commons, the House of
locally elected Members of Parliament (MPs),
known as the Lower House, wields virtually
all the power but inhabits only half the building. Jutting out towards Parliament Square is
Westminster Hall, with the offices, dining
rooms and libraries of the Commons; in the
centre is the Commons' debating chamber.
To the right of Westminster Hall is the domain
of the Lords, whose role is to examine and
sometimes block bills proposed by the Lower
House, although a bill can be reintroduced.
Until recently, most lords governed by
birthright, as descendants of the previous ruling classes, but the voting rights of many
hereditary peers have been abolished and
the make-up of the Lords has changed. Most
members are now life peers, ennobled for
services to the nation, and their titles can not

be passed to their children. Former MPs are
often made peers in recognition of years of
public service.

There are 650 elected MPs, yet the Commons seats only about 450. This is not usually a problem since MPs attend sessions
when they wish. The governing party sits on
one side, facing the opposition. Cabinet ministers sit on the front bench, opposite the
"Shadow Cabinet" (the leading members of
the opposition). The Cabinet, consisting of
up to two dozen ministers and chaired by the
prime minister, meets at 10 Downing Street
weekly to review major issues.

Major parties represented are the Con-
servatives, Labour and the Liberal Democrats.
General elections are run on the basis of local
rather than proportional representation.
Therefore, a party's presence in the house
may not reflect its overall national standing.
A party, however, needs an overall majority in
the house to push through its bills, hence the
need for the coalition after the 2010 election.
The procedure of law making is so complex
that a bill usually takes more than six months
to be enacted. If it is still incomplete at the
end of the parliamentary year, it is dropped.
Various techniques are employed by the opposition to delay a bill.

The press can report on Parliament and
the business of both houses is televised. A
select group of journalists ("lobby correspon-
dents") have daily informal "background"
briefings with ministers.

Parliament meets from October to July. In
November, the government's plans for the
year are announced in the Queen's Speech
at the State Opening of Parliament. From the
Visitors' Gallery, the public can watch the
House of Commons at work, though seats are
limited and security precautions tight. The
weekly Prime Minister's Question Time – an
unruly affair – usually attracts a full house. ❑

**LEFT:** the Queen's speech at the State Opening of
Parliament. **ABOVE:** the Commons in action.

Recommended Restaurants, Pubs & Bars on page 85

## Churchill War Rooms ❻

✉ Clive Steps, King Charles Street; www.cwr.iwm.org.uk ☎ 7930 6961 ⏱ daily 9.30am–6pm ⓒ charge 🚇 Westminster

This was the wartime bunker from which Sir Winston Churchill conducted World War II. Many of the 21 rooms were abandoned in 1945 and left untouched until the museum opened in 1984; others have been meticulously restored to their wartime condition, "down to the last paper clip". The Central Map Room and the rooms that served as a round-the-clock typing pool illustrate the problems of communications in the 1940s.

A converted broom cupboard housed a pioneering hotline to the White House, enabling Churchill to have confidential talks with President Roosevelt, despite air raids.

The **Churchill Museum** within includes a selection of letters and other memorabilia, as well as an interactive table on which visitors can find information about Churchill's life.

### PARLIAMENT SQUARE

Parliament Street empties out into **Parliament Square**, with its tall trees and lawns lined with statues of illustrious statesmen. This, the country's first official roundabout, is surrounded by national landmarks.

### The Houses of Parliament ❼

✉ www.parliament.uk ☎ 0844 847 1672 (for summer hours) ⓒ see panel, page 76 ⓒ charge for tours; free for UK residents if arranged through their MP 🚇 Westminster

The clock tower of the **Houses of Parliament** has become a symbol of London. Its elaborately fretted stone sides rise up nearly 330ft (100

*The transatlantic telephone in the Churchill War Rooms.*

**LEFT:** the Central Map Room. **BELOW:** Big Ben behind Boudicca's statue.

**BELOW RIGHT:**

The Union flag on top of Victoria Tower indicates that Parliament is in session. Night sessions are indicated by a light shining over the clock tower.

metres) to a richly gilded spire and a 13.5-tonne hour bell supposedly nicknamed **Big Ben** after a rather fat government official called Sir Benjamin Hall who was commissioner of works when the bell was installed. Its chimes first rang out across Westminster in 1859, after an earlier bell was damaged while being tested three years previously.

Facing Big Ben is the odd-looking **Portcullis House**, a £250 million office block for members of Parliament; its prominent and much criticised "chimneys" form part of the air-conditioning system.

The oldest part of the Houses of Parliament and one of the oldest buildings in London is **Westminster Hall**, begun in 1097. The thick buttressed walls are spanned with a magnificent hammer-beamed oak roof. This hall has witnessed many seminal events in British history: coronation celebrations, lyings-in-state and treason trials. Among those condemned to death were Sir Thomas More, who fell foul of King Henry VIII; King Charles I, accused of treason against Parliament; and the 17th-century revolutionary Guy Fawkes, who tried to blow up the buildings (see page 29).

### Fire and reconstruction

In 1834 a fire achieved what Guy Fawkes had failed to do and most of the ancient Palace of Westminster was destroyed. Westminster Hall, a small crypt chapel and the Jewel Tower (see page 77) survived. Following this conflagration, the current purpose-built structure was created in exuberant Gothic style by Sir Charles Barry and Augustus Pugin.

The houses are embellished with gilded spires and towers, mullioned windows and intricate stone carving and statues. The complex, which took some 30 years to complete, covers 8 acres (3.2 hectares); there are 100 staircases and more than 1,100 rooms. Apart from the ceremonial state rooms and the two main debating chambers, the House of Lords and the House of Commons, there are libraries, dining rooms, offices and secretarial facilities for government ministers, opposition leaders and ordinary Members of Parliament.

## Visiting the Houses of Parliament

**G**uided tours of the Houses of Parliament are held during Parliament's summer recess in August and September (Aug: Mon–Tue, Thur–Sat 9.15am–4.30pm, Wed 1.15–4.30pm; Sept: Mon, Fri, 9.15am–4.30pm; Tue–Thur 1.15–4.30pm. Also Sat all year 9.15am–4.30pm). To watch parliamentary debates at other times of the year from the public galleries overlooking the Commons or Lords chambers, queue by St Stephen's Gate on the western side of the building. Note that Parliament is also in recess at Christmas and Easter.

Entry times vary depending on when Parliament is in session, but normal sitting times for the Commons are Mon–Tue 2.30–10.30pm; Wed 11.30am–7.30pm; Thur 10.30am–6.30pm. The Commons does not normally sit on Friday, but when it does the hours are 9.30am–3.30pm. Expect to queue for 1–1½ hours, less in the evenings. The longest queues are for Prime Minister's Question Time (held at noon on Wednesday); UK residents should contact their MP for an advance ticket.

*Recommended Restaurants, Pubs & Bars on page 85*

## Main points of interest

**St Stephen's**, on the western side of the building, is the main entrance to the House of Commons, and anyone can watch debates from the visitors' gallery, though there are almost always queues *(see box, page 76)*. Beneath **St Stephen's Hall** is the ancient crypt chapel that survived the 1834 fire. Members can take their marriage vows and have their children baptised here. The **Commons chamber** was bombed in 1941; the current chamber only opened in 1950.

The immense **Victoria Tower** marks the grand entrance to the

House of Lords. It is also the entrance used by the Queen when opening a new session of government.

Opposite Parliament is the moated **Jewel Tower ❽**, a relic of the Palace of Westminster dating from 1365. Its small museum of Parliament Past and Present (Apr–Oct 10am–5pm, Nov–Mar 10am–4pm; charge) has more information panels than artefacts.

Opposite Parliament is the **Supreme Court** (Parliament Square, www.supremecourt.gov.uk; Mon–Fri 9.30am–4.30pm; charge), the UK's highest court of appeal. Guided tours are available on Fridays at 10am, 11.30am, 1.30pm and 3pm. Booking is advised.

### Westminster Abbey ❾

✉ www.westminster-abbey.org
📞 7222 5152 🕐 Mon–Tue, Thur–Fri 9.30am–4.30pm, last admission 3.30pm; Wed 9.30am–7pm, last admission 6pm; Sat 9am–2.30pm, last admission 1.30pm 🅲 charge; guided tours extra 🚇 Westminster

The most historic religious building in Britain is **Westminster Abbey**. It is

*The Jewel Tower has had several functions over the centuries. It was used to test official standards of weights and measures from 1869 until the 1930s, and its moat once supplied fish for the sovereign's table.*

**LEFT:** sightseeing from the top of a tour bus.
**BELOW:** the opulent House of Lords.

**TIP**

For art lovers in a hurry, a 220-seat catamaran runs every 40 minutes between Tate Britain on the Thames' north bank and Tate Modern on the south bank. It stops at the London Eye. Tel: 7887 8888.

**ABOVE AND BELOW**
Rodin's *The Kiss* and *The Cholmondeley Ladies*, artist unknown, in Tate Britain.
**RIGHT:** the towers of Westminster Abbey.

also an outstanding piece of Gothic architecture, which is probably more striking from the detail on the inside than from its outward aspects. So many eminent figures are honoured in this national shrine that large areas of the interior have the cluttered appearance of an overcrowded sculpture museum. *For full coverage of the abbey, see pages 86–7.*

## St Margaret's Church

On the northeast side of Westminster Abbey facing the Houses of Parliament is **St Margaret's Church,** used by MPs for official services and for high-society weddings. Sir Walter Raleigh (1552–1618), the sea captain, poet and favourite of Queen Elizabeth I, who established the first British colony in Virginia and introduced tobacco and potatoes to Britain, was interred here after his execution. William Caxton (*c.*1421–92), who ran the first English printing presses nearby, is also buried here.

Beyond Westminster Abbey and Victoria Gardens a short street leads to one of London's most unobtrusive but notable concert halls, **St John's,**

**Smith Square.** This former 18th-century church has fine acoustics and a reputation for a varied programme of classical music. In the crypt is a good wine bar-cum-restaurant *(see page 85).*

## Tate Britain ⑩

✉ Millbank; www.tate.org.uk/britain
☎ 7887 8888 🅒 daily 10am–6pm, until 10pm every Fri 🄴 free, but charge for feature exhibitions
🅿 Pimlico

*Recommended Restaurants, Pubs & Bars on page 85*

A 10–15-minute walk along Millbank from the Houses of Parliament is **Tate Britain,** founded in 1897 by Henry Tate, of the Tate & Lyle sugar empire, and today the storehouse for the Tate's collection of British art from 1500 to the present. It is complemented by Tate Modern, further down the river on Bankside, which houses most of the Tate's modern and contemporary international collection *(see pages 198–199).*

The galleries within Tate Britain are arranged by date and theme. The only criticism is that there isn't enough space: the majority of the collection has to be kept in storage out of the public view. A much-needed extension is being considered.

Among the British paintings are portraits by William Hogarth (1697–1764) and Thomas Gainsborough (1727–88), views of the English countryside by John Constable (1776–1837) and, in the Clore Gallery, seascapes and landscapes by J.M.W. Turner (1775–1851). Turner bequeathed the paintings to the nation on his death, with the stipulation that they should all be hung in one place, and should be available for the public to see, without charge.

The most popular 19th-century painters represented are the Pre-Raphaelites, including Millais, Holman Hunt, Rosetti and Burne-Jones. Modern British artists represented include Stanley Spencer, Francis Bacon and David Hockney. Sculptures include works by Jacob Epstein, Barbara Hepworth and Henry Moore. The Tate also stages free lectures and film shows, and has a reputation for the avant-garde, with the award of an annual Turner Prize. Its Rex Whistler-designed restaurant is a great place to have lunch *(see page 85).*

Across the river from Millbank, to the right, the modern green-and-cream building is **Vauxhall Cross,** headquarters of MI6's spymasters; this secret services building, designed by Terry Farrell, is built in a "Faraday Cage" which stops electro-magnetic information passing in or out.

## VICTORIA STREET

The west door of Westminster Abbey opens on to **Victoria Street,** important commercially but, since its re-building, a long grey canyon of undistinguished office blocks. Down this street, close to the Victoria Station end, is **Westminster Cathedral.**

## Westminster Cathedral ⓫

✉ www.westminstercathedral.org.uk
☎ 7798 9055  ⓒ cathedral daily 7am–7pm; tower Mon–Fri 9.30am–5pm, weekends 9.30am–6pm
ⓒ charge for tower  🚇 Victoria

This is the most important Catholic church in London. Its bold red-and-white brickwork makes it look like a gigantic layer cake. Built at the end of the 19th century in an outlandish Italian-Byzantine style not seen elsewhere in London, it has a 273ft (83-metre) tower incorporating a lift. The views from the top are superb. The

*Fine views from the top of Westminster Cathedral's tower.*

**BELOW:** the Italian-Byzantine-style facade of Westminster Cathedral.

interior is sumptuous, with many chapels clad in coloured marble, but the decor was never finished; the numerous mosaics included in the original designs are absent, and the ceiling is largely bereft of decoration.

On the north side of Victoria Street behind St James's Park Underground station is **Queen Anne's Gate**, a small, quiet street which has retained much of its 18th-century atmosphere. Lord Palmerston, who became prime minister in 1855, was born at No. 20.

## ST JAMES'S PARK AND BUCKINGHAM PALACE

The formal arrangement of lakes and flora at **St James's Park** is one of the most delightful in London. Formerly the grounds of St James's Palace acquired by Henry VIII in 1531, it was laid out in 1603, then re-landscaped in formal style by John Nash in 1827. It has always had a collection of ducks and water fowl, including black swans and pelicans, fed every day at 3pm. Another entertainment is the lunch-time concerts played in the bandstand.

*A carved canopy on one of the elegant terraced houses in Queen Anne's Gate.*

**ABOVE RIGHT AND BELOW:** St James's Park.

Continuing the ornithological theme is **Birdcage Walk**, which takes its name from an 18th-century aviary, running along the south side of the park from Parliament Square to Buckingham Palace and dividing the park from the drilling ground of the **Wellington Barracks**, the home of the Royal Grenadier Guards and the Coldstream Guards. Here the **Guards' Chapel and Museum** (www.theguardsmuseum.com; daily 10am–4pm, tel: 7414 3271; charge) are on the site of a former chapel which was hit by a bomb in 1944, killing 121 members of the congregation.

There are five of these aristocratic infantry regiments of Guards, first formed during the English Civil War (1642–9), and the museum provides a social history in uniform (including a uniform worn by the Duke of Wellington), as well as a large collection of toy soldiers.

## Buckingham Palace

✉ Buckingham Palace Road; www.royalcollection.org.uk ☎ 7766 7300 ⏰ late July–late Sept only, 9.30am–6.30pm, last admission 4.15pm; tickets are timed, and a visit lasts 2–2½ hours 💷 charge Ⓜ Green Park, Hyde Park Corner, Victoria

Buckingham Palace has been the main London home of the royal family since Queen Victoria acceded to the throne in 1837. George IV had earlier employed John Nash (responsible for many of the grander parts of

*Recommended Restaurants, Pubs & Bars on page 85*

central London) to enlarge the building which had been built in the 17th century for the Duke of Buckingham (it originally became the property of the Crown when George III bought it for his wife in 1761). Nash added two wings that were later enclosed in a quadrangle, while the main facade came later still, being designed by Aston Webb in 1913.

## A tour of the palace

The sumptuous **State Rooms** are open to the public for a few weeks in late summer when the Queen is not in residence. These include the Dining Room, Music Room, White Drawing Room and Throne Room, where there are paintings by Vermeer, Rubens and Rembrandt. The tour includes a stroll through part of the 40-acre (16-hectare) Palace Gardens where the cream of society mingles with the good and the worthy from all walks of life at the celebrated garden parties. The guests are invited because of some commendable contribution made to the nation, but few of the 8,000 people a year get to shake the Queen's hand.

Only the invited get further into the 775-room palace, although one enterprising intruder penetrated as far as the Queen's bedroom one night in 1982. She talked to him quietly while managing to summon palace security. The Queen and the Duke of Edinburgh occupy about 12 of the rooms, on the first floor of the north wing, overlooking Green Park. If the Queen is in residence, the royal standard flies from the flagpole.

Next to the Royal Mews on Buckingham Palace Road, the **Queen's Gallery** (daily 10am–5.30pm; tel: 7766 7301; charge, combined tickets with admission to Buckingham Palace and the Royal

*At a typical palace garden party, guests consume more than 27,000 cups of tea, more than 20,000 sandwiches and around 20,000 pieces of cake.*

**ABOVE:** Buckingham Palace. **BELOW LEFT AND RIGHT:** Longcase equation clock next to a portrait of King George III; State Banquet table.

**SHOP**

The gift shop next to the Queen's Gallery on Buckingham Palace Road is the place to buy souvenirs such as "God Save the Queen" pillow-cases, Queen Victoria china, Buckingham Palace biscuits, and a variety of Windsor-endorsed luxury foodstuffs.

**RIGHT:** *Portrait of Agatha Bas* (1641) by Rembrandt, the Queen's Gallery.
**BELOW:** ornamental gate to Green Park on the Mall.

Mews are available late July–late Sept) was refurbished in 2002 to coincide with the Queen's Golden Jubilee. The Queen has one of the top private art collections in the world, including an exceptional collection of Leonardo da Vinci drawings, portraits by Holbein and Rubens, and watercolour views of Windsor by Paul Sandby. Exhibitions are changed periodically and the works displayed vary in number.

The adjoining **Royal Mews** (late Mar–end Oct, daily 10am–5pm, Nov–mid-Dec Mon–Sat 10am–4pm; tel: 7766 7302; charge) contain royal vehicles, ranging from coaches to Rolls-Royces. The Gold State Coach, built for George III in 1762, is still used by the Queen on major state occasions.

Most of the everyday crowds come to see the **Changing of the Guard** which takes place outside the palace on alternate mornings at 11.30am, and daily in May, June and July. The New Guard, which marches up from Wellington Barracks, meets the Old Guard in the forecourt of the palace and they exchange symbolic keys to the accompaniment of regimental music. The Foot Guards are distinctive for their bearskin hats.

The **Queen Victoria Memorial** ⓕ in front of the palace was built in 1901. It encompasses symbolic figures glorifying the achievements of the British Empire and its builders.

## THE MALL

**The Mall**, the wide thoroughfare leading from Buckingham Palace to Trafalgar Square, was laid out by Charles II as a second course for the game of *paille maille* (a kind of croquet which spread from Italy to France, and then to Britain), when the one in Pall Mall *(see page 83)* became too rowdy. The Mall is the venue for the autumn **State Opening of Parliament**, when the Queen rides in a gold stagecoach surrounded by more than 100 troopers of the Household Cavalry wearing armorial breastplates. A further eccentricity are two farriers who accompany the procession, bearing spiked axes that would once have been used to kill any horse lamed in the parade and chop off its hooves to prevent the horse flesh being sold to a butcher.

*Recommended Restaurants, Pubs & Bars on page 85*

The Mall is lined with a succession of grand buildings and historic houses reflecting different styles and periods. The ducal palaces have been used as royal residences: **Clarence House** ⓰ is home to Prince Charles; at **Lancaster House** Chopin gave a recital for Queen Victoria; **Marlborough House** ⓱, designed by Sir Christopher Wren, was the home of Queen Mary, consort of George V (1865–1936) until her death in 1953. Now it is a Commonwealth conference and research centre. The brick Tudor **St James's Palace** faces on to Pall Mall *(see page 84)*.

Near the end of the Mall is **Carlton House Terrace**, built by John Nash, part of which houses the headquarters of **The Royal Society**, a learned body for the promotion of natural sciences. The oldest society of its kind, it was founded in 1660.

At the Trafalgar Square end, the terrace incorporates the **Mall Gallery** and the **Institute of Contemporary Arts** ⓲, a venue for avant-garde exhibitions, cinema and theatre, held in the restored Nash House.

The reinforced concrete structure across the Mall on the corner of the park is a bomb-proof shelter built for the Admiralty and nicknamed the Citadel, or Lenin's Tomb.

**Admiralty Arch** ⓳, leading from The Mall to Trafalgar Square, is a five-arched gateway commissioned by King Edward VII in memory of his mother, Queen Victoria, and completed in 1911. Traffic passes through the two outer arches: the central arch is opened only for state occasions, letting royalty in and out of the city.

*The Queen Victoria Memorial in front of Buckingham Palace.*

## PALL MALL AND ST JAMES'S

Along elegant **Pall Mall** ⓴ exclusive gentlemen's clubs mingle with the grand homes of royalty. Their lofty

**LEFT:** Horse Guards on the Mall.
**BELOW:** Admiralty Arch.

ANNO·DECIMO·EDWARDI·SEPTIMI·REGIS·
VICTORIÆ·REGINÆ·CIVES·GRATISSIMI·MDCCCCX·

*The bronze statue of Frederick, the Duke of York, at the top of the Duke of York Steps.*

**BELOW RIGHT:** St James's Palace. **FAR RIGHT:** Boisdale (top), display in the Cinnamon Club (bottom).

book-lined rooms, elegant, picture-lined dining rooms and chandeliered lounges can be seen from the street. The area has been the haunt of men of influence since the 17th century, and it is reassuring to learn that the clubs generally enjoy a reputation for dull food and snobbish company.

In **Waterloo Place**, at the east end of Pall Mall and the bottom end of Regent Street, the statue of Frederick, the "grand old" Duke of York (whose 10,000 men are fruitlessly marched up and down hill in a popular nursery rhyme), overlooks the Mall and St James's Park from its 124ft (37-metre) column. His monument's cost was met by extracting a day's wages from every man in the armed services.

One building that is unmistakable in Pall Mall is the red-brick **St James's Palace** ㉑ at the western end, built by Henry VIII in 1540 in a style that echoes his palace at Hampton Court. The state apartments are not open to the public and the chief relic of the original Tudor palace, the **Gatehouse** or **Clock Tower**, one of the finest examples of Tudor architecture in the city, is best viewed

from the street. Clarence House is part of the complex.

North of St James's Palace **St James's Street** ㉒ leads into an area traditionally associated with gentlemen's tailors and shoemakers. The characterful shop frontages include **Berry Bros and Rudd**, at No. 3, which could be straight out of a Dickens novel. **James Lock and Co**, at No. 6, is the birthplace of the bowler hat. A few doors up is **Lobb's**, shoemakers to Queen Victoria, and now to the Duke of Edinburgh.

### St James's Square

Also off the north side of Pall Mall is **St James's Square** ㉓ laid out by Henry Jermyn, the first Earl of St Alban in about 1660. The Dukes of Norfolk had a town house in the square from 1723 until 1938. The building was used by General Eisenhower when he was preparing to launch the invasions of North Africa and northwest Europe in World War II. Also here is the London Library, an independent subscription library whose past members have included Dickens and George Eliot. ❏

## Club Land

**E**ach of London's members' clubs has its own character and attracts a certain type of person. It is said that bishops and Fellows of the Royal Society join the Athenaeum (see picture), the foremost literary club, while actors and publishers opt for the Garrick or Saville Club. Diplomats, politicians and spies prefer Brooks', the Traveller's, Boodles or White's, while journalists gather at the Groucho Club in Soho. The novelist Jules Verne used the Reform Club (Pall Mall), the leading liberal club, as the setting for Phileas Fogg's wager that he could travel around the world in 80 days.

Dukes join the Turf Club, while top Tories like to dine together at The Carlton on St James's Street. The majority of London's clubs are the near-exclusive preserve of men. Their continuing influence in the social, commercial and political life of the capital should not be underestimated.

# BEST RESTAURANTS, PUBS AND BARS

## Restaurants

Prices for a three-course dinner per person with a half-bottle of house wine:
**£** = under £20
**££** = £20–30
**£££** = £30–50
**££££** = over £50

## British

### Boisdale
15 Eccleston St, SW1
℡ 7730 6922; www.bois dale.co.uk ©L Mon–Fri, D Mon–Sat. **££££** [p332, A1]
Scottish dishes such as lobster bisque, haggis, and Aberdeen Angus steaks. There is always fresh fish and game and a full malt whisky line-up.

### Goring Dining Room
Goring Hotel, Beeston Place, SW1 ℡ 7396 9000; www. thegoring.com ©L Sun–Fri, D daily. **££££** [p332, A1]
Traditional fare such as potted shrimps, filet of venison, and proper puddings. Sunday roast lunch is a speciality.

### Smith Square Restaurant
St John's, Smith Square, SW1 ℡ 7222 2779

©L Mon–Fri, D on weekday concert evenings and weekends. **££–£££** [p332–3, C1]
Beneath one of London's top concert venues, this brick-vaulted restaurant offers good food and excellent service. Sand-wiches and snacks are also on offer, and there is a long wine list.

### Tate Britain Restaurant
Millbank, SW1 ℡ 7887 8825 ©L daily. **£££** (set menu **££**) [p332–3, C2]
Traditional fare such as fish of the day, veal escalope and steak-and-kidney pudding are well prepared and reliably good. Has an excellent wine list.

## French

### Le Caprice
Arlington House, Arlington St, SW1 ℡ 7629 2239; www.le-caprice.co.uk ©L & D daily. **££££** [p318, A4]
Chic, buzzy bistro with Art Deco decor. The food – sophisticated salads, seafood and wonderful desserts – is more for

picking over than wolfing down. Vegetarian dishes are also available.

### Quaglino's
16 Bury St, SW1 ℡ 7930 6767; www.quaglinos-restaurant.co.uk ©L & D Mon–Sat. **£££** [p318, B4]
Glamorous brasserie that also does a set lunch menu. Live music most days (when it closes at 1am) adds to the atmosphere.

## Indian

### The Cinnamon Club
Old Westminster Library, Great Smith St, SW1 ℡ 7222 2555; www. cinnamonclub.com ©L & D Mon–Sat. **££££** (set lunch **££**) [p332–3, C1]
Set in a beautifully refurbished Victorian library. The menu has a fine selection of speciali-ties, ranging from Wagyu beef to tandoori lamb.

## Pubs and Bars

As one might expect, Westminster has a good choice of pubs, includ-ing **St Stephen's Arms** (10 Bridge St) and the **Red Lion** (48 Parliament St), both popular with politicians. There are also wine bars aplenty. **Tapster** (3 Brewers Green, Buckingham Gate), offers a traditio-nal wine bar setting and menu, as does **Balls Brothers** (50 Bucking-

ham Palace Road), one of a small chain of Lon-don wine bars. For a sleeker environment, try **Cinnamon Club Bar**, the high-tech downstairs bar of the restaurant (see main listings) or **Zander** (45 Buckingham Gate). For speciality whiskies, as well as cocktails, try **Millbank Lounge** (30 John Islip St), a modern bar decked out in red and chrome.

# WESTMINSTER ABBEY

**More than 3,000 notable people are buried here. The clutter of monuments make it seem like an ecclesiastical Madame Tussauds, with stone replacing wax**

Monarchs were interred here until George II in 1760, and they are still crowned here. Among the royal tombs, look out for those of Elizabeth I and her half-sister Queen Mary, both in the Lady Chapel. Poets lie close by, beginning with Geoffrey Chaucer in 1400, who had been Clerk of the King's Works to the Palace of Westminster.

Other tombs include those of the naturalist Charles Darwin, the explorer David Livingstone and the scientist Sir Isaac Newton.

The Tomb of the Unknown Warrior *(above)* houses a body brought back from France at the end of World War I, along with the soil for the grave. As the national shrine, Westminster Abbey was the natural resting place for this anonymous representative of the countless war dead.

Royal weddings also take place here – most recently Prince William's to Kate Middleton.

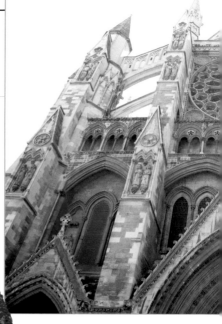

**ABOVE:** much of the present abbey, the third on the site, was built in the 13th century in early English Gothic style by Henry III. In the 16th century, Henry VII added the chapel in the late Gothic Perpendicular style. During the 18th century, Nicholas Hawksmoor designed the towers at the main west entrance.

**ABOVE:** the marble effigy of Queen Elizabeth I sits over her tomb and that of her half-sister, Queen Mary Tudor, in the Lady Chapel. Originally buried in the vault of King Henry VII, Elizabeth's tomb was moved here in 1606. Her crown, collar, orb and sceptre are replacements, the originals having been stolen.

## The essentials

✉ *www.westminster-abbey.org*

☎ *7222 5152*

🕐 *Mon–Fri 9.30am–4.30pm, Wed until 7pm (last admission 6pm), Sat 9am–2.30pm*

💰 *charge; guided tours are extra*

🚇 *Westminster*

## SOME HIGHLIGHTS

**Poets' Corner.** The remains of Chaucer, Edmund Spenser, Samuel Johnson, Dryden, Sheridan, Browning, Tennyson, Dickens and Kipling lie here. Ben Jonson is buried standing up because he didn't wish to occupy too much space.
**Coronation Chair.** This has been used for every coronation in the Abbey since 1308.
**Henry VII's Chapel.** Contains exquisite fan-vaulting and the statues of nearly 100 saints.
**Chapter House.** Parliament met here in the 14th century. It has a fine tiled floor from 1259 and some lurid wall paintings based on the Apocalypse.
**Undercroft Museum.** This 11th-century room contains many of the Abbey's treasures as well as waxworks and death masks of various monarchs.
**Sculptures.** There are superbly carved angels in the south transept, and the chapels of Henry V and Henry VII are packed with saints and philosophers.
**Brass band concerts** are often held in a garden off the Cloisters in July and August.

**ABOVE:** the Lady Chapel where King Henry VII is buried. **CENTRE TOP:** shrine of St Edward the Confessor. **CENTRE BOTTOM:** Poets' Corner consists of a mixture of burials and commemorations of playwrights, poets and writers. Shakespeare's memorial comprises the central feature of this group memorial. **RIGHT:** the choir is the part of the abbey where the monks worshipped. This area includes the abbey organ; famous organists who played here include Henry Purcell, who is also buried in the abbey.

*Recommended Restaurants, Bars, Pubs & Cafés on pages 95–7*

# SOHO AND CHINATOWN

Soho, Chinatown and Leicester Square form London's main entertainment centre, where you'll find abundant clubs, pubs, cinemas and theatres, and cuisines from all over the globe

The West End has long been seen as the place to head for a night out in London. Piccadilly Circus is a springboard for London's theatreland while Leicester Square is the gateway to Chinatown and the location of the Empire cinema, the venue for UK film premieres. Over the past few decades, however, as tacky shops and chain restaurants have muscled in on these famous squares, their glamour has begun to look a little tarnished. Neighbouring Soho, on the other hand, has largely shed its once-dubious image as London's dark underbelly to become one of the capital's foremost destinations for drinking and dining.

## PICCADILLY CIRCUS

At the heart of the West End is **Piccadilly Circus ❶**, star of millions of postcards. The first illuminated advertising signs appeared here in 1890, offering lucrative rental income to shopkeepers but contrasting harshly with the elegant architecture of neighbouring Regent Street. The statue of Eros, Greek god of love, was erected in 1893 as the Angel of Charity in honour of the philanthropic seventh Earl of Shaftesbury (1801–85) who drove

the broad thoroughfare bearing his name through the squalid slums that had grown up to the northeast.

Adding to Piccadilly's bright lights are the refurbished Criterion theatre on the south side, a huge branch of fashion retailer The Sting on the west and the 19th-century facade of the London Pavilion, a former music hall, on the east, which is now part of the **Trocadero Centre ❷**, a complex of shops and restaurants on Holland Street. It includes **Ripley's Believe It or Not!**

**Main attractions**
PICCADILLY CIRCUS
OLD COMPTON STREET
SOHO SQUARE
BERWICK STREET MARKET
CARNABY STREET
CHINATOWN

**LEFT:** gateway to Chinatown.
**RIGHT:** sitting under Eros, Piccadilly Circus.

Created by the Belgian-born Madam Valerie, **Pâtisserie Valerie** (open until 11pm) at No. 44 Old Compton Street sells mouthwatering sweet and savoury pastries. If you're in need of a caffeine fix but don't like London prices, the **Algerian Coffee Shop** on Old Compton Street serves great coffee at low prices. It also sells freshly roasted coffee. Take your pick from the jars of beans that line the shelves like an old-fashioned sweet shop.

**BELOW:** Bar Italia in Soho's Frith Street.

(daily 10am–midnight; charge), a collection of hundreds of weird objects from fossilized dinosaur eggs to a replica of Tower Bridge made from matchsticks.

The Trocadero also contains **Funland** , a huge indoor entertainment complex (daily 10am–1am), consisting of five floors of video games, slot machines, dodgems, 10-pin bowling, a sports bar, and a pool hall, all of which have seen better days**.**

## BUSTLING SOHO

On the north side of Shaftesbury Avenue lies **Soho**, a bustling area of narrow streets long popular with immigrants. Flemish weavers, French Huguenots, Greeks, Italians, Belgians, Maltese, Swiss, Chinese and Russian Jews have sought refuge here at various times. Their influence is still felt in the patisseries, delicatessens, restaurants and shops.

Four hundred years ago Soho was an area of open fields, and its name

is said to come from a hunting cry: "So-ho, so-ho!".

## Bars and clip joints

Once infamous as the centre of London's sex industry, Soho occupies a middle-ground between the edgy, seedier Soho of its past and the tourist-friendly hotspot of smart bars and restaurants that populate the area today. "Anything you like, sir" is still a phrase murmured to passers-by, but most of the strip joints and sex shops have been pushed towards the side streets. There are also venues for drag artists and transvestites that have been going long enough to have become almost respectable, and several of the attractive late-night bars and restaurants designed for the discerning gay crowd draw visitors of all persuasions.

## Old Compton Street ❸

This is Soho's main artery, where a few of the celebrated continental

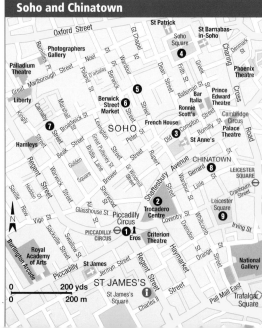

*Recommended Restaurants, Bars, Pubs & Cafés on pages 95–7*

ing arrangements at the Colony Club in Dean Street. At 22 Frith Street, opposite Ronnie Scott's jazz club, is Bar Italia, a narrow café-bar with pavement seating and a retro Italian feel, which serves the best cappuccino in town and is open 24 hours a day. It is also a great place to watch international football matches; the large screen at the back of the bar is visible from the street.

### Soho Square ❶

At the top of Frith Street, **Soho Square** was one of London's best addresses when it was built in the 17th century. Today various film, new media and design companies are based here, their minimalist receptions lit up by plasma screens or statement art. During the summer the garden at the heart of the square is crowded with office workers grabbing a bit of sun with their sandwich. In the centre of the square are a 17th-century statue of Charles II and a 19th-century mock-Tudor gardeners' tool shed from which steps lead down to an underground cavern, used as a

food stores, cafés and specialist shops which once dominated the street, live on. Most have been replaced by modern coffee shops, bars and more outlandish establishments, such as the body-piercing shop.

Situated at the Charing Cross Road end of Old Compton Street, the **Prince Edward Theatre** dates back to 1930. It was here that cabaret artiste Josephine Baker made her London debut in 1933.

Just off Old Compton Street is the French House in Dean Street, the centre of the Free French in World War II, an artists' haunt and still fiercely French. Artists such as Francis Bacon and Lucian Freud used to take advantage of the liberal licens-

**TIP**

A few of Soho's bars and pubs are still predominantly gay: two examples are the Admiral Duncan and Comptons in Old Compton Street. Among the clubs is Candy Bar, a lesbian venue in Carlisle Street (*also see page 302*).

**LEFT:** Soho Square was originally named King's Square due to the statue of Charles II in the centre. **BELOW:** Old Compton Street.

## Historic Streets

**M**any famous people are associated with Soho, from the painters Thomas Gainsborough (1727–88) to Francis Bacon (1909–92), from Casanova (1725–98) to Oscar Wilde (1854–1900). A blue plaque reminds you that 41 Beak Street was the home of Canaletto, the Venetian painter, from 1749 to 1751. In 1926 John Logie Baird transmitted the first television images from an attic at 22 Frith Street (now Bar Italia), next door to where Mozart stayed as a boy. The house at 26 Dean Street, now Quo Vadis restaurant, is where Karl Marx (above) wrote *Das Kapital*.

# The Royal Wedding

"We're supposed to have just a small family affair," Prince William jokes to the bride's father, Michael Middleton, at the altar. (Daily Telegraph)

It might have been less lavish than his father's wedding to Princess Diana in 1981, but when a future king gets married a low-key wedding just isn't an option. So when Prince William married Kate Middleton on 29th April 2011, the ceremony was held at Westminster Abbey, in front of 2,000 guests and a worldwide television audience of around 2 billion people.

Thousands of onlookers descended on London to share in the party atmosphere, with many spending the night sleeping in the streets to ensure a good view of the procession the next day. Most made for the processional route along Whitehall and the Mall. However, those desperate for a look at 'the dress' – a closely guarded secret – tried to get as close as possible to the Goring Hotel, where the bride spent her last night as a commoner. The exclusive hotel was block-booked by the Middletons for two days.

The next morning Kate emerged with her father to be driven to Westminster Abbey, and the fashion world was delighted to discover that her dress was an elegant ivory satin creation, designed by Sarah Burton of Alexander McQueen (the late 'bad boy' of British fashion). It was decorated with lace hand-made by the Royal School of Needlework at Hampton Court; such was the secrecy that even the lace-makers didn't know Burton was the designer.

The wedding was an intriguing mix of the ancient and modern: while the couple were making their vows, for instance, the internet practically melted as people tweeted their admiration for Pippa Middleton's bottom – the chief bridesmaid's rear inspiring many Facebook tribute sites. The couple emerged from the cathedral with new titles, the Duke and Duchess of Cambridge, and later delighted the crowds in the Mall with two balcony kisses. After a buffet reception at Buckingham Palace for around 650 guests, hosted by the Queen, William drove his new bride to Clarence House in his father's borrowed Aston Martin.

The honeymoon, another strictly guarded secret, took place a week after the wedding with William and Kate jetting off to the secluded island of Desroches in the Seychelles.

Interest in the wedding is predicted to give a boost to Britain's economy, with an extra 4 million visitors expected. Tourist numbers to Britain should grow even further in 2012, due to London hosting the Olympics and the celebrations surrounding the Queen's Diamond Jubilee (marking her 60-year reign as Queen). The highlight of this will be the Thames Jubilee Pageant on 3rd June, when the Queen will process along the river in a Royal Barge at the head of a flotilla of around 1,000 boats. ❑

**LEFT:** Prince William and Kate Middleton process down the aisle in Westminster Abbey.
**ABOVE:** crowds of well-wishers line the Mall.

*A detail from the exterior of the French Protestant Church of London at Soho Square, which holds an archive of books and records related to the French Huguenots.*

workshop during World War II and now waiting to be put to good use.

The red-brick tower of St Patrick's Catholic Church lends a bit of variety to the architectural proceedings. Established in 1893 on the site of an earlier church, St Patrick's has recently had a £3.5 million restoration.

A hint of Soho Square's former glory can be seen in the 18th-century house of charitable works, caring for the destitute, **St-Barnabas-in-Soho**, on the corner of Greek Street. Once a residential hostel, it is now a "life skills" centre for homeless people. Its elegant interior of fine woodcarvings, fireplaces and plasterwork is not open to the public but a monthly series of events are held here.

## Wardour Street ❺

Continuing west from Soho Square past Dean Street, the next main road is **Wardour Street**, once sarcastically known as the only street in the world which was shady on both sides. It is still the heart of London's film and recording industries, and during weekday lunch times the surrounding bars and restaurants are full of 30-something media bods discussing the next big thing.

Wardour Street has become something of a restaurant hotspot in recent years, and venues such as Busaba Eathai and Floridita ensure the street is busy long after office hours.

At the Shaftesbury Avenue end of Wardour Street, a tower is all that remains of Sir Christopher Wren's church of **St Anne's**, bombed in the war, though its beautifully kept gardens provide some shade and benches for a rest on a hot day.

## Berwick Street Market ❻

The fruit and vegetable market in parallel **Berwick Street** is well laid out and inexpensive, and its stalls also sell cheese and flowers. The traders represent the most dense concentration of cockneys in central London apart from the taxi cafés, and their language is colourful.

## Carnaby Street ❼

A detour away from Soho via Broadwick Street will take you towards **Carnaby Street**. The street now hosts up-market branches of some of the hipper high-street chains (Office, Fornarina, Lee Jeans and American

**LEFT:** the mock-Tudor 19th-century tool shed in the centre of Soho Square. **BELOW:** Berwick Street Market.

**SHOP**

The 1920s mock-Tudor facade of Liberty is visible at the end of Carnaby Street (turn onto Great Marlborough Street for the main entrance). In recent years, it has shed its slightly stuffy image to combine eccentric English charm with edgy, high-fashion clothing and decor. It is well worth a look (also see page 52).

**RIGHT:** the small park at the centre of Leicester Square.
**BELOW:** Gerrard Street in Chinatown. **BELOW RIGHT:** the statue of Charlie Chaplin on Leicester Square.

Apparel, for example). You will still find examples of the sort of fashion creativity that first put the area on the map, but for this you'll need to leave Carnaby Street itself and explore the pedestrianised streets to the east.

## CHINATOWN ❽

Returning to Soho and continuing down Wardour Street, walk along the south side of Shaftesbury Avenue to **Gerrard Street** and parallel **Lisle Street**, home of Chinese grocers, restaurants and stores. Kitsch Chinese street furniture, lamps and archways in Gerrard Street make this the heart of Chinatown. Established in the 1950s after the first Chinatown in Limehouse was damaged by WWII bombing, it has some of the best Oriental cuisine in town, although quality varies.

There are also herbal and medicine shops. On Sundays, a family outing day for the city's Chinese, there is a Chinese food market. Chinese New Year in late January or early February is celebrated in style, with massive papier-mâché lions dancing through the streets.

## LEICESTER SQUARE ❾

Just south of Chinatown, Leicester Square is home of the big cinemas and host to the capital's film premieres. Until the 17th century, this was the garden of Leicester House and at the four corners of the garden are busts of famous people associated with the square. At the centre is the **Shakespeare monument** (1874), surrounded by brass plates in the ground giving distances to cities all over the world. Facing the bard is a **statue of Charlie Chaplin**, born in Southwark, south London, in 1889. Around the square is a regular contingent of caricature artists, buskers, Bible-thumpers and, on special occasions, a funfair carousel and amusement rides. ❏

# BEST RESTAURANTS, BARS, PUBS AND CAFÉS

## Restaurants

Prices for a three-course dinner per person with a half-bottle of house wine:
£ = under £20
££ = £20–30
£££ = £30–50
££££ = over £50

## American

### Ed's Easy Diner

Old Compton St, W1
📞 7434 4439; www.eds
easydiner.com 🍽 daily, all day from noon. £ [p319, C2]
Beefburgers, veggie burgers, chicken burgers dished up in 1950s American-style surroundings. There is another Ed's diner at the Trocadero on Rupert Street.

## Chinese

### Harbour City

46 Gerrard St, W1 📞 7439 7859 🍽 daily, all day. ££ (set menu £–££) [p319, C3]
A recommended choice with a window table overlooking Gerrard Street. Dim sum served from noon–5pm.

### Joy King Lau

3 Leicester St, WC2 📞 7437 1133; www.joykinglau.com 🍽 daily, all day. £££ (set menu ££–£££) [p319-20, C3]
This is a popular choice for those who know Chinese food well. Set

menus from around £28 feature sizzling veal with black pepper sauce, plus a range of noodle dishes. Dim sum is available until 5pm.

### Mr Kong

21 Lisle St, WC2H 📞 7437 7341; www.mrkong restaurant.com 🍽 daily, all day till 2.45am, Sun until 1.45am. ££ (set menu £–££) [p319, C4]
This is one of the more authentic (and claustrophobic) Chinese restaurants in the area. It offers many unusual dishes such as baked lobster with black beans and chilli, and deep fried oysters. Has a lively vegetarian selection too.

### Royal Dragon

30 Gerrard St, W1 📞 7734 1388; www.rdklondon.co.uk

🍽 D daily, until 3am. ££ (set menu £) [p318, C3]
A noisy place where sizzling, quick-fire dishes descend from on high. Set menus are reliable. Dim sum served from noon–5pm.

### Yauatcha

15 Broadwick St, W1 📞 7494 8888; www. yauatcha.com 🍽 daily, all day. £££ [p318, B2]
This stylish, Michelin-starred tearoom and dim sum emporium offers delicious, if expensive, dim sum from noon until midnight (until 10.30pm on Sun). Created by the founder of Wagamamas, the popular chain of noodle restaurants.

## Fish

### Randall & Aubin

16 Brewer St, W1 📞 7287 4447; www.randallandaubin. com 🍽 L & D daily. £££ [p318, B2]
Piles of lobster, crab and oysters greet you as you enter this bustling place. The menu also includes roasts.

### Zilli Fish

36–40 Brewer St, W1V 📞 7734 8649; www.zilli restaurants.com 🍽 L & D Mon–Sat. £££ (set menu ££) [p318, B3]
Not cheap, but a great lunch venue. Try the lobster spaghetti or the chargrilled swordfish. The chocolate fondant with ice cream is divine.

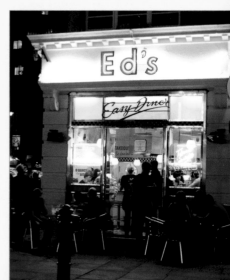

**ABOVE:** dim sum in Chinatown.
**RIGHT:** American fare on Old Compton Street.

by for steaks, cocktails and house music.

### French

**L'Escargot
Marco Pierre White**
48 Greek St, W1 ☎ 7439
7474; www.lescargot
restaurant.co.uk Ⓒ L Mon–
Fri, D Mon–Sat. £££ (set
menu ££ ) [p319, C2]
The *grand-père* of
London's French
restaurants, with its
lovely 1920s decor, is
now run by Marco Pierre
White. It offers a choice
between the exciting
hubbub of the ground
floor or the more
intimate Picasso room
upstairs, with à la carte
and set menus.

### Hungarian

**Gay Hussar**
2 Greek St, W1 ☎ 7437
0973; www.gayhussar.co.uk
Ⓒ L & D Mon–Sat. £££
[p318–9, C2]
In polished, gentleman's
club surroundings, a mix
of hearty British and
Hungarian dishes are
served. Pork and
potatoes are prominent.

### Indian

**Indian Masala Zone**
9 Marshall St, W1 ☎ 7287
9966; www.masalazone.
com Ⓒ L & D daily. £–££
[p318, B2]
Bright and always busy,
this offers reasonably
priced, if slightly
sanitised, Indian food in
fast-paced surroundings.

### International

**Balans**
60 Old Compton St, W1
☎ 7439 2183; www.
balans.co.uk Ⓒ daily
(Mon–Thur and Sun
8am–5am, Fri–Sat
8am–6am). ££ [p318, C2]
Sets out to bring a buzz
and glamour to gay eating
in Compton Street with its
range of New York brunch-
style dishes – including
melt-in-your-mouth eggs
benedict – and an
extensive all day menu.

**Café Emm**
17 Frith St, W1 ☎ 7437
0723; www.cafeemm.com
Ⓒ L & D daily. £ [p318, C2]

Buzzy, intimate and
exceptionally good value,
Café Emm is packed out
every night. Portions are
large, and dishes range
from salmon fish cakes
to lamb shank with
ratatouille and mash. Be
prepared for boisterous
birthday parties.

**Floridita**
100 Wardour St, W1 ☎ 7314
4000; www.floridita.co.uk
Ⓒ Tue–Wed 5.30pm–2am,
Thur–Sat 5.30pm–3am.
£££. Admission £10 after
8pm on Fri and Sat.
[p318, B2]
Eat to a Latin beat in this
buzzy, Cuban-themed
restaurant – a reincarna-
tion of the cavernous
Mezzo that used to
occupy the site. Live
music from musicians
sourced in Havana.

**Profile**
84–6 Wardour St, W1
☎ 7734 3444; www.profile
soho.com Ⓒ L & D daily. £
[p318, B2]
A New York-style diner/
bar that's worth stopping

### Italian

**Amalfi**
29–31 Old Compton St, W1
☎ 7437 7284; www.amalfi-
restaurant.co.uk Ⓒ L & D
daily. ££ [p318–9, C2]
The cooking is of the
1970s bistro variety, but
pizzas, vegetable pastas
and other Italian fare are
filling and you can be sure
of quick service and a
table without reservation.

**Bocca di Lupo**
12 Archer St, W1 ☎ 7734
2223; www.boccadilupo.com
Ⓒ L daily, D Mon–Sat.
££–£££ [p318, B3]
Popular restaurant serv-
ing regional dishes such
as courgette flower risotto
and Florentine steaks.

**Kettners**
29 Romilly St, W1 ☎ 7734
6112; www.kettners.com
Ⓒ daily, all day. ££ [p318, C2]

Prices for a three-course dinner per person with a half bottle of house wine:

**£** = under £20
**££** = £20–30
**£££** = £30–50
**££££** = over £50

This sprawling, always busy *grande dame* fuses an extensive champagne list with a menu of dishes such as pearl barley risotto or seared turbot. Pudding bar, too.

## Quo Vadis
26–29 Dean St, W1 ☎ 7437 9585; www.quovadissoho. co.uk Ⓔ L Mon–Fri, D Mon–Sat. **£££–££££** [p318, C2] A venerable institution in the one-time home of Karl Marx serving high-end modern Italian food. Brit art on the walls, and an expensive but excellent wine list.

## Japanese
### Satsuma
56 Wardour St, W1 ☎ 7437 8338; www.osatsuma.com Ⓔ daily, all day. **££** [p318, C2] Fast food but well presented, with some good *udon* and *ramen* noodle dishes, plus sushi.

## Mediterranean
### Hummus Bros
88 Wardour St, W1 ☎ 7734 1311; www.hbros.co.uk Ⓔ L & D daily. **£** [p318, B2] Very popular budget café serving, as its name suggests, hummous with

various toppings such as salad or Mexican beef. Ideal mopped up with fresh pitta bread.

### Leon
36/38 Old Compton, W1 ☎ 7434 1200; www.leon restaurants.co.uk Ⓔ B, L & D daily. **£–££** [p318, C2] Branch of popular Mediterranean chain attracting lunchtime workers for its reasonably priced wraps, soups and salads. Hot dishes include Moroccan meatballs and sweet potato falafel. Sustainably-sourced fast food.

## Modern European
### Bar du Marché
19 Berwick St, W1 ☎ 7734 4606; www.bardumarche. co.uk Ⓔ all day, Mon–Sat. **££** [p318, B2] Tucked behind Berwick Street Market, this is a surprisingly unpretentious Soho hangout. Serves a mix of French brasserie-style food, salads and seafood.

### Mildred's
45 Lexington St, W1 ☎ 7494 1634; www.mildreds.co.uk Ⓔ Mon–Sat noon–11pm. **££** [p318, B2] This is a friendly, laid-back place. The vegetarian food ranges from veggie burgers to tofu stir fries and ale pie, accompanied by organic beer and soft drinks.

## Bars, Pubs and Cafés

### Bars
If you're in search of a hip hang-out, head for West Soho and **Alphabet** (*61–3 Beak St*). Arranged over two floors, it caters for a media in-crowd. A quality Martini and an excellent selection of wines can be found at **Café Boheme** (*13–17 Old Compton St*), while cigar lovers should make for **Le Casa del Habano** (*100 Wardour Street*) where cocktails are served, and cigars sampled, in the Cigar Boutique.

### Pubs
If it's Soho history you're after, **The French House** (*49 Dean St*) offers a decadent and beautiful old bar that was the centre of the French Resistance in London during World War II, and the regular haunt of painter Francis Bacon and writer Samuel Beckett. The upstairs restaurant serves good French fare (*tel: 7437 2799*). **The Experimental Cocktail Club** (*13A Gerrard St*) is a newly opened and already popular plush bar offering top cocktails and absinthe. Vintage gins add a classy flavour. **Bar Code** (*3–4 Archer St*) is a late-night gay dance and cruise bar.
  For those who like their ale from a barrel

and not a bottle, Soho has plenty of classic Victorian pubs – **The Argyll Arms** (*18 Argyll St*), the **Coach & Horses** (*29 Greek St*), the **Dog & Duck** (*18 Bateman St*) are just three.

### Cafés
The best in Soho are found in and around Compton Street. **Bar Italia** (*22 Frith St*) is a Soho legend, serving great Italian coffee and snacks around the clock. The most wonderful, boho French café this side of the Channel is **Maison Bertaux** (*28 Greek St*) where the surroundings appear as if they'll crumble to the touch, just like their exquisite cakes; for a gentle French experience amid the bustle of gay Compton Street, **Pâtisserie Valerie** (*44 Old Compton St*) belongs to another age.

**ABOVE LEFT:** Amalfi on Old Compton Street.
**LEFT:** a beacon of good taste on Dean Street.
**RIGHT:** The French House pub, also on Dean Street.

# TRAFALGAR SQUARE AND COVENT GARDEN

With its shooting fountains and soaring column, Trafalgar Square is one of London's most popular open spaces. It is also a short hop from vibrant Covent Garden

S outh of Leicester Square is Trafalgar Square, from where the Strand heads east, flanked on one side by Covent Garden and on the other by the riverside Victoria Embankment leading down to Waterloo Bridge.

## TRAFALGAR SQUARE ❶

The closest that London has to the kind of large public square common in other European capitals was designed in 1838 by Sir Charles Barry. In 1841 it was named **Trafalgar Square** to commemorate Admiral Lord Nelson's 1805 victory against Napoleon's navy at Trafalgar, off the Atlantic coast of Spain.

At the centre of the square is **Nelson's Column**, a 169ft (51.5-metre) monument, made up of a Corinthian column topped by a statue of Horatio Nelson, battle-scarred with only one arm but without a patch on his blind eye. He is gazing towards the Mall, inspecting the fleet of model ships attached to pillars on the avenue. The four iconic lions (1847) are by Edwin Landseer.

Around the square, Canada House, South Africa House and Uganda House are memories of distant Empire days. Also celebrating the old Empire are statues of General Charles Napier and Major General Sir Henry Havelock, on the plinths in the two southern corners of the square. The statue in the northeast corner depicts George IV.

Controversy over who should occupy the northwest-corner's fourth plinth – left empty after plans in 1841 to erect an equestrian statue collapsed through lack of funds – recently caught Londoners'

**Main attractions**
TRAFALGAR SQUARE
NATIONAL GALLERY
NATIONAL PORTRAIT GALLERY
ST MARTIN-IN-THE-FIELDS
COVENT GARDEN MARKET
ROYAL OPERA HOUSE
ST PAUL'S, THE "ACTORS' CHURCH"
LONDON TRANSPORT MUSEUM
LONDON COLISEUM
CHARING CROSS BOOKSHOPS

**LEFT:** an open-top bus tour passes Nelson's Column in Trafalgar Square.
**RIGHT:** one of Trafalgar Square's pools and fountains in front of the National Gallery.

**RIGHT:** Holbein's *The Ambassadors* in the National Gallery. **BELOW:** the entrance to the National Gallery, seen from the side.

imaginations. A committee was formed to commission works of art that could take their turn on the plinth, with *Alison Lapper Pregnant* and Thomas Schütte's *Hotel for the Birds* the first two installations. In 2009 artist Antony Gormley put a succession of local people on the plinth – each with an hour to do whatever they wished.

The square has long been the site of public gatherings, political demonstrations and New Year celebrations. A mayoral campaign to rid it of its traditional plague of pigeons was largely successful, and in 2003 the north side of the square was pedestrianised to give people a sporting chance of reaching the fountains without being mown down by traffic.

In the southwest corner of the square, Admiralty Arch marks the start of The Mall, leading to Buckingham Palace (see pages 82–3). Whitehall, the other exit, will lead

you to the Houses of Parliament (see page 75).

## The National Gallery ❷

✉ Trafalgar Square; www.national gallery.org.uk 📞 7747 2885 🕒 Sat–Thur 10am–6pm, Fri 10am–9pm 🎫 free except some special exhibitions 🚇 Charing Cross

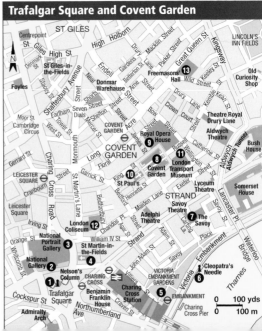

**Trafalgar Square and Covent Garden**

*Recommended Restaurants, Pubs, Bars & Cafés on pages 106–7*

Dominating the north side of Trafalgar Square is the neoclassical **National Gallery**, designed by William Wilkins in 1838 with a modern wing by Robert Venturi completed in 1991. This is the country's most important art gallery, home to around 2,000 west European masterpieces, including works by Rembrandt, Rubens, El Greco, Vermeer and Van Gogh. *For full details, see pages 108–9.*

## The National Portrait Gallery ❸

St Martin's Place; www.npg.org.uk
7306 0055 or 7312 2463
Mon–Wed and Sat–Sun 10am–6pm, Thur–Fri 10am–9pm
free except for some special exhibitions   Charing Cross

Behind the National Gallery is the **National Portrait Gallery**, housed in a Florentine Renaissance building originally designed by architect Ewan Christian and opened in 1896. Only a fraction of the collection's 10,000 artworks, plus half a million photographs of the nation's illustrious men and women, is on display at any one time. *For full details, see pages 110–11.*

## St Martin-in-the-Fields ❹

Trafalgar Square; www.stmartin-in-the-fields.org   box office (evening concerts): 7766 1100   daily 8am–6pm   free except evening concerts   Charing Cross

Across the road is the church of **St Martin-in-the-Fields**, the oldest building in Trafalgar Square, built in 1726 by a Scottish architect, James Gibbs, when this venue was in fields outside the city. Nell Gwynne, the mistress of Charles II, is one of several famous people buried in this parish church of the royal family, which was so chic in the 18th century that pews were rented out on an annual basis. The royal box is on the left of the altar. The crypt, which houses a soup kitchen for the homeless, a café and the London Brass Rubbing Centre, was used as an air-raid shelter during the bombing blitz of World War II.

Regular classical music concerts are held in the church on Wednesday, Thursday, Friday and Saturday,

*The spire of St Martin-in-the-Fields.*

**BELOW:** soaking up the sunshine on the entrance steps to St Martin-in-the-Fields.

## Nelson's Column

Horatio Nelson (1758–1805) is the country's greatest naval hero. A tiny figure, he was partially blinded in his right eye in Corsica, had his right arm amputated at Santa Cruz and was pacing the deck of HMS *Victory*, when he was fatally shot by a French sharpshooter off Cape Trafalgar. He could be insubordinate, famously putting a telescope to his blind eye at the Battle of Copenhagen and pretending he could not read an order to disengage from battle. He is also remembered for his affair with Emma Hamilton, the wife of the British Ambassador to Naples. The three shared a *ménage à trois*.

*It took until 1878 before Cleopatra's Needle was towed in a specially constructed pontoon to London, where its intended site outside Parliament was not strong enough to bear the 180-tonne weight. Buried beneath it are newspapers from the day it was erected, a set of coins, four Bibles in different languages, a railway timetable and photographs of the 12 best-looking English women of the time.*

**BELOW:** one of the sphinxes flanking Cleopatra's Needle, (**RIGHT**) on the Victoria Embankment.

at either 7.30pm or 8pm. There are also free lunch time concerts.

## AROUND THE STRAND

The mundane modern architecture in the Strand, the main thoroughfare connecting the West End with the City, camouflages the fact that it was once a very fashionable street, home in the 18th and 19th centuries to the poet Samuel Taylor Coleridge and the novelist George Eliot. Although the street is well past its glory days, a sense of history is not altogether lost: you can still dine in traditional style at Simpson's, opened in 1848, or take tea in the Thames Room of the Savoy.

At the Strand's western end, near Trafalgar Square, is **Charing Cross** railway station. In front of it is a replica of the last of 12 crosses set up by Edward I in 1291 to mark the funeral procession of his queen, Eleanor of Castile, from Nottinghamshire to Westminster Abbey. "Charing" is thought by some to come from "*chère reine*" (dear queen) Eleanor, although it is more likely to have come from the Old English word "*cierran*", meaning to turn.

## Victoria Embankment

At this point, cut down Villiers Street, which for a while was home to Rudyard Kipling, author of *The Jungle Book* (a blue plaque marks the spot). Nearby is Craven Street, where the Founding Father of the USA, Benjamin Franklin, lived from 1757–75. His Georgian mansion is now a museum, the **Benjamin Franklin House** (36 Craven Street; www.benjaminfranklinhouse.org; Wed–Sun noon–4.15pm; guided tours Mon noon–4.15pm; tel: 7839 2006; charge; book in advance).

Back on Villiers Street, at its southern end, is **Victoria Embankment**, built in 1870 to ease traffic congestion and carry sewage pipes needed to improve London's crude sanitation system. In the **Victoria Embankment Gardens ❺** a restored **Water Gate** once marked the river entrance to York House, London home of the archbishops of York, birthplace of philosopher and statesman Francis Bacon (1561–1626) and home of the dukes of Buckingham.

On the river front is **Charing Cross Pier**, a starting point for boats

*Recommended Restaurants, Pubs, Bars & Cafés on pages 106–7*

heading east to Greenwich. This is also the site of the 60ft (18-metre) **Cleopatra's Needle** ❻, carved in Aswan, Egypt, *c.*1475BC and presented to Britain in 1819 *(see margin note, left)*. The needle is flanked by two bronze sphinxes.

## The Savoy

Back on the Strand are several theatres, including the **Adelphi**, opened in 1806. Richard D'Oyly Carte (1844–1901), sponsor of Gilbert and Sullivan operas at the splendid Art Deco **Savoy Theatre**, also financed the building of the **Savoy Hotel** ❼, which opened in 1889 as one of the first in London with private bathrooms, electric lights and lifts (elevators). From the Strand, the Savoy is unimposing, but it is grand enough to have its own private forecourt and the only road in Britain where traffic drives on the right.

D'Oyly Carte is commemorated in a stained-glass window in the **Queen's Chapel of the Savoy** (www.duchyof lancaster.co.uk; Tue–Sun; services: Oct–July Sun 11am, Wed 12.30pm), behind the hotel. It was founded in

the 16th century when the former Savoy Palace became a hospital. Built by Peter, ninth Count of Savoy, in 1246, the palace had its heyday under John of Gaunt (1340–99), when it was "the fayrest manor in Europe, big enough for a large part of an army".

## Covent Garden ❽

Named after a convent whose fields occupied the site, **Covent Garden** was for centuries the principal market in London for vegetables, fruit and flowers, and the workplace of Eliza Doolittle, the flower girl in George Bernard Shaw's *Pygmalion*, who later burst into song in the film and musical *My Fair Lady*. The main

**TIP**

Hitch a ride with one of Covent Garden's rickshaw bicycles *(left)*. They're not cheap, but they offer a novel, ecologically-efficient and dry method of transport for short trips.

*Charing Cross is the spot from which distances to and from London are measured.*

**BELOW:** browsing at Apple Market in Covent Garden piazza.

**KIDS**

On the second Sunday in May, a service at St Paul's commemorates the Punch and Judy puppet tradition, first noted here in 1662 by diarist Samuel Pepys. There's a brass band procession around the area at 10.30am and puppetry performances in the afternoon. For adults, the Punch & Judy pub inside the market marks the spot where the puppet show was first mounted.

**ABOVE RIGHT:** old-fashioned telephone boxes near the Opera House. **BELOW:** the Royal Opera House. **BELOW RIGHT:** Neal's Yard, off Shorts Gardens road in Covent Garden.

piazza was originally laid out with colonnaded town houses designed by Inigo Jones c.1630, and inspired by the 16th-century Italian architect Andrea Palladio. A small market was founded here as early as 1656.

After the market moved out in 1974, the area became a blueprint for turning old commercial buildings into a mall of stores and stalls. Restaurants, cafés and shops occupy the old warehouses in the streets around the market square. There is a good line in street entertainers, who undergo auditions before they are granted a licence to perform here.

## Royal Opera House ❾

✉ Bow Street; www.roh.org.uk 📞 7304 4000 🕐 Mon–Sat 10am–3.30pm 🎫 free except for tours 🚇 Covent Garden

In 1733, a theatre was established in the northeast corner of Covent Garden, on the site now occupied by the **Royal Opera House**. A fire ravaged the first building in 1808, consuming Handel's organ and many of his works. The Opera

House has had to contend with unimpressed audiences: price riots were common in the 19th century, and in 1809 lasted 61 nights. The Floral Hall, which acts as a reception space prior to performances and during intervals, is spectacular.

## St Paul's Church ❿

✉ Bedford Street; www.actorschurch.org 📞 7836 5221 🕐 Mon–Fri 9am–4.30pm, Sun 9am–1pm and for services 🎫 free 🚇 Covent Garden

The portico of **St Paul's**, the actors' church, built in 1633 by Inigo Jones, and used as a backdrop in *My Fair*

*Recommended Restaurants, Pubs, Bars & Cafés on pages 106–7*

*Lady*, dominates the western end of the square. The vaults and grounds of this Tuscan-style church are said to contain the remains of more famous people than any other church except Westminster Abbey. The headstones have long been removed, but residents include master wood carver Grinling Gibbons (died 1720), the composer of *Rule Britannia*, Thomas Arne (1778) and the actress Ellen Terry (1928).

## London Transport Museum ⑪

✉ Covent Garden Piazza; www. ltmuseum.co.uk ⓒ daily 10am–6pm, opens 11am Fri ☏ 7379 6344 or 7565 7299 ⓔ charge but free to accompanied children under 16 🚇 Covent Garden

The old flower market, in the south-eastern corner of the square, is now occupied by **London Transport Museum**, which has a large collection of horse-drawn coaches, buses, trams, trains and rail carriages. It effectively traces the social history of modern London, whose growth was powered by transport, and deals with issues such as congestion and pollution. This is a great museum for children.

## Around Drury Lane

Neighbouring **Drury Lane** is closely linked with the theatre. Its principal venue is the Theatre Royal, which, when it opened in 1663, was only the second legitimate playhouse in the city. The mistress of Charles II, Nell Gwynne, depicted by cartoonists as a voluptuous orange seller, trod the boards here. Being one of the largest in the West End, its stage can mount blockbuster musicals.

Opposite its white Corinthian portico is the former **Bow Street police station**, home in the 18th century of the scarlet-waistcoated Bow Street Runners, the prototype policemen.

## Long Acre and St Martin's Lane

Long Acre cuts through Covent Garden, from Neal Street to Leicester Square tube station. At 12–14 Long Acre is Britain's best travel bookshop, **Stanford's**. South of Long Acre is St Martin's Lane, home of the English National Opera's **London Coliseum** ⑫ *(see page 299)*, where productions are sung in English, with subtitles.

Great Queen Street is the site of the **Freemasons' Hall** ⑬ (www.ugle.org. uk, Mon–Fri 11am–4pm; tel: 7831 9811), an imposing white behemoth that houses a museum on the history of freemasonry, a library and tavern.

### CHARING CROSS ROAD

Long Acre leads to **Charing Cross Road**, a centre for rare and second-hand books. **Foyles** is a maze of more than 4 million volumes but has become better organised, if duller, since the death of its eccentric former owner, Christina Foyle. **Zwemmer's** is known for fine art and photography books, while Denmark Street is known as **Tin Pan Alley**, a home of early British rock 'n' roll.  ❏

*The iconic revolving globe on top of the London Coliseum measures 12ft (4 metres) in diameter and weighs around 5 tonnes.*

**BELOW:** Foyles, the largest bookshop in Britain in terms of numbers of books stocked.

# BEST RESTAURANTS, PUBS, BARS AND CAFÉS

## Restaurants

Prices for a three-course dinner per person with a half-bottle of house wine:

**£** = under £20
**££** = £20–30
**£££** = £30–50
**££££** = over £50

## American

### Christopher's

18 Wellington St, WC2
7240 4222; www.
christophersgrill.com B
Sat–Sun, L & D daily. £££
(set menus £–££)
[p319, E3]
The dishes on the contemporary American menu are imaginative and usually well prepared, but the elegant dining rooms are the main attraction. Has

good-value pre- and post-theatre menus.

### Joe Allen

13 Exeter St, WC2  7836 0651; www.joeallen.co.uk
daily noon–midnight. £££
(brunch, pre-theatre and late supper menus £–££)
[p319, E3]
Tucked away below street level, this relaxed diner has a predictable enough menu – salads, steaks, spareribs, pecan pie – and average-quality food, but it's ever popular with customers, who sip cocktails until 12.45am.

## British

### Rules

35 Maiden Lane, WC2
7836 5314; www.rules.

co.uk L & D daily.
£££–££££ [p319, E3]
Rules (est. 1798) is London's oldest restaurant, and the decor, notably the wonderful Art Nouveau stained-glass ceiling and the wood panelling, reflects its heritage. The robust food is very English, with beef, lamb and a variety of game from Rules' own estate in the Pennines.

### Simpson's-in-the-Strand, Grand Divan

100 The Strand, WC2
7836 9112; www.
simpsonsinthestrand.co.uk
B Mon–Fri, L & D daily.
££££ (breakfast £, set menu ££) [p319, E3]
This bastion of Britishness retains all the grandeur of bygone days – chandeliers, oak panelling and tail-coated waiters – while managing a surprisingly relaxed atmosphere. The menu is traditional (beef fillet, duck and Dover sole); for many the famed roast beef, wheeled in on a silver-domed carving trolley is the only choice. A good place to breakfast like a king.

## Fish

### J. Sheekey

28–32 St Martin's Court,
WC2  7240 2565; www.

j-sheekey.co.uk L & D
daily. ££££ (weekend lunch menu ££) [p319, D3]
Think chargrilled squid with gorgonzola polenta, Cornish fish stew and New England baby lobster, followed by rhubarb pie, or the famed Scandinavian iced berries with white chocolate sauce. Impressive wine list. Chic. Booking essential.

## French

### L'Atelier de Joel Robuchon

13–15 West St, WC2
7010 8600; www.joel robuchon.co.uk L & D
daily. £££–££££ (pre-theatre menu available) [p319, C2]
French food with Spanish influences at this two Michelin-starred restaurant. Foie gras ravioli, free range quail, Scottish scallops, lobster and steak are just some of the offerings. Diners sit at a counter surrounding the kitchen.

## International

### Asia de Cuba

St Martin's Lane Hotel, 45 St Martin's Lane, WC2  7300 5500 or 7300 5588 B, L & D daily. ££££ [p319, D3]
Attached to one of London's hippest hotels is this buzzing restaurant, with eccentric decor and

**LEFT:** Asia de Cuba. **RIGHT:** J. Sheekey, famous for fish.

fusion menu. Lobster parcels, pot-roast pork and melt-in-your-mouth tuna are a few of the treats on offer.

## Modern European

### Belgo Centraal
50 Earlham St, WC2
☎ 7813 2233; www.belgo-restaurants.co.uk ⓒ L & D daily. ££ [p319, D2]
Belgian fare of mussels and chips and excellent beers. Long benches, shared tables and waiters dressed as monks add to the atmosphere. The "Beat the Clock" option offers great value from 5–6.30pm.

### Carluccio's
Garrick St, WC2 ☎ 7836 0990; www.carluccios.com ⓒ B, L & D daily. ££ [p319, D3]
The flagship *caffè* of the Italian chain, this location comprises a bar, café and shop spread over two floors. The dishes are authentic, change seasonally and gluten-free versions are available. Try the Sicilian rice balls or some of the best pasta outside Italy.

### The Ivy
1 West St, WC2 ☎ 7836 4751; www.the-ivy.co.uk ⓒ L & D daily. ££££ (set menu ££) [p319, D2]
Begun in 1917, The Ivy is one of London's best-known celebrity haunts. The menu is British but includes international favourites. The wine list is strong and the surreptitious star-spotting irresistible. Open late so useful for post-theatre meals. The only problem is getting a table – reserve months, not just days, ahead.

### The Portrait Restaurant
National Portrait Gallery, St Martin's Place, W1 ☎ 7312 2490; www.npg.org.uk ⓒ L daily, D Thur–Sat. £££ [p319, D4]
When it comes to location, few can beat the top floor of the National Portrait Gallery. It offers views of Trafalgar Square, Big Ben and the Millennium Wheel. The food is above average by gallery restaurant standards. The menu includes game, pork belly and fish, with a delicious array of desserts.

### Sarastro
126 Drury Lane, WC2 ☎ 7836 0101; www.sarastro-restaurant.com ⓒ L & D daily. ££–£££ [p319, E2]
"The show after the show" is this restaurant's slogan. The flamboyant decor, with velvet drapes, golden chairs, opera boxes, chandeliers and props, is a stage set in itself. The Turkish-influenced menu is more straightforward, and there is live music most evenings.

## Vegetarian

### Food for Thought
31 Neal St, WC2 ☎ 7836 9072; www.foodforthought-london.co.uk ⓒ B Mon–Sat, L daily, D Mon–Sat until 8pm. £ [p319, D2]
This pleasant eatery does an imaginative selection of dishes, with a daily changing menu. Tom-yam soup might be followed by gnocchi with gorgonzola and oyster mushrooms. A BYOB (no corkage) policy keeps the cost down. No credit cards.

## Pubs, Bars and Cafés

Cafés, wine bars and pubs are ten a penny in the Covent Garden area – ideal for a relaxed lunch or a night on the town, with happy hours/late closing hours commonplace.

For location, it's hard to top **The Portrait Bar** *(National Portrait Gallery)*, with wonderful views over Trafalgar Square, or **The Opera Terrace Bar** *(Royal Opera House)* above the Piazza.

Londoners' old favourites, such as the **Cork & Bottle** *(44–46 Cranbourn St)*, pull in the crowds for their comfort factor and excellent wine lists, while venues such as **Brasserie Max** *(10 Monmouth St)* and **Christopher's Martini Bar** *(18 Wellington St)* appeal to trendy urbanites. If beer is your thing, try the **Lowlander** *(36 Drury Lane)*, boasting an impressive lager and ale list.

Historic pubs around Covent Garden include the **Lamb and Flag** *(33 Rose Street)*, tucked away down the tiniest of alleyways, and **The Punch & Judy**, on the upper level of the Market itself. Villiers Street, which leads to Embankment tube, shelters the wonderful **Gordon's Wine Bar**, where drinkers sit under the arches on chilly nights (though keep an eye on your bag) and out on the terrace in summer. Sherry and port are specialities here.

Some of the most exclusive bars are found in hotels, from classics such as the **American Bar** *(Savoy Hotel, Strand)* to the ultra-fashionable **Lobby Bar** at One Aldwych.

# THE NATIONAL GALLERY

Dominating Trafalgar Square is one of the world's finest art collections, bringing together masterpieces from over seven centuries – and entry is free

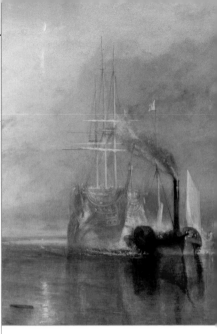

The National Gallery was founded in 1824, when a private collection of 38 paintings was acquired by the British Government for the sum of £57,000 and exhibited in the house of the owner, banker John Julius Angsterstein, at 100 Pall Mall. Included in the collection were *Bacchanal* by Poussin, *St Ursula* and *The Queen of Sheba* by landscape master Claude, paintings by Van Dyck, two admirable Rembrandts, a superb Aelbert Cuyp, and William Hogarth's narrative, *Six Pictures called Marriage à la Mode*.

As the collection grew, a new building was needed. William Wilkins' long, low construction, with its neoclassical facade and dome, opened in 1834 in the then-recently created Trafalgar Square. The building has been remodelled in various ways. The most prominent addition is the Sainsbury Wing, added by the American architect Robert Venturi in 1991.

## The essentials

✉ *Trafalgar Square; www.nationalgallery.org.uk*
📞 *7747 2885*
🕐 *Mon–Thur and Sat–Sun 10am–6pm, Fri 10am–9pm*
🎟 *free except for some special exhibitions*
🚇 *Charing Cross*

**ABOVE:** the **West Wing** contains paintings from 1500–1600, including Raphael's *Saint Catherine of Alexandria* (c.1507), above, Michelangelo's *The Entombment* (c.1500–1), Leonardo's *The Virgin of the Rocks* (1491–1508), Titian's *Bacchus and Ariadne* (1520-23), and Holbein's double portrait of *The Ambassadors* (1533).

## GALLERY LAYOUT

**ABOVE:** J.M.W. Turner's *The Fighting Téméraire*, voted the nation's favourite picture in a poll in 2005.

The National Gallery's collection is arranged chronologically, from the 13th century to the end of the 19th century, through four wings, starting in the Sainsbury Wing containing works from the 13th–15th centuries.

Many people enter the gallery through its grand main entrance, however, from where a magnificent flight of stairs offers you a choice of three directions. Take the left flight to the West Wing and the Renaissance galleries. Go straight ahead, through the Central Hall, for the North Wing, where you will find several portraits by Rembrandt as well as Velázquez's *Rokeby Venus*, the Spanish painter's only surviving nude, or turn right for the East Wing. Here you will find portraits and landscapes, including work by Gainsborough, Constable (see *The Hay Wain* above), J.M.W. Turner and Stubbs.

For special exhibitions held in the main wing, it is best to take the Getty Entrance, which also offers level access and wheelchairs.

**ABOVE LEFT:** among the gallery's Post-Impressionist works is Georges Seurat's *Bathers at Asnières*.
**LEFT:** Botticelli's *Venus and Mars* (c.1485) in the Sainsbury Wing.

# NATIONAL PORTRAIT GALLERY

## A showcase for five centuries of top British portraiture

A British Historical Portrait gallery was founded in 1856, the initiative of the 5th Earl of Stanhope. With no collection as such, it relied on gifts and bequests, the first of which was the "Chandos" picture of William Shakespeare, attributed to John Taylor, c.1610, and arguably the only portrait of Britain's most famous playwright done from life. From the start, additions to the collection (initially comprising traditional paintings, drawings and sculpture, with photography a later addition) were determined by the status of the sitter and historical importance of the portrait, not by their quality as works of art; these criteria still pertain today. Portraits of living people were not admitted until 1968, when the policy was changed to encourage younger artists and a fresh exploration of the genre.

**LEFT:** this portrait of Elizabeth I by an anonymous artist was almost certainly painted from direct observation, when she was about 40. There are about 50 portraits of Elizabeth II in the collection.

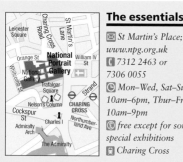

## The essentials

✉ St Martin's Place; www.npg.org.uk
📞 7312 2463 or 7306 0055
🕐 Mon–Wed, Sat–Sun 10am–6pm, Thur–Fri 10am–9pm
💷 free except for some special exhibitions
🚉 Charing Cross

## SPECIAL EXHIBITIONS

Changing exhibitions are held on the ground floor, and it is worth checking the website to see if anything interesting is on. Recent examples include "Glamour of the Gods – Hollywood Portraits", and the annual Taylor Wessing Photographic Portrait Prize, showcasing the work of professional and amateur portrait photographers. Other recent displays featured portraits in Pop Art, such as Andy Warhol's *Marilyn*.

## GALLERY LAYOUT

The displays are broadly chronological, starting on the second floor (reached by the vast escalator from the main hall) and ending on the ground floor. There are thematic sub-divisions within each

**ABOVE:** Room 12 is devoted to portraits of those closely involved with the arts in the late 18th century, such as Samuel Johnson, Handel and the prolific landscape architect Capability Brown. A self-portrait of the artist Gainsborough, and a bust of poet Alexander Pope, can also be found here.

**LEFT:** among the 17th- and 18th-century portraits on the second floor is this one of Lady Emma Hamilton, the wife of the British Ambassador to Naples and the mistress of Lord Nelson *(see page 101),* painted by George Romney in 1785. Emma Hamilton was known for her great beauty and vitality; there are 28 portraits of her in the gallery's collection.

**RIGHT AND BELOW:** the official portraits of the Victorian and Edwardian periods, which fill the bulk of the first floor, are some of the last examples of stylish formality. Works are organised by theme, from the arts, in Room 24, home to this Romantic portrait of poet Alfred Tennyson by Samuel Laurence (above right), and science and technology in Room 27, featuring evolutionist Charles Darwin (right), to politics, expansion and empire.

period: the Tudors, 17th-century and 18th-century portraits on the second floor; the Victorians and 20th-century portraits until 1990 (including special displays on the Balcony Gallery and landing) on the first floor, and, on the ground floor, the ever-popular British portraits since 1990 and temporary shows.

# MAYFAIR TO OXFORD STREET

Mayfair has consistently retained its social prestige since the building of its great estates began in the 1660s. With its Georgian residences, gentlemen's clubs and exclusive shops, it is synonymous with wealth

**W**est of Trafalgar Square and Piccadilly Circus is Mayfair, the smartest part of town. This is where a broom cupboard costs as much as a house in the country, where shoes are handmade and where life is bespoke.

The area is divided in two by Piccadilly. To the south of this famous thoroughfare lies St James's *(see page 84),* which grew up around the life of the royal court; to the north Mayfair, the most expensive place to land on the English Monopoly board. The second most expensive, Park Lane, forms the western boundary of the area, while Oxford Street, the capital's most famous shopping street, is on its northern side.

## PICCADILLY

Court fops and dandies were a source of moneymaking for London's traders. In the 18th century Robert Baker grew rich by selling them "pickadils", fashionable stiff collars, and built a mansion on what was then Portugal Street. It became known as **Piccadilly**, and it remains a fashionable street and a favourite location for airline and national tourist offices.

**LEFT:** getting shoes shined inside Burlington Arcade, a classy place to shop.
**RIGHT:** the Royal Academy of Arts.

## Royal Academy of Arts ❶

✉ Burlington House, Piccadilly; www. royalacademy.org.uk ☎ 7300 8000 ⏰ daily 10am–6pm, Fri until 10pm; John Madejski Fine Rooms (guided tours) Tue 1pm, Wed–Fri 1pm and 3pm, Sat 11.30am ⓔ charge except for permanent collection 🚇 Green Park

Behind the imposing Renaissance-style facade of **Burlington House** on the north side, fronted by a handsome courtyard, the Academy stages big, thematic exhibitions and is

**Main attractions**
ROYAL ACADEMY OF ARTS
FORTNUM & MASON
THE RITZ
BURLINGTON ARCADE
BOND STREET
CORK STREET GALLERIES
HANDEL HOUSE MUSEUM
SHEPHERD MARKET
OXFORD STREET
SELFRIDGES
HAMLEYS
LIBERTY

*The Royal Academy is famous for its Summer Exhibition, the largest open contemporary art exhibition in the world.*

**RIGHT:** entrance to The Ritz hotel.

famous for its Summer Exhibition to which any artist may present work for selection. The fun of this massive assemblage of paintings is that it ranges from the sublime to the risible.

In the **John Madejski Fine Rooms**, tucked to the rear of the main staircase, much of the RA's little-known permanent collection is rotated on a yearly basis. In contrast to the Academy's top-lit galleries, these smaller rooms have been restored to reveal heavy gilding and panelled doors crowned by plaster putti – the *gusto italiano* as interpreted by William Kent in the 1720s. The Academy's most famous bequests include Michelangelo's marble *Taddei Tondo* (in the high-tech Sackler wing), Constable's *The Leaping Horse* and Gainsborough's *A Romantic Landscape*.

### Fine living

At No. 181 Piccadilly is **Fortnum & Mason ❷**, grocers to the Queen and famous for its food hampers, food

hall and shop assistants in tails. A tercentenary refurbishment has seen the food hall expand into the basement, with a new wine bar and an ice-cream parlour. The hourly changing of the guard on the mechanical clock above the shop front is a free attraction.

A little further along Piccadilly is **The Ritz ❸**, where afternoon tea in

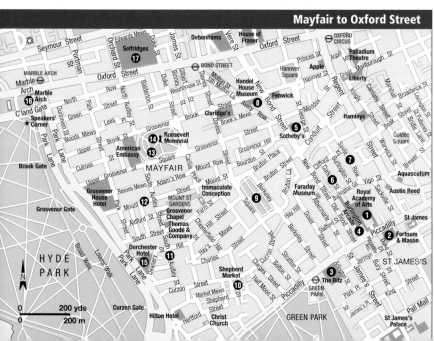

**Mayfair to Oxford Street**

the Palm Court is a tradition. The hotel, built in 1906, was fashionable in the 1930s, but lacks the cachet it used to have. In 1995 it was bought for £75 million by the low-profile Barclay brothers, David and Frederick. Its casino, probably the city's classiest, remains popular. The elegant Louis XVI dining room overlooks Green Park.

**Piccadilly Arcade**, known for its glass and chinaware shops, has graceful, bow-fronted Regency windows which belie the fact that it was built in 1910. Almost opposite and beside the Academy, **Burlington Arcade ❹** was built in 1819.

## MAYFAIR

The region bounded by Piccadilly and Park Lane, Oxford and Regent streets, has been a place of wealth and power since the early 18th century, when it was first laid out by the Grosvenor family, dukes of Westminster. **Mayfair** takes its name from the fair which was held annually on the site of what is now Shepherd Market. In the best British tradition, it clings to its exclusivity, although many of the magnificent Georgian homes of business barons and princes of property are now overrun with hotels, luxury offices, embassies and clubs.

The high street of Mayfair is **Bond Street**, divided into Old Bond Street at its southern end leading north to New Bond Street. Here are London's most exclusive couturiers and designer boutiques, jewellery shops, antiques emporia and art galleries.

The headquarters of **Sotheby's ❺**, the auctioneers founded in 1744 and now American-owned, is at No. 34. World record prices for art works are notched up here, but not every sale is for millionaires. Admission is free, as long as you look reasonably presentable, and there is a small café.

Asprey the jeweller and Fenwick's the department store are also part of

Bond Street's fabric and are worth checking out. Art galleries proliferate in Bond Street and adjacent Bruton Street, but the best place for art is **Cork Street ❻**, parallel to Bond Street to the east, with such prestigious premises as Waddington's and The Gallery in Cork Street, where Britain's top artists are represented.

Just beyond is **Savile Row ❼**, the home of several gentlemen's outfitters, where even off-the-peg items are highly priced. The offices of Apple, the Beatles company, were at No.3 Savile Row, and in 1969 the group staged what was to be their last ever live concert from its roof, included in the film *Let It Be*.

### Handel House Museum ❽

✉ 25 Brook Street; www.handel house.org ☎ 7495 1685 ◯ Tue–Sat 10am–6pm, Thur until 8pm, Sun noon–6pm ⓖ charge ⬚ Bond Street/Oxford Circus

On **Brook Street**, which runs from the west side of New Bond Street, stands the house in which Handel wrote his *Messiah*. His home for 35

*The Burlington Arcade was built in 1819. This Regency promenade of Lilliputian shops is patrolled by Beadles. In their top hats and livery, they ensure good behaviour, with "no undue whistling, humming or hurrying". Only a Beadle knows what constitutes undue humming.*

**BELOW:** the place to come for gentlemen's bespoke tailoring.

**KIDS**

On Saturday afternoons at Handel House children can drop in free and have the chance to dress up in Georgian costume. Special sessions with the Composer in Residence are sometimes geared towards older children; past events have included workshops where children created their own "water music".

**RIGHT:** the entrance to Claridge's.
**BELOW:** Italian restaurant Da Corradi on Shepherd Market.

years until his death in 1759, it has been refurbished in early 18th-century style. While the composer's life and work is well documented with information sheets, CD listening posts, and paintings, prints and old musical scores, the sparsely furnished rooms come into their own as evocative settings for intimate chamber music concerts – often with the Handel House harpsichord as their focus – and other special events.

Another musical resident here was Jimi Hendrix, who occupied a flat at No.23 from 1968 to 1969 (now the museum's private offices, although tours are available once a year). A small corner of the museum is given over to a series of photographic portraits showing the guitar legend at home.

### Smart addresses

Brook Street is also home to **Claridge's Hotel**, one of London's premier luxury hotels, built in the 1890s, though mostly in Art Deco style. Here also is the **Savile Club**, haven of the literary establishment; past members include Thomas Hardy and the poet Yeats.

### BERKELEY SQUARE ❾

Nightingales rarely sing in **Berkeley Square**, though they may have done when the song was written in 1915, and this once highly aristocratic square has been much spoilt by dull office buildings. In 1774 Lord Clive

of India committed suicide at No. 45. The Earl of Shelburne, the prime minister who conceded the independence of the United States in 1783, lived in Lansdowne House, now the site of the private members' Lansdowne Club. Berkeley Square House is built on the site of the house where Queen Elizabeth II was born in 1926.

## SHEPHERD MARKET ❿

From Berkeley Square, Curzon Street leads to Shepherd Market, Mayfair's "village centre", by way of a side passage. This small pedestrian enclave is incongruous amid the grand town houses and exclusive hotels. Built around 1735 by the architect Edward Shepherd, it was established to supply the daily needs of local residents and obliterated the open space which had accommodated the May Fair – commemorated by a blue plaque at 7 Trebeck Street – whose riotousness offended the well-off residents.

Even today Shepherd Market maintains a quaint air. There are specialist shops, pubs and restaurants, all on a village scale. At night, the area is a haunt of up-market prostitutes.

## SOUTH AUDLEY AND MOUNT STREETS

Along **South Audley Street** ⓫ is the former residence of Charles X, the last Bourbon king of France, who lived here 1805–14. At No.19, **Thomas Goode & Co**, the china, silverware and crystal shop once almost exclusively the preserve of international royalty, has occupied its own block here since the 1840s.

Behind neat miniature hedges, a marble colonnade frames the window displays. Stealing the show are the pair of howdah-bearing ceramic elephants, 7ft (2.1 metres) tall in their regalia, which are the establishment's trademark. Produced by Minton for Thomas Goode, they took the Paris Exhibition of 1889 by

storm. The shop incorporates a design archive and museum section.

The original wood pannelling and chandeliers of the Audley pub set the tone for the unbridled Victoriana of **Mount Street** ⓬, whose eastern portion especially, lined with fine shops, is strikingly homogeneous: wholly rebuilt from 1880–1900 in the pink terracotta Queen Anne style, its red-brick facades are enthusiastically decked out with terracotta features.

## GROSVENOR SQUARE ⓭

A pleasing, friendly statue of General Eisenhower and Winston Churchill having a chat on a bench

*In 1875 architects Messrs Ernest George and Peto were commissioned to design a frontage for Thomas Goode and Co. Many of the unusual features they incorporated still remain. One is the mechanical front door, which opens automatically under the weight of anyone standing on the platform. This rare piece of Victorian design is believed to be the only example still in use in the world.*

**ABOVE LEFT:** the lavish interior of Thomas Goode & Co. **BELOW:** the window of Thomas Goode & Co.

*The entrance to Selfridges on Oxford Street. The store opened in 1909. The present American neoclassical emporium was completed in 1926.*

in Bond Street is a sign of the interest Americans have always had in Mayfair. In 1785 John Adams, the first United States Minister to Britain and later the nation's president, took up residence at **9 Grosvenor Square**. No fewer than 31 of the 47 households in the square then belonged to titled families. Plans were made in 2007 to move the United States embassy to a larger and more secure suburban location south of the Thames; the move is hoped to be complete by 2017.

The cost of the statue of **Franklin D. Roosevelt** ⑭ in the gardens was met by grateful British citizens after World War II.

## PARK LANE

**Park Lane**, running from Hyde Park Corner to Marble Arch, forms the western boundary of Mayfair. Its once magnificent homes overlooking Hyde Park *(see page 211)* have largely been replaced by modern hotels and apartments. These include the **Hilton Hotel** and the **Dorchester Hotel** ⑮, General Dwight D. Eisenhower's HQ in

World War II, and popular with visiting film stars. To the north, the residence of the Grosvenor family (owners of a 300-acre/120-hectare estate covering Mayfair and Park Lane) was knocked down in 1928 to make way for the **Grosvenor House Hotel**, whose Great Room is London's largest banqueting hall.

## MARBLE ARCH AND OXFORD STREET

At the top of Park Lane, the **Marble Arch** ⑯, designed by John Nash and based on the Arch of Constantine in Rome, was placed here, then known as Tyburn, in 1851 after being removed from the front of Buckingham Palace where it was originally erected in 1827. It now sits in the middle of a busy traffic island.

Crowds first came to **Oxford Street** to see the condemned being taken to Tyburn *(see box below left)*: this produced a ready clientele for shopkeepers, and stores first appeared along "Ladies' Mile" between Tottenham Court Road and Marylebone Lane, just short of Bond Street Underground station. This

## Hangman's Haunt

A stone slab on a traffic island opposite Marble Arch at the west end of Oxford Street, London's principal shopping thoroughfare, marks the spot where public hangings took place – the first recorded in 1196. The last in 1783 was of a highwayman, John Austin. Up to 50,000 convicted felons died here. The site of London's main place of execution took its name from Tyburn Brook, which flowed into the Westbourne River at what is now the Serpentine in Hyde Park. The condemned were transported here along what is now Oxford Street (formerly Tyburn Street) from Newgate Prison or the Tower of London.

Hanging days were public holidays: the victims dressed in their best, carried nosegays of flowers and took a last mug of ale. Felons were allowed to speak to the crowd before being hanged. The site of the now demolished Newgate Prison contains the Central Criminal Court.

*Recommended Restaurants, Pubs, Bars & Cafés on pages 120–1*

was where the first department stores were built. One of the finest to this day, **Selfridges ⑰**, was built further west by Gordon Selfridge, a Chicago retail millionaire. Marks & Spencer, the drapers, opened their largest shop next door in 1930, still the site of their flagship store.

Only buses and taxis are allowed to drive down most of Oxford Street and its widened pavements are usually packed with tourists. Near Bond

Street Underground station, designer boutiques in St Christopher's Place – with its pavement cafés and hanging baskets – offer an escape from the masses, as do Bond Street and South Molton Street on the south side.

At Oxford Circus, Oxford Street crosses over **Regent Street** which continues north, part of Nash's scheme to connect the Prince Regent's home at Carlton House with his newly acquired property at Regent's Park. Among Regent Street's restaurants are **Veera-swamy's** (entrance on Swallow Street), London's first Indian restaurant, and the former **Café Royal**, at No. 68, which was used by *belle-époque* figures such as George Bernard Shaw, Oscar Wilde, James Whistler and Aubrey Beardsley.

The Café Royal was also a haunt of Winston Churchill, and the high-living Edward VIII (when he was Prince of Wales) and George VI. The building closed in 2008 after 143 years and its famous artefacts were auctioned off – including the café's original boxing ring. It is due to be converted into an hotel by 2012. ❑

**SHOP**

Oxford Street is known for its department stores and chain stores, but Regent Street is also worth exploring. Shops include **Hamleys**, the world's biggest toy store, at Nos. 188–96, **Aquascutum**, legendary for creating the trench-style raincoat, at No. 100, and the gigantic **Apple Store** at No. 235. **Austin Reed**, at No. 103–13, has an Art Deco barber's in its basement (now a beauty salon). Just off Regent Street on the fringes of Soho is **Liberty** *(see pages 52 and 94)*.

**LEFT:** view from the Hilton Hotel. **BELOW:** Hamleys toy shop on Regent Street.

# BEST RESTAURANTS, PUBS, BARS AND CAFÉS

## Restaurants

Prices for a three-course dinner per person with a half-bottle of house wine:
**£** = under £20
**££** = £20–30
**£££** = £30–50
**££££** = over £50

### American

#### Hard Rock Café

150 Old Park Lane, W1
📞 7514 1700; www.hardrock.com 🕐 L & D daily. **££** [p325, E4]
Long established member of the global chain. Expect long queues, huge portions of nachos, chicken wings, sundaes and hamburgers, and homage to rock 'n' roll memorabilia. The "vaults museum" next door exhibits guitars belonging to Hendrix, Presley *et al*.

### Chinese

#### Kai

65 South Audley St, W1
📞 7493 8988; www.kaimayfair.co.uk 🕐 L & D daily. **££££** (set lunch **£££**) [p325, E3]
Opulence pitched at a wealthy clientele. Specialities include abalone in a white truffle jus reduction and tiger prawns with crisp curry leaves. Holder of one Michelin star.

### Fish

#### Scotts

20 Mount St, W1 📞 7495 7309; www.scotts-restaurant.com 🕐 L & D daily; Oyster Bar daily all day. **££££** [p325, E2]
This restaurant is more than 150 years old. Seafood (good fish pie, scallops, and Dover sole) in grand surroundings. Popular celebrity hangout, so book if you can.

### French

#### Alain Ducasse

The Dorchester, Park Lane, W1 📞 7629 8866 🕐 L Tue–Fri, D Tue–Sat. **££££** [p325, E3]
Three Michelin stars at this elegant hotel restaurant. Dishes might include Anjou pigeon, or wild sea bass.

#### Hélène Darroze

The Connaught, Carlos Place, W1 📞 7107 8880 🕐 Brunch Sat, L Tue–Fri, D Tue–Sat. **£££–££££** [p325, E2]
Hélène Darroze has earned two Michelin stars for her modern French cuisine. Service is formal and prices are high in the evening, but the lunch time set menu represents good value.

#### Le Gavroche

43 Upper Brook St, W1 📞 7408 0881; www.le-gavroche.co.uk 🕐 L Mon–Fri, D Mon–Sat. **££££** [p325, E2]
French haute cuisine is given a lighter touch with hints of Asian influence. A chic, civilised operation with polished service.

Male diners are expected to wear a jacket.

#### Truc Vert

42 North Audley St, W1
📞 7491 9988; www.trucvert.co.uk 🕐 Mon–Fri 7.30am–10pm, Sat 9am–10pm, Sun 9am–4pm. **£££** [p325, E2]
Informal, buzzy restaurant in a wonderful deli, offering salads, pâtés, quiches and pastries plus charcuterie/cheese plates made to order.

### Indian

#### Benares

12a Berkeley Square House, Berkeley Sq, W1 📞 7629 8886; www.benaresrestaurant.com 🕐 L & D daily. **£££** [p326, A2]
Hits on the menu include butter poached lobster tail with mussel kedgeree. Recipient of a Michelin star. All lamb and chicken is halal.

### Italian

#### Cecconi's

5A Burlington Gardens, W1 📞 7434 1500; www.cecconis.co.uk 🕐 B, L & D daily, also brunch Sat–Sun. **£££** [p318, A3]
Specialises in classic regional gems. Menu features tartares, carpaccios and Italian tapas.

**LEFT:** chef at work in Momo.
**RIGHT:** Ye Grapes in Shepherd Market.

### Rocket

4–5 Lancashire Court, W1
7629 2889; www.rocket
restaurants.co.uk L & D
daily. ££ [p326, A2]
Modern Italian serving
wood-fired pizzas and
pasta in a pretty enclave
off New Bond Street.

### Japanese

#### Nobu

Metropolitan Hotel, 19 Old
Park Lane, W1 7447
4747 L & D daily. ££££
[p325, E3]
Haunt of A-list celebrities.
Great Japanese food with
a Peruvian twist, but
tables are close and there
are two-hour time limits.

#### Umu

14–16 Bruton Place, W1
7499 8881; www.umu
restaurant.com L Mon–
Fri, D Mon–Sat. £££–££££
[p326, A2]
The food here has been
awarded a Michelin star,
and consists of sushi,
sashimi and a Kaiseki
tasting menu.

### Middle Eastern

#### Fakhreldine

85 Piccadilly, W1 7493
3424; www.fakhreldine.
co.uk L & D daily. £££
[p326, A3]
Modern interpretation of
traditional dishes, with a
Lebanese brunch menu
on Sundays.

### Modern European

#### The Albemarle

Brown's Hotel, 33 Albemarle
St, W1 7518 4004 B,

L & D daily. ££££ (set menu
£££) [p318, A4]
This restaurant has a
modern feel, impeccable
service and cutting-edge
cuisine. Has a great
cheeseboard and seri-
ous wine cellar. Holder of
2 AA rosettes.

#### Criterion Grill

224 Piccadilly, W1 7930
0488; www.criterion
restaurant.com L & D
daily. £££ (set menu ££)
[p318, C3]
The Criterion has a
please-all menu, featuring
British produce such as
Scottish beef and Cornish
crab. The real draw is the
neo-Byzantine interior.

#### Dover Street
#### Restaurant & Jazz Bar

8–10 Dover St, W1 7629
9813; www.doverst.co.uk
D Mon–Sat until 2am.
£££ [p318, A4]
Attracts an affluent post-
work crowd who come
here to unwind over
drinks and the live jazz,
soul and Latin sounds.
The brasserie-style menu
is unadventurous but reliable. Charge after 10pm;
no jeans or trainers.

#### Gordon Ramsay
#### at Claridge's

Claridge's Hotel, Brook St,
W1 7499 0099 L & D
daily. ££££ (set lunch £££)
[p325, E2]
Working under Ramsay's
supervision, head chef
Steve Allen cooks dreamy
rich, intricate dishes. The
set lunch is a relative bargain. Booking essential.
Dress code smart.

### Maze

10–13 Grosvenor Sq, W1
7107 0000; www.gordon
ramsay.com L & D daily.
££££ (set lunch £££)
[p325, E2]
This Rockwell-designed,
Gordon Ramsay-owned
restaurant is a runaway
success. Dishes are
intensely flavoured, for
example boiled beef
cheeks with cardamom
and star anise.

### Others

#### Momo

25 Heddon St, W1 7434
4040; www.momoresto.com
L Mon–Sat, D daily;

tearoom daily noon–1am.
£££ (set lunch ££)
[p318, A3]
Theatrical decor, authen-
tic Moroccan cuisine and
a party atmosphere.
Share excellent *pastilla*
(sweet and sour pigeon
pie), couscous or tagines.

### The Wolseley

160 Piccadilly, W1 7499
6996; www.thewolseley.
com B, L & D daily.
£££–££££ [p318, A4]
Always busy, always
glamorous, The Wolseley
is the place to come for
afternoon tea and pre-
theatre light meals as
well as lunch or dinner.

### Pubs, Bars and Cafés

Mayfair drinkers fre-
quent some of London's
grandest hotel bars
where the scale of the
free nibbles can offset
the steep drinks prices.
Try the stately **Coburg
Bar at the Connaught**
*(Carlos Place)*, the mirrored piano **Dorchester
Bar** *(53 Park Lane)*, the
fashionable **Claridge's
Bar** *(55 Brook St)* or the
**Rivoli Bar** at The Ritz
*(150 Piccadilly)*.

Old-fashioned booz-
ers are thin on the
ground, but there are a
few gems. The posh,
high Victoriana **Audley**
(41–43 Mount St)
attracts the Mayfair rich.
More cosy is the **Coach
& Horses** *(5 Bruton St)*
and most lively is **Ye
Grapes** *(16 Shepherd
Market)*. **Eagle Bar
Diner** *(3–5 Rathbone

*Place)* has tongue-in-
cheek chic and a long
list of cocktails.

Head to the **Met Bar**
*(Metropolitan Hotel,
19 Old Park Lane)*,
newly reopened after
refurbishment, for
creative cocktails. This
former celeb hang-out
no longer restricts
entry to members and
hotel guests only.

# LONDON'S PARKS

The city has more green spaces than any comparable conurbation – and they're used for everything from sunbathing to speechmaking

London's eight major parks – Hyde Park, Kensington Gardens, Regent's Park, St James's Park, Green Park, Greenwich Park, Richmond Park and Bushy Park – are all owned and run by the Crown. Many were once royal hunting grounds, and they retain an elegant air.

The largest park is Hyde Park (350 acres/140 hectares), a vast open space only a few paces away from bustling Oxford Street. The corner of the park near Marble Arch is known as Speakers' Corner, where freedom of speech is given full rein on Sunday afternoons.

Hyde Park adjoins Kensington Gardens, which have the air of a Victorian children's playground, with model boats on the Round Pond. The oldest park is St James's, beautifully landscaped with fountains and views of Buckingham Palace and Whitehall. Regent's Park, in Marylebone, houses London Zoo and has a very fine rose garden.

In addition there are several good suburban parks, some of them established in the 19th century to alleviate the unhealthy living conditions of the poor. The other great open space is Hampstead Heath in north London.

**ABOVE:** lavender beds at Kew Gardens. Main attractions include the Palm House (the Victorian glasshouse containing a tropical rainforest), a rose garden next to the Palm House, the Temperate House and the Princess of Wales conservatory.

**BELOW:** Kew Gardens' treetop walkway allows you to view different species of tree while 18 feet up in the air, as well as journeying underground to see trees' roots. Another feature of the gardens is the 163ft (50m) -high pagoda.

**ABOVE:** one of the Royal Parks, Green Park consists of 47 acres (19 hectares) of trees and grassland. Formerly a famous duelling site, this is where the 41-gun royal salute takes place in June for the Queen's birthday.

**RIGHT:** Richmond Park *(see page 238)* was once a royal hunting ground, but today more than 600 red and fallow deer graze in peace. The 2,470-acre (1,000-hectare) park has extensive facilities for horse riders, cricketers, golfers and footballers. Adam's Pond is used for model boats, and two Pen Ponds are reserved for anglers.

## MUSIC AND THEATRE IN THE PARK

The sight of people sitting in striped deckchairs in a park on a warm summer's day listening to a brass band is reassuringly English. Five of the royal parks have their own bandstands and hold regular, free afternoon concerts at weekends. Throughout the summer, jazz and woodwind recitals are given at Kensington Gardens and the last night of the Proms (the summer Henry Wood Promenade Concerts in the Albert Hall) spills over into Hyde Park. Concerts in Greenwich Park are held in a special park arena by the Royal Observatory. The evening concerts are held in mid-July and feature well known musicians.

Great houses provide other venues for music and theatre, with picnic concerts at Kenwood House featuring artists such as Tom Jones. Concerts are also held in the grounds of Holland House in Holland Park, west London, and make a delightful evening, as do the open-air Shakespeare productions in Regent's Park (*left*) in the summer.

Some of the Royal Parks will also host events at the 2012 Olympics, with Hyde Park being the setting for the triathlon, for instance.

*Recommended Restaurants, Pubs, Bars & Cafés on pages 130–1*

# MARYLEBONE AND FITZROVIA

North of Oxford Street lies Marylebone,
a characterful area of elegant squares and
terraces bordered by Regent's Park. Among
its attractions are Madame Tussauds, London
Zoo and the Sherlock Holmes Museum

The residential area of **Marylebone** (pronounced *marry-le-bun*) lies between Oxford Street and Regent's Park. It is largely Georgian in character, its streets and squares named after the Cavendish, Harley and Portland families, who progressively developed the district from the beginning of the 18th century. The need to relieve congestion in Oxford Street inspired the creation of a new road running from Paddington to Islington through the parish of St Mary-by-the-bourne.

Today, Marylebone still retains an air of genteel village dwelling, an oasis framed by multicultural Edgware Road to the west, Oxford Street to the south and Tottenham Court Road to the east. The section known as Fitzrovia, traditionally an artists' enclave and retaining a bohemian atmosphere, nestles around the BT Tower.

## NORTH OF OXFORD STREET

St Christopher's Place, a pedestrian enclave lined with boutiques and cafés, is accessible through a narrow passageway on Oxford Street *(see pages 118–9)* and leads via cobbled James Street to Wigmore Street. The latter contains several good restaurants as well as various medical specialists spilling over from **Harley Street**, the preferred haunt of private physicians since the 1840s.

On the north side of the road stands **Wigmore Hall ❶** *(see page 300)*, a delightful concert venue, particularly at lunchtimes. BBC Radio 3 broadcasts live from here on Mondays. The Art Nouveau building, which has notable acoustics, was erected in 1901 by a German piano company.

**Main attractions**

WIGMORE HALL
WALLACE COLLECTION
MARYLEBONE HIGH STREET
MADAME TUSSAUDS
ROYAL ACADEMY OF MUSIC
SHERLOCK HOLMES MUSEUM
REGENT'S PARK
LONDON ZOO
LORD'S CRICKET GROUND
LONDON CENTRAL MOSQUE
BT TOWER
FITZROY TAVERN
CHARLOTTE STREET

**LEFT:** Fitzrovia's BT Tower rises over 18th-and 19th-century terraces.
**RIGHT:** the entrance to Wigmore Hall, a fine Art Nouveau concert hall.

*The Great Gallery in the Wallace Collection contains Old Master paintings and French and Italian furniture.*

## Wallace Collection ❷

✉ Hertford House, Manchester Square, W1; www.wallacecollection. org ☏ 7563 9500 ⏰ daily 10am–5pm 🎫 free 🚇 Bond Street

This remarkable display of art ranges from 17th- and 18th-century English and European paintings to Sèvres porcelain. In addition to pictures by Velázquez, Boucher and Fragonard, it contains Rembrandt's *Self-Portrait in a Black Cap*, Rubens' *Rainbow Landscape*, Poussin's *Dance to the Music of Time*, and Frans Hal's *The Laughing Cavalier*.

The collection was bequeathed to the British nation by the widow of Sir Richard Wallace, whose family originally amassed these works.

## MARYLEBONE VILLAGE

Tucked amongst quiet residential terraces, **Marylebone High Street ❸** is a hub of homeware shops, boutiques and restaurants, its urban village atmosphere providing an oasis from the surrounding bustle. It also has several specialist food shops, from charcuteries to fishmongers. On Sundays there is a **farmers' market** (10am–2pm) at Cramer Street car park.

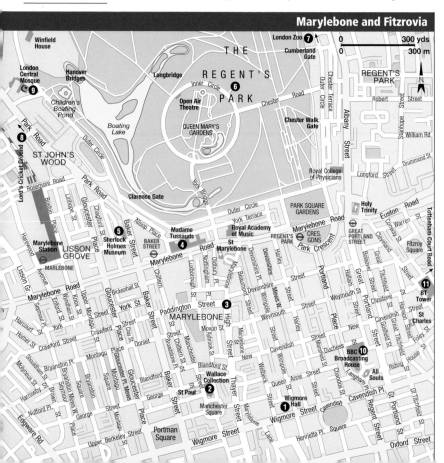

### Marylebone and Fitzrovia

*Recommended Restaurants, Pubs, Bars & Cafés on pages 130–1*

More pubs and small shops are dotted along narrow **Marylebone Lane**, which winds along the course of the subterranean River Tyburn.

## MARYLEBONE ROAD AND BAKER STREET

Marylebone Road is one of London's busiest east-west thoroughfares. Its intersection with north-south Baker Street is marked by two attractions, Madame Tussauds and the Sherlock Holmes Museum.

## Madame Tussauds ❹

✉ Marylebone Road; www.madametussauds.com  📞 0871 894 3000  🄲 Mon–Fri 9.30am–5.30pm, Sat–Sun 9am–6pm, school summer holidays daily 9am–7pm  🄶 charge  🚇 Baker Street

With its high tech special effects and increasing emphasis on contemporary celebrities, Madame Tussauds waxwork museum is one of London's top attractions, especially for teenagers. *For more information, see the photo feature on pages 132–3.*

Not far past the scrum outside Madame Tussauds is the **Royal Academy of Music**, which hosts daily recitals, workshops, seminars and concerts, most of which are free (tel:

7873 7300). Opposite the Academy stands **St Marylebone Parish Church**, which was depicted by Hogarth in the wedding scene of *A Rake's Progress*. Lord Byron (1788) was baptised here, and Lord Nelson worshipped here.

## Sherlock Holmes Museum ❺

✉ 221b Baker Street; www.sherlock-holmes.co.uk  📞 7224 3688  🄲 daily 9.30am–6.30pm  🄶 charge  🚇 Baker Street

On Baker Street, north of the intersection with Marylebone Road, this museum re-creates the Victorian home of Arthur Conan Doyle's fictional detective. Some rooms are detailed representations of his living quarters, others contain waxwork tableaux of characters and scenes described in the stories. A Victorian "maid" is on hand to answer questions.

## REGENT'S PARK

Baker Street, Marylebone High Street and Portland Place all lead to **Regent's Park ❻**, an elegant 470-

*Regent's Park's rose garden in the heart of the Inner Circle contains some 20,000 roses. They bloom from June through to Christmas.*

**LEFT:** falconry display at London Zoo. **BELOW:** exhibits in the Sherlock Holmes Museum.

**TIP**

An alternative and more romantic route to London Zoo is to take a canal boat from Camden Lock or Little Venice along Regent's Canal. The London Waterbus Company runs regular services in summer (tel: 7482 2660, bookings 7482 2550; www.londonwaterbus.com) with a reduced service during winter.

acre (190-hectare) space surrounded by John Nash's Regency terraces. Shakespeare plays are performed at the Open Air Theatre in summer. The boating lake is a tranquil spot, and Regent's Canal runs through the north of the park.

## London Zoo ❼

✉ Outer Circle, Regent's Park; www.zsl.org/london-zoo ☎ 7722 3333 �🕐 daily Mar–Oct 10am–5.30pm, until 6pm mid-July–early Sept, Nov–Feb 10am–4pm ⓔ charge 🚇 Camden Town

Increasingly placing an onus on conservational breeding, London Zoo includes a tropical birdwalk in the Blackburn Pavilion, the Gorilla Kingdom, and the Clore Rainforest Lookout displaying South American mammals, birds and reptiles. The new Penguin Beach has a pool allowing you to watch the colonies of Humboldt and Macaroni penguins swimming underwater. On a more tactile level, the children's enclosure allows visitors to handle animals such as goats and llamas.

### Around the Park
On the northwest side of the park is **Lord's Cricket Ground ❽** (nearest tube: St John's Wood), belonging to the Marylebone Cricket Club, which runs the English game. To access the ground and the portrait-packed Long Room through which players walk on their way to the field, see the honours boards in the players' dressing rooms and visit the **museum**, you must take the 100-minute tour (www.lords.org; daily noon

**RIGHT:** London Zoo's new Penguin Beach.
**BELOW:** the dome and minaret of London Central Mosque.

*Recommended Restaurants, Pubs, Bars & Cafés on pages 130–1*

and 2pm, except on major match or preparation days, also 10am Apr–Sept; tel: 7616 8595; charge).

Nearby is the **London Central Mosque** and Islamic Cultural Centre. The site for the mosque was a gift from the government to the Muslim community during World War II, in recognition of the substantial Islamic population of the British Empire, although the building of the mosque was not completed until 1977. Visitors are welcome but note that clothing to below the knee is required; women can borrow headscarves from the bookshop.

## PORTLAND PLACE

The eastern stretch of Marylebone leads to Park Crescent and **Portland Place**, conceived by the Adam brothers as a home for the rich. John Nash included it in his grand design to connect Regent's Park with St James's but the plan was never realised. The Adam houses in Portland Place house several embassies, institutes and learned societies, such as the Royal Institute of British Architects (RIBA).

**Langham Place**, which curves round to connect Portland Place with Regent Street, has a trio of dramatic buildings: the circular **All Souls' Church** built by Nash in 1822–24, the Langham hotel and **Broadcasting House**, headquarters of the BBC, where the first public television transmission was made in 1932. The TV studios are now at White City in west London, but the corporation's main radio studios are still here.

## FITZROVIA

Dominating the skyline of this former bohemian enclave is the 620ft (189-metre) -high **BT Tower**, one of the tallest structures in London. **Fitzroy Square** is central to the area's literary heritage *(see below)*; George Bernard Shaw, Virginia Woolf and Ian McEwan have all lived here.

Cosmopolitan **Charlotte Street** used to be known mainly for Greek eateries but now has a variety of chic restaurants. Running parallel is **Tottenham Court Road**, home to electrical goods and home furnishing stores such as Heal's, and the eastern boundary of Fitzrovia. ❏

**KIDS**

**Pollock's Toy Museum** (Mon–Sat 10am–5pm; tel: 7636 3452; www. pollockstoymuseum. com) has a great variety of toy exhibits and puppet theatres, spread over an eccentric building accessible by a small entrance on Scala Street, off Charlotte Street. There is an old-fashioned toy shop on the ground floor.

**BELOW LEFT:** All Souls' Church, Langham Place.

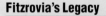

## Fitzrovia's Legacy

**F**itzrovia has long attracted countercultures; in the mid-19th century, for example, it was a hub of working men's clubs and Chartist activity. However, it is most famous for attracting a bawdy bohemian set between the 1920s and 1950s. Welsh poet Dylan Thomas and the painter Augustus John frequented the Fitzroy Tavern, while writer Julian Maclaren-Ross drank away his publishing advance at The Wheatsheaf, ultimately becoming better known for his "King of Fitzrovia" persona, complete with silver-topped cane, than for his short stories.

George Orwell was another regular and the Newman Arms on Rathbone Street features in his novels *Nineteen Eighty-Four* and *Keep the Aspidistra Flying*. Others inhabitants included Anthony Powell, Wyndham Lewis and Francis Bacon. The scene dissolved in the 1950s. Today creativity comes in other forms: many media companies are based here.

# BEST RESTAURANTS, PUBS, BARS AND CAFÉS

## Restaurants

Prices for a three-course dinner per person with a half-bottle of house wine:
**£** = under £20
**££** = £20–30
**£££** = £30–50
**££££** = over £50

## British

### Langan's Bistro
26 Devonshire St, W1
☎ 7935 4531; www.langans restaurants.co.uk © L Mon–Fri, D Mon–Sat. **££** [p321, C4]
Old-timer and former celebrity haunt serving simple, old-fashioned bistro fare with considerable aplomb. No culinary fireworks in the kitchen but good for more romantic occasions.

### Riding House Café
43 Great Titchfield St, W1
☎ 7927 0840; www.riding housecafe.co.uk © B, L & D daily. **££** [p321, E4]
A shabby chic look, with British/Mediterranean dishes and good puddings. Lively atmosphere.

## Fish

### Back to Basics
21a Foley St, W1 ☎ 7436 2181; www.backtobasics.uk. com © L & D Mon–Sat. **£££** [p321, E4]
A blackboard menu has a dozen or so fish dishes in this excellent neighbourhood venue.

### Fishworks
89 Marylebone High St, W1
☎ 7935 9796 © L Mon–

Fri, D Mon–Fri and Sun. **££** [p321, C4]
Member of a well-regarded chain selling fresh fish and seafood in the front, with a restaurant behind.

### Golden Hinde
73 Marylebone Lane, W1
☎ 7486 3644 © L Mon–Fri, D Mon–Sat. **£** [p325, E1]
Vintage chippie (1914), with a magnificent 1930s fryer now purely decorative. Fabulous glisteningly fresh fish in crispy golden batter. BYOB. No corkage.

## French

### Galvin Bistrot de Luxe
66 Baker St, W1 ☎ 7935 4007; www.galvin restaurants.com © L & D daily. **£££** [p325, D1]
Critically adored brasserie serving traditional Gallic dishes. Has a reasonable set menu served 6–7pm.

### Pied à Terre
34 Charlotte St, W1 ☎ 7636 1178; www.pied-a-terre. co.uk © L & D Mon–Sat. **££££** (set lunch **£££**) [p321, E4]
Michelin-starred cuisine. A sample dish is roast pigeon with red chard and cherry and thyme sauce. Has a vegetarian tasting menu, too.

## Italian

### Caffe Caldesi
118 Marylebone Lane, W1
☎ 7487 0754; www. caldesi.com © L & D Mon–Sat. **£££** [p325, E1]
This is a gem, with a ground floor café/wine bar and a first floor restaurant. A sample dish is sea bass with saffron sauce. Set lunch available.

### Da Paolo
3 Charlotte Place, W1
☎ 7580 0021; www. dapaolo.co.uk © L Mon–Fri, D daily. **£££** [p321, E4]
Italian village atmosphere, dishes that include linguine with langoustines and beef fillet with blue cheese, and desserts such as Sicilian lemon cheesecake.

### Locanda Locatelli
Churchill Intercontinental, 8 Seymour St, W1 ☎ 7935 9088 © L & D daily. **££££** [p325, D1]
Italian classics from Giorgio Locatelli.

## Japanese

### Roka
37 Charlotte St, W1
☎ 7580 6464; www.roka restaurant.com © L daily, D Mon–Fri and Sun. **££££** [p321, E4]

**LEFT:** Fishworks on Marylebone High Street.
**ABOVE RIGHT:** the Golden Hinde, a vintage chippie.

See and be seen at this rustic-style, uber-stylish place, where the food is based on *robatayaki* cuisine (cooked on an open charcoal grill).

### Modern European

#### Odin's Restaurant

27 Devonshire St, W1
7935 7296; www.langans restaurants.co.uk L Mon–Fri, D Mon–Sat. £££ [p321, C4]
Grand antique-filled dining room that's good for an intimate dinner as tables are hidden behind old-style screens. Famed for its delicious chocolate pudding.

#### Orrery

55 Marylebone High St, W1
7616 8000; www.orrery-restaurant.co.uk L & D daily. All menus are set ££–££££ [p321, C4]
Dinner here is a romantic gastro experience. Roast rabbit with poached apricots and white chocolate vacherin are examples of typical dishes.

### North African

#### Original Tagines

7a Dorset St, W1 7935 1545; www.original-tagines.com L daily, D Mon–Sat. ££ [p320–1, C4]

A buzzy little restaurant which specialises in deliciously spiced Moroccan tagines. Laid-back atmosphere.

### Spanish

#### Navarro's

67 Charlotte St, W1 7637 7713; www.navarros.co.uk L Mon–Fri, D Mon–Sat. ££ [p321, E4]
A choice of some 50 tapas in a cheerful restaurant. Seafood dishes generally excel and there are plenty of vegetarian options.

#### The Providores and Tapa Room

109 Marylebone High St, W1
7935 6175; www.the providores.co.uk L & D daily. Tapa Room ££, Providores ££££ [p321, C4]
Interesting ingredients are used to create exciting fusion dishes. The downstairs Tapa Room is more informal. Try the chocolate, raisin and sherry brownie.

#### Salt Yard

54 Goodge St, W1 7637 0657; www.saltyard.co.uk L Mon–Fri, D Mon–Sat. £–££ [p321, E4]
Bar and restaurant serving tapas, with inventive options such as cour-

gette flowers stuffed with goats' cheese. Charcuterie and bar snacks available too.

### Vegetarian

#### Manna

Erskine Rd, NW3 7722 8028; www.mannav.com L Sat–Sun, D Tue–Sun. ££ [off map]
Good vegetarian restaurant in Primrose Hill. Chic interior and seasonal dishes from around the

world, from Japanese pickle salad to fajitas.

#### Reuben's

79 Baker St, W1 7486 0035; www.reubens restaurant.co.uk L & D Mon–Fri and Sun. ££ [p320, C4]
Kosher food served in no-frills surroundings. Famed for its traditional favourites such as salt beef and chicken soup. There's a deli and café, plus a takeaway menu.

### Pubs, Bars and Cafés

At the **Fitzroy Tavern** (16 Charlotte St) they still display George Orwell's journalists' union card. The **Newman Arms** (23 Rathbone St) is famed for its pies and **The Marquis of Granby** (2 Rathbone St) offers a choice of real ales.

Modish bars range from the **Long Bar** in the Sanderson Hotel (50 Berners St) to the cultish basement **Jerusalem** (33–34 Rathbone Place), and the conspiratorial **Bradley's Spanish Bar** (42–44 Hanway St). **Coco Momo** (79 Marylebone High St) is a good gastro-bar.

For sheer indulgence, visit **Artesian** at Langham Hotel (1 Portland Place) and choose from the extensive cocktail menu. It includes the Langham Cobbler, made with sake. For a down to earth, old-fashioned pub try the small **Golden**

**Eagle** (59 Marylebone Lane) with its traditional ales and regular piano sing-songs.

---

#### CAFÉS

**La Fromagerie** (2–6 Moxon St) is a cheese shop with a tasting café. For a daytime treat, tuck into a gâteau at **Pâtisserie Valerie** at Maison Sagne (105 Marylebone High St) or visit **The Wallace** (The Wallace Collection, Manchester Sq) for a civilised lunch or tea break, in an airy glass-roofed courtyard. In Fitzrovia, **Lantana** (13–14 Charlotte Place) offers Aussie-style brunches.

# SEEING STARS AT MADAME TUSSAUDS

**When computer animation creates miraculous images on cinema screens, what is the appeal of a collection of mute effigies with fibreglass bodies and wax heads?**

A key ingredient in the success of Madame Tussauds is that the models are no longer roped off or protected by glass cases. You can stroll right up to them – an impertinence their body-guards would never permit in real life. You can be photographed with your arm around the Queen (pictured) or Tom Cruise. Whatever impulse draws crowds to see a minor television personality declare a supermarket open is at work here in over-drive, and the reactions are similar. Is Lady Gaga really wearing a telephone hat? Is Beyoncé's skin really that perfect? An additional talking point is provided by the fact that, while the best models are astonishingly lifelike, a surprising proportion just aren't all that good.

To ring the changes, Tussauds mounts temporary groupings based on films such as *Pirates of the Caribbean* or TV shows such as *The X Factor*.

**ABOVE:** it can take 800 hours of specialist sculpting to create figures such as Princes William and Harry. If the subjects are willing, a cast of their teeth is taken to ensure accuracy. Some donate clothing for their waxwork – Nicolas Cage provided a pair of jeans, Kylie Minogue a mini-dress and Tony Blair a suit.

**RIGHT:** a waxwork of the R'n'B star Rihanna was unveiled in autumn 2011, in the museum's Pop Stars section where she joins Justin Bieber and the late Amy Winehouse, amongst others.

## The essentials

✉ *Marylebone Road; www.madametussauds. com* 🕑 *Mon–Fri 9.30am–5.30pm, Sat–Sun 9am–6pm, daily 9am–7pm during school summer hols*
📞 0871 894 3000
🎟 *Child: £24.60 (or £17.22 if book online)*
🚇 *Baker Street*

**ABOVE:** the Beatles – age cannot wither them, nor will they be melted down while fans want to pose with them.

**RIGHT:** Humphrey Bogart's likeness is passable, though Marlon Brando and Alfred Hitchcock fare less well. You can hug Marilyn Monroe as her skirt billows up as it did in *The Seven Year Itch.*

## THE WOMAN BEHIND THE WAXWORKS

The story began during the French Revolution in 1789 when Marie Grosholtz, trained by a doctor in modelling anatomical subjects in wax, was asked to prepare death masks of famous victims of the guillotine. She married a French engineer, François Tussaud, in 1795, but left him in 1802 to spend the next 33 years touring Britain with a growing collection of wax figures. The London waxworks began in Baker Street and moved to Marylebone Road in 1884.

Today those gory beginnings are echoed in the waxworks' Chamber of Horrors, which contains the blade that sliced off Marie Antoinette's head and recreates various none-too-scary tableaux of torture.

You can enter a dark section of the chamber where actors portraying deranged serial killers lunge at you and yell in your face. Since you are forewarned that this will happen and assured that they won't touch you, it's hard to be seriously terrified.

A better bet is the audio-animatronic Spirit of London ride, which carries you past well-made historical tableaux.

**BELOW:** sport is represented mainly by football celebrities such as Wayne Rooney, pictured, and David Beckham.

*Recommended Restaurants, Pubs, Bars & Cafés on pages 142–3*

# BLOOMSBURY AND KING'S CROSS

Home to the British Museum and the traditional base of publishing in London, Bloomsbury has an intellectual reputation. But a new wind is blowing through the area with the regeneration of neighbouring King's Cross and the opening of the Eurostar rail terminal at St Pancras

The eastern side of Tottenham Court Road marks the beginning of Bloomsbury, London's literary heart, and home to the British Museum and the University of London. The area was laid out in the late 17th and early 18th centuries, initially by Thomas Wriothesley, Earl of Southampton, and later by the Russell family, the Dukes of Bedford. Both are commemorated in the place names of the area.

Publishing houses occupy many of the fine Georgian properties lining the streets and squares. Bloomsbury is blue plaque territory *par excellence (see page 138)*. Charles Dickens lived in Doughty Street between 1837 and 1839 *(see the Charles Dickens Museum, page 139)* and in the early part of the 20th century it nurtured the Bloomsbury set, a group of writers who laid the foundations for modernism in Britain. Virginia Woolf, Vanessa Bell, Duncan Grant, Dora Carrington, E.M. Forster, Roger Fry, Maynard Keynes and Queen Victoria's biographer, Lytton Strachey, all lived at addresses in the area. They probably had more influence as a body than as individuals,

and were bookish men and women in a bookish world.

## The British Museum ❶

✉ Great Russell Street; www.thebritishmuseum.org ☏ 7323 8299 ◷ daily 10am–5.30pm, until 8.30pm Fri ⒢ free except some special exhibitions ⒭ Russell Square

The British Museum on Great Russell Street is the nation's greatest treasure house. It opened in 1759, in smaller premises in South Kensington, and

**Main attractions**
THE BRITISH MUSEUM
CORAM'S FIELDS
THE FOUNDLING MUSEUM
CHARLES DICKENS MUSEUM
KING'S CROSS
ST PANCRAS STATION
LONDON CANAL MUSEUM
THE BRITISH LIBRARY

**LEFT AND RIGHT:** the glass-roofed Great Court and the ever popular Egyptian mummies at the British Museum.

> *London thou art a jewel of jewels, a jasper of jocundity, music, talk, friendship, city views, publishing, something central & inexplicable, all this is within my reach...*
>
> Virginia Woolf 1924

now owns more than 6½ million items, ranging from the oldest neolithic antiquities to 20th-century manuscripts *(see pages 144–9)*.

Access to the collections is via the **Great Court**, roofed with a steel and glass canopy in 2000 and one of the most spectacular spaces in London. The museum's famous circular Reading Room, where Karl Marx did much of his research for *Das Kapital*, is open to all as an information centre and a home to temporary exhibitions, its library having moved to Euston Road *(see page 141)*.

In Room 95 are 1,700 examples of Chinese ceramics, dating from the 3rd to the 10th century. They were collected by Sir Percival David.

## Near the museum

From the museum three short streets (**Museum Street**, **Coptic Street** and **Bury Place**) lead to Bloomsbury Way. Among their antiquarian bookshops and cafés look out for the **London Review Bookshop** (14 Bury Place), which regularly hosts author readings and interviews; **Blade Rubber** (12 Bury Place), selling a huge range of rubber stamps as well

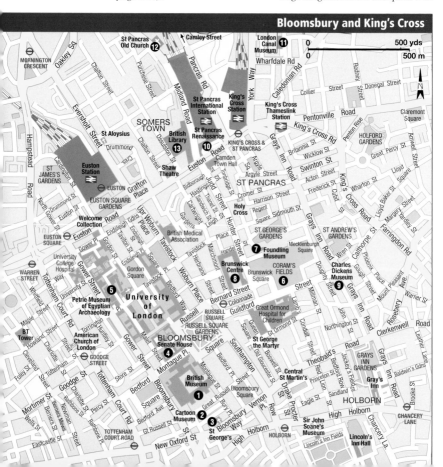

**Bloomsbury and King's Cross**

as everything needed to make home-made greetings cards; and, next door to one another at the northern end of Bury Place, **It's All Greek** and **Parthenon**. These both sell quality replicas of ancient artefacts (though the British Museum's own shop is also very good for these).

In Little Russell Street, running between Museum Street and Coptic Street, the **Cartoon Museum ②** (35 Little Russell St; www.cartoonmuseum. org; Tue–Sat 10.30am–5.30pm, Sun noon–5.30pm; tel: 7580 8155; charge) charts the history of British cartooning from Hogarth and Bate-

man to Steve Bell and Gerald Scarfe, taking in comic book characters such as Dennis the Menace and comic postcards by Donald McGill.

The British Museum's collection had an effect on the architecture of the area. Nicholas Hawksmoor's **Church of St George ③** (1731) in Bloomsbury Way was inspired by the Mausoleum of Halikarnassos, one of the Seven Wonders of the Ancient world, remnants of which can be seen in the museum *(see page 146)*. This is best appreciated by looking at its unusual stepped tower with lions and unicorns at its base and a statue of George I wearing a toga on top. The church often holds free choral performances on Sunday afternoons (www.stgeorgesbloomsbury.org.uk).

## THE UNIVERSITY OF LONDON

Just north of the British Museum is the University of London, identified by the grey turret of **Senate House ④**, built in 1936, on the western side of Russell Square.

Close by, at 46 Gordon Square, is the house to which Virginia Woolf and her siblings moved after their

**TIP**

The Tavistock Hotel on Tavistock Square sits above a wonderful retro-look bowling alley (entrance Bedford Way, not part of the hotel). This is a great option for children on a wet day, but be aware that they are not admitted after 4pm. In the evenings and at weekends it is essential to book (tel: 7183 1979; www.bloomsbury bowling.com).

**LEFT:** a few of the thousands of rubber stamps for sale at Blade Rubber on Bury Place. **BELOW LEFT:** Nicholas Hawksmoor's tower on the Church of St George. **BELOW:** literary bookshop on Bury Place.

# Blue Plaques

**Numerous famous writers, artists and intellectuals have made Bloomsbury their home. Commemorating their presence are scores of blue plaques**

**O**ne of many pointers to London's varied past are the blue plaques slapped on sundry sites to commemorate famous people, events and buildings. There are plenty in Bloomsbury, but they are strewn all across London. Almost 900 have appeared on the former homes of the famous and the long dead, and about 20 new ones are added each year. The first plaque was erected by the Royal Society of Arts in memory of the poet Lord Byron in 1867. In 1901 the London County Council took over the service, which is today administered by English Heritage.

Bona fide plaques are ceramic with white lettering on a circular blue base. They are bald statements of fact, giving little biographical information – simply the name, dates, profession and usually the period he or she lived in the building.

The awarding of a plaque is almost haphazard: there is no overall register of famous people who have lived in London. Many plaques are put up because descendants or adherents of the deceased put forward the suggestion to English Heritage. Thus plaques function as a barometer of public taste, as notions change about what constitutes fame. The range has been dominated by 19th-century politicians and artists, but in 1997 the first plaque to commemorate a rock star – Jimi Hendrix – went up in Brook Street.

A plaque-spotting tour would not lack variety. Captain William Bligh of Bounty fame lived at 100 Lambeth Road, SE1; Charlie Chaplin lived at 287 Kennington Road, SE1; Sir Winston Churchill lived at 34 Eccleston Square, SW1; Benjamin Franklin lived at 36 Craven Street, WC2; Charles Dickens lived at 48 Doughty Street, WC1; Henry James lived at 34 De Vere Gardens, W8; Karl Marx lived at 28 Dean Street, W1; George Bernard Shaw lived at 29 Fitzroy Square, W1; and Mark Twain lived at 23 Tedworth Square, SW3.

Most candidates for traditional plaques are submitted to lengthy scrutiny. They must have been dead for at least 20 years; they must be regarded as eminent by luminaries in their profession; they should have made an important contribution to human welfare; the well-informed passer-by should recognise their name; and they should, by the kind of infuriatingly nebulous "general agreement" that has characterised British decision-making, deserve recognition.

More recently the borough of Southwark began placing its own blue plaques to locals who received most votes in a public poll. This enabled the living as well as the dead to be commemorated murally. ❑

**ABOVE:** Bloomsbury hostess Lady Ottoline Morrell lived at 10 Gower Street. **LEFT:** the Borough of Southwark recognises the living as well as the dead.

*Recommended Restaurants, Pubs, Bars & Cafés on pages 142–3*

father's death in 1904, thus becoming a magnet for other "Bloomsberries".

The **Petrie Museum of Egyptian Archaeology ⑤** (University College London, Malet Place; Tue–Sat 1–5pm; free) is a two-room collection of treasures, of interest mainly to students and academics.

### CORAM'S FIELDS ⑥

East of the British Museum, across **Russell Square**, the area is dissected by Southampton Row. On the east side of the square, just beyond the children's hospital in Great Ormond Street, are Coram's Fields, where children rule the roost (adults may only enter the park if accompanied by children). As well as playgrounds, sports facilities, and a nursery, it has rabbits, chickens and sheep.

Thomas Coram was a sea captain who started a hospital and school for foundling children and persuaded artists of the day, including William Hogarth, to donate works of art to raise funds. The collection, which includes paintings by the great 19th-century portraitists Thomas Gainsborough and Joshua Reynolds, is displayed in **The Foundling Museum ⑦**, adjacent to the site of the old Foundling Hospital on the north side of Coram's Fields (40 Brunswick Square; www.foundlingmuseum.org.uk; Tue–Sat 10am–5pm, Sun 11am–5pm; tel:

7841 3600; charge; children free).

The ground floor traces the history of the hospital and of the philanthropic movement set against the background of 19th-century social conditions. Upstairs, in a fine rococo drawing room, are items belonging or related to George Frideric Handel, one of the hospital's benefactors.

### Shopping and eating

The **Brunswick Centre ⑧**, a 1960s shopping-cum-housing development on the west side of Coram's Fields, has recently been given a makeover. It includes several good eating options as well as the Renoir, an art-house cinema. Alternatively, south of Coram's Fields is **Lamb's Conduit Street**, a characterful street with interesting shops and The Lamb pub.

### CHARLES DICKENS MUSEUM ⑨

✉ 48 Doughty St; www.dickens museum.com  📞 7405 2127  🕐 daily 10am–5pm (closed Mar–Nov 2012)  💷 charge  🚇 Russell Square

A five-minute walk southeast of Coram's Fields is the house-museum

**BELOW LEFT:** portrait of Dickens in a window of the Charles Dickens Museum. **BELOW:** Charles Dickens Museum.

**DRINK**

Among the many eating and shopping options in St Pancras is the longest champagne bar in Europe. It is situated just below the clock inside the station.

**RIGHT:** inside the St Pancras Renaissance hotel. **BELOW:** St Pancras, brought back to life by the Eurostar terminal. **BELOW RIGHT:** opposite Euston Station, on Euston Road, look out for St Pancras New Church. Its eight caryatids (four on each side) were inspired by the Erechtheum on the Acropolis in Athens.

where Dickens lived with his family between 1837 and 1839 and wrote *Oliver Twist* and *Nicholas Nickleby*. In a reverential atmosphere, visitors can inspect a huge collection of furniture, memorabilia, paintings, books and documents. The displays on the upper floors illustrate his one great passion besides literature – the plays, which he produced, directed and acted in at various times.

South of Dickens Museum, **John Street**, lined with handsome Georgian properties, some with a full complement of 18th-century ironwork, leads to Theobald's Road and Holborn *(see pages 150–1)*. North of Coram's Fields, and best reached along Hunter Street, lies the newly booming area of King's Cross and St Pancras.

## KING'S CROSS AND ST PANCRAS

Just as Southwark and Bankside became the focus for redevelopment in the late 20th century, the area around St Pancras and King's Cross stations, for many years run down and sleazy, is undergoing massive

regeneration in the 21st century. Triggered by the construction of the Eurostar rail terminal, which opened in 2007, the area is fast becoming a new cultural zone, attracting creative industries and contemporary art galleries, as well as bars, restaurants and luxury apartments.

Housing the new terminal, **St Pancras Station ⑩**, an immense redbrick edifice by Sir Gilbert Scott, the

*Recommended Restaurants, Pubs, Bars & Cafés on pages 142–3*

master of Victorian Gothic, has been superbly restored, with a 5 star hotel and a spa.

## Regent Quarter

The area behind the two stations, for long an industrial backwater crossed by roads and railway lines, is also being regenerated, especially the so-called Regent Quarter, near the Regent Canal. Occupying an old icehouse on the wharf of **Battlebridge Basin**, is the **London Canal Museum** ⓫ (12–13 New Wharf Road, accessed from Wharfdale Road; www.canalmuseum.org.uk; Tue–Sun 10am–4.30pm; tel: 7713 0836; charge). As well as portraying canal life, the museum tells the hard story of London's 19th-century ice trade, when ice was imported from Norway. One of two ice pits is open to view.

## Camley Street

Behind St Pancras Station, Camley Street leads north towards Camden. On the left is **St Pancras Old Church** ⓬, one of the oldest Christian sites in London. Its cemetery

contains the graves of several notable figures, including the celebrated architect and art collector Sir John Soane *(see page 153)*.

Also on Camley Street, opposite the cemetery and flanking the canal is a slim **nature park** (free) with a trail, wildlife pond and child-friendly activities at weekends.

## The British Library ⓭

✉ 96 Euston Road; www.bl.uk
☎ 0843 208 1144 🕐 Mon–Fri 9.30am–6pm, until 8pm Tue, 5pm Sat, tours available 💷 free
🚇 King's Cross

Back on Euston Road, next door to St Pancras, is the British Library, which moved here from the British Museum in 1998. It houses over 14 million books and periodicals, including a Gutenberg Bible, the Magna Carta and original texts by Shakespeare, Dickens and da Vinci. In addition to guided tours of the highlights, the library holds temporary exhibitions. The spacious courtyard (with café) is a peaceful refuge from busy Euston Road. ❑

**TIP**

Opposite Euston Station is the excellent Wellcome Collection (183 Euston Road; www.wellcomecollection.org; Tue–Sat 10am–6pm, until 10pm Thur, Sun 11am–6pm; tel: 7511 2222; free), a museum-cum-art space devoted to medicine and its relationships with art and society. It mixes items from Henry Wellcome's (1853–1936) eclectic collection of objects, interactive exhibits, paintings and much more. Other draws include a stylish café and a bookshop.

**BELOW:** one of the 11 reading rooms in the British Library.

## Using the British Library

Researchers can use the reading rooms by applying in person or through the website (www.bl.uk) for a reader's pass. Two forms of identification, including proof of home address and proof of signature must be produced. Your need to use the library will be ascertained, so documentation or a business card supporting your application is useful. Free 45-minute induction sessions help users find their way around the vast resources.

Members of any local library in the UK can also access the collection, if the book required cannot be obtained from any other library. This is done through the local library service.

# BEST RESTAURANTS, PUBS, BARS AND CAFÉS

## Restaurants

Prices for a three-course dinner per person with a half-bottle of house wine:

£ = under £20
££ = £20–30
£££ = £30–50
££££ = over £50

## American

### All Star Lanes

Victoria House, Bloomsbury Place, WC1 ☎ 7025 2676; www.allstarlanes.co.uk ◎ L Fri–Sun, D daily. ££ [p322, B4]
Smart American-style diner serving good steaks, burgers and crab cakes with 10-pin bowling on the side. Red leather cocktail bar boasting the largest selection of bourbons in

the city adds to the glamorous 1950s effect. DJs play every Fri–Sat 8pm onwards.

## British

### The Brill

6–8 Caledonian Rd, N1 ☎ 7833 7797; www.the brill.co.uk ◎ L & D Mon–Fri. £ [p322, B2]
Just a couple of minutes walk from King's Cross station, this restaurant serves simply-done British food at reasonable prices. There are hearty sandwiches available at lunchtime, while main dishes range from pan fried fish to sausage and mash. Menu features traditional puddings, too.

### The Gilbert Scott

St Pancras Hotel, Euston Rd, NW1 ☎ 7278 3888 ◎ B, L & D daily. ££–£££ [p322, A2]
Marcus Wareing's restaurant has a spectacular gothic interior. The menu celebrates British dishes such as Dorset jugged steak, and Yorkshire fishcakes.

## Fish

### North Sea Fish Restaurant

7–8 Leigh St, WC1 ☎ 7387 5892; www.northseafish restaurant.co.uk ◎ L & D Mon–Sat. £–££ [p322, B3]
Veteran chippie serving straightforward fish and chips. Good range of fish, plus British puddings.

## Indian

### Malabar Junction

107 Great Russell St, WC1 ☎ 7580 5230; www.malabar junction.com ◎ L & D daily. ££ [p326, C1]
Much classier than its frontage suggests, this elegant Indian restaurant specialises in spicy and nutty Keralan cuisine. Lovely atrium for light-filled dining.

### Salaam Namaste

68 Millman St, WC1 ☎ 7405 3697; www. salaam-namaste.co.uk ◎ L & D daily. ££ [p322, B3]
A light and modern restaurant. Excellent pan-Indian cuisine with a special emphasis on seafood. Lots of familiar

Indian dishes, but many inventive options too.

## Italian

### Cosmoba

9 Cosmo Place, off Southampton Row, WC1 ☏ 7837 0904; www. cosmoba.co.uk ⓒ L & D Mon–Sat. ££ [p322, B4]
A hidden gem in an alley connecting Southampton Row and Queen Square. Plain, family-run and specialising in homely Italian food, such as gnocchi with gorgonzola, or grilled sea bream.

### Pizza Express

30 Coptic St, WC1 ☏ 7636 3232; www.pizzaexpress. com ⓒ L & D daily. £ [p322, D1]
This branch of the quality pizza-pasta chain occupies a fabulous old dairy decorated in Art Nouveau tiles. A stone's throw from the British Museum.

## Japanese

### Abeno

47 Museum St, WC1 ☏ 7405 3211; www. abeno.co.uk ⓒ L & D daily. ££ [p326, C1]
Oriental pancake house specialising in okonomiyaki, which are tasty, if messy, omelettes and pancakes crammed with meat, vegetables or fish, cooked on a hotplate at the table.

### Wagamama

4a Streatham St, WC1 ☏ 7323 9223; www.waga mama.com ⓒ L & D daily. £ [p322, D1]
This was the original of the chain. Canteen-like basement with communal tables and bench seating, serving wholesome budget noodles and garnishes such as dumplings and salads.

## Spanish

### Cigala

54 Lamb's Conduit St, WC1 ☏ 74051717; www.cigala. co.uk ⓒ L & D daily. £££ (set lunch £) [p322, B4]
Set up by Jake Hodges, founder of Moro, Cigala serves real Spanish food in an attractive modern dining room. Excellent Spanish wine list, including many sherries. Tapas served in the basement.

## Others

### Konaki

5 Coptic St, WC1 ☏ 7580 9730; www.konaki.co.uk ⓒ L Mon–Fri, D Mon–Sat. £–££ [p326, C1]
Long-established and popular Greek restaurant near the British Museum. Serves Greek staples and has a small terrace for summer dining.

### Perseverance

63 Lamb's Conduit St, WC1 ☏ 7405 8278; www.the-perseverance.moonfruit. com ⓒ L daily, D Mon–Sat.

£–££ [p322, B4]
Popular gastro-pub offering light, inventive, tasty and well-presented dishes in a crowded bar or the more secluded first-floor dining room.

### The Brunswick Centre

This shopping mall [p322, B3] in the heart of Bloomsbury has several of the better chain restaurants, offering good-value dining. They include **Strada** (Nos 15–17; tel: 7278 2777; £) for good wood-oven pizzas, **Carluccio's** (No

1, tel: 7833 4100; £–££), for pastas, which also has a small Italian deli-cum-bakery attached; and **Giraffe** (Nos 19–21; tel: 7812 1336; £–££), a café-bar with a global menu including great breakfasts and healthy options for children. Also popular with families is **Nando's** (No. 3, tel: 7713 0351; £) serving spicy Portuguese-style chicken with salads, rice or chips, followed by frozen yoghurts and cheesecake for pudding.

## Pubs, Bars and Cafés

Bloomsbury has several traditional pubs tucked into its quiet corners. One of the best sources is pedestrianised Lamb's Conduit Street where **The Lamb**, a classy old-timer, serves Young's beer and pub food and has a small pavement terrace. Also see **Perseverance** (see main listings), a gastro-pub at No. 63.

Just along the street is another long-time favourite, **Vats Wine Bar**, offering a convivial atmosphere, quality food (fish, hearty casseroles, home-made pies, etc) and a lengthy wine list. Closer to the British Museum, Pied Bull Yard, just off Bury Place, offers **Truckles** (Mon–Fri only), a wine bar with a light and airy

ground floor, a sawdust-sprinkled basement, and a large courtyard.

For traditional English or Viennese afternoon tea, try the British Museum's **Court Restaurant**, high up under the spectacular glass roof; some tables have views into the circular Reading Room. Also pleasant for lunch.

**LEFT:** chef at work in Wagamama.

# THE BRITISH MUSEUM

**Opened in 1759, this world-class institution on Great Russell Street contains some 6½ million objects**

Devote just 60 seconds to each object owned by the British Museum and you'd be there, without sleep or meal breaks, for more than 12 years. Even though only 50,000 objects are on display at any given time, this is not a place to "do" in a couple of hours. It is a treasure house that caters for scholars as well as tourists and, as the scholars do, it is best to concentrate initially on what interests you most. A tour of the highlights is a good start (see right-hand column or join one of the organised tours). As you seek out any particular objects in the 100 or so galleries, you will be diverted by enough intriguing displays to justify future visits.

The British Museum is the most traditional of institutions, with most objects in glass cases and few buttons and levers for children to manipulate, but it is rarely boring. The best time to visit is soon after opening. This is also

## The essentials

✉ *Great Russell Street, WC2; www.thebritish museum.org*
📞 *7323 8299*
🕐 *daily 10am–5.30pm, until 8.30pm Fri*
💷 *free except for some special exhibitions*
🚇 *Russell Square*

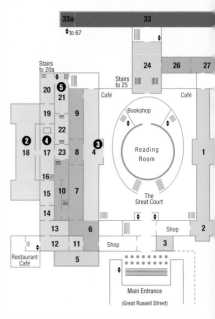

**Ground Floor**

Montague Place Entrance

## Highlights

1 Egyptian Mummies
2 Sculptures of the Parthenon
3 Rosetta Stone
4 Nereid Monument
5 Mausoleum of Halikarnassos
6 Sutton Hoo Ship Burial
7 Lewis Chessmen
8 Lindow Man
9 Benin Bronzes
10 Cassiobury Park Turret Clock

## Key

Exhibitions/Themes
Egypt
Middle East
Greece & Rome
Americas
Asia
Europe
Africa
Prints & Drawing
↕ Lift

an ideal time to appreciate the Great Court, a dramatic glassed-over space in the heart of the complex, added for the millennium, and the round Reading Room, where Marx and Lenin once studied, which now functions as an information and research centre.

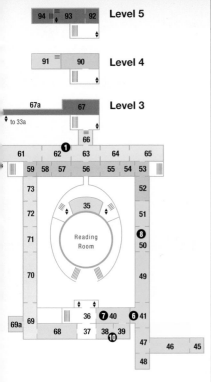

Level 5
Level 4
Level 3

61 62 ❶ 63 64 65

59 58 57 56 55 54 53

73 52

72 35 51

71 Reading Room ❽ 50

70 49

❼ 40 ❻ 41

69a 69 68 36 37 38 39 ❿

47 46 45

48

**Lower Floors**

78 77

❾ 25

25 25 25

Stairs to 24

Clore Education Centre

Ford Centre for Young Visitors

Stairs to Great Court

**LEFT:** the Portland Vase, a superbly crafted cameo glass vessel from the early 1st century.

**TOP RIGHT:** the gilded wooden inner coffin of Henutmehyt, a Theban priestess, dating from c.1250 BC.

**RIGHT:** the 12th-century Lewis Chessmen, found in the Outer Hebrides.

## TOP 10 HIGHLIGHTS

**The Egyptian mummies**
This is the richest collection of Egyptian funerary art outside Egypt.

**The Sculptures of the Parthenon**
Commonly known as the Elgin Marbles, these 5th century BC sculptures have a wondrous muscular detail.

**The Rosetta Stone**
This granite tablet from the 2nd century BC provided the elusive key to deciphering ancient Egypt's hieroglyphic script.

**The Nereid Monument**
The imposing facade of this 4th-century monument from Xanthos in Turkey was reconstructed after an earthquake.

**The Mausoleum of Halikarnassos**
This giant tomb, finished around 350 BC in southwest Turkey, was one of the Seven Wonders of the Ancient World.

**The Sutton Hoo Ship Burial**
The richest treasure ever dug from British soil, an early 7th-century longboat likely to have been the burial chamber of an East Anglian king.

**The Lewis Chessmen**
82 elaborately carved 12th-century chess pieces, found in the Outer Hebrides, off the Scottish coast.

**Lindow Man**
A well-preserved 2,000-year-old body found in a peat bog in England and dubbed Pete Marsh.

**The Benin Bronzes**
Brass plaques found in Benin City, Nigeria, in 1897. They depict court life and ritual in extraordinary detail.

**The Cassiobury Park Turret Clock**
This intricate 1610 weight-driven clock is part of a remarkable collection of timepieces.

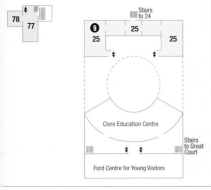

## THE MAIN COLLECTIONS

### Greece and Rome

The museum's vast holdings from the Classical world are divided between Rooms 11–23 on the ground floor (off the left-hand side of the Great Court as you enter the museum), where the larger objects are found, and Rooms 69–73 on the first floor.

Room 18, the **Parthenon Gallery**, is lined with an exquisitely detailed frieze from the colonnade of the Parthenon *(see right)*, removed from the Acropolis by Lord Elgin, British Ambassador in Constantinople, at the end of the 18th century. The Parthenon was dedicated to the goddess Athena Parthenos and the frieze is said to depict the Great Panathenaia, a procession held every four years in honour of the goddess. It was carved under the direction of the master sculptor Pheidias.

Nearby, in Room 17, is the **Nereid Monument**, a magnificent Lycian tomb (*c.*390–380 BC) from Xanthos, and, in Room 21, fragments and sculptures from the **Mausoleum of Halikarnassos** (modern day Bodrum; mid-4th century BC), the tomb of Maussollos, considered to have been one of the Seven Wonders of the Ancient World. A large-scale model of the mausoleum shows how it would have looked in its splendid entirety.

**ABOVE:** head of a horse of Selene (the Moon) from the Parthenon (5th century BC). **MAIN PICTURE:** a section from the north frieze of the Parthenon.

### Ancient Near East

This section covers the ancient civilisations of Mesopotamia, Anatolia and the Levant. Among the highlights are tablets containing the inscription of Nebuchadnezzar II, King of Babylon, found in the ruins of Babylon in the early 19th century. Other highlights are the carved Assyrian reliefs and gateway figures from the palaces at Khorsabad, Nineveh and Nimrud.

**BELOW:** human-headed winged bull, one of a pair of marble bulls that guarded either side of a gateway at Khorsabad, Assyria (710 BC), in modern day Iraq.

## TREASURES OF ANCIENT EGYPT

The Egyptian Galleries filled with funerary artefacts (Rooms 61–66, on the upper floor), are the rooms to see first, simply because they can get wildly over-crowded as the day goes on – 98 percent of visitors want to see the Egyptian mummies in rooms 62–63. They're worth seeing, too: thanks to the enthusiastic plundering by 19th-century explorers, this is the rich-est collection of Egyptian funerary art outside Egypt.

The size and ornamentation of the coffins and sar-cophagi are immediately striking. The richly gilded inner coffin of the priestess Henutmehyt *(see page 145)*, for example, dating from 1250 BC, is a work of considerable art. Scans displayed beside the coffin of Cleopatra (not *the* Cleopatra) show how well the body inside is preserved, and the process of embalming is explained in detail. Apart from the noble humans who were destined to spend their afterlife in London's Bloomsbury, there are various mummified cats, dogs, fish and crocodiles, plus amulets and assorted jewellery.

Look out for the paintings from the Tomb of Nebamun, a Theban official, dat-ing from the 18th Dynasty (*c.*1350 BC), in Room 61.

### Early Europe
As well as highly crafted Celtic artefacts and Roman treasures, look out for Lindow Man, a 1st-century man discovered in a peat bog in Cheshire.

### Medieval and Modern Europe
Apart from the Sutton Hoo treasure, objects include richly decorated ecclesiastical artefacts such as an intricately decorated 12th-century gilt cross from Germany.

**ABOVE:** the ceremonial helmet from the Sutton Hoo treasure.
**TOP RIGHT:** Nebamum hunting birds in the marshes (1450 BC).
**ABOVE RIGHT:** Lindow Man, the 1st-century bog man.

## TOURS WORTH TAKING

Free "eye-opener" tours (30–40 minutes) focus on different areas of the collection, and a variety of multimedia sets can be hired, including one for children. Handling sessions take place daily in various galleries, and there are free lunch time talks Tue–Sat at 1.15pm.

## Africa

The Sainsbury African Galleries in the basement combine ancient and modern, showing how cultural traditions are still alive today. This is one of the most colourful and vibrant collections in the museum. Of special interest are the Benin Bronzes, from the Kingdom of Benin (now in Nigeria), a powerful state in West Africa between the 13th and 19th centuries. As well as the beautifully detailed bronze plaques depicting life in the royal court there are bronze heads and figures.

Other highlights of this section include Asante goldwork, from the gold-rich Ghanaian kingdom of Asante, Afro-Portuguese ivories, African textiles and funerary screens from the eastern Niger Delta.

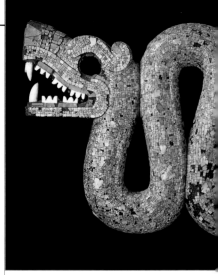

## The Americas

The museum has superb collections from Central and North America in Rooms 26–27 on the ground floor (far-right corner off the Great Court). There are a number of impressive Olmec statues and other works from around 1000 BC, plus magnificent carved Mayan slabs from the 8th century AD. Relics from the Aztec civilisation include turquoise mosaic work that may have been given to Hernán Cortés by Moctezuma II and a very rare pre-Conquest manuscript painted on deer skin.

**TOP AND ABOVE:** two of the freestanding Benin bronzes. The bronzes were discovered, languishing in an outbuilding, by British forces making a retaliatory attack on Benin following the massacre of a British diplomatic mission there. Only some of the bronzes found their way to Britain; others were sold to museums around the world.

**RIGHT:** an ivory mask, also made by the Edo peoples of Benin.

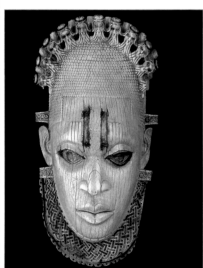

## Prints, Drawings

For conservation and space reasons, only a fraction of the museum's 3 million works on paper are displayed at any one time. Highlights include Old Master prints and drawings, and satires of the 18th and 19th centuries.

**RIGHT:** Raphael's *Virgin and Child* cartoon, one of numerous drawings by Raphael held by the museum.

## Asia

The museum's collections of Chinese, Japanese and Korean artefacts are astonishingly large, with a series of vast galleries given over to them (33–33b on the ground floor, 67 and 92–95 on the upper floors). Exhibits from India include the Amaravati Sculptures (1st–3rd century AD) that adorned a *stupa* (Buddhist temple) in Andhra Pradesh, southeastern India, and exquisite Mughal miniatures (from 16th–17th century).

## Money and Medals

A collection of 750,000 coins dates from the 7th century BC to the present day, and there are notes dating back to 14th-century China (Room 68).

**MAIN PICTURE:** double-headed serpent (1400–1521), Mexico. It is carved in wood and covered with turquoise mosaic. Turquoise was highly prized as a symbol of fertility by the Aztecs.

**LEFT:** Assistant to a Judge of Hell, stone figure from the Ming Dynasty (16th century), China. The figure is holding a bundle of scrolls recording the sins of the deceased.

## REFRESHMENTS

The ground level of the Great Court has two refreshment areas, but for something more special head up the stairs to the Court Restaurant. Breakfast, lunch and tea are served. Try to get a table looking down upon the circular Reading Room.

# HOLBORN AND THE INNS OF COURT

Once the haunt of Samuel Johnson, Dickens and Thackeray, this area on the cusp of the City is packed with history. It has long been the centre of the legal profession and was for centuries the irrepressible hub of Britain's newspaper industry

### Main attractions
SOMERSET HOUSE
THE INNS OF COURT
LINCOLN'S INN FIELDS
SIR JOHN SOANE'S MUSEUM
DR JOHNSON'S HOUSE
ST BRIDE'S CHURCH

**BELOW:** judges wait outside Westminster Abbey for the annual service at the start of the judicial year.

olborn encompasses what can be termed legal London, with landmarks such as the Royal Courts of Justice, the Old Bailey and the historic Inns of Court clustered around Fleet Street, the former centre of the national newspaper industry. The area is wedged in between London's financial and political centres, and is markedly different from both: away from the busy thoroughfares, quiet courtyards, leafy parks and some of the city's oldest buildings lend a sense of a bygone London.

## KINGSWAY AND THE EASTERN STRAND

### Somerset House ❶

✉ The Strand; www.somersethouse.
org.uk; www.courtauld.ac.uk ☎ 7845
4600 ⓒ Courtauld Institute of Art
daily 10am–6pm ⓐ charge, but free
Mon 10am–2pm ⓡ Temple

**Somerset House** became the city's first office block in 1775 when the original 16th-century palace was rebuilt. For many years it housed the official registry of births, marriages and deaths; the inland revenue offices remain, but the northern and southern wings now accommodate a series of galleries and museums. The complex is divided into two main sections by its large courtyard, which contains a fanciful statue of George III wearing a toga. In December and January the courtyard is turned into a **skating rink**, the classical facade providing a magical setting.

Entering from the Strand, you'll come to the **Courtauld Institute**, home to a collection of 20th-century European art, notably some major Impressionist and post-Impressionist paintings: works include Van Gogh's *Self-Portrait with Bandaged Ear* and Manet's *A Bar at the Folies-Bergère*. Temporary exhibitions are held in the Embankment galleries.

*Recommended Restaurants, Pubs & Bars on page 157*

The Seamen's Hall gives access to the splendid **River Terrace**, which in summer has a café with great views.

Across the Strand from Somerset House is **Bush House** ❷, the headquarters of the BBC's World Service, which broadcasts across the world in a babelesque variety of languages. To the north, **Kingsway** marks the western boundary of Holborn and legal London. It was named after George V, and its tunnel, opened in 1906 for trams to dive beneath the buildings of Aldwych before emerging at Waterloo Bridge, was a miracle of urban engineering in its day.

Two baroque churches sit on traffic islands in the Strand: by Bush House is **St Mary le Strand**, built by James Gibbs from 1715; a short distance further east by a statue of Gladstone is **St Clement Danes** ❸, completed by Wren in 1682. The name is a reference to the first structure on the site, built by the Vikings in the 9th century. The church has an association with the Royal Air Force, who rebuilt it after bomb damage in WWII.

At the end of the Strand on the left are the **Royal Courts of Justice** ❹, which deal with libels, divorces and all civil cases. The courts moved here from Westminster Hall in 1884. The neo-Gothic confection of towers and spires has around 1,000 rooms, and newspaper and television journalists often hang around its entrance awaiting verdicts. Visitors are free to sit in the public galleries of the 58 courts when trials are in session. There are public tours of the building on the first and third Tuesday of each month, running at 11am and 2pm. It is necessary to book in advance (tel: 7947 7684; charge).

**TIP**

There are free guided tours of the buildings of Somerset House every Thursday at 1.15 and 2.45pm, and Saturday at 12.15, 1.15, 2.15 and 3.15pm. Tickets are available on the day from 10.30am from the Information Desk.

**LEFT:** the Royal Courts of Justice.
**ABOVE AND BELOW:** winter ice skating and summer fountains in the courtyard of Somerset House.

*The Inns of Court buildings were originally leased as hostels to trainee lawyers by the Knights Hospitaller (who succeeded the Templars, earlier owners of this land).*

**RIGHT:** inside Temple Church, the church of Middle and Inner Temples.
**BELOW:** Lincoln's Inn.

## THE INNS OF COURT

All around this area are the **Inns of Court**, home of London's legal profession. The "Inns" were once, much as they sound, places of rest and comfort for trainee lawyers. From the 19th century onward, law was taught at King's College, next to Somerset House in the Strand, and at University College in Gower Street. Before then, the only way to obtain legal training was to serve an apprenticeship in one of the Inns.

Four still remain, and still function as accommodation and offices for the legal profession: **Middle Temple ⑤** and **Inner Temple ⑥** between Fleet Street and the Embankment, and **Gray's Inn** *(see page 154)* and **Lincoln's Inn** further north. With their cobbled lanes and brass plaques bearing Dickensian names, they are atmospheric places to stroll around. Note that the entrances to Middle Temple Lane and Inner Temple Lane are easily missed – the gates are usu-ally closed and access is via a small side passageway.

These Inns take their name from the crusading Knights Templar, who bought land here in the 12th century and built the **Temple Church** (charge), inspired by the Church of the Holy Sepulchre in Jerusalem. There are a number of the knights' tombs inside, and a tiny punishment cell by the altar. Sloping down to the Embankment, the grassy swards of the Temple Gardens are a pleasant place to take a break from sightseeing.

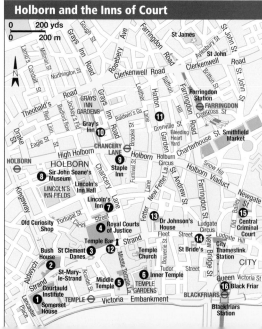

**Holborn and the Inns of Court**

*Recommended Restaurants, Pubs & Bars on page 157*

North of the Royal Courts of Justice, between Kingsway and Chancery Lane, is **Lincoln's Inn ❼**, alma mater of Oliver Cromwell, and the two great 19th-century prime ministers, William Gladstone and Benjamin Disraeli.

**Lincoln's Inn Fields** were created for the students' recreation, but the best sport was watching the early city planners try to outmanoeuvre each other: Inigo Jones sat on a 17th-century Royal Commission to decide the area's fate.

## Sir John Soane's Museum ❽

✉ 13 Lincoln's Inn Fields; www.soane.org 📞 7405 2107
🕐 Tue–Sat 10am–5pm; 6–9pm (candlelit opening) first Tue of each month 💲 free except Tue evenings
🚇 Holborn

This marvellous museum is a self-endowed monument to John Soane (1753–1837), one of London's most important architects and collectors, who left his house and collection much as they had been during his lifetime. He built his private home

on three sites along the edge of Lincoln's Inn Fields (No.13) and it is a delight to visit, like being in a miniature British Museum.

Among the highlights are an Egyptian sarcophagus, Hogarth's *Rake's Progress* and some fine Canalettos, but much of the pleasure of visiting is derived from the building itself.

As the museum is undergoing phased restoration until 2014, some rooms may be closed during your visit, although the first phase should be completed in early 2012.

*Soane's collections range from Roman bronzes believed to have come from Pompeii and a fragment of the frieze on the Acropolis in Athens, to a statuette from Florence's Medici Palace and paintings by Watteau and J.M.W. Turner.*

**ABOVE:** *An Election Entertainment,* part of William Hogarth's Election sequence painted in 1754–55.
**BELOW:** Sir John Soane's Museum.

A sign outside a Fleet Street opticians. This part of London has retained a core of shops selling a particular item: opticians and other optical-related goods (such as camera lenses) as well as watch repair shops along Fleet Street, and diamonds in Hatton Garden.

**BELOW:** The Old Curiosity Shop.
**BELOW RIGHT:** the spire of St Bride's, said to have inspired the first tiered wedding cake.

## Dickens's world

The ghost of the great Victorian writer Charles Dickens (1812–70) haunts the streets of Holborn. Just south of Lincoln's Inn Fields is the **Old Curiosity Shop**, a tiny 16th-century structure – now a shoe shop – likely to have been the inspiration for Little Nell's antiques shop.

On the other side of Lincoln's Inn, Dickens's first marital home was on the site of the neo-Gothic Prudential Assurance building in Holborn, opposite a half-timbered row of shops at the bottom of Gray's Inn Road. This is **Staple Inn** ❾, one of the former Inns of Chancery that dealt with commercial law. Dating from 1586 and a survivor of the Great Fire of London, it shows how much of the city must have looked before 1666.

Dickens underwent his legal apprenticeship at **Gray's Inn** ❿ (Mon–Fri 10am–4pm), one of Holborn's four Inns of Court. Dating from the 14th century, its grounds lie just to the west of Gray's Inn Road. The magnificent garden (Mon–Fri noon–2.30pm) was laid out by Francis Bacon, the Elizabethan essayist. With an irony that must have tickled Dickens's sense of the law's ridiculousness, Gray's Inn Hall saw the first production of Shakespeare's *Comedy of Errors*.

Further east is **Bleeding Heart Yard**, scene of much of the domestic action in *Little Dorrit*. Only a step or two away is **Hatton Garden** ⓫, the centre of London's diamond trade, and **Leather Lane**, where market stalls sell fresh food and household goods.

## FLEET STREET

Just beyond the Temple Inn and the Royal Courts of Justice is **Temple Bar** ⓬, where a mean-looking heraldic dragon *(see picture on page 156)* marks the boundary between Westminster and the City of London, beyond which, theoretically, the monarch cannot pass without the Lord Mayor's permission.

Stretching eastwards is **Fleet Street**, home of Britain's national newspapers from 1702, when the first daily newspaper, the *Daily Courant*, was published here. In the

Recommended Restaurants, Pubs & Bars on page 157

**DRINK**

Drinkers in Ye Olde Cheshire Cheese pub on Fleet Street (the entrance is on an alley-way called Wine Office Court), close to Dr Johnson's House, can raise a glass to the great man's memory. This is one of London's oldest inns – Johnson and, later, Dickens and Thackeray all came here. *For details see page 157.*

nary. **Dr Johnson's House** ⓭ is an evocative museum of this great man of letters (www.drjohnstonehouse.org; Mon–Sat 11am–5.30pm, Oct–Apr until 5pm; tel: 7353 3745; charge). The creaky old building dates from 1700; Johnson paid rent to the tune of £30 per year, equivalent to around £3,000 today. (The alleyway leading to Gough Square is immediately east of No.167 Fleet Street.)

The crime writer Edgar Wallace (1875–1932) is immortalised on a plaque on the northwest corner of **Ludgate Circus**, at the far end of Fleet Street. As an 11-year-old he sold newspapers at this junction.

1980s, new technology enabled the press barons to move to cheaper sites in Docklands and elsewhere.

There is still evidence of the street's illustrious past. Dr Samuel Johnson ("A man who is tired of London is tired of life") lived in the back courts at 17 Gough Square from 1748 to 1759 where, with the help of six assistants, he compiled the first comprehensive English dictio-

Wedged in behind the **Reuters Building** designed by Sir Edwin Lutyens in 1935 is "the journalists' and printers' church", **St Bride's** ⓮ (www.stbrides.com; tel: 7427 0133). It was near here that the aptly named Wynkyn de Worde, an associate of William Caxton, set up the street's first press. There is a small museum of Fleet Street in the crypt, where a magpie collection of Roman mosaics

**LEFT:** Ye Olde Cheshire Cheese pub is just off Fleet Street.
**BELOW LEFT:** Johnson portrayed in a window of his former home.

## Dr Johnson's Dictionary

Samuel Johnson (1709–84) was one of the great figures of the Enlightenment, rising from a humble background to become a member of London's intellectual elite. Having arrived in the city in 1737, he was commissioned in 1746 to produce a dictionary for a fee of £1,575 – a large sum at the time, but the work ended up taking 10 years, and Johnson had to pay for his staff and materials out of it. In 1762, however, his financial stability was assured with the award of a £300 annual pension by the king in recognition of his efforts (and thanks to some very influential friends).

While some words in the dictionary have changed in meaning over the years (for example, "nice" was defined as "superfluously accu-rate"), many of his pithy definitions still fit the bill. One of the more oblique entries is for "lexicographer", which Johnson ruefully defined as "a harmless drudge".

*On top of the Old Bailey's dome, a golden figure of justice stands with a sword in her right hand and, in her left, scales to weigh the evidence.*

**RIGHT:** Blackfriars Bridge with St Paul's behind. **BELOW:** the dragon at Temple Bar.

from a villa on this site, Saxon church walls, and human remains are stored – much was revealed when the building was bombed in World War II. The ossuary is visible if you join a guided tour (Tue 3pm; charge; check website for dates). Samuel Pepys was baptised at St Bride's (he was born in 1633 in Salisbury Court, off Fleet Street) and he records in his diary how he had to bribe the sexton to find room for his brother's corpse here. The church's elegant spire is Sir Christopher Wren's tallest and is said to have inspired the first tiered wedding cake. Lunch time concerts are often held here during the week.

## LUDGATE HILL

The River Fleet, which once marked the division between Westminster and The City, used to be a "disembouging stream" according to the 18th-century poet Alexander Pope. Acting as a sluice for Smithfield Market, and notorious since the 14th century for its foetid stench, it was bricked over in the 18th century, although the subterranean

waters still have the propensity to make their presence felt by periodically flooding basements in the area.

The Fleet Prison for debtors was on the Fleet's right bank, Newgate Prison on the left. Public executions took place here until 1868, when a law brought an end to the rowdy spectacles they had become.

On the site of the former prison, just beyond Ludgate Circus, is the **Central Criminal Court** ⑮, universally known by the name of the street in which it is located, **Old Bailey**. Some of the country's most unpleasant criminals have been brought to account here, and in the forbidding No. 1 Court, until the abolition of the death penalty in 1965, convicted murderers were sentenced to be hanged, the judges placing black caps on their heads as they passed sentence. You can still watch cases from the visitors' gallery (Mon–Fri 10am–1pm and 2–5pm approx, closed Aug).

## BLACKFRIARS

The underground river enters the Thames at Blackfriars Bridge, named after a monastery that was here from 1278 to 1538. A fine monument to this monastic order is the 1905 **Black Friar** ⑯, on the corner of Queen Victoria Street: a most spectacular Arts and Crafts pub.

Heading west along Victoria Embankment from Blackfriars takes you back to Somerset House, past the permanently moored ships HMS *President* and HQS *Wellington*, opposite the gardens of the Inns of Court. ❑

# BEST RESTAURANTS, PUBS AND BARS

## Restaurants

Prices for a three-course dinner per person with a half-bottle of house wine:
£ = under £20
££ = £20–30
£££ = £30–50
££££ = over £50

## Asian

### Asadal

227 High Holborn, WC1
7430 9006; www.asadal.
co.uk ⓒ L Mon–Sat, D daily.
££–£££ [p319, E1]
Basement restaurant by Holborn tube station, offering a wide choice of Korean dishes. Try *kalbi* (beef and sauce), *kimchi* (seasoned vegetables) or *hae mool jeon gol* (a spicy seafood and tofu stew).

### Chi Noodle and Wine Bar

5 New Bridge St, Bride Court EC4 7353 2409;
www.chinoodle.com ⓒ L & D Mon–Fri. ££ [p327, E2]
Airy restaurant and takeaway offering pan-Asian noodle and rice dishes.

### Pu's Thai Brasserie

10 Gate St, WC2 7404 2126; www.pus-brasserie.
com ⓒ L & D Mon–Sat.
£–££ [p319, E1]
Reasonable Thai restaurant located around the corner from Sir John Soane's Museum.

### Wagamama

109 Fleet St, EC4 7583 7889; www.wagamama.
com ⓒ L & D Mon–Fri. £ [p327, E1]
A branch of the popular chain offering inexpensive noodles, soups, salads and rice dishes at communal tables.

## British

### Ye Olde Cheshire Cheese

145 Fleet St, EC4 7353 6170 ⓒ L daily, D Mon–Sat.
££–£££ [p327, E1]
This is easily dismissed as a tourist trap, but its age and history are impressive: it was frequented by Dickens and Samuel Johnson. A warren of nooks and crannies, its cosy chop room serves good steak and kidney pies.

## French

### Bleeding Heart Restaurant and Bistro

Bleeding Heart Yard, Greville St, EC1 7242 2056 for restaurant; www.bleeding
heart.co.uk ⓒ L Mon–Sat, D daily. £££ [p323, D4]
Comprises three establishments: the tavern, the bistro (No. 7) and the restaurant, each in separate premises. The latter is the place to go for superb French cuisine

and alfresco dining in the cobbled courtyard.

## Other

### Gaucho

125–126 Chancery Lane, WC2 7242 7727; www.
gauchorestaurants.co.uk ⓒ L Mon–Fri, D Mon–Sat.
£££ [p327, E2]
An Argentinian-style chain specialising in steaks, but the odd pasta, fish and chicken dish are also available.

## Pubs and Bars

This area has several historic pubs. Two of the most atmospheric are **Ye Olde Cheshire Cheese** off Fleet Street *(see restaurants)* and **Black Friar** *(174 Queen Victoria St)*, whose Arts and Crafts interior (stained glass, wood panelling, marble and mosaics) is worth a visit in itself, but it is also known for its good choice of ales.

Another striking interior, this time Victorian, is offered by the **Punch Tavern** *(99 Fleet St)* which has a tiled entrance, dark panelling and serves decent food. An ex-bank turned boozer is the opulent **Old Bank of England** at 194 Fleet Street.

Also worth mentioning are **Davy's of Creed Lane** *(100 Creed Lane)*, offering quality wines and wine bar fare, and **El Vino** *(47 Fleet St)*, once the favourite wine bar of hard-drinking journalists and now of lawyers. Its cellar restaurant serves traditional British food and tapas.

Offering a different ambience is **Pearl Bar** *(Chancery Court Hotel, 252 High Holborn)*, part restaurant, part high-end cocktail bar, with over 50 wines available by the glass.

**ABOVE RIGHT:** the courtyard of Bleeding Heart.

*Recommended Restaurants, Pubs, Bars & Cafés on pages 174–5*

# ST PAUL'S AND THE CITY

The City, covering just one square mile, is Britain's main financial centre. This was the original London, once contained by Roman walls, and it retains its own government and police force

T he City, London's financial quarter, is a world apart from the rest of the capital. It runs its own affairs, has its own police force and a distinct set of hierarchies. Even the Queen treads carefully here: on her coronation drive in 1953, she was obliged – if only by tradition – to stop at Temple Bar and declare that she came in peace. The name "Square Mile" is given to this financial district that was at one time regarded as "the clearing-house of the world", but it signifies far more than a limited geographical area. For most of its 2,000-year history, the City *was* London.

Today, more than 300,000 workers stream into the City every weekday. Known for their work-hard-play-hard attitude, they are driven by competition and substantial annual bonuses. On weekends, under 9,000 City residents are left to savour the stillness that settles across the Square Mile, an area where a strong sense of tradition has helped a potentially faceless financial world retain a certain degree of character.

The City has been devastated twice. In 1666 the Great Fire devoured four-fifths of the area, and during the winter of 1940–1 Germany's Luftwaffe left one-third of it in ruins.

**LEFT:** St Paul's Cathedral. **RIGHT:** looking down on to Finsbury Circus in the City.

## St Paul's Cathedral ❶

✉ www.stpauls.co.uk  ☎ 7246 8350
🕐 Mon–Sat 8.30am–4pm, tours at 10.45am, 11.15am, 1.30pm, 2pm
💷 charge  🚇 St Paul's

At the top of Ludgate Hill, the western approach to the City, stands St Paul's, the first cathedral built after the English Reformation and Sir Christopher Wren's greatest work. A tablet above his plain marble tomb reads: *Lector, si monumentum requiris, circumspice* ("Reader, if you wish to see

**Main attractions**
ST PAUL'S CATHEDRAL
BARTS HOSPITAL
ST BARTHOLOMEW THE GREAT
SMITHFIELD MEAT MARKET
CHARTERHOUSE SQUARE
ST JOHN'S GATE
BUNHILL FIELDS
MUSEUM OF LONDON
GUILDHALL
BANK OF ENGLAND
LEADENHALL
MONUMENT
TOWER OF LONDON

**TIP**

Like any closed world, the City doesn't open up easily to outsiders. Peering out of a tourist bus at acres of glass and concrete is far too superficial an examination; time and legwork in the network of alleys and backstreets which thread through the office blocks will reveal much more.

his memorial, look around you"). *For full coverage of St Paul's, see the feature on pages 176–7.*

## Paternoster Square

St Paul's needs room to breathe, but the area around it – in particular the ancient market site known as **Paternoster Square** – has been intensively developed. In spite of recent remodelling, it forms a disappointing setting for Wren's masterpiece.

In 2004 the **London Stock Exchange** abandoned its long-held base near the Bank of England in Threadneedle Street for new premises

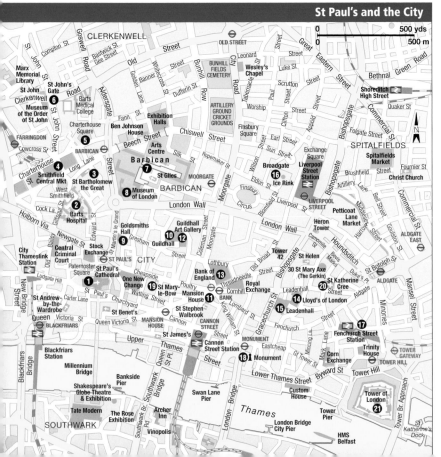

### St Paul's and the City

in Paternoster Square that were better suited to electronic trading.

With origins going back to merchants trying to raise money for a Far Eastern trip in 1553, the Stock Exchange has changed enormously since the Big Bang reforms of 1986 when it agreed to radically change its practices. Fixed commission systems were abolished, and jobber and broker functions were merged and transferred to a computerised quotation system. The trading floor, once crowded with frantic pin-striped figures engaged in open outcry, fell silent. As a result, the Stock Market is a fairer but duller place. It is no longer open to the general public.

## Historic churches

In the warren of roads that lead from St Paul's to the river, there are several Wren churches. **St Andrew-by-the-Wardrobe** in St Andrew's Hill was so named because it stood near a royal storage area. **St Nicholas Cole Abbey** is followed by **St Benet's**, which serves as the Metropolitan Welsh Church.

On the other side of Queen Victoria Street is the **College of Arms**

*The Stock Market trading floor has vanished but a new spectacle, The Source, now spans the height of the building's atrium. Composed of rising and falling spheres suspended on cables, this computer-controlled kinetic sculpture is said to represent market forces.*

(www.college-of-arms.gov.uk; entrance hall open when receptionist is present Mon–Fri 10am–4pm, free; Record Room tours by arrangement, tel: 7248 2762; charge), which has a handsome, refurbished 17th-century interior by William Emmett and a library of heraldry and genealogy which, for a fee, deals with genealogy enquiries.

Other Wren churches in the vicinity include **St James Garlickhythe** on busy Upper Thames Street, which was disastrously struck by a crane

**LEFT:** setting up an outside office.
**ABOVE:** sign on the College of Arms.
**BELOW:** Paternoster Square and its column.

*A carved wooden figure in the museum of Barts Hospital.*

**BELOW:** tomb of the monk Rahere, founder of St Bartholomew's Hospital, in St Bartholomew the Great.

that demolished its rose window in 1991, and **St Michael Paternoster Royal**, the burial place of Dick Whittington (1423), a Lord Mayor of London, who, with his cat, has entered British mythology as a pantomime figure. This rags-to-riches story sets out to prove that even country bumpkins could be elected Lord Mayor of the City, though the real Whittington came from a wealthy county family and amassed a fortune as a merchant.

## WEST SMITHFIELD

Northwest of St Paul's is the great block of St Bartholomew's Hospital.

### Barts Hospital ➋

✉ Museum, North Wing 📞 3465 5798 🕐 Tue–Fri 10am–4pm, tours by arrangement Fri 2pm 🎫 free, charge for tour 🚇 Barbican or St Paul's

Founded in 1123, St Bartholomew's Hospital is the oldest in London. Like many early hospitals, it was founded as a monastery offering "hospitality" to pilgrims and the needy. The care provided was initially a combination

of shelter, comfort, food and prayer, and only in later centuries evolved into medical treatment. Patients were tended by monks and nuns (hence the term "sister" still in use today).

The hospital includes an interesting little **museum** on changes in medicine over the centuries. A door at the rear of the museum opens to reveal two William Hogarth murals dressing the staircase of the entrance hall of the North Wing. Some of the figures are believed to have been modelled on patients. For a closer look, book one of the guided Friday tours.

Opposite the hospital, on the wall at the corner of **Giltspur Street** and **Cock Lane**, is a golden figure of a urinating boy, symbolising the extinguishing of the 1666 Great Fire at this point. Just beyond, in **West Smithfield**, are memorials to the Scottish hero William Wallace, victim of a spot of judicial butchery here in 1305, and to the 270 "Marian martyrs", Protestants burned at the stake for religious heresy by Queen Mary in the 1550s.

*Recommended Restaurants, Pubs, Bars & Cafés on pages 174–5*

Bartholomew Fair, immortalised in Ben Jonson's play of the same name. Film-makers, too, have been drawn to this corner of London: scenes in *Four Weddings and a Funeral* and *Shakespeare in Love* were filmed inside the church. The monk Rahere, who founded St Bartholomew's Hospital, is buried here.

## SMITHFIELD TO CLERKENWELL

The unlikely confection of iron and plaster adjacent to St Bartholomew's is **Smithfield Central Markets ❹**, at its busiest early in the morning. Here the porters and workers known as "bummarees" thunder about with barrow loads of carcasses and the knife grinders shower sparks out of the backs of their vans. Through all the commotion, it's still possible to hear "backchat", Smithfield's equivalent of Billingsgate profanity, designed to fool unwanted listeners.

The last of the great markets still on its original site, Smithfield is now one of the most modern meat markets in the world, thanks to a £70 million overhaul. The renovation was accomplished without sacrificing the Victo-

### St Bartholomew the Great ❸

✉ West Smithfield; www.greatstbarts. com ☎ 7606 5171 🕐 Mon–Fri 8.30am–5pm (4pm mid-Nov–mid-Feb), Sat 10.30am–4pm, Sun 8.30am–8pm 🎫 charge 🚇 Barbican

One of the oldest and finest churches in the City stands in a corner of the square, perhaps a trifle shocked by what has passed before, for this was also the site of the

*As late as the mid-19th century cattle were still being driven through the streets of London to be slaughtered in Smithfield meat market. Some unruly animals would charge into shops and houses if the doors were open, hence the possible origin of the phrase "bull in a china shop".*

**ABOVE LEFT:** gateway leading to St Bartholomew the Great. **BELOW LEFT:** Smithfield butcher.

## A Street by Any Other Name

**S**mithfield meat market originally traded in live animals herded in from the country. But the gore of slaughter proved too much for the Victorians, and they moved the industry outside the city, leaving Smithfield to deal in carcasses only. They also changed the names of the area's lanes, so that Stinking Lane, later Blow Bladder Lane, became King Edward Street.

Other street names hark back to the livery companies who plied their trades in the area. A flavour of the City's trading past remains in the main shopping thoroughfare, Cheapside, behind St Paul's. In medieval times, Cheapside (from the Old English word "ceap" or "cepe" – to buy) was the City's mercantile heart: the names of the side streets, Bread Street, Milk Street and Honey Lane, give an idea of the merchandise. Just beyond Cheapside was the poulterers' area, now known as Poultry. Cannon Street (a corruption of candlewick) was the candlemakers' area. Garlick Hill could be smelled from Cheapside.

*Tombstones in Bunhill Fields, where many famous people are buried, including John Bunyan, author of* The Pilgrim's Progress.

**BELOW:** get your bearings and find key attractions.

rian shell of the Central Markets. Although Smithfield has resisted becoming a shopping piazza like Covent Garden, the area has gone up-market, with a number of good quality restaurants in St John Street.

Just north of Smithfield is Georgian **Charterhouse Square ❺**. With its gas lamps and cobbles, it is a favourite location for period film-makers. The Carthusian order **London Charterhouse** still has around 40 residents, some of whom conduct guided tours between April and August (www.the charterhouse.org; Wed at 2.15pm, book in advance; tel: 7253 9503; charge).

### St John's Gate ❻

✉ St John's Lane; www.museumstjohn. org.uk 📞 7324 4005 🕐 Mon–Sat 10am–5pm, tours Tue, Fri–Sat 11am, 2.30pm 💷 free 🚇 Farringdon

To the left of London Charterhouse, approached through the medieval St John's Gate off Clerkenwell Road, is **St John's Priory**, founded by the crusading Order of the Knights of St John. Little remains of the buildings dissolved by Henry VIII, but there is a small **museum** in the Gate House, and guided tours of the Grand Hall and remains of the Priory Chapel which, like the Temple Church off Fleet Street, was round.

### Clerkenwell

Further north, beyond Old Street is **Clerkenwell**, historically a district of immigrants (notably Italian) and revolutionary traditions, as well as the traditional centre of the city's watchmaking industry. In the 19th century, Chartists and campaigners for Home Rule collected around Clerkenwell Green.

Guiseppe Mazzini, the Italian revolutionary, lived at No. 10 Laystall Street and Lenin edited a newspaper in what is now the Marx Memorial Library at 37a Clerkenwell Green (www.marx-memorial-library.org; open to the public for guided tours Mon–Thur 1–2pm only; tel: 7253 1485).

To the east, just south of Old Street Underground station on City Road, is **Bunhill Fields** (closes 7pm Apr–Sept, 4pm Oct–Mar), the burial ground for many notable nonconformists including Daniel Defoe, William Blake and

John Bunyan. Across the road is **Wesley's Chapel** (www.wesleyschapel.org.uk; Mon–Sat 10am–4pm, Sun 12.30–1.45pm, closed Thur lunch time; tel: 7253 2262), built by the founder of Methodism, John Wesley, in 1778. There is a museum in the crypt and Wesley's house, next to the chapel, is also open to the public. In the men's public toilets are Victorian fixtures manufactured by Thomas Crapper.

## THE BARBICAN

Based around three 42-storey towers, the **Barbican Centre** ❼ (www.barbican.org.uk; tours Wed 4pm, Sat 11am and 2pm, Sun 2pm, depart from ticket desk on level G; charge) is the main residential block in the City and contains Europe's largest arts centre. It was devised as council housing by the Corporation of London in the 1950s to attract residents and boost a falling City population. It took more than 20 years to build and is renowned for its inaccessibility and maze-like design. Later the flats were sold at exorbitant prices. The complex contains two art galleries, a cinema, two theatres and the London Symphony Orchestra, and is now listed.

Beside the Barbican Centre, on the site of a Roman fort, is the Museum of London.

## Museum of London ❽

✉ London Wall; www.museumof london.org.uk ☏ 7001 9844
🕑 daily 10am–6pm, last entry 5.30pm
🎫 free 🚇 Barbican

With more than a million objects in its stores, this is the world's largest urban history museum and an essential stop for understanding how the City developed.

**ABOVE:** detail from Edward Penny's *A City Shower* (c.1764), the Museum of London.
**LEFT:** John Wesley, the father of Methodism.
**BELOW:** the Barbican.

## The Romans

The Romans established the City in AD 43, but there are few remains of the original Roman settlement. The Roman Wall, which was 2 miles (3km) long, 20ft high and 9ft wide (6 by 3 metres) and had six magnificent gates (Ludgate, Aldersgate, Cripplegate, Newgate, Bishopsgate and Aldgate) is now found only in fragments. Good sections can still be seen at London Wall, Noble Street, Cooper's Row and the Museum of London. There are also remains on the approach to the Tower of London from Tower Hill Underground station. The wall's course can be traced with the help of maps which have been set up on the City's pavements.

**KIDS**

The Museum of London holds a good range of free activities and workshops for children, especially during school holidays.

*It is a myth that the City walls halted the Great Fire of 1666. In fact, the flames leapt across the Fleet River, destroying around 63 acres (25.5 hectares) outside the walled area.*

**BELOW:** the Lord Mayor's Coach in the Museum of London.

Aside from important prehistoric and Roman collections, it has a vast archaeological archive, a costume and decorative arts collection, a photographic archive of 280,000 images and more than 5,000 hours of oral life-story recordings.

London's history is presented chronologically from prehistory to the early Stuarts. The same thematic threads run through each period: architecture, trade and industry, transport, health, religion, fashions, leisure pursuits. There are many detailed information panels; you may find that, an hour into your visit, you're still with the Romans.

Here are some highlights:

### London Before London

This surveys life in the Thames Valley from 450,000 BC–AD 50. The centrepiece of the exhibition is the "River Wall" displaying 300 artefacts found in the Thames.

### Roman London

This gallery has a hoard of gold coins (1st–2nd century AD), a Roman leather bikini, and the gilded arms of what must have been a life-size statue of a god or emperor.

### Medieval London

Telling the story of London from the end of Roman rule to the accession of Elizabeth I, this gallery displays items such as a gold and garnet brooch found in a Covent Garden grave, and some extremely pointy medieval shoes.

### War, Plague and Fire

This tells the story of London in the turbulent 17th century, when Civil War, plague and then the Great Fire of 1666 ravaged the city. Objects include a death mask of Oliver Cromwell, primitive fire fighting equipment and fire-damaged floor tiles from Pudding Lane (where the fire began in a baker's shop).

### Galleries of Modern London

These new galleries bring the story of London up to the present day, and display the stunning Lord Mayor's Coach. There is also a reconstructed 18th-century pleasure garden and pavilion, a cell from a debtors'

*Recommended Restaurants, Pubs, Bars & Cafés on pages 174–5*

prison. an Art Deco lift from Selfridges, and exhibits such as the elaborate Fanshawe dress made from Spitalfields' woven silk.

## THE GUILDS

Craftsmen with the same trade tended to congregate in small areas, and clubbed together to form medieval guilds. Like trade unions, the guilds operated to ward off foreign competition and established an apprenticeship system. They set standards for their goods and working practices, and ran mutual-aid schemes which helped members in difficulty. The more prosperous guilds built halls to meet and dine in and wore lavish uniforms or "liveries", in due course becoming livery companies.

Down the centuries the livery companies joined the establishment, promoting charities and founding some of England's better educational institutes, including Haberdashers' College and Goldsmiths' College.

### The Livery Halls

Today some of the most impressive portals in the City belong to livery halls. Behind their elaborate carvings members dine as lavishly as ever.

Most spectacular is **Goldsmiths Hall** ❾ in Foster Lane (www.the goldsmiths.co.uk/hall; tel: 7606 7010), between the Museum of London and St Paul's, where the integrity of coins made by the Royal Mint are checked in an annual ceremony. The use of the word "hallmark" as a seal of value originated here and the company is still responsible for assaying gold. Unfortunately, visitors are not usually allowed inside the livery halls, except on open days held a few times a year (tel: 7606 3030 to book). While the 108 livery companies today have little connection with their original crafts, they

## TIP

Postman's Park delivers a soothing antidote to the high walkways and municipal signage of the over-scale Barbican. Small, secluded and a short walk from the Museum of London walkway exit, this is a good place to take a break. Rows of hand-lettered Doulton plaques placed in an open gallery by socialist artist George Watts (1817–1904) commemorate tragic acts of bravery by ordinary people. The General Post Office, from which the park derives its name, closed long ago.

**LEFT:** gold leopard, Skinners Hall.
**BELOW:** the ceiling of the Livery Hall of the Drapers' Company.

## At Sixes and Sevens

For years there was fierce rivalry between the craftsmen's guilds. In 1515 the Lord Mayor interceded and named a top 12 who could process in that order at the Lord Mayor's Show: Mercers (dealers in fine cloth), Grocers, Drapers, Fishmongers, Goldsmiths, Skinners, Merchant Taylors, Haberdashers, Salters, Ironmongers, Vintners and Clothworkers. Competition between the Skinners and Merchant Taylors, who both claimed the number six slot, was particularly fierce. The Lord Mayor decreed they should alternate positions six and seven every year, which is said to have originated the expression "at sixes and sevens", meaning "uncertain".

*Behind Mansion House is **St Stephen Walbrook**, the Lord Mayor's church, rebuilt after the Great Fire and considered by many to be Christopher Wren's best. Its dome is believed to be a dry run for St Paul's and its controversial "cheeseboard" altar is by Henry Moore.*

still exert influence in their home territory. The City is governed by the City Corporation, chaired by the **Lord Mayor** (whereas the rest of the capital comes under the wing of the Mayor of London, who presides over the Greater London Authority). The office of Lord Mayor dates from 1189. The new Mayor is elected each year on Michaelmas Day, 29 September, when the reigning Lord Mayor and his aldermen parade through the streets carrying posies of flowers to ward off the stench which filled the City in medieval times.

## Guildhall ❿

✉ Gresham Street; www.cityoflondon. gov.uk ☎ 7606 3030 🕒 Mon–Sat 10am–4.30pm all year; Sun 10am–4.30pm May–late Sept 🎫 free 🚇 St Paul's

In November the Mayor is sworn in here, taking up his symbols of office in a ceremony known as the Silent Change, so called because no words are spoken. The Guildhall is the best place to glimpse the guilds'

past. Dating from the 15th century, and several times restored, the Great Hall is decorated with the liveries' banners and shields, and contains statues of Gog and Magog, the legendary founders of London. A small museum (Mon–Sat 9.30am–4.30pm; free) in a room adjacent to the Library displays the timepieces owned by the Clockmakers' Company. This splendid collection is the oldest and largest of its kind. There are 15 marine timekeepers, including one by John Harrison.

The Lord Mayor's Show is held a day after his swearing in. This colourful parade starts at the Guildhall and passes through the City, culminating at **Mansion House ⓫**, opposite the Bank of England. This is the Lord Mayor's official residence, designed by George Dance the Elder in 1758, but its magnificent rooms are not open to the public. However, there are guided tours every Tuesday at 2pm (charge) – meet at the A-board near the porch entrance to Mansion House, in Walbrook.

**BELOW:** the Guildhall. **BELOW RIGHT:** the West Wing entrance of the Guildhall.

*Recommended Restaurants, Pubs, Bars & Cafés on pages 174–5*

western corner, the **Royal Exchange** building to the east and Sir John Soane's implacable facade of the Bank of England to the north.

All the City's great institutions grew from the fulfilment of the most basic needs and only later acquired their grandiose headquarters. Banking first came to the City in the 12th century when Italian refugees set up lending benches (*banca* in Italian) in **Lombard Street**, running eastwards from the Bank of England.

## The Bank of England ⑬

✉ Museum entrance in Bartholomew Lane; www.bankofengland.co.uk
☎ 7601 5545 ⓒ Mon–Fri 10am–5pm
ⓔ free 🚇 Bank

The **Bank of England** dominates the Bank square as it does the British financial scene. Popularly known as the Old Lady of Threadneedle Street, a nickname which probably originates from a late 18th-century cartoon depicting an old lady (the bank) trying to prevent the then prime minister, Pitt the Younger, from securing her gold. The name stuck because it

*One of several striking ornamental signs on Lombard Street. The signs were put up in 1902 to mark Edward VII's coronation.*

## Guildhall Art Gallery ⑫

✉ Guildhall Yard; www.guildhallart gallery.cityoflondon.gov.uk ☎ 7332 3700 ⓒ Mon–Sat 10am–5pm, Sun noon–4pm 🚇 Mansion House or St Paul's

Established in 1886, the Guildhall's gallery was destroyed in the Blitz but reopened in 1999. John Singleton Copley's immense *The Defeat of the Floating Batteries at Gibraltar,* around which the new gallery was designed, commands attention, but allow time to linger over the smaller-scale works depicting London life. You can take a free tour of the collection's highlights on Fridays (hourly between 12.15–3.15pm).

Shortly before work began on the present building, the remains of a **Roman amphitheatre** were discovered under the yard. The arena, including well-preserved timber drains bearing original carpentry tool marks, may now be viewed in a lower-level gallery.

### BANK AND BEYOND

The triangular intersection known as **Bank** can intimidate. Imposing civic architecture abounds, with Sir Edwin Lutyens' **HSBC** building on the north west side, Mansion House on the

**LEFT:** Rossetti's *La Ghirlandata* (1873), Guildhall Art Gallery.
**BELOW:** an ornate memorial to Admiral Horatio Nelson (1758–1805), the Guildhall.

**SHOP**

The Royal Exchange, where animated young traders in traditional garish blazers once shouted and waved instructions, is now occupied by a clutch of luxury retailers including Cartier, Bulgari, Tiffany, Hermès, De Beer and Chanel. To round off a spree here, head for one of the Exchange's posh restaurants or bars.

aptly describes the conservative, maternalistic role the bank played in stabilising the country's economy – a role strengthened in 1997 when the new Labour government freed it from direct government control.

The Bank of England was set up in 1694 to finance a war against the Dutch. In return for a £1.2 million loan, it was granted a charter and became a bank of issue (with the right to print notes and take deposits). Today it prints 5 million notes daily, destroys another 5 million and stores the nation's gold reserves. Its present home was largely rebuilt between 1925 and 1939.

It covers 3 acres (1.2 hectares) and contains the **Bank of England**

**RIGHT:** the Bank of England Museum.
**BELOW LEFT AND RIGHT:** exterior and interior of the Lloyd's of London building.

**Museum** (Mon–Fri 10am–5pm). The presentations narrate how the bank helped to finance Britain's war effort against France in 1688, how it became one of the first institutions in the City to employ women and how it controlled government borrowing during World War II. There is a display of gold, including Roman and modern bars.

## Lloyd's of London

The Big Bang brought immediate demands for new office buildings which would be purpose-built for modern communications and, by 1991, 1.7 sq miles (4.4 sq km) of office space had been built in the City. One of the first, and the most dramatic, was the 1986 **Lloyd's of London**  building in Lime Street, designed by Sir Richard Rogers (now Lord Rogers).

For so long the biggest insurance group in the world, Lloyd's started in the 17th-century coffee house of Edward Lloyd, where underwriters, shippers and bankers gathered and began to strike deals. Its practices remained largely unchanged for

*Recommended Restaurants, Pubs, Bars & Cafés on pages 174–5*

The building is no longer open to visitors, but the exterior is a highlight of the City. Hidden from sight on a magnificent marble floor is a rostrum housing the **Lutine Bell**, which was rung once for bad news and twice for good. It was rung following the 9/11 terrorist attacks in 2001.

Beside this modern building is the more accessible **Leadenhall ⓯**, once the wholesale market for poultry and game, and now a handsome commercial centre. The magnificent airy Victorian cream and maroon structure has a collection of up-market chain shops, book shops, sandwich bars and stylish restaurants, attracting City workers at breakfast and lunch time.

*Leadenhall Market sits on the site of the Roman Forum.*

300 years, but in the late 1980s sundry international disasters led to some huge payouts and millions of pounds were lost. Many of the "names" – investors who shouldered the insurance risks, often through syndicates – lost life savings and owed more than they could ever possibly pay; tragically a few committed suicide.

## Grand stations

London's other steel-and-glass Victorian constructions – the railway stations – were also given facelifts during the 1980s building boom. **Liverpool Street** was overhauled along with neighbouring **Broadgate ⓰**, one of the most ambitious developments in the City, with 16 office-block buildings around three squares

**LEFT:** Leadenhall Market. **BELOW:** Broadgate Circle.

including, at Broadgate Square, an ice rink with sushi, coffee and sandwich stalls dotted around the perimeter. There are now plans afoot to redevelop the site.

**Fenchurch Street** with its arched roof and graceful windows was the City's first railway station. Originally situated in the Minories, it moved in 1854 to its present location and has the 1930s Manhattan-style office building, **1 America Square**, over its railway lines.

To stand out in such an architectural playground, new buildings have to be innovative. One recent example is the distinctive **30 St Mary Axe building**, a 40-storey tapering

glass tower designed by Lord Foster and known affectionately as "the gherkin". The only piece of curved glass used in the structure forms the tip of the dome, under which is an exclusive (members only) restaurant giving 360-degree views.

Less obvious is **One New Change** on Cheapside, the City's newly opened shopping centre designed by Jean Nouvel. Its 6th floor roof terrace offers stunning views of the City and St Paul's.

## Monument ⑱

✉ Monument Yard; www.the monument.info ☎ 7626 2717
🕒 viewing gallery daily 9.30am–5pm
💷 charge 🚇 Monument

Erected according to Wren's designs to commemorate the 1666 fire, this Roman Doric column stands 202ft (61 metres) high. The height happens to be the same as the distance between the monument's base and the king's baker's house in Pudding Lane where the fire began.

The Great Fire lasted four days and spread through 460 streets,

*Monument, commemorating the Great Fire of London. Climb its 311 steps for superb views.*

**RIGHT:** view of St Paul's from One New Change. **BELOW:** summer in the City.

destroying 87 churches and more than 13,000 houses. Inside the column, 311 steps wind up to a small platform, from which the view is spectacular. Appropriately enough, the gallery affords a chance to appreciate the remarkable vision Wren imposed on the City through his spires. There are so many Wren spires that you risk severe Wren-fatigue if you attempt to see them all.

**St Mary-le-Bow ⓲** is the home of the famous Bow bells, which define a true cockney – you have to be born within earshot. There have been many sets of bells over the centuries; the current ones were cast after WWII. The church interior after restoration is rather plain, but the Norman crypt, now a restaurant called The Café Below, is worth a visit. Wren was able to leave his significant mark on London because so much of it had been destroyed in the Great Fire, but some churches survived the conflagration, including **St Katherine Cree ⓴**, a mix of Classical and Gothic, in Leadenhall Street. Henry Purcell played its fine 17th-century organ, and the painter Hans

Holbein, a plague victim, was buried here in 1543.

## Tower of London ㉑

✉ Tower Hill; www.hrp.org.uk ☏ 0844 482 7777 ⏰ Mar–Oct Tue–Sat 9am–5.30pm, Sun–Mon 10am–5.30pm; Nov–Feb Tue–Sat 9am–4.30pm, Sun–Mon 10am–4.30pm ⓒ charge 🚇 Tower Hill

East of the Monument, across the river from the oval-shaped City Hall, from which the Greater London Authority's power is exercised, is the City's oldest structure. At first sight the **Tower of London** can look like a cardboard model rather than a former seat of power, but closer inspection reveals an awesome solidity which encompasses much of Britain's history. The Tower has contained at various times a treasury, public record office, observatory, royal mint and zoo, and was so frequently remodelled for these purposes that its interiors look less ancient than one expects.

*For full coverage of the Tower of London, see pages 178–181.* ❏

**DRINK**

Visits to the Tower of London are exhausting, but refreshment is within easy walking distance. The Ship pub in Talbot Court off Eastcheap, and The Samuel Pepys pub down Stew Lane, off Upper Thames Street on the river, have real character and real ale.

**BELOW LEFT:** the 30 St Mary Axe building, aka the Gherkin.
**BELOW:** the Tower of London.

# BEST RESTAURANTS, PUBS, BARS AND CAFÉS

## Restaurants

Prices for a three-course dinner per person with a half-bottle of house wine:

£ = under £20
££ = £20–30
£££ = £30–50
££££ = over £50

### British

#### The Café Below

St Mary-le-Bow, Cheapside, EC2 ☏ 7329 0789; www.cafebelow.co.uk © B, L & D Mon–Fri. £–££ [p328, B2]
An excellent café in the church crypt of St Mary-le-Bow, with seats in the churchyard in summer. The menu changes daily, is seasonal, includes plenty of vegetarian options, and all food is home-made.

#### Hix Oyster and Chop House

36–37 Greenhill Rents, off Cowcross St, EC1 ☏ 7017 1930; www.hixoysterand chophouse.co.uk © L Mon–Fri and Sun, D daily £££ [p323, D4]
Chef Mark Hix showcases his modern British cooking. Dishes, which vary with the seasons, might include beef and oyster pie, Porterhouse steaks and grilled fish.

#### One New Change

Cheapside ☏ www.onenewchange.com [p328, B2]
The City's new shopping centre has several bars and restaurants. These include a Searcy's Champagne Bar (tel: 7871 1213), Madison

Restaurant (tel: 8305 3088) on the roof terrace, and the chic café Bea's of Bloomsbury (tel: 7242 8330).

#### St John

26 St John St, EC1 ☏ 7251 0848; www.stjohn restaurant.com © L Mon–Fri and Sun, D Mon–Sat. ££££ [p323, D4]
This little restaurant, a stone's throw from Smithfield's meat market, is a Clerkenwell favourite. It offers simple but curious dishes such as Middle White belly and dandelion. One Michelin star.

### Fish

#### Sweetings

39 Queen Victoria St, EC4 ☏ 7248 3062; www.sweetingsrestaurant.com © L only Mon–Fri. ££ [p328, B2]
First-rate restaurant with bags of traditional City atmosphere, and well-prepared dishes such as grilled skate or turbot in mustard sauce, and old-fashioned puddings such as treacle tart.

### French

#### Café du Marché

22 Charterhouse Sq, Charterhouse Mews, EC1 ☏ 7608 1609; www.cafedu

marche.co.uk © L Mon–Fri, D Mon–Sat. £££ [p323, D4]
Rustic ambience, including a countrified courtyard, and traditional French menu. The food can seem a little on the rich side. Ideal for a romantic meal or lunch time treat. Has three restaurants, each with a different atmosphere, under the same roof.

#### Club Gascon

57 West Smithfield, EC1 ☏ 7796 0600; www.club gascon.com © L Mon–Fri, D Mon–Sat. £££ [p328, A1]
Though tradition is not totally dispensed with, there's more to this Michelin-starred restaurant than the foie gras and *magret de canard* standards. Dishes and ingredients of southwestern France are prepared with an inventive touch and served tapas style, with a fine selection of regional wines to match. Booking essential.

### Italian

#### Caravaggio

107 Leadenhall St, EC3 ☏ 7626 6206; www.etrusca restaurants.com © L & D Mon–Fri. ££££ [329, C2]
Grand and rather showy Italian restaurant in a converted bank. Fish is a

**LEFT:** Café du Marché on Charterhouse Square.
**RIGHT:** St John on St John Street, near Smithfield.

good option and the fillet steak with aubergine and gorgonzola is a carnivore's dream.

## Modern European

### Bonds
5 Threadneedle St, EC2
**C** 7657 8088; www.theeton collection.co.uk ©L & D Mon–Fri. ££££ (set lunch ££) [p328, C2]
Set in the classy Threadneedles boutique hotel, overlooking the Bank of England, this top-class restaurant draws clients of the silk-lined wallet variety. Dishes include plenty of British fish and meat. There is a tapas menu too.

### The Don
20, St Swithin's Lane, EC4
**C** 7626 2606; www.thedon restaurant.com ©L & D Mon–Fri. £££–££££ [p328, C2]
Hidden in a courtyard off St Swithin's Lane, this is a cosy and welcoming brick-walled bistro. The food is a flavour-packed mélange of influences,

with a French bias. There is also a more formal restaurant.

### Eagle
159 Farringdon Rd, EC1
**C** 7837 1353 ©L daily, D Mon–Sat. ££ [p323, C3]
This was the pub that launched a thousand gastropubs with its pioneering menu of inventive dishes. The food has a Mediterranean bias and a good choice of European beers.

### Little Bay
171 Farringdon Rd, EC1
**C** 7278 1234; www.little bay.co.uk ©daily, all day. £ [p323, C3]
For honest food, keenly priced, this bizarre little bistro, lit by hand-crafted copper sculptures, is hard to beat.

### Searcy's
Level 2, Barbican, Silk St, EC2 **C** 7588 3008; www. barbican.org.uk ©L Mon–Fri, D Mon–Sat. £££ [p323, E4]
A classy place that serves up well-executed

dishes for an arts-centre restaurant. Ring first as it doesn't open at night if there's no performance.

## Pan-Asian

### Cicada
132–136 St John St, EC1
**C** 7608 1550; www.ricker restaurants.com ©L Mon–Fri, D Mon–Sat. ££ [p323, D3]
Offers a range of well-executed pan-Asian dishes such as black cod with sweet miso.

## Spanish

### Moro
34–36 Exmouth Market, EC1
**C** 7833 8336; www.moro. co.uk ©L & D Mon–Sat. £££ [p323, C3]
Laid-back restaurant serving Moorish cuisine, where lamb is charcoal grilled, tuna is wind-dried, monkfish wood-roasted, and manzanilla sherry partners prawns and garlic. Tapas available all day.

## Pubs, Bars and Cafés

Given that some of London's oldest streets as well as its newest buildings are here, the mix of watering holes is diverse, ranging from hip bars and contemporary cafés to quaint pubs full of character and history. Fewer and farther between are the no-nonsense Victorian pubs, but with a bit of effort, traditionalists or anyone craving a quiet pint and a packet of peanuts can root them out. Fashionable cocktail bars include **Fluid** (40 Charterhouse Lane, near Smithfield), **1 Lombard Street** (that's the address too), the sleek Harvey Nichols-run **Prism** (147 Leadenhall Street) and the capacious **Smiths of Smithfield** (67–77 Charterhouse Street).
  **Ye Olde Watling** (Watling Street) serves real ales and food. **Vertigo 42** (Tower 42,

Old Broad Street) lives up to its name by serving Champagne and Champagne-based cocktails to accompany great views from on high in the 42-storey skyscraper. The down-to-earth **Vinoteca** (7 St John Street) has an excellent wine list, good, unpretentious food and reasonable prices. **Royal Exchange Grand Café and Bar** (The Courtyard, Royal Exchange, Bank) offers breakfast, lunch, dinner and drinks in opulent surroundings with prices to match. **Jerusalem Tavern** (55 Britton Street) is an intimate little pub dating from 1720, with cubicles, Georgian-style furniture and a selection of real ales and fruit beers. **The Counting House** (50 Cornhill) is a bank-turned-pub, with high ceilings and chandeliers.

# St Paul's Cathedral

Sir Christopher Wren built more than 50 churches in London after the Great Fire of 1666, but this is the one that remains his masterpiece

Historians believe that the first church on the St Paul's site was built in the 7th century, although it only really came into its own as Old St Paul's in the 14th century, and by the 16th century it was the tallest cathedral in England. Much of the building was destroyed in the Great Fire of 1666.

Construction on the new St Paul's Cathedral began in 1675, when its architect, Sir Christopher Wren (pictured), was 43 years old.

The architect was an old man of 76 when his son Christopher finally laid the highest stone of the lantern on the central cupola in 1710. In total, the cathedral cost £747,954 to build, and most of the money was raised through taxing coal imports. Prior to the 300th anniversary of the "topping out" of the cathedral in 2008, centuries of soot and grime were scrubbed away as part of a £40 million restoration project.

### The essentials

- ✉ *www.stpauls.co.uk*
- ☎ 7246 8350
- 🕐 *Mon–Sat 8.30am–4pm, tours begin at 10.45am, 11.15am, 1.30pm and 2pm*
- 💲 *charge*
- 🚇 *St Paul's*

**ABOVE:** Just below the 24 windows in the dome is the Whispering Gallery, nearly 100ft (30 metres) of perfect acoustic. A whisper can be heard across the gallery, 107ft (33 metres) away.

**ABOVE:** the superb craftsmanship was supervised during the 35-year construction by one master builder, Thomas Strong, and by Wren himself.

## THE HIGHLIGHTS

**Features**: marble steps (**A**); oak pulpit (**Q**); High Altar (**R**); Dean's pulpit and stairs to crypt (**U**); stairs to dome (**V**). **Chapels**: St Dunstan's (**B**); All Souls' (**C**); St Michael & St George's (**D**); American Chapel of Remembrance (**S**). **Tombs & Monuments**: Lord Leighton (**E**); General Gordon (**F**); Viscount Melbourne (**G**); Duke of Wellington (**H**); Joshua Reynolds (**I**); Dr Samuel Johnson (**J**); Admiral Earl Howe (**K**); Admiral Collingwood (**L**); J.M.W. Turner (**M**); Sir John Moore (**N**); General Abercromby (**O**); Lord Nelson (**P**); John Donne (**T**).

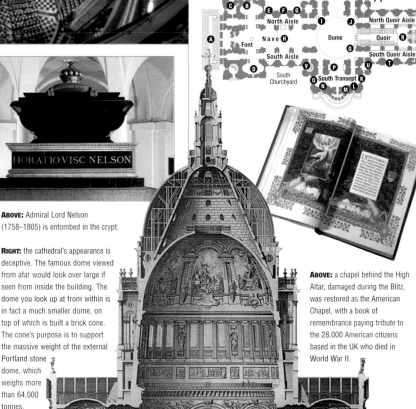

**ABOVE:** Admiral Lord Nelson (1758–1805) is entombed in the crypt.

**RIGHT:** the cathedral's appearance is deceptive. The famous dome viewed from afar would look over large if seen from inside the building. The dome you look up at from within is in fact a much smaller dome, on top of which is built a brick cone. The cone's purpose is to support the massive weight of the external Portland stone dome, which weighs more than 64,000 tonnes.

**ABOVE:** a chapel behind the High Altar, damaged during the Blitz, was restored as the American Chapel, with a book of remembrance paying tribute to the 28,000 American citizens based in the UK who died in World War II.

# THE TOWER
# OF LONDON

Queens were beheaded here,
princes murdered and traitors
tortured. Once a place to be
avoided, it is now one of
London's top visitor attractions

Encircled by a moat (now dry), with 22 towers, the Tower, begun by William the Conqueror around 1078, is Britain's top military monument and a reminder of how power was once exercised in the nation.

Two of Henry VIII's wives, Anne Boleyn and Catherine Howard, were beheaded here, in 1536 and 1542. So were Sir Thomas More, Henry's principled Lord Chancellor (1535), and Sir Walter Raleigh, the last of the great Elizabethan adventurers (1618). The uncrowned Edward V, aged 12, and his 10-year-old brother Richard were murdered here in 1483, allegedly on the orders of Richard III. William Penn, the future founder of Pennsylvania, was imprisoned here in 1669, and the diarist Samuel Pepys in 1679. As recently as 1941, Rudolph Hess, Germany's deputy führer, was locked in the Tower.

Given that the Tower's 18 acres (7.3 hectares) contain enough buildings and collections to occupy three hours, you may prefer to skip the one-hour Beefeater-led tour and strike out on your own. A multimedia guide can be hired.

In summer, it's best to arrive early to beat the queues, giving priority to the Crown Jewels and the Bloody Tower. Note that the spiral staircases in some of the towers require a degree of agility. Within the Tower walls, picnics are permitted on any of the seats. There are also snack kiosks and a restaurant in the New Armouries.

**ABOVE:** the meticulously restored interior of the Medieval Royal Residence uses replica furniture and textiles, rich colours, scents, sound and lighting effects to create an impression of 13th-century life in the palace. Edward I probably slept here, in the King's Bed Chamber, when he stayed at the Tower in 1294.

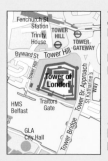

## The essentials

✉ Tower Hill;
www.hrp.org.uk
☎ 0844 482 7777
🕐 Mar–Oct Tue–Sat
9am–5.30pm, Sun–Mon
10am–5.30pm; Nov–Feb
Tue–Sat 9am–4.30pm,
Sun–Mon 10am–4.30pm
💷 charge
🚇 Tower Hill

## THE SIGHTS WORTH SEEING

### The Medieval Palace

Just before Traitor's Gate is the entrance to the residential part of the Tower, used by monarchs when they lived here. St Thomas's Tower, built in 1275–79 but much altered, displays archaeological evidence of its many uses. Parts of the Wakefield Tower (1220–40), such as the King's Bed Chamber, are furnished in 13th-century style and a torture exhibition has been added. A spiral staircase leads to a walkway on top of the south wall, which provides a good view of the riverside defences. The wall runs to the Lanthorn Tower (1883) containing 13th-century artefacts.

### The White Tower

The oldest part of the fortress, the White Tower, was probably designed in 1078 by a Norman monk, Gandulf, a prolific builder of castles and churches. It has walls 15ft (5 metres) thick. Its original form remains, but nearly every part has been refurbished or rebuilt: the door surrounds and most windows were replaced in the 17th and 18th centuries, and much of the Normandy stone was replaced with more durable Portland stone from Dorset. The first floor gives access to the austere Chapel of St John the Evangelist, a fine example of early Norman architecture. Much of the remaining space is devoted to displays of armour, swords and muskets, taken from the Royal Armouries. Legend has it that London will fall if the ravens who nest here ever leave the Tower – so their wings are clipped to ensure they stay.

**ABOVE:** at the centre of the fortress is the imposing White Tower with its four weathervane-topped turrets, each of a different style. The name followed Henry III's order to whitewash the exterior.

**ABOVE:** Tower Green is the grassy area, west of the White Tower, that gives access (but only for guided tours) to the much rebuilt Chapel Royal of St Peter ad Vincula. In front of the chapel is the Scaffold Site where nobles were beheaded (the less illustrious were executed in public on Tower Hill, outside the castle walls).

## MORE MODERN THAN MEDIEVAL

Given that so much of the country's turbulent history was played out within these walls, the Tower conspicuously lacks the romantic aura that many visitors expect. The reason is that, until comparatively recently, its buildings were functional – as well as serving as a fort, arsenal, palace and prison, it also contained at various times a treasury, public record office, observatory, royal mint and zoo. As a result, it was frequently remodelled and renovated, especially in the 19th century, so that many floors and staircases, for example, look more modern than medieval. But then, how could the boards that Henry VIII trod hope to survive the footfalls of 2½ million tourists a year?

Any sense of awe is also undermined by the brightly uniformed "Beefeaters" *(see right)*. Although all have served in the armed forces for at least 22 years, some have enthusiastically embraced showbiz, apparently auditioning for the role of pantomime villain by alternating jocular banter with visitors and melodramatically delivered descriptions of torture and beheadings. In contrast, pike and musket drills by the English Civil War Society are conducted with the masterful lethargy of confirmed pacifists.

**ABOVE:** the upper chamber of Wakefield Tower was used as a throne room by Henry III and later converted into an anteroom of the King's private chambers by his son, Edward I. Wakefield Tower also housed the state archives from 1360 to 1856 and, for a time, served as the Jewel House.

**RIGHT:** attired in Tudor uniforms, Yeoman warders first took up their posts under Edward VI and have been guarding the Tower for more than 500 years. Their nickname "Beefeaters" may derive from the French word *buffetier*, meaning servant, although an "eater" was also used in English to describe a servant. In 2007 the first female Beefeater, Moira Cameron, was appointed. Like her fellow male Beefeaters she has a military background. Among the perks of the job of a Beefeater is the use of a subsidised apartment within the Tower of London.

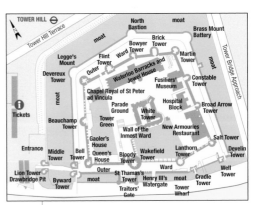

**ABOVE:** in 2006 a new memorial was erected to commemorate the 10 prisoners beheaded on Tower Green, including Anne Boleyn and Catherine Howard, the unfortunate wives of Henry VIII. A glass pillow rests on two discs of glass and granite.

**BELOW RIGHT:** Sir Walter Raleigh's room in the Bloody Tower (1603–16).

## THE HIGHLIGHTS

### The Wall Walk
The walk along this defensive outer wall takes in the eastern towers. Access is through the Salt Tower, often used as a prison. Next are the Broad Arrow Tower, also once a lock-up, the Constable Tower, which contains a model depicting the Tower in the 14th century, and the Martin Tower, which houses an exhibition on the Crown Jewels.

### The Royal Fusiliers' Museum
In the centre of the Tower is the modest but elegantly housed Royal Fusiliers' Museum. Opened in 1962, it follows the regiment's campaigns from its first battle for William of Orange against the French in Walcourt up to its more recent peacekeeping involvement in the Balkans and Northern Ireland. The regiment was almost destroyed in the American War of Independence.

### The Crown Jewels
These are displayed in the neo-Gothic Waterloo Barracks, built in 1845. The queues here can be long, with airport-style barriers. At the centre of the display are a dozen crowns and a glittering array of swords, sceptres and orbs used on

royal occasions. A moving walkway ensures that visitors cannot linger over the principal exhibits, but many other glass cases contain gold dishes, chalices and altar dishes that can be viewed at leisure. The collection includes the notorious Koh-i-Noor diamond.

# SOUTHWARK AND THE SOUTH BANK

The historic area south of the Thames has been transformed into a vibrant entertainment centre. Its multiple attractions, ranging from the London Eye and Tate Modern to Tower Bridge, are linked by an attractive riverside walk

**S**outhwark is one of the oldest parts of the capital. The first bridge across the Thames was built by the Romans near London Bridge, and the community around it developed separately from the City, as it lay beyond the City's jurisdiction. In Shakespeare's day it was the place for putting on unlicensed plays and for setting up brothels, and it retained its reputation as an area of vice well into the 19th century. The regeneration around Tate Modern, Borough Market and Butler's Wharf – coupled with Renzo Piano's new giant tower, The Shard – has transformed the area.

The Shard will be the tallest building in Western Europe, at 310m (1,016ft) high, and will mix residential and office space, and include a 5-star hotel. It has transformed the London skyline even before completion, and its viewing galleries will offer unobstructed views of the city and its suburbs.

## AROUND LAMBETH BRIDGE

Opposite the Houses of Parliament, beside Lambeth Bridge, is the red-brick **Lambeth Palace ❶**, which has been the London residence of the Archbishops of Canterbury since the 12th century. The fine Tudor brickwork of the entrance tower dates from 1485, but much of the rest is Victorian. The rare occasions on which the palace is open to the public include the annual Open House weekend *(see page 57)*.

Adjacent, by Lambeth Bridge on Lambeth Palace Road, the garden and deconsecrated church of **St Mary** contains the **Garden Museum** (www.gardenmuseum.org.uk; Sun–Fri 10.30am–5pm, Sat until 4pm, closed first Mon of every month;

| Main attractions |
| --- |
| IMPERIAL WAR MUSEUM |
| LONDON SEA LIFE AQUARIUM |
| LONDON EYE |
| ROYAL FESTIVAL HALL |
| HAYWARD GALLERY |
| BFI SOUTHBANK |
| NATIONAL THEATRE |
| TATE MODERN |
| SHAKESPEARE'S GLOBE |
| SOUTHWARK CATHEDRAL |
| BOROUGH MARKET |
| TOWER BRIDGE |
| DESIGN MUSEUM |

**LEFT:** Gabriel's Wharf.
**RIGHT:** Lambeth Palace.

The Garden Café, within the Garden Museum, is a great option for a bite to eat in the Lambeth Bridge area. The café serves home-cooked, vegetarian food, from aubergine and black bean chilli to delicately spiced soups and good cakes.

**ABOVE RIGHT:**
recalling the Crimea at the Florence Nightingale Museum. **BELOW:** exhibition at the Garden Museum.

tel: 7401 8865; charge). It is based on the work of two 17th-century royal gardeners, the elder and younger John Tradescant, father and son, who introduced exotic fruits such as pineapples to Britain. The old-fashioned roses and herbaceous perennials are delightful, and the church's rich history is evident in its memorials, including one remembering HMS *Bounty*'s Captain William Bligh, who lived locally in his later years.

## Imperial War Museum ❷

✉ Lambeth Road; www.iwm.org.uk
📞 7416 5000  🕐 daily 10am–6pm
ⓔ free except some special exhibitions
🚇 Elephant & Castle, Lambeth North

A 15-minute walk south from Lambeth Bridge, along Lambeth Road, leads to the **Imperial War Museum**. This impressive building, opened in 1815 to house the Bethlem hospital for the insane (popularly known as

Bedlam), was an inspired choice for a museum that chronicles the horrors of modern warfare. *For full details, see pages 200–1.*

## St Thomas's Hospital

Back by the river, close to Westminster Bridge, **St Thomas's Hospital** includes a reminder of warfare's nobler side: the **Florence Nightingale Museum ❸** (2 Lambeth Palace Road; www.florence-nightingale.co.uk; daily 10am–5pm; tel: 7620 0374; charge). Don't be deterred by the walk down Lambeth Palace Road, which is unattractive at this point; this small museum is worth the detour. It has a rich collection of memorabilia,

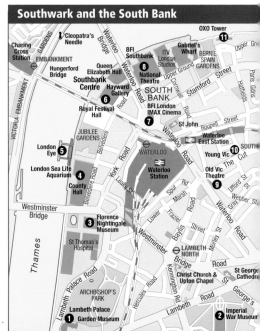

### Southwark and the South Bank

*Recommended Restaurants, Pubs, Bars & Cafés on pages 196–7*

and there are audio hot-spots around the museum on the life and achievements of the woman whose work in the Crimean War of 1853–6 helped transform nursing.

## COUNTY HALL ❹

Just downstream from Westminster Bridge and facing the Houses of Parliament is the majestic **County Hall**, designed in 1908 by architect Ralph Knott and for years the seat of the Greater London Council, which ran London until the government of

Margaret Thatcher abolished it in 1986. Now owned by Japan's Shirayama Shokusan Corporation, it incorporates an up-market hotel (the five-star Marriott), a budget hotel (a Premier Inn), the London Aquarium, a recording studio, a games arcade and several restaurants.

The first attraction as you walk eastwards along the river is **Namco Station** (10am–midnight; www.namco experience.com), home to bumper cars, video games and a bowling alley.

The top attraction in County Hall, especially for children, is the **London Sea Life Aquarium** (www. visitsealife.com/london;   Mon–Thur 10am–6pm, last entry 5pm, Fri–Sun 10am–7pm, last entry 6pm; tel: 0871 663 1678; charge). Thousands of specimens represent some 500 species of fish, and atmospheric sounds, smells and lighting are all employed to great effect. Highlights include the sharks and touch pool.

**KIDS**

At the London Sea Life Aquarium, it's worth catching the feeding times. For example, otters may be fed at 11.30am, 1.30pm and 3.30pm, but do check times beforehand.

**LEFT:** fish at the London Sea Life Aquarium.

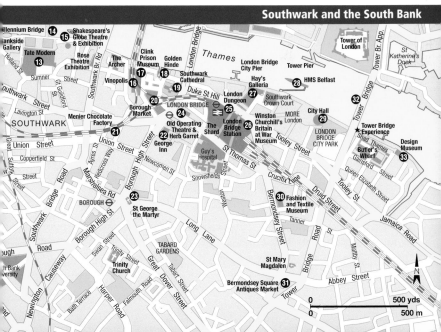

**Southwark and the South Bank**

*At 450ft (135 metres), the London Eye is one of the highest structures in London. The hub and spindle weigh 330 tonnes – more than 40 double-decker buses. On average, a whopping 10,000 people take a "flight" on it every day – that's around 3.5 million people per year.*

**BELOW:**
spectacular views from the top of the London Eye. Each pod holds up to 25 people.

## London Eye ❺

✉ County Hall; www.londoneye.com
☎ 0870 5000 600 ⊙ daily Sept–Mar 10am–8.30pm, Apr–June 10am–9pm, Jul–Aug 10am–9.30pm
⊙ charge 🚇 Waterloo

Towering over County Hall is the **London Eye**, the world's second largest observation wheel (the largest being the newer Singapore Flyer), designed by architects David Marks and Julia Barfield for the turn of the millennium.

The 32 enclosed capsules take 30 minutes to make a full rotation – a speed slow enough to allow passengers to step in and out of the capsules while the wheel keeps moving. On a clear day, you can see for 25 miles (40km). Book ahead (by phone or online) if you hope to ride the Eye at busy periods, although check the weather forecast first.

## SOUTHBANK CENTRE ❻

The **Southbank Centre** (bookings tel: 0844 875 0073; www.southbankcentre.co.uk) is Europe's largest arts complex. Its policy of maintaining an

"open foyer" means that its cafés, bars, book and record shops are open throughout the day.

## Concert halls

The 2,900-seat **Royal Festival Hall** (RFH), the oldest and largest of the three concert halls on the South Bank, was constructed on the site of the Lion Brewery, destroyed by bombing during World War II. The building was opened in 1951 as part of the Festival of Britain, intended to improve the country's morale after years of post-war austerity. Reopened in 2007 after extensive renovation, the hall now has improved acoustics, better facilities in the foyer and a renovated restaurant, Skylon.

There are two other concert halls within the complex, the 917-seater **Queen Elizabeth Hall**, opened in 1967 for music theatre and opera, and the 372-seater **Purcell Room**, intended for solo recitals and chamber music.

## Hayward Gallery

Set on the upper level of the South-bank Centre complex is the **Hayward Gallery** (Sat–Wed 10am–6pm, Thur–

*Recommended Restaurants, Pubs, Bars & Cafés on pages 196–7*

Fri 10am–8pm; tel: 0844 875 0073; charge), which has changing exhibitions. Its cutting-edge programme focuses on four areas: single artists, artistic movements, other cultures, and contemporary themes. Recent exhibitions have focused on William Eggleston, Dan Flavin, Antony Gormley, Ray Lichtenstein, Tracey Emin and Sam Taylor Wood.

The Hayward's mirrored **Waterloo Sunset Pavilion**, designed by Dan Graham as part of the regeneration of the Southbank, remains open in between main exhibitions. The gallery roof is often used as exhibition space.

## BFI Southbank

Next door is **BFI Southbank** (the former National Film Theatre; www.bfi.org.uk), Britain's leading art house cinema since 1952. With three auditoria and an intimate studio cinema, it holds over 2,400 screenings and events each year, from restored silent movies (with live piano accompaniment) to world cinema productions.

In 2007, new areas of the building were opened, including a "Mediathèque", where visitors can

browse the British Film Institute's archive free; a studio cinema, for the screening of archive and contemporary film and talks; a research area, and a shop. The Riverfront Bar in front of the building, with trestle tables sheltering under Waterloo Bridge, is complemented by the chic Benugo Bar & Kitchen.

The BFI also runs the **BFI London IMAX Cinema ❼**, which rises from the roundabout at the south end of Waterloo Bridge. Large format film is projected onto a screen 66ft high by 85ft wide (20 by 26 metres), the biggest in the UK. It also specialises in screening films in 3-D.

*The revitalised Royal Festival Hall, a post-war addition to London, is one of the capital's finest concert halls. It is connected to the north bank of the Thames by the Hungerford Footbridge.*

**BELOW LEFT:** the British Film Institute.
**BELOW:** Hayward Gallery, part of the Southbank Centre.

## THE NATIONAL THEATRE ❽

On the other side of **Waterloo Road**, still by the river, is the concrete **National Theatre** (www.national theatre.org.uk; see page 299). Built largely by women during World War II and opened in 1976, it houses three theatres: the large 1,200-seater **Olivier**; the 900-seater **Lyttelton**, a two-tier proscenium theatre; and the **Cottesloe**, a more intimate space, accessed at the side of the building.

For a peek behind the scenes, book a backstage tour (tours run six times a day Mon–Fri, twice on Sat

**ABOVE:** the National Theatre. **BELOW RIGHT:** the Oxo Tower.

and once on Sun, and last 1 hour 15 mins; tel: 7452 3400; charge).

At this point, a detour down Waterloo Road, past the IMAX cinema (see page 187), leads to The Cut and the elegant **Old Vic Theatre** ❾ (www.oldvictheatre.com), erected in 1811. A music hall in its early days, it became the first home of the National Theatre and is now a repertory theatre with Hollywood star Kevin Spacey as artistic director and musician Elton John as chairman. Backstage tours are available (tel: 7928 2651 for dates; charge).

Located a little further along The Cut is the **Young Vic** ❿, a theatre especially known for nurturing the talent of young theatre directors.

## GABRIEL'S WHARF TO BANKSIDE

Back on the riverfront, to the east of the National Theatre, is **Gabriel's Wharf**, a cluster of shops and restaurants. East again is the Art Deco **Oxo Tower** ⓫. Architect Albert Moore had grand ideas for this project: as well as erecting what was to become London's second highest

## The National Theatre

The idea of a National Theatre was suggested in 1848, but it wasn't until 1912, when Lilian Baylis became manager of the Old Vic Theatre, that the basis for a National Theatre was established. Baylis turned the old Victorian music hall into "the home of Shakespeare and opera in English", but finding a site for a permanent theatre proved difficult. During World War II, the government introduced funding for the arts as part of the war effort, the London County Council made land available on the South Bank, and in 1949 the National Theatre Bill was passed through Parliament. In 1962 Laurence Olivier was named artistic director.

The Old Vic remained the company's home while the new theatre was being built, by architect Denys Lasdun. In 1976, after more than a century of controversy, the National Theatre was opened by the Queen, by which time Peter Hall was the director. He was succeeded by Richard Eyre in 1988 and Trevor Nunn in 1997. The current director, Nicholas Hytner, has had some success in broadening the theatre's appeal by offering some cheaper seats.

*Recommended Restaurants, Pubs, Bars & Cafés on pages 196–7*

commercial building, he wanted to use electric lights to spell out the product's name. When planning permission was refused due to an advertising ban, Moore came up with the idea of using three letters – O, X and O – as 10ft (3-metre) -high windows looking out north, south, east and west. Inside the tower are several smart restaurants.

Beyond Blackfriars Bridge, the riverside walk leads past the **Bankside Gallery** ⓬ (tel: 7928 7521; www.banksidegallery.com; daily 11am–6pm), home of the Royal Watercolour Society and the Royal Society of Painter-Printmakers, which holds exhibitions.

## Tate Modern ⓭

✉ Bankside; www.tate.org.uk
☎ 7887 8888 ⓒ Sun–Thur 10am–6pm, Fri–Sat 10am–10pm ⓔ free except for special exhibitions
🚇 Southwark or London Bridge

Easily identifiable by its tall brick chimney, **Tate Modern** occupies the former Bankside Power Station and houses the Tate's international mod-ern art collection and part of its contemporary collection. The main entrance, to the west of the building, takes you onto the ground floor through a broad sweep of glass doors, then down a massive concrete ramp. The space in front of you is the Turbine Hall, the old boiler room, which is now used to house sculptural works and large installations. *(For full coverage, see pages 198–9.)*

**TIP**

A novel way to travel between Tate Modern and Tate Britain *(see page 78)* is to take the Tate Boat. It runs every 40 minutes during gallery hours and also stops at the London Eye.

*Bankside Power Station – which, like Battersea Power Station, was designed by Sir Giles Gilbert Scott – was built in two phases between 1947–1963. It ceased generating electricity in 1981.*

**ABOVE:** Tate Modern.
**BELOW:** the BFI London IMAX Cinema.

On the third weekend in December, Bankside holds a Frost Fair (with an ice slide, stalls and free events at the Globe), inspired by the Frost Fairs of centuries past, held on the frozen Thames.

*We wanted a platform, a flying carpet that is as thin as possible.*

Roger Risdill-Smith, of Ove Arup and Partners, engineers of the Millennium Bridge

**ABOVE RIGHT:**
*The Frozen Thames* (1677) by Abraham Hondius. **BELOW:** the Millennium Bridge.

## Millennium Bridge

Giving easy access to Tate Modern from St Paul's Cathedral, the Millennium Bridge was the first new river crossing in central London since Tower Bridge opened in 1894.

Designing the footbridge was tricky: it had to be slender enough so as not to spoil the view of St Paul's from Bankside, yet it also had to make an impact as a significant millennial sculpture. The solution, a sort of stainless-steel scalpel, was provided by architect Norman Foster, sculptor Anthony Caro and engineers Ove Arup and Partners. However, opening-day crowds caused the bridge to sway excessively, and it had to be closed for two years for adjustments.

## Shakespeare's Globe ⑮

✉ New Globe Walk; www.shakespeares globe.com ☎ box office: 7401 9919 🕒 tours regularly 💰 charge for tours 🚇 London Bridge or Southwark

Bankside and Southwark are the most historic areas of the South Bank. They grew up in competition

with the City opposite, but by the 16th century had become vice dens. Bankside was famous for brothels, bear- and bull-baiting, prize fights and the first playhouses, including the Globe.

The replica of the 1599 building opened in 1996 and is worth a visit even if you're not seeing a play. It has been painstakingly re-created using the original methods of construction. The season of the open-air galleried theatre runs from May to early October. It can accommodate around 1,500 people – 600 standing (called "groundlings" and liable to get wet if it rains) and the rest

seated. The wooden benches feel rather hard by Act III, but you can bring or rent cushions.

**Shakespeare's Globe Exhibition**, to the right of the theatre, is well worth a visit. There are traditional displays, but touch screens and hands-on exhibits provide the fun element.

## The Rose Theatre

Shakespeare also acted at the Rose Theatre, whose foundations were discovered close to the Globe in 1989. Turn down New Globe Walk (by the Globe's box office) and then left into Park Street. This was Bankside's first theatre, built in 1587. Events are staged here and tours take place when guided tours of the Globe are not possible (charge).

## BANKEND

Back on the riverside walk, past Southwark Bridge on the stretch known as Bankend, is the **Anchor Inn**. The present building (1770–5) is the sole survivor of the 22 busy inns that once lined Bankside. Dr Samuel Johnson, of dictionary fame, drank here.

## Vinopolis, City of Wine ⑯

✉ 1 Bank End; www.vinopolis.co.uk
☎ 7940 8301 ⏰ Thur–Fri 2–10pm, Sat noon–10pm, Sun noon–6pm; last tour 2 hours before closing 💲 charge
🚇 London Bridge

Opposite the eastern side of the pub, occupying 2½ acres (1 hectare) of cathedral-like space under railway arches, the sprawling Vinopolis, City of Wine offers a visual wine tour through exhibits of the world's wine regions. Individual audio units give access to four hours of recorded commentary in six languages, and the admission charge includes tickets for wine tastings. Guided tours are held on Sundays at 1pm.

## Clink Street

Like most country bishops, the bishops of the powerful see of Winchester had a London base. A single

*Note that there are no tours of Shakespeare's Globe theatre during performances. If you are visiting when a matinée is on, you will be given a tour of the Rose, Bankside's first playhouse, instead.*

**LEFT:** signs at Vinopolis. **BELOW:** Shakespeare's Globe.

*The Bishops of Winchester were the first authority in England to lock up miscreants. "In the clink", now a euphemism for being in jail, is thought to stem from the sound made by the clanking of the prisoners' chains. The bishops' prison operated from 1151 to 1780.*

London Borough of Southwark

**The Clink**
**1151-1780**

**Most notorious**
**medieval prison**

Voted by the People

**ABOVE RIGHT:** remnant of Winchester Palace on Clink Street. **BELOW:** Southwark Cathedral. **BELOW RIGHT:** the *Golden Hinde*.

gable wall remains of **Winchester Palace**, their former London residence. They had their own laws, regulated the many local brothels and were the first authority in England to lock up miscreants. The prison they founded, in what is now Clink Street, remained a lock-up until the 18th century. The **Clink Prison Museum** ⑰ (www.clink.co.uk; Mon–Fri 10am–6pm, Sat–Sun until 7.30pm; tel: 7403 0900; charge) recalls the area's seedy past.

Clink Street leads on to Pickfords Wharf, built in 1864 for storing hops, flour and seeds, and now converted into an apartment block. At the end of the street, in the **St Mary Overie Dock**, is a replica of Sir Francis Drake's splendid galleon, the *Golden Hinde* ⑱ (www.goldenhinde.com; Mon–Sat 10am–5.30pm; tel: 7403 0123; charge).

Launched in 1973, the ship is the only replica to have completed a circumnavigation of the globe, and has now clocked up more nautical miles than the original, in which Drake set sail on his voyage of discovery in 1577.

## Southwark Cathedral ⑲

✉ London Bridge; www.southwark.cathedral.org.uk ☎ 7367 6700
☺ daily 8am–6pm ☺ free
🚇 London Bridge

Southwest of London Bridge and hemmed in by the railway, Southwark Cathedral is a rich fund of local history. A memorial to Shakespeare in the south aisle, paid for by public subscription in 1912, shows the bard reclining in front of a frieze of 16th-century Bankside. Above it is a modern (1954) stained-glass window depicting characters from his plays. Shakespeare was a parishioner for several years. John Har-

*Recommended Restaurants, Pubs, Bars & Cafés on pages 196–7*

vard, who gave his name to the American university, was baptised here, and is commemorated in the Harvard Chapel.

The cathedral holds free organ recitals every Monday (1pm) and classical concerts on Tuesday (3.15–4pm).

## BOROUGH

The area around London Bridge is in the throes of a regeneration programme. Much of its Dickensian character lingers, adding greatly to its appeal. In addition to Borough Market, there are several quirky museums and many restaurants, cafés and specialist shops.

## Borough Market ⑳

✉ Southwark Street; www.borough market.org.uk ☎ 7407 1002 ⏰ Thur 11am–5pm, Fri noon–6pm, Sat 8am–5pm 🚇 London Bridge

The highlight of the area is Borough Market, a wholesale food market dating from the 13th century. On Thursday, Friday and Saturday (the last two are the busiest days) a popular retail market offers gourmet and organic products. Apart from basics such as fruit and vegetables, you will find stalls specialising in seafood, game, oils and vinegars, cakes, preserves, fresh pasta, juices, wines and beers.

## Southwark Street

A brief diversion down Southwark Street is the splendid Victorian **Hop Exchange** (now offices), with The Wheatsheaf in its cellar. A cross between bar and pub, it serves hearty pub grub, shows Sky sports, has black and white photographs decorating its walls and is often lively.

Further along Southwark Street, the **Menier Chocolate Factory** ㉑ (51–3 Southwark Street; www.menier chocolatefactory.com; box office: 7378 1713) sits on the corner of O'Meara Street. Housed within this 1870s

chocolate factory is a 150-seat theatre, plus bar and restaurant.

## Borough High Street

Situated on Borough High Street, the main road south from London Bridge, is the 17th-century **George Inn** ㉒ (No. 77), the only remaining galleried coaching inn in London and mentioned in Dickens' *Little Dorrit*. Further down the street is the renovated **Church of St George the Martyr** ㉓ (www.stgeorge-themartyr. co.uk/history), also known as "Little Dorrit's Church", because Dickens' heroine was baptised and married there. She is represented in stained glass in the east window. There are free recitals at 1pm on Thursdays.

## LONDON BRIDGE AREA

Back towards London Bridge, at 9a St Thomas Street, is the **Old Operating Theatre Museum & Herb Garret** ㉔ (www.thegarret.org.uk; daily 10.30am–5pm; tel: 7188 2679; charge), the only surviving 19th-century operating theatre in Britain. It offers insights into the fearsome medical techniques of the day. The Herb Garret displays

**FOOD**

There are lots of opportunities to sample the produce free at Borough Market. Many stalls also do takeaway food, from venison burgers to scallops that are pan-fried while you wait. For a posh sit-down meal, try Roast *(see page 196)*, on the first floor; breakfast (Mon–Fri till 11am, later on Saturday) is a great way to enjoy the up-market dining experience at a fraction of the cost of lunch or dinner.

**RIGHT:** *Golden Hinde* figurehead. **BELOW:** Borough Market.

**KIDS**

The tour of the **London Dungeon** begins with an obligatory photo opportunity – head in the stocks, a blackened chopper at your neck. It's lots of fun for kids who are keen on the macabre, but it is pretty scary and the entire visit is spent in darkened corridors (often made more atmospheric by bloodcurdling shrieks), so it's not recommended for children under eight. Even under-15s must be accompanied by an adult. Queues tend to be long, so book in advance.

**RIGHT:** asking for information at the London Dungeon.
**BELOW:** HMS *Belfast*.

herbs and equipment used in the preparation of medicines.

## Tooley Street attractions

Parallel to the river, on Tooley Street, is the **London Dungeon** ㉕ (28–34 Tooley St; www.thedungeons.com; daily Sept–Oct, Apr–May, June–mid-July 10am–5.30pm; mid-July–Aug and Easter 9.30am–6.30pm; Nov–Dec 10am–5pm; tel: 7403 7221; charge). Lasting about 1½ hours, the actor-led tour features ghoulish exhibits of the Black Death, the Great Fire of 1666, Jack the Ripper's exploits, Sweeney Todd the barber's gruesome deeds, and a boat ride to hell. Guaranteed to make you jump at some point.

Nearby, **Winston Churchill's Britain at War Museum** ㉖ (www.britainatwar.co.uk; Apr–Oct 10am–5pm, Nov–Mar 10am–4.30pm, last entry one hour before closing; tel: 7403 3171; charge) recreates the sounds and smells of the Blitz.

Opposite is **Hay's Galleria** ㉗, a setting for shops, craft stalls and restaurants. The 60ft (18-metre) kinetic sculpture in the centre is David Kemp's *The Navigators*.

## HMS *Belfast* ㉘

Downstream from Hay's Galleria is HMS *Belfast*, the last of the warships to have seen action in World War II (http://hmsbelfast.iwm.org.uk; Mar–Oct 10am–6pm, Nov–Feb 10am–5pm; last entry one hour before closing; tel: 7940 6300; charge). Its tour ranges from the bridge to the engine rooms, capturing the cramped facilities of its 950-man crew.

To its east, the oval-shaped building is **City Hall** ㉙, seat of the Greater London Authority, the body that governs London. In front is **The Scoop**, a sunken amphitheatre staging free theatre, music and films in summer.

## Bermondsey Street

A 10-minute detour southeast leads to hip Bermondsey Street, where, at

### London Bridge

The present London Bridge, dating from 1967–72, is the latest of many on this site. Until Westminster Bridge opened in 1750, the crossing here was the only bridge across the Thames in London. A wooden bridge had existed here since the Romans, but the first stone bridge, later lined with houses, was erected in 1176 and completed 33 years later. In 1823–31 a new bridge of five stone arches was built, but in 1972, having been sold to American businessman Robert P. McCulloch for US$2.46 million, it was dismantled and re-erected in Arizona. Some claimed that McCulloch bought London Bridge in error, thinking that it was the much grander Tower Bridge. He denied this.

*Recommended Restaurants, Pubs, Bars & Cafés on pages 196–7*

No. 83, you can't miss the pink-and-orange **Fashion and Textile Museum** ③⓪ (www.ftmlondon.org; Tue–Sat 11am–6pm; tel: 7407 8664; charge), the creation of British designer Zandra Rhodes. It celebrates fashion via exhibitions and its own academy.

At the other end of the street, on Friday morning only, is **Bermondsey Square Antiques Market** ③①, which has successfully shed its bad reputation. Arrive early if you are after a bargain as the hundreds of traders start gathering at 4am.

## TOWER BRIDGE ③②

Dating from 1894 the Victorian Gothic **Tower Bridge** is one of London's most iconic structures. Despite its mock-medieval cladding, it contains 11,000 tons of steel, and sophisticated engineering raises its middle portion to allow tall ships through. When the capital was a flourishing port, it opened several times a day. In 1954 a bus driver was awarded a medal for putting his foot on the accelerator when, to his horror, he saw the bridge yawn

open before him. The bus leapt over a 3ft (1-metre) gap. These days the bridge opens around 500 times a year, with its bascules taking 90 seconds to lift.

The structure contains **Tower Bridge Experience** (www.towerbridge.org.uk; Apr–Sept 10am–6.30pm, Oct–Mar 9.30am–6pm; tel: 7403 3761; charge), an exhibition detailing the history of the bridge and explaining how the mechanism works. The view from Tower Bridge's high walkways is magnificent.

## Around Butlers Wharf

The old warehouses east of Tower Bridge contain a gourmet's delight. The gourmet in question is Habitat founder Sir Terence Conran, who opened several restaurants, such as Le Pont de la Tour (*see page 197*) in the biscuit-coloured **Butlers Wharf**.

The adjacent **Design Museum** ③③ (www.designmuseum.org; daily 10am–5.45pm; tel: 020 7940 8790; charge), inspired by Conran, showcases influential (mainly 20th-century) design through its permanent collection and excellent changing exhibitions. ❑

**DRINK**

Further east along the south bank from Tower Bridge and the Design Museum is Rotherhithe, which has several good traditional pubs, including the Mayflower, where the Pilgrim Fathers moored their ship before sailing to Plymouth and America in 1620. It is close to the Brunel Museum (Railway Avenue; www.brunel-museum.org.uk; daily 10am–5pm) on the site of the Thames Tunnel: built by Isambard Kingdom Brunel it was the world's first under-river tunnel.

**BELOW:** Tower Bridge raised to let a large vessel through.

# BEST RESTAURANTS, PUBS, BARS AND CAFÉS

## Restaurants

Prices for a three-course dinner per person with a half-bottle of house wine:

**£** = under £20
**££** = £20–30
**£££** = £30–50
**££££** = over £50

### British

#### Chop House

Butlers Wharf Building, 36e Shad Thames, SE1 [ 7403 3403; www.chophouse-restaurant.co.uk © L & D daily. **££££** (set menu **££**) [p329, D4]
Carnivores should go straight for the steak and kidney pudding, served with oysters, or pork loin and crackling. There are fish dishes for non-meat eaters. Other attractions

include great river views and a terrace.

#### Roast

Floral Hall, Stoney St, SE1 [ 0845 034 7300; www.roast-restaurant.com © B Mon–Sat, bar brunch Mon–Thur, L daily, D Mon–Sat. **£££** [p328, B3]
Spectacularly set on the upper floor of Borough Market, with gorgeous views. Sourced from the market, the excellent food is resolutely British.

### Fish

#### fish!

Cathedral St, SE1 [ 7407 3803; www.fishkitchen.com © L & D daily. **£££** [p328, B3]
Specialises in tasty GM-free fish in the shadow of

Southwark Cathedral. Bar seats are fun but noisy.

#### Livebait

43 The Cut, SE1 [ 0844 692 3901; www.livebait restaurants.co.uk © L & D daily. **£££** [p327, E4]
Luvvies from the Old and Young Vic theatres cram into the cool, all-over tiled rooms for good fish prepared in creative ways.

#### Masters Super Fish

191 Waterloo Rd, SE1 [ 7928 6924 © L Tue–Sat, D Mon–Sat. **£** [p327, E4]
Need a taxi? You'll find cabbies galore tucking into huge portions of fish and chips in this old-fashioned eatery.

### French

#### RSJ

33a Coin St, SE1 [ 7928 4554; www.rsj.uk.com © L Mon–Fri, D Mon–Sat. **££–£££** [p327, E3]
This pretty restaurant offers pleasant dishes such as Gressingham duck with beetroot salad, but the real attraction is the excellent selection of wines from the Loire.

### Modern European

#### The Anchor and Hope

36 The Cut, SE1 [ 7928 9898 © L Tue–Sun, D Mon–Sat. **££** [p327, E4]

Meat and offal feature strongly on the gastro-pub menu. Reasonable prices, hefty portions and friendly staff. The no-booking policy can mean long queues.

#### Cantina Vinopolis

1 Bank End, SE1 [ 7940 8333; www.cantina vinopolis.com © L Thur–Sat, D Mon–Sat. **£££** [p328, B3]
Full marks to the wine list (over 150 choices) at the restaurant in London's only wine museum. Then comes the decor – soaring cathedral-style arches. Appealing menu, too, with some dishes suitable for vegetarians.

#### Delfina

50 Bermondsey St, SE1 [ 7357 0244; www.the delfina.co.uk © B & L Mon–Fri, D Fri. **££–£££** [p328–9, C4]
Creatives flock to this light, airy restaurant in a former chocolate gallery for well-prepared dishes and the calm atmosphere. Artworks adorn the walls and outdoor seating is available in summer.

#### Oxo Tower

Oxo Tower Wharf, Barge House St, SE1 [ 7803 3888; www.harveynichols.com © L & D daily. **££££** (set lunch **£££**) [p327, E3]

**LEFT:** George Inn. **ABOVE RIGHT:** Cantina Vinopolis.

Some find it overpriced, but this iconic spot is still hugely popular. The biggest draw is the fabulous view of the Thames through huge windows.

### Le Pont de la Tour
Butlers Wharf Building, 36d Shad Thames, SE1 ☎ 7403 8403; www.lepontdela tour.co.uk ⓒ L & D daily. ££££ (set lunch £££) [p329, D4]
Prime ministers and presidents have enjoyed the splendid view of Tower Bridge from here, where the stress is on seafood. Impeccable but very expensive.

### Southwark Cathedral Refectory
Southwark Cathedral, London Bridge, SE1 ☎ 7407 5740 ⓒ B & L daily. £ [p328, B3]
This restaurant does hearty, well-priced soups and main dishes. The terrace is a bonus in summer. Open for morning coffee and afternoon tea (10am–6pm).

### Tate Modern Restaurant
Bankside, SE1 ☎ 7887 8888 ⓒ L daily, D Fri–Sat (last order 9.30pm). ££££ [p328, A3]

Great views, a buzz and an arty crowd are the attractions here. Level 2 Café is good for lunch, too, but lacks the views.

### Others

### Baltic
74 Blackfriars Rd, SE1 ☎ 7928 1111; www.baltic restaurant.co.uk ⓒ L & D daily. £££ [p327, E4]
A cool bar filled with media types leads to the skylit dining room. Eastern European dishes feature, such as roast pork and spiced meatballs. Alternatively, try vodka and blinis at the bar.

### The Cut Bar
Young Vic Theatre, 66 The Cut, SE1 ☎ 7928 4400; www.thecutbar.com ⓒ B, L & D Mon–Sat. ££ [p327, E4]
Set over 2 floors this stylish bar/restaurant serves burgers alongside an eclectic mix of dishes, such as Alpine salad or watermelon curry.

### Mesón Don Felipe
53 The Cut, SE1 ☎ 7928 3237; www.mesondonfelipe. com ⓒ L & D Mon–Sat. ££ [p327, E4]
Londoners in the know

flock to this excellent tapas bar. Tables fill up fast, but there's often room at the bar.

### Tapas Brindisa
18–20 Southwark St, SE1 ☎ 7357 8880; www. brindisa.com ⓒ B Fri–Sat, L daily, D Mon–Sat. £££ [p328, B3]
Connected to one of the most popular stalls in Borough market, this restaurant is usually

packed. Authentic tapas and a buzzing ambience. No reservations taken.

### Pubs, Bars and Cafés

In Chaucer's *Canterbury Tales*, the Miller declares, "And if the words get muddled in my tale, just put it down to too much Southwark ale." Sobriety has never been a characteristic of this area, which still has many pubs. The **George Inn** *(77 Borough High St)*, owned by the National Trust, is London's only galleried coaching inn. The **Market Porter** *(9 Stoney St)* is famous for opening its doors 6–8.30am for Borough Market workers.

For a traditional wine bar, try the **Boot and Flogger** *(10–20 Redcross Way; closes 8pm),* named after a corking device. Reminiscent of a gentleman's club, it was until recently a Free Vintner, meaning that it did not need a licence.

Other good places to drink include the Old Vic Theatre's **Pit Bar** *(The Cut; closed Sun),* which

opens late. The **Wine Wharf** *(Stoney St; closed Sun),* part of Vinopolis, offers great wines and light meals, while next door the **Brew Wharf** has a micro-brewery and does gastro-pub style food.

For cafés, try **Monmouth Coffee Co**. *(Stoney St),* **Konditor & Cook** *(22 Cornwall Rd and 10 Stoney St)* or **Café 171** *(171 Union Street)* for salads, omelettes and soup.

# TATE MODERN

**Once it generated electricity. Now it is is a powerhouse of modern and contemporary art**

Tate Modern has caught the public's imagination in a quite unprecedented way, both for its displays and its building, a magnificent presence on the South Bank. In 1998 the decision was taken to transform the redundant Bankside Power Station, a massive horizontal block with a huge central tower, into a gallery showcasing the Tate's collection of modern and contemporary art.

Machinery from within the power station was removed to create an entrance the height of the building; three gallery floors, shops and cafés, a restaurant and an auditorium were piled into a compact bank on one side. Visitors pour into the museum down a huge ramp, which is part of the towering Turbine Hall, used to accommodate large-scale installations.

On the way round, visitors can enjoy views into the Turbine Hall from the mezzanine bridge on level 2 and various gallery levels. Between the two suites on each of the gallery floors is seating where one can rest, read and watch the boats go by on the Thames.

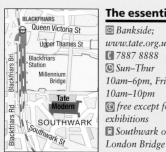

**ABOVE:** *Whaam!* by Roy Lichtenstein (1923–97), on show at Tate Modern. Lichtenstein's interest in Americana dated from the early 1950s, but his involvement in pop art received a crucial boost from one of his young sons, who showed him a Mickey Mouse comic book and said: "I bet you can't paint as good as that."

**LEFT:** *Lobster Telephone* by Salvador Dalí (1904–89). The gallery also owns four of Dalí's paintings and one of his prints, but do check beforehand if there is a piece you particularly wish to see, as some works may be out on loan.

## The essentials

✉ *Bankside;*
*www.tate.org.uk*
☎ *7887 8888*
🕐 *Sun–Thur 10am–6pm, Fri–Sat 10am–10pm*
🎟 *free except for special exhibitions*
🚇 *Southwark or London Bridge*

**ABOVE:** Chinese artist Ai Weiwei's *Sunflower Seeds*, one of the many installations that have graced the Turbine Hall. This installation was made up of around 100 million individually crafted ceramic 'seeds' that covered 1000 sq m (10,764 sq ft).

## THE COLLECTION

In order to make the permanent collection more accessible to, and more popular with, the general public, the works are ordered by theme. Note that the displays change from time to time, so the examples picked out here may not all be on show when you visit.

The permanent collection is hung in four suites, over two floors. On level 3 are "Material Gestures" and "Poetry and Dream". The former covers post-war European and American painting and sculpture, and includes work by Anish Kapoor, Barnett Newman, Claude Monet and Tacita Dean, while "Poetry and Dream" focuses on Surrealism, thus embracing the work of artists from Joan Miró, Max Ernst and Salvador Dalí to Francis Bacon, Joseph Beuys and Giorgio de Chirico. On level 5 are "Energy and Process" and "States of Flux", with the former showcasing artists, such as the Italian Arte Povera movement, who are interested in transformation and natural forces. "States of Flux" is devoted to Cubism, Futurism and Vorticism, with work by Georges Braque, Paul Cézanne, Fernand Léger, Roy Lichtenstein, Auguste Rodin, Henri Matisse and Bridget Riley.

**ABOVE:** *Little Dancer Aged Fourteen* by Edgar Degas (1834–1917). The original wax version outraged propriety when first exhibited in Paris in 1881.

**BELOW:** power station turned art gallery.

**ABOVE:** Kandinsky's *Swinging* (1925). Kandinsky began his artistic career as a figurative landscape painter in Russia, but moved towards abstraction through the influence of German Expressionism. He used colour for emotional effect. Also in Tate Modern's permanent collection is Kandinsky's *Cossacks* (1910–11).

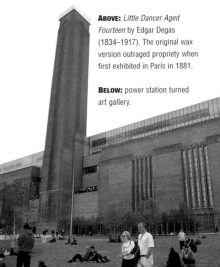

# THE IMPERIAL WAR MUSEUM

## It vividly chronicles a century of conflict around the world

The building that now houses the Imperial War Museum opened in 1815 as Bethlem Royal Hospital for the insane, popularly known as Bedlam. After the hospital moved out of London in the 1930s, the central block of the building was turned over to the Great War collection of the Imperial War Museum, previously housed in South Kensington. The former psychiatric hospital was an inspired choice for a museum chronicling the horrors of modern warfare.

After World War II the museum began to gather material from this and later conflicts, and three smaller sites, including the warship HMS *Belfast (see page 194)*, were acquired.

In recent years, the museum has expanded its remit from the purely military to include a rolling programme of exhibitions covering many aspects of modern history, some only loosely connected with conflict – from code breaking and refugees to fashion and sport.

**ABOVE:** the Imperial War Museum, formerly Bethlem Royal Hospital.

**LEFT:** some parts of the museum are harrowing and not recommended for young children. The **Holocaust Exhibition**, built around the testimonies of survivors and with poignant exhibits, is not recommended for children under 14.

**BELOW:** the details of the trench warfare of World War I are imaginatively conveyed in the "Trench Experience".

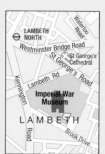

## The essentials

- ✉ *Lambeth Road;*
- *www.iwm.org.uk*
- 📞 *7416 5000*
- 🕐 *daily 10am–6pm*
- 💷 *free except for some special exhibitions*
- 🚇 *Elephant & Castle or Lambeth North*

## MUSEUM LAYOUT

As you enter the main hall, your direction will depend on where your interest lies. The stairs at the back of the **Large Exhibits Gallery** lead down to exhibitions on the two world wars. Here artefacts, art, photography, film and sound recordings weave an atmosphere as close as possible to the mood of the time, while interactive screens give access to further information. On the first floor is an extension of the Large Exhibits Gallery, along with the fascinating **Secret War** exhibit on counter-intelligence. The second floor holds one of Britain's leading collections of

**4**    Lord Ashcroft Gallery: The Extraordinary Heroes

**3**    Holocaust exhibition

**2**    Art galleries
Crimes against humanity
John Singer Sargent room
Temporary exhibitions

**1**    Secret War
Survival at Sea
Explore History Centre
Large exhibits

**G**    Ticket and Information desk
Large exhibits
Temporary exhibitions
Multimedia galleries
Shop and café

**Main entrance**

**LG**    First World War
Second World War
Conflicts Since 1945
Monty: Battlefield Master
Trench Experience
Blitz Experience

**West entrance**

**20th-century art** – the World War I gallery is to the right; World War II to the left. Many of the works were officially commissioned for propaganda purposes, including the famous painting *Gassed* in the **John Singer Sargent** room. The top floors house the **Holocaust Exhibition** and the **Lord Ashcroft Gallery**.

**ABOVE:** one of the museum's exhibits is the Blitz Experience, complete with realistic sounds and smells.
**BELOW AND RIGHT:** the Large Exhibits Gallery displays weapons, vehicles and planes from both World Wars, such as a gun from HMS *Lance* which fired the first British shot in WWI and a Spitfire and V2 rocket from WWII.

*Recommended Restaurants, Bars & Pubs on pages 212–13*

# KNIGHTSBRIDGE, KENSINGTON AND NOTTING HILL

**Wealthy and elegant, Knightsbridge and Kensington have long been the London home of the British upper classes, and the areas' cultural attractions reflect their dilettantish interests. Neighbouring Notting Hill Gate is more diverse and younger, with more edge**

These three areas of London encompass many of its best features: Knightsbridge has grand architecture, designer shops and two of London's top department stores; Kensington is home to three world-class museums and Queen Victoria's monuments to her husband Prince Albert; Notting Hill Gate, the stamping ground of the young, hip and famous, has Portobello Road, one of London's funkiest street markets.

In the heart of all this is a huge area of parkland, where you can skate, jog, hire a boat or just stroll around and forget you're in the city, and throughout the area are pretty cobbled mews and squares lined with elegant town houses that make venturing off the main streets rewarding.

This chapter begins at Hyde Park Corner, proceeds via Knightsbridge to Kensington and Notting Hill Gate, and then dips into Kensington Gardens and Hyde Park.

## HYDE PARK CORNER

At the junction of Piccadilly, Park Lane and Knightsbridge, **Hyde Park Corner** is a major hub of traffic now, but it used to stand on the outskirts of London.

## Apsley House ❶

✉ 149 Piccadilly, Hyde Park Corner; www.english-heritage.org.uk 📞 7499 5676 🕒 Apr–Oct Wed–Sun 11am–5pm, Nov–Mar weekends only 10am–4pm 💷 charge 🚇 Hyde Park Corner

The mansion on the northern side of Hyde Park Corner is known colloquially as No. 1, London, as it was the first house you came to after passing through the tollgates at the top of Knightsbridge. Built in 1770 by Robert Adam, and owned by

| Main attractions |
| --- |
| APSLEY HOUSE |
| HARRODS |
| VICTORIA AND ALBERT MUSEUM |
| NATURAL HISTORY MUSEUM |
| SCIENCE MUSEUM |
| ROYAL ALBERT HALL |
| ALBERT MEMORIAL |
| KENSINGTON SQUARE |
| HOLLAND PARK |
| NOTTING HILL |
| PORTOBELLO ROAD MARKET |
| KENSINGTON PALACE |
| KENSINGTON PALACE GARDENS |
| HYDE PARK |

**LEFT:** the Royal Albert Hall, a Grade I listed building, in South Kensington.
**RIGHT:** Apsley House at Hyde Park Corner.

*You can take a lift inside Wellington Arch up to the galleried balconies, from where there are good views all around, including into the gardens of Buckingham Palace.*

Arthur Wellesley, the first Duke of Wellington, in 1816, just after he had defeated Napoleon at Waterloo, it is still lived in by the Wellington family. Inside are collections of furniture, silver and porcelain, and paintings by Velázquez, Rubens, Van Dyck and Goya. Among its sculptures is a huge nude of Napoleon by Canova.

**Wellington Arch ❷** (Apr–Oct Wed–Sun 10am–5pm, until 4pm Nov–early Dec; may close for functions so ring ahead, tel: 7930 2726; charge), in the middle of Hyde Park Corner, was designed in 1828 as part of a grand approach to London. The huge bronze statue of a charioteer and four horses (the *Quadriga*) depicts the angel of peace descending on the chariot of war.

## KNIGHTSBRIDGE

Running west of Hyde Park Corner is Knightsbridge, where you'll find two of London's most famous stores: Harrods and Harvey Nichols.

**Harvey Nichols ❸**, well known for its innovative window displays, opened on the corner of Knightsbridge and Sloane Street in the 1880s; with eight floors of fashion, beauty and home collections, it caters to a discerning – and affluent – clientele. The Fifth Floor is a very smart place to eat (*see page 213*).

## Harrods ❹

✉ 87–135 Brompton Road; www.harrods.com ☏ 7730 1234 🕐 Mon–Sat 10am–8pm, Sun noon–6pm Ⓤ Knightsbridge

Nearby in Brompton Road, **Harrods** is hard to miss, especially at night when it is brightly illuminated. The food hall is ornately decorated and sells a wide range of gourmet items; it's worth looking, even if you only come out with a tin of speciality tea. The store's famous January sales see the British lose their dignity in the scramble to save hundreds of pounds.

**Knightsbridge, Kensington and Notting Hill**

*Recommended Restaurants, Bars & Pubs on pages 212–13*

The store was started by Henry Charles Harrod when his grocery business opened in 1849, although the present building was opened in 1905. The Egyptian Al-Fayed brothers bought the store and other House of Fraser outlets for £615 million in 1983, and the flamboyant Mohamed Al-Fayed (whose son Dodi died with Princess Diana in the 1997 Paris car crash) owned the store until 2010, when he sold it to Qatar Holdings.

**Beauchamp Place ❺** (pronounced *Beecham*), a stylish street west of Harrods lined with designer stores and expensive restaurants, is the stamping ground of the well-heeled, including sundry royals.

Beyond Harrods, at the point where Brompton Road branches left, is the Roman Catholic **Brompton Oratory ❻** (www.bromptonoratory.com; daily 6.30am–8pm), a flamboyant Italian baroque building designed by a 29-year-old architect, Herbert Gribble. Opened in 1884, its huge dome, extravagant decor and gilded mosaics are seldom seen in British churches.

## SOUTH KENSINGTON

South Kensington exudes affluence; Christie's has an auction house here, in Old Brompton Road, and there are plenty of designer shops and up-market restaurants.

It's also very cosmopolitan: the Lycée Français is at 35 Cromwell Road, teaching the children of the many French people who live in the area, and the German Goethe Institute is in Princes Gate.

### Three Victorian museums

At the heart of South Kensington are three world-class museums: The Victoria and Albert Museum, The Natural History Museum and the Science Museum, which owe their existence to the spirit and enterprise of the Victorian age. In 1851, the Great Exhibition, held in Hyde Park, was an astonishing success. For the first time elements of the far-flung Victorian Empire were brought under the curious gaze of the public. The idea for the exhibition had come from Henry Cole (1808–82), chairman of the Society of Arts, and it had been taken up enthusiastically by Prince Albert.

More than 6 million visitors came to the park to see the Crystal Palace, and after it moved to Sydenham, south London, the following year, the profits were used to purchase 87

*A cabmen's shelter in front of the V&A Museum, one of 13 still dotted around London. Now Grade II-listed, they provide shelter and refreshment for cab drivers.*

**LEFT:** luxury fragrances at Harrods, which lights up at night (**BELOW**).

*Figures in the Cast Court at the V&A.*

acres (35 hectares) of land in adjoining South Kensington to build a more permanent home for the arts and sciences.

Greatest of them all is undoubtedly the **Victoria and Albert Museum** ❼, popularly known as the V&A, which Henry Cole began assembling the year after the Great Exhibition, though Queen Victoria did not lay the foundation stone of the current building until 1899, 38 years after Albert died. It was the first museum to be gas-lit, allowing working people to visit in the evening after finishing their jobs. *For a detailed guide to its collections, see pages 216–17.*

On the other side of Exhibition Road is the neo-Gothic pile of the **Natural History Museum** ❽, built between 1873 and 1880. With its collection of 75 million plants, animals, fossils, rocks and minerals and, of course, its dinosaurs, it is justly celebrated and a big hit with children. *For details, see pages 218–19.*

The **Science Museum** ❾, round the corner in Exhibition Road, traces the history of inventions from the first steam train – Stephenson's Rocket –

**RIGHT:** detail on the intricately carved stonework of the Natural History Museum.
**BELOW LEFT AND RIGHT:** central hall and facade of the Natural History Museum.

to the battered command module from the Apollo 10 space mission, and is a particular favourite of children. The Wellcome Wing focuses on contemporary science and technology. *See pages 214–15 for more details.*

On the corner of Queen's Gate Terrace, opposite the Natural History Museum, is **Baden-Powell House**, with a statue of the Boy Scouts' founder standing on watch outside. It is now a budget hostel, but there is a small exhibition area dedicated to Lord Baden-Powell (1857–1941).

*Recommended Restaurants, Bars & Pubs on pages 212–13*

## Music and geography

Further up Exhibition Road, on Prince Consort Road, is the **Royal College of Music**, containing the **Museum of Instruments**  (www. rcm.ac.uk; Tue–Fri 2–4.30pm in term time and summer holidays only; tel: 7591 4300; free), a collection of over 1,000 instruments from 1480 to the present.

On the corner of Exhibition Road and Kensington Gore is the **Royal Geographical Society** (www.rgs.org; Tue–Fri 10am–5pm; tel: 7591 30 00). Exhibitions are held in the new extension, and for a small fee you can visit the library, which holds many antiquarian maps.

## Royal Albert Hall ⑪

✉ Kensington Gore; www.royalalbert hall.com ☎ 0845 401 5045 (tickets and tours) 🚇 South Kensington

The **Royal Albert Hall**, an ornate building with a capacity of 5,500, was opened in 1871 in honour of Prince Albert. The frieze around the outside illustrates "The Triumph of Arts and Sciences". Events here range from boxing to rock concerts, but the hall is best known for the Proms, a series of BBC-sponsored classical concerts. Named after the promenading audience, they provide a rich diet of affordable music.

Queen Victoria's most expressive tribute to her husband is the **Albert Memorial** ⑫ in Kensington Gardens, opposite the Albert Hall. Designed by Sir George Gilbert Scott, it depicts the prince as a god or philosopher, clutching in his right hand the catalogue of the Great Exhibition which he masterminded. Marking the corners of the monument are symbols for the spread of the British Empire: a camel for Africa, a bull bison for America, an elephant for Asia and a cow for Europe (Australia, then the Empire's dumping ground for convicts, failed to merit a mention).

In a 1960s building next door to the Albert Hall is the **Royal College of Art**, where annual graduation exhibitions allow the public to buy the works of future greats. David Hockney and Henry Moore studied here.

*The Albert Memorial has been restored to its former gilded – some say gaudy – glory.*

**BELOW:** frieze running around the Albert Hall.

## Prince Albert

**A**lbert of Saxe-Coburg-Gotha (pictured), born in Germany in 1819, was Queen Victoria's first cousin. When they married in 1839, both aged 20, his English was limited, but he worked to improve it. He enjoyed hunting and winter sports, and sired nine children. His great interest in the sciences and the natural world made him a typical Victorian and he was largely responsible for establishing the museums in South Kensington. Victoria was shattered when he died in 1861, spending the next 40 years mourning.

**KIDS**

Holland Park is great for kids. As well as the wildlife – rabbits, peacocks and squirrels – there is an adventure playground (for ages 6–15 approximately), and a smaller sand pit play area for children under 8. After they've let off steam, take them to the Japanese garden, which has a waterfall and stepping stones.

**RIGHT:** detail of an Islamic tile in Leighton House Museum.
**BELOW:** Edward Burne-Jones's house in Kensington Square.

## KENSINGTON HIGH STREET

Kensington Gore runs into Kensington High Street, a useful shopping area, more compact and stylish than Oxford Street but with most of the big-name stores and fewer people. **Kensington Church Street**, branching off to the right towards Notting Hill Gate, is the place for antiques. On the corner behind the flower stall stands **St Mary Abbots Church** ⓭, designed by Victorian architect Sir George Gilbert Scott, and a fine example of Victorian Gothic Revival. Walk through the cloisters to reach St Mary Abbots Gardens, a quiet spot away from the crowds. To the right, Kensington Church Walk is lined with exclusive boutiques. At the top, Holland Street, running off Kensington Church Street, has designer shops and a pretty pub, the Elephant and Castle.

Back on Kensington High Street, walk down Derry Street to the entrance to the **Roof Gardens** (tel: 7937 7994; call to check opening hours), a members' club and restaurant (Babylon, *see page 213*), six storeys above street level. With 1½ acres of ornamental gardens and

views over west London, this is one of the most original places to eat in the city. The gardens are themed with Spanish and English woodland areas and have resident flamingos.

Further down Derry Street is **Kensington Square** ⓮, one of the oldest in London, and an elegant mix of architectural styles dating from the late 17th century. The Pre-Raphaelite painter Edward Burne-Jones lived at No. 41, and the philosopher John Stuart Mill, another eminent Victorian, at No. 18.

At the other end of Kensington High Street is **Leighton House Museum** ⓯ (12 Holland Park Road; Wed–Mon 10am–5.30pm, free guided tour Wed 3pm; tel: 7602 3316; charge). The red-brick exterior conceals an extraordinary interior. The home of the Victorian artist Lord Leighton (1830–96), president of the Royal Academy, it is a mix of lavish Orientalism and conventional Victorian comforts. It contains his highly romanticised works, as well as many by fellow Pre-Raphaelites, but the centrepiece of the house is the grand Arab Hall, displaying Leighton's collection of Islamic tiles.

South of here is cosmopolitan **Earl's Court**, named after the earls of Oxford who owned the land in the 12th century. It is famous for its massive exhibition centre, built in

*Recommended Restaurants, Bars & Pubs on pages 212–13*

1937, which will host the volleyball events in the 2012 Olympics.

To the west is **Olympia**, another exhibition centre. To the north is **Holland Park** ⓰, the grounds of the Jacobean Holland House, mostly destroyed in World War II. Peacocks preen among the formal gardens, and the ruins provide an appealing set for open-air concerts. For refreshments, try the restaurant in the Orangery, or the more informal café nearby.

## NOTTING HILL

The northeastern exit of Holland Park leads to Holland Park Avenue, at the top of which is Notting Hill Gate, one of the hip areas of London.

## Portobello Road Market ⓱

Portobello Road; www.portobello road.co.uk  Mon–Wed and Fri–Sat 8am–6pm, Thur 8am–1pm; antiques market Sat 8am–6pm  Ladbroke Grove or Notting Hill Gate

On Saturdays, Notting Hill's Portobello Road is home to a vast antiques market. The antiques are concentrated in the more genteel southern end of the street, while further north, under the Westway flyover, a flea market mixes junk, cutting-edge fashion and arts and crafts (Fri–Sun). Between these two, the traditional fruit, veg and flower stalls mix with traders selling global foodstuffs.

As a backdrop to the stalls, the refurbished **Electric Cinema** is London's oldest surviving cinema (1905).

Off Portobello Road, on Blenheim Crescent, is the **Travel Bookshop**, the setting for the 1999 romantic comedy *Notting Hill*, in which Hugh Grant improbably wooed Julia Roberts. What the film didn't convey is that Notting Hill is a melting pot in which several races and just about every social class rub shoulders.

### Ladbroke Grove

Notting Hill's main north–south artery, **Ladbroke Grove**, is the parade route for the **Notting Hill Carnival**, a three-day Caribbean festival which takes over the area on the last weekend of August. West of Notting Hill (Shepherd's Bush or White City tube stations) is **Westfield**, Europe's largest shopping centre with over 300 shops.

*Turquoise Island in Westbourne Grove is home to Notting Hill's funkiest public toilets and a florist's.*

**BELOW LEFT:** Farm Place, Notting Hill Gate. **BELOW:** antiques dealers' shops line Portobello Road.

*Dating from 1912, Peter Pan's statue in Kensington Gardens was erected secretly one night so it might seem as if it had appeared by magic.*

**RIGHT:** Kensington Palace's sunken garden. **BELOW:** Horse Guards near Kensington Palace.

## QUEENSWAY AND KENSINGTON GARDENS

Westbourne Grove heads eastwards to **Queensway** ⑱, home to Whiteleys Shopping Centre, which has cafés, restaurants and a cinema. At the top of Queensway, past the ice rink, is Kensington Gardens.

London's great green lung is **Hyde Park** and **Kensington Gardens**, which cover 1 sq mile (2.5 sq km) – the same area as the City of London. Although they are a single open space, they are two distinct parks, divided by West Carriage Drive.

### Kensington Palace ⑲

✉ Kensington Gardens; www.hrp.org.uk ⏱ daily 10am–6pm
📞 0844 482 7777 @ charge
Ⓣ Notting Hill Gate or Queensway

On the west side of Kensington Gardens, overlooking the Round Pond, is **Kensington Palace**, the former home of Diana, Princess of Wales.

The palace was given its present appearance by Sir Christopher Wren and Nicholas Hawksmoor, and was the centre of the Court after William

III bought the mansion in 1689. Several monarchs were born here, the last of them Victoria in 1819, who 18 years later was called from her bed to be told she had become Queen.

The palace has just undergone a £12 million redevelopment, making previously unseen areas open to the public. A new display focuses on Princess Diana's clothes and style, while another new exhibition explores Queen Victoria's story, with visitors being able to see the room in which she was born and the spot where she met Prince Albert.

Around the palace grounds are an attractive sunken garden and an **Orangery**, designed by Nicholas Hawksmoor in 1704 and modified by Sir John Vanbrugh. It has wood carvings by Grinling Gibbons and is now a café *(see page 212)*.

A path east of the gilded main gates of Kensington Palace leads to **Kensington Palace Gardens**. The lake on the eastern side (called The Long Water here, and the Serpentine in Hyde Park) has, at its northern edge, the delightful **Italian Garden**, commissioned by Prince Albert, with fountains and a statue of Edward Jenner, who developed the vaccination against smallpox. The loggia in Italian Renaissance-style was originally the fountains' pumphouse.

*Recommended Restaurants, Bars & Pubs on pages 212–13*

Along the path by the water is a statue, by George Frampton, of J.M. Barrie's **Peter Pan** – the full title of this classic children's story is *Peter Pan in Kensington Gardens*.

The **Serpentine Gallery 20** (www. serpentinegallery.org; daily 10am–6pm; tel: 7402 6075; free) by the road bridge is a dynamic exhibition space for contemporary art.

## HYDE PARK

Across the road is **Hyde Park** which, as the *Domesday Book* of 1086 records, was inhabited by wild bulls and boars. First owned by the monks of Westminster Abbey, it was turned into a royal hunting ground

by Henry VIII and then opened to the public in the 17th century. The **Serpentine 21** was created in the 1730s as a royal boating lake, and boats can still be hired from the north bank. **Rotten Row**, William III's Route du Roi, running along the southern edge, is where the Household Cavalry, based in the barracks on Knightsbridge, exercise their horses.

The **Princess Diana Memorial Fountain 22**, a ring of flowing water surrounding a landscaped area, was designed by Seattle-based landscape architect Kathryn Gustafson.

At the northeast corner, near Marble Arch, is **Speakers' Corner 23**, where anyone can pull up a soap box and sound off, especially on Sunday afternoons. This tradition goes back to when the Tyburn gallows stood here (1388–1783; *see page 118*) and condemned felons were allowed to make a final unexpurgated speech to the crowds before being hanged. Close by, in Park Lane, is the monument **Animals in War**, a reminder of the role played by millions of animals in warfare.                  ❑

**KIDS**

In the northwestern corner of Kensington Gardens is the popular Diana Memorial Playground, perhaps a more fitting tribute to the princess than the Princess Diana Memorial Fountain.

**LEFT:** marking the 7-mile (11km) -long urban parkland Memorial Walk.
**BELOW:** the Italian Garden, Hyde Park.

# BEST RESTAURANTS, BARS AND PUBS

## Restaurants

Prices for a three-course dinner per person with a half bottle of house wine:
**£** = under £20
**££** = £20–30
**£££** = £30–50
**££££** = over £50

### British

#### Geales
2 Farmer St, Notting Hill Gate, W8 ℂ 7727 7528; www.geales.com ⓒ L Tue–Sun, D daily. **££** [p334, B3]
An up-market fish and chip restaurant which has been keeping locals happy for years.

#### The Orangery
Kensington Gardens, W8 ℂ 0844 482 7777 ⓒ Mar–Sept daily 10am–6pm, Oct–Feb 10am–5pm. **£££** [p324, A3]
In a magnificent building designed for Queen Anne in 1704, this is the place to come for traditional afternoon tea. Light lunches also served.

### French

#### Bibendum
Michelin House, 81 Fulham Rd, SW3 ℂ Restaurant: 7581 5817; Oyster Bar: 7589 1480; www. bibendum.co.uk ⓒ L & D daily. **££££** (set lunch **£££**) [p331, C2]
Opened by Sir Terence Conran and Paul Hamlyn in 1987, Bibendum continues to thrive; there's an oyster bar on the ground floor and a restaurant on the first floor of this individual Art Deco-style building.

#### Racine
239 Brompton Rd, SW3 ℂ 7584 4477; www.racine-restaurant.com ⓒ L & D daily. **££–£££** [p331, C1]
A real taste of France in the heart of London. The menu features classic French dishes like steak tartare, while indulgent desserts might include rich chocolate terrine.

### Indian

#### Bombay Brasserie
Courtfield Rd, SW7 ℂ 7370 4040; www.bombay brasserielondon.com ⓒ L & D daily, last orders midnight. **£££** (set lunch **££**) [p330, B2]
This up-market Indian has rejuvenated its classic menu and deserves its reputation for good, if expensive, food. Book a table in the conservatory.

#### Malabar
27 Uxbridge St, Notting Hill Gate, W8 ℂ 7727 8800; www.malabar-restaurant. co.uk ⓒ L & D daily. **££** [p334, B2]
Uses fresh herbs, whole spices and gives an innovative twist to traditional dishes. Good value buffet lunch on Sundays.

#### Zaika
1 Kensington High St, W8 ℂ 7795 6533; www.zaika-restaurant.co.uk ⓒ L Tue–Sun, D daily. **££££** (set lunch **££**) [p334, C2]
The name translates as "sophisticated flavours" and this is what you get, with the menu mixing traditional favourites with "new" Eastern dishes. Plenty of unusual vegetarian options too.

### Italian

#### Osteria Basilico
29 Kensington Park Rd, Notting Hill, W11 ℂ 7727 9957; www.osteriabasilico. co.uk ⓒ L & D daily. **£££** [p334, A1]
Established in 1992, this place buzzes with a Notting Hill crowd. Friendly staff serve classic Italian home cooking and pizzas. Booking is recommended.

#### San Lorenzo
22 Beauchamp Place, SW3 ℂ 7584 1074; www.san lorenzo.com ⓒ L & D Mon–Sat. **££££** [p331, D1]
A swanky Knightsbridge venue patronised by fashion, music and media moguls, as well as royals. The food is not as noteworthy as the clientele.

**LEFT:** the Orangery, Kensington Gardens. **ABOVE RIGHT:** salads in Ottolenghi. **RIGHT:** Elbow Room, Notting Hill.

Chef Marcus Wareing has 2 Michelin stars for his cooking at this hotel restaurant. Serves plenty of British produce, such as Aberdeen Angus beef and Cornish seabass.

### Ottolenghi
63 Ledbury Rd, Notting Hill W11 ☎ 7727 1121. Also at 1 Holland St, Kensington W8 ☎ 7937 0003. ◷ Mon–Fri 8am–8pm, Sat 8am–7pm and Sun 8.30am–6pm. ££ [p334, B1]
Fabulous fresh food made on the premises – sit at the communal table or take away. The Kensington branch is take away only, perfect for a picnic.

### The Terrace
33c Holland St, Kensington W8 ☎ 7937 3224; www.theterracerestaurant. co.uk ◷ Brunch Sat–Sun, L & D Mon–Sat. £££ [p334, B3]
On fine days you can sit outside at this small restaurant. Serves main courses such as duck breast with spring onion mash and cabbage.

## Modern European

### Babylon
The Roof Gardens, 7th Floor, 99 Kensington High St, W8 ☎ 7368 3993; www.roof gardens.virgin.com ◷ L daily, D Mon–Sat. ££££ (set lunch ££) [p334, C4]
This Richard Branson-owned modern restaurant overlooks 1½ acres of gardens, with great views of London. The food lives up to the spectacular setting.

### Clarke's
122–4 Kensington Church St, W8 ☎ 7221 9225; www.sallyclarke.com ◷ L daily, D Mon–Sat. ££££ (set menu £££) [p334, B3]
Colchester crab with Irish smoked salmon, dill flat-bread and pea leaves is a classic dish. High-quality ingredients treated simply is key to the restaurant's success. A bakery supplies divine fresh bread.

### Fifth Floor
Harvey Nichols, 109–125 Knightsbridge, SW1 ☎ 7235 5250 ◷ L daily, D Mon–Sat. £££–££££ [p325, D4]
A postmodern space popular with media types and models offering an effective combination of big flavours and light dishes.

### Kensington Place
201–9 Kensington Church St, W8 ☎ 7727 3184; www.kensingtonplace-restaurant.co.uk ◷ L & D daily. £££ (set lunch £–££) [p334, B2]
A trailblazer of the Modern European scene, it still serves simple yet inventive good food. Noise levels are high.

### Marcus Wareing at The Berkeley
Wilton Place, Knightsbridge, SW1 ☎ 7235 6000 ◷ L Mon–Fri, D Mon–Sat, ££££ (set lunch £££) [p325, D4]

## Bars and Pubs

The best bars are found in the area's grand hotels where extravagant cocktails are mixed in the elegant and refined spaces of sumptuous living – places such as the **Library Bar** in the Lanesborough Hotel on Hyde Park Corner, the **Blue Bar** in the Berkeley Hotel in Wilton Place, and the **Mandarin Bar** in the Mandarin Oriental in Knightsbridge. Those looking for something a bit more funky can try the **Beauchamp** (43 Beauchamp Place), **Montgomery Place** (31 Kensington Park Road) or **The Elbow Room** (103 Westbourne Grove) with its plasma TVs and seven pool tables.

Good food is to be found in pubs these days, especiallly in "gastro-pubs", where the quality of the food is high on the agenda.

Here are a few of the best: **Anglesea Arms** (15 Selwood Terrace, South Kensington), the **Cross Keys** (1 Lawrence St, Chelsea), **The Abingdon** (54 Abingdon Rd), **Churchill Arms** (119 Kensington Church Street), **Windsor Castle** (114 Campden Hill Road), **The Cow** (89 Westbourne Park Road, and **The Fat Badger** (310 Portobello Road).

# THE SCIENCE MUSEUM

This museum is an astounding tribute to the ingenuity of human beings over the centuries

With more than 10,000 exhibits, plus additional attractions such as an IMAX theatre and "Launchpad", an interactive play area for children, this museum could take days to explore, so it is best to assign priorities before you start.

An important point to note is the distinction between the main wing, dating to 1928 and containing the classic steam engines and planes, and the Wellcome Wing, opened in 2000, concentrating on information technology. You can walk between the two wings at five of the museum's seven levels, but the ambience of the wings is quite different and it is more satisfying to explore one wing at a time.

**ABOVE:** The Making the Modern World gallery brings together many of the museum's most exciting exhibits. "Modern" is defined as post-1750 and the stars include the world's oldest surviving steam locomotive, the coal-hauling Puffing Billy (circa 1815), a Ford Model T (1916), a Lockheed Electra airliner hanging in silvery splendour from the ceiling (1935), a copy of Crick and Watson's DNA double helix model (1953) and the Apollo 10 command module (left, 1969).

**BELOW:** the first gallery you enter is the Energy Hall, dominated by a 1903 mill engine.

## The essentials

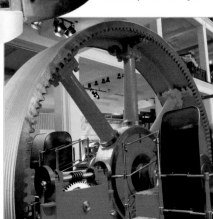

✉ *Exhibition Road, SW7; www.sciencemuseum. org.uk*

☏ *0870 870 4868*

🕐 *daily 10am–6pm*

🎟 *free except for some special exhibitions, the IMAX cinema and simulators*

🚇 *South Kensington*

## OTHER HIGHLIGHTS

The Wellcome Wing *(above)* looks to the future rather than the past. On the ground floor, Antenna is a series of changing exhibits based around current science news, while an IMAX film theatre conjures up dinosaurs or outer space. The theme of the first floor is "Who am I?", asking such questions as "How does your brain make you so special?" and "Do we all come from Africa?". In Future, on the third floor, is a series of large digital board games on which contestants are invited to vote on health, communications and lifestyle topics – for example, "Should men be allowed to give birth?".

The Flight Gallery (third floor) is a favourite with all ages; exhibits range from a seaplane to a Spitfire, from hot-air balloons to helicopters. The 1919 Vickers Vimy in which Alcock and Brown made the first non-stop transatlantic flight is here, as is Amy Johnson's *Gipsy Moth Jason*. There's also a replica of the Wright Flyer in which Wilbur and Orville Wright pioneered powered flight in 1903.

The Launchpad (third floor) for older kids is packed with experiments they can try out; "explainers" help them understand what's going on. There are over 50 interactive exhibits from the world of physics, such as a thermal imaging camera.

The Secret Life of the Home (basement) displays domestic appliances and gadgets, with buttons to press and levers to pull, two of which show the internal workings of a flushing lavatory and a CD player.

**ABOVE:** the ever-popular Exploring Space gallery has been revamped to include a range of new exhibits, including the huge Spacelab 2 x-ray telescope – the actual instrument that was flown on the Space Shuttle – and full-size models of the Huygens Titan probe and Beagle 2 Mars Lander. The replica of the Apollo 11 lunar excursion module has been reconfigured to a new level of accuracy.

**RIGHT:** The Rocket, George Stephenson's 1829 passenger locomotive, is on display in the Making of the Modern World gallery.

# VICTORIA AND ALBERT MUSEUM

**The world's largest collection of decorative and applied arts covers everything from massive sculptures to knitting**

With 5 million objects and almost 8 miles (13km) of galleries, the Victoria and Albert Museum (founded in 1852) is colossal. Its exhibits range from exquisite Persian miniatures to a whole room designed by Frank Lloyd Wright. One minute one can be admiring Raphael's cartoons for the tapestries in the Sistine Chapel, and the next examining E.H. Shepard's illustrations for *Winnie-the-Pooh* or admiring a plaster cast of Michelangelo's *David* (left).

The museum is undergoing a 10-year refurbishment. So far, the British Galleries have received a major overhaul and the Islamic Galleries have been redesigned with the superb Ardabil carpet, the oldest carpet in the world, as a centrepiece. The Ceramics galleries include porcelain animals crafted for Augustus the Strong, while highlights from the Gilbert collection (gold and silver objects, and enamel portrait miniatures), are in rooms 70–73.

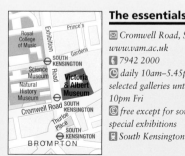

## The essentials

✉ *Cromwell Road, SW7; www.vam.ac.uk*
📞 *7942 2000*
🕐 *daily 10am–5.45pm, selected galleries until 10pm Fri*
🎟 *free except for some special exhibitions*
🚇 *South Kensington*

**ABOVE:** an immense glass sculpture by the American glass artist Dale Chihuly hangs in the foyer of the Cromwell Road entrance.

**RIGHT:** a British Empire builder is savaged in *Tippoo's Tiger* (Mysore, 1793), in the South Asia Gallery.

**TOP:** the British Galleries document British taste, exploring "what was hot and what was new from the time of Henry VIII and the Tudors to William Morris". The exhibits include the Great Bed of Ware, a 16th-century four poster.

**Above:** the Iranian Ardabil carpet (1539–40) in the Jameel Gallery of Islamic arts.

## OTHER HIGHLIGHTS

**The Sculpture Courts.** British and neoclassical works from the late 18th and early 19th centuries.
**Plaster Casts.** Fine copies, from Trajan's Column to Michelangelo's *David*.
**Raphael Cartoons (1515–6).** Templates for a series of tapestries in the Sistine Chapel.
**Medieval and Renaissance.** Renaissance pieces include Andrea Briosco's 16th-century *Shouting Horseman*.
**The Fashion Galleries.** Fashions through the ages from the 18th century to the present day.
**The Ceramic Staircase.** Completed in 1869, it symbolises the relationship between art and science.
**The Hereford Screen.** An intricate choir screen (1862) studded with semi-precious stones.
**Henry Cole Wing.** Prints, drawings, paintings and photographs ranging from John Constable's paintings to Beatrix Potter's watercolours. Don't miss the Frank Lloyd Wright Gallery.
**Refreshment Rooms.** Three fabulously ornate café interiors from the 19th century, interlinked and opening onto the courtyard garden.
**The Museum Shop.** Quite simply irresistible.

**ABOVE:** platform shoes in stamped leather by Vivienne Westwood (1993). Recently re-opened after restoration, the Fashion Galleries display temporary exhibitions.

# THE NATURAL HISTORY MUSEUM

This colossal collection has 75 million plants, animals, fossils, rocks and minerals – and it's growing by 50,000 new specimens a year

If any of London's museums encapsulates the Victorians' quest for knowledge and passion for cataloguing data, it's this one. Yet, in spite of its vast size, the layout is easy to master due to colour coded zones: the Red Zone (entrance on Exhibition Road), the Green Zone, which looks at Earth's ecology, the Blue Zone, which investigates earth's biodiversity, and the Orange Zone covering the wildlife garden and the Darwin Centre.

One of the museum's greatest delights is the way it presents high-tech exhibits alongside beautifully kept Victorian-style galleries filled with meticulously labelled cabinets. Many of the latter are found in quiet by-ways of the museum, but one vintage member of the collection is the wood and plaster model of a blue whale, which has been the centrepiece of the Mammals section since being built in 1938.

**ABOVE:** the Central Hall of the museum. The extravagant Gothic Romanesque building, by architect Alfred Waterhouse, was the first in Britain to be faced entirely in terracotta. Its soaring arches and rich ornamental detail bring to mind a cathedral, an effect intended by Sir Richard Owen, the superintendent of the collection. Owen wanted the building to be a temple of nature.

**ABOVE:** the skeleton and dramatic full-size model of a blue whale is a big attraction. Many families also make a bee-line for the Dinosaurs section (Life Galleries), the highlight of which is a full-scale animatronic T-Rex that roars and twists convincingly, impressing most children.

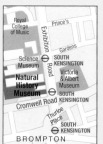

## The essentials

✉ *Cromwell Road, SW7; www.nhm.ac.uk*
☎ *7942 5000*
🕐 *daily 10am–5.50pm*
🎫 *free except for some special exhibitions*
🚇 *South Kensington*

## OTHER HIGHLIGHTS

**Investigate (basement)**. Here *(above)* children can touch, weigh, measure and examine under a microscope a range of specimens. A team of explainers is on hand to help. There is also an outdoor section where children can inspect pond life close up.

**Human Biology**. This section is packed with interactive exhibits: you can test your memory and senses or be tricked by optical illusions.

**Mammals**. As well as displaying an astonishing array of taxidermy, these galleries contain sobering statistics on the rapid rate at which species are becoming extinct.

**Creepy Crawlies**. Wander through a house and learn about the many uninvited housemates in an average home. Sit in a life-size model of a termite mound or watch a colony of leaf-cutter ants.

**Earth's Treasury**. This conveys the planet's beauty, displaying rocks, gems and minerals glittering in the gallery's semi-darkness.

**The Jerwood Gallery**. This houses a superb collection of watercolours, oils, prints and drawings, some of which are the original illustrations to books by 19th-century explorers.

**The Darwin Centre**. Opened in 2009, this new, cocoon-shaped centre for scientific study and repository for 20 million specimens gives visitors the opportunity to see scientists in action.

**The Wildlife Garden** *(the West Lawn)*. There's a tour twice daily in spring and summer. This lush spot is a refreshing way to end a visit.

**LEFT:** a cross-section of a giant redwood.
**BELOW:** An escalator transports visitors into a vast globe, the entrance to the Earth Galleries, where Restless Surface covers earthquakes and volcanoes. The tremors of an earthquake are simulated in a mock-up of a Japanese mini-market.

BANHAM
0171
637 1414

24

Recommended Restaurants, Pubs, Bars & Cafés on pages 228–9

# CHELSEA

Backing on to a secluded stretch of the Thames, Chelsea has tranquil gardens, royal connections and a village feel. It also has a strong bohemian side. Running through it is the King's Road, the centre of Swinging London in the 1960s and, later, of punk

S andwiched between Kensington and the Thames, Chelsea's tranquil enclaves still hint at the riverside hamlet it was until the late 18th century. Despite a modest character, by the 16th century Chelsea had become known as a "Village of Palaces", with strong royal links – King Henry VIII among them – and was destined to be the site of Wren's Royal Hospital in 1682.

A reputation for art took root with the Chelsea Porcelain Works and the illustrations generated by the Chelsea Physic Garden's botanical publications. By the 19th century, a bohemian set had moved in wholesale, including the painters Rossetti, Whistler and Sargent and writers such as George Eliot (and later, T.S. Eliot).

## BELGRAVIA TO SLOANE SQUARE

When the squares and terraces of Belgravia were built around 1824, these streets west of Hyde Park Corner were intended to rival Mayfair. From Knightsbridge, the best entrance to Belgravia is via **Wilton Place**. The stucco terraces were developed by architect Thomas Cubitt, who gave his name to the modern construction company known for its motorway

bridges. Like much of Mayfair, **Belgrave Square** is largely occupied by embassies and various societies and associations. The square usually has a heavy police presence.

**Eaton Square**, to the south, is more residential. However, many of its supposed residents live in other parts of the world and the houses are dark and obviously under-used. Chopin gave his first London recital here at No. 88.

In 1895 the playwright Oscar Wilde was arrested in the Cadogan Hotel in Sloane Street, tried and sent

**Main attractions**

SLOANE SQUARE
ROYAL COURT THEATRE
KING'S ROAD
DUKE OF YORK SQUARE
OLD CHELSEA TOWN HALL
ST LUKE'S CHURCH
ROYAL HOSPITAL
NATIONAL ARMY MUSEUM
CHELSEA PHYSIC GARDEN
CHEYNE WALK
THE EMBANKMENT
CARLYLE'S HOUSE
CHELSEA OLD CHURCH

**LEFT:** Chelsea has a large number of mews houses. **RIGHT:** fashionista in Chelsea.

to prison for his homosexual conduct. Sloane Street leads from Knightsbridge to **Sloane Square ❶**, where **Chelsea** proper begins. On the east side of the square is the **Royal Court Theatre**, where John Osborne's mould-breaking anti-establishment play *Look Back in Anger* was first staged in 1956. The company still has a robust reputation for shaping the classics of the future.

Sloane Square was named after a physician, Sir Hans Sloane (1660–1753), whose personal collection formed the basis of what is now the British Museum. He laid out much of

this area and his name crops up often on street plans. He also unwittingly gave his name to a typical young upper-class urbanite living in Chelsea in the 1980s: the Sloane Ranger, a lady in flat shoes, pearls, gathered skirt and a quilted jacket.

## ALONG THE KING'S ROAD

Until 1829 the **King's Road ❷**, leading west from Sloane Square, was a private royal road leading from Hampton Court to the court of King James. It rose to fame during the 1960s, and was later linked to punk fashions, after Vivienne Westwood

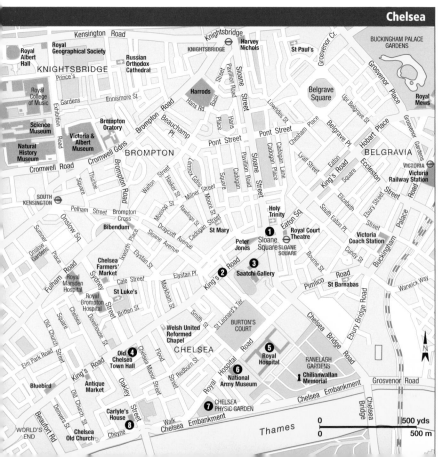

now houses the **Saatchi Gallery**, which moved here in 2007 (www.saatchi-gallery.co.uk). It contains the work of contemporary British artists assembled by former advertising mogul Charles Saatchi. In recent years the collection's bias has shifted towards paintings and away from works such as Damien Hirst's celebrated sheep in formaldehyde solution.

## Old Chelsea Town Hall ❹

Prettily painted 18th- and 19th-century terraces leading off the King's Road have a tradition of housing artists and intellectuals. On the left-hand side of the road opposite Sydney Street stands the Old Chelsea Town Hall. The old borough of Royal Kensington, given its royal appellation by Queen Victoria in 1901, was merged much against its wishes with Chelsea in 1965, and took over the administration of both. The Old Chelsea Town Hall continues to provide a cultural and social focus for residents. The Register Office next door is well-known for society and celebrity weddings.

Duke of York Square includes a pedestrian enclave of up-market homeware and fashion units (Myla, Joseph, Space.nk, etc), cafés and a seasonal ice rink. Partridges the grocers organises a regular Saturday food market outside their shop (10am–4pm).

and Malcolm McLaren opened their designer shop, Sex, at No. 430 in 1972. Westwood still sells her designs from these premises, renamed World's End, which is what this part of Chelsea is called. Sloane Square's GTC (General Trading Company), and Peter Jones department store are also long-established shops.

## Duke of York Square ❸

Lately, the biggest innovation on the King's Road's retail front has been the redevelopment of the Duke of York's Headquarters, formerly a military campus. The main building with its Tuscan portico (1801), designed as a school for the orphans of soldiers,

**FAR LEFT:** the Royal Court Theatre.
**LEFT:** home furnishings on the King's Road.
**BELOW LEFT AND RIGHT:** a wedding at Chelsea Register Office.

*The Chelsea Pensioners, who live in the Royal Hospital, are service veterans. They are given board and lodging, nursing care and a small allowance, including a pint of beer a day.*

**BELOW:** enjoying a drink at Chelsea Farmers' Market.

## SYDNEY STREET

In 1836, Charles Dickens was married more conventionally – in **St Luke's**, a stunning Gothic church halfway up Sydney Street, running north of the King's Road. Eagle-eyed Disney fans may recognise it from the 1996 film version of *101 Dalmatians*. If the weather is fine its gardens are a lovely spot to unwind.

Sydney Street is also home to the popular Chelsea Gardener nursery and the **Chelsea Farmers' Market**, a small shopping enclave with a boho feel thanks to its organic supermarket and one-storey clapboard units where the emphasis is on natural remedies and ingredients.

At the top of Sydney Street is

**Brompton Cross**, a network of streets containing up-market shops and restaurants, including Bibendum *(see page 212)*, in the Art Deco-style former headquarters of the Michelin Tyre Company on Fulham Road.

## HOSPITAL ROAD

Among the leggy would-be models gliding along the King's Road are uniformed old gents with the initials RH on their caps. These are Chelsea Pensioners, retired war veterans who live in the **Royal Hospital**, built by Christopher Wren in 1692 on Royal Hospital Road. From the King's Road, a practically uninterrupted vista is afforded down the length of **Royal Avenue**, the hospital perfectly framed in the distance. The gravelled boulevard now lined with 19th-century houses was laid out by Wren with the purpose of providing a direct route from the hospital to Kensington Palace. The scheme failed to materialise when Charles II, the sponsor, died, and this first and only section now stands as testimony to Wren's grand vision. Royal Avenue was the fictional home of James Bond.

## Royal Hospital ❺

✉ Royal Hospital Road; www.chelsea-pensioners.org.uk 📞 7881 5200
🕐 Mon–Sat 10am–noon and 2–4pm; grounds year round Mon–Sat 10am–sunset, Sun from 2pm 💷 free
🚇 Sloane Square

The idea behind this magnificent building housing the Chelsea Pensioners was inspired by the Hôtel des Invalides in Paris. The main buildings, two residential wings linked by the Great Hall and Chapel, were designed in English baroque style.

The wood-panelled Great Hall, the dining room, features a vast mural with Charles II on horseback, painted by Verrio. It was in this hall in 1852 that Wellington lay in state. Decorated with regimental colours, the adjoining Chapel features *Christ Rising from the Tomb*, a fresco by Sebastiano Ricci. A huge painting of the Battle of Waterloo by George Jones hangs in the entrance to a small museum. It overlooks a 1:300 scale model that, with an audio presentation, illustrates the hospital and its massive grounds in the 18th century.

## National Army Museum ❻

✉ Royal Hospital Road; www.nam.ac.uk 📞 7730 0717
🕐 daily 10am–5.30pm 💷 free
🚇 Sloane Square

The permanent exhibition follows the history of the British Army from the defeat of the French at Agincourt in 1415 to the present day, although with much less emphasis on the latter. Massive flamboyant paintings, some as long as 20ft (6 metres), celebrate soldiers' greatest and worst moments, while portraits by Gainsborough, Reynolds and lesser artists crowd

**KIDS**

The National Army Museum's Kid Zone is a free interactive learning and play space designed to unleash children's imaginations. There's a medieval castle to explore, life in a forest army camp to negotiate, and a variety of activity areas to challenge and entertain the under-10s. A soft play area for babies is also included. Entry is by timed ticket.

**ABOVE LEFT:** the Great Hall, Royal Hospital.
**BELOW:** produce market on Duke of York Square, off the King's Road.

## The Chelsea Flower Show

The Chelsea Flower Show (www.rhs.org.uk), one of the largest of its kind in the world, is a great social event held in the Royal Hospital's spacious gardens during May. First held in 1862, the Royal Horticultural Society show has grown to encompass an impressive number of show gardens, hastily but immaculately assembled in the days running up to the show, plus an astonishing variety of plants and flowers.

The show lasts for five days. The first two are open only to members of the RHS, but the remaining days are open to all.

*Chelsea Physic Garden can lay claim to having the oldest rock garden in England, if not Europe. Dating back to 1773, it is made of salvaged building stone from the Tower of London and basaltic lava from Iceland.*

**ABOVE RIGHT:**
Florence Carlyle's portrait of Thomas Carlyle, in Carlyle's House. **ABOVE AND BELOW:** Cheyne Walk.

other walls. There is also the skeleton of Napoleon's favourite horse, Marengo. You can feel the weight of a Tudor cannonball or try on a soldier's helmet, while the replica World War I trench is a place for quiet reflection. Three sections of the Berlin Wall stand outside the museum.

## Chelsea Physic Garden ❼

✉ 66 Royal Hospital Road; www.chelseaphysicgarden.co.uk
☎ 7352 5646 ◷ Apr–Oct Tue–Fri noon–5pm, Sun noon–6pm; closed Nov–Mar ◎ charge Ⓡ Sloane Square

Behind a high wall is the Chelsea Physic Garden, founded in 1673 for the study of medicinal plants. The 3½-acre (1.5-hectare) garden is divided into four contrasting sections: a Garden of World Medicine, a Pharmaceutical Garden, and systematic order beds in the two southern quadrants. The Pharmaceutical Garden displays plants according to their medical uses while the Garden of World Medicine details the use of specific plants in different parts of the world.

You will also find a pond rockery, perfumery and aromatherapy borders, glasshouses, and herb and vegetable gardens. A woodland area has birds' nesting boxes, and there are themed trails for adults and children.

### CHELSEA EMBANKMENT

At the foot of **Royal Hospital Road**, a fine row of Queen Anne houses make up **Cheyne Walk** *(see box below)*. Cheyne Walk sits back from the flagstoned, windblown sweep of **Chelsea Embankment**, roaring with traffic in the shadows of old plane trees but beautiful nonetheless. Flanked by greenery it is also known as Chelsea

## The Ultimate Des Res

Cheyne Walk has long been one of London's most exclusive streets. A host of famous people have lived in its fine, mainly 18th-century, properties, from writers George Eliot and Hilaire Belloc to the artist J.M.W. Turner and the engineer Isambard Kingdom Brunel. It is still a choice address today, with Paul Getty, Mick Jagger and Keith Richards having all been resident at one time.

The pre-Raphaelite artist Dante Gabriel Rossetti lived with the poet Swinburne in No. 16, and they kept peacocks in their back garden. The birds so disturbed the neighbours that nowadays every lease on the row prohibits tenants from keeping them.

Gardens and opened to great fanfare in 1874. It retains its sculptural lampposts with their fat, milky globes, and its cast-iron benches with end supports shaped like sphinxes. The views stretch out across the Thames to the Battersea Park Peace Pagoda on the opposite bank, built by Japanese monks and nuns in 1985; east to the iconic chimneys of the Battersea Power Station; and west to the pink-and-cream confection of the **Albert Bridge** (1873).

## Carlyle's House ❽

✉ 24 Cheyne Row; www.nationaltrust. org.uk ☎ 7352 7087 ☺ mid-Mar– early Nov Wed–Sun 11am–5pm ☺ charge 🚇 Sloane Square

A statue of the Scottish essayist Thomas Carlyle (1795–1881) watches the traffic grind by further down the Embankment. The dour essayist lived here between 1834 and 1881. The house is preserved exactly as it was – to the point of not having electricity – and it is easy to imagine Mr and Mrs Carlyle sitting in their kitchen, although it may not have been a cosy scene. It was fortunate the Carlyles married each other, it was said, otherwise there would have been four miserable people in the world instead of two. Yet leading intellectuals, including Charles Dickens, John Ruskin and Alfred, Lord Tennyson, used to visit Carlyle here.

Sir Hans Sloane's tomb is outside **Chelsea Old Church** (All Saints) on Cheyne Walk. The church has several fine Tudor monuments and was painstakingly rebuilt after being destroyed by a landmine in 1941.

The site was formerly occupied by a 12th-century Norman church. Henry VIII, who had a large house on the river where Cheyne Walk now is, supposedly married Jane Seymour in secrecy here, several days before the official ceremony. Thomas More (1478–1535), author of *Utopia*, which sketched out an ideal commonwealth, had a farm here. His stormy relationship with Henry VIII, which resulted in his execution, was the subject of Robert Bolt's 1960 play *A Man For All Seasons*. ❑

*The telltale enormous windows looking out onto Tite Street (off Royal Hospital Road) betray the origins of these houses: in the 1870s, this street was crammed with artists' studios, including The Studios, at No. 33. These were once used by the American painter John Singer Sargent (1856–1925) who died at No. 31, while Oscar Wilde once occupied No. 34.*

**BELOW:** a statue of Sir Thomas More in front of Chelsea Old Church.

# BEST RESTAURANTS, PUBS, BARS AND CAFÉS

## Restaurants

Prices for a three-course dinner per person with a half-bottle of house wine:
**£** = under £20
**££** = £20–30
**£££** = £30–50
**££££** = over £50

### British

#### Cadogan Arms
298 King's Rd, SW3
📞 7352 6500; www.the
cadoganarmschelsea.com
💻 L & D daily. **£££**
[p330, C2]
Traditional Victorian pub turned fashionable gastro-pub, offering real ales along with good food. Dishes might include rack of Welsh lamb or pan fried sea bass. Good selection of British cheeses.

### Tom's Kitchen
27 Cale St, SW3
📞 7349 0202; www.toms
kitchen.co.uk 💻 B and L
Mon–Fri, brunch Sat–Sun, D
daily. **££–£££** [p331, C3]
Relaxed brasserie run by award-winning chef Tom Aikens. The menu changes daily, but features classic British dishes such as Cumberland sausages and mash, steak sandwiches, fish pie and macaroni cheese.

### Chinese

#### Eight Over Eight
392 King's Rd, SW3
📞 7349 9934; www.ricker
restaurants.com 💻 L & D
daily. **£££** [p330, B4]
This stylish restaurant offers Asian dishes with a modern twist. Dim sum, sushi, king prawn curry, and chocolate pudding with green tea ice cream are just some of the delights on offer.

### Ken Lo's Memories of China
65–9 Ebury St, SW1
📞 7730 7734; www.atoz
restaurants.com 💻 L & D
daily. **£££–££££** (set lunch available) [p332, A1]
Ken Lo's menus, skewed towards western tastes, have stood the test of time, though the final bill invariably comes as a costly surprise.

### Fish

#### Poissonnerie de L'Avenue
82 Sloane Avenue, SW3
📞 7589 2457; www.
poissonneriedelavenue.com
💻 L & D daily. **£££** (set menu
**££**) [p331, C2]
Run by the same family for over 40 years, it serves fresh fish and seafood from the adjoining fishmonger's. Dishes are old-school French, although some come with an Italian flourish.

### French

#### Cheyne Walk Brasserie
50 Cheyne Walk, SW3
📞 7376 8787; www.cheyne
walkbrasserie.com
💻 L Tue–Sun, D Mon–Sat.
**£££** (weekday lunch menu
**££**) [p330–1, C4]
The flavours of Provence are cooked up over the central grill of this Belle Époque dining room. Also offers views of the Albert Bridge and a sumptuous cocktail lounge.

#### La Poule au Pot
231 Ebury St, SW1 📞 7730
7763 💻 L & D daily. **£££**
(set lunch **££**) [p331, E2]
The £19 fixed-price lunch menu features dishes such as escargots or soupe de poisson with *bifteck et frites* to follow. In the evening, candlelight and romantic nooks make it a hit with couples.

### Indian

#### Chutney Mary
535 King's Rd, SW10
📞 7351 3113; www.chutney
mary.com 💻 L Sat–Sun, D
daily. **£££** (set lunch **££**)
[p330, A4]
At the sister restaurant to Veeraswamy (the UK's oldest Indian eatery), take your pick of regional dishes from Goa to Delhi, Kerala to Bombay. The Sunday jazz brunch is popular. Meat is halal.

#### Quilon
41 Buckingham Gate, SW1
📞 7821 1899; www.quilon.
co.uk 💻 L Mon–Fri and

**LEFT:** Tom Aikens' restaurant. **TOP RIGHT:** Itsu.

Sun, D Mon–Sat. £££ (set lunch ££) [p332, B1]
The lunch menu at this Michelin-starred, South Indian restaurant is good value, though an evening meal of, say, pepper shrimps followed by Manglorean chicken or duck roast, is pricier. Menu blends traditional and more progressive dishes.

### Rasoi

10 Lincoln St, Sloane Sq, SW1 ☎ 7225 1881; www.rasoir-uk.com
◐ L Mon–Fri and Sun, D daily. £££ [p331, D2]
Run by celebrated chef Vineet Rasoi and holder of a Michelin star, this restaurant offers the ultimate Indian dining experience. It serves superb food in a traditional Chelsea townhouse.

## *Japanese*

### Itsu

118 Draycott Avenue, SW3 ☎ 7590 2400; www.itsu.com
◐ Mon–Sat noon–11pm, Sun noon–10pm. £ [p331, C2]
If the offerings on the conveyor-belt plates don't appeal, try a dish from the hot grill such as chicken teriyaki. Bookings not accepted.

## *Modern European*

### Elistano

25–27 Elystan St, SW3 ☎ 7584 5248; www. elistano.com ◐ L & D daily. £££ [p331, C2]
The menu features dishes such as tuna carpaccio with dandelion salad, and herb crusted rack of lamb with new potatoes. Vanilla pannacotta might appear in the dessert section.

### Gordon Ramsay

68 Royal Hospital Rd, SW3 ☎ 7352 4441; www.gordon ramsay.com ◐ L & D Mon–Fri. ££££ (lunch menu £££) [p331, D4]
The celebrity chef's gastronomic offerings – such as roasted sea scallops with octopus, black pudding tempura, cauliflower purée and parmesan velouté – are exquisite. The lunch time set menu costs £45 for 3 courses. No jeans or trainers.

## *Others*

### Patara

181 Fulham Rd, SW3 ☎ 7351 5692; www.patara london.com ◐ L & D daily. ££ [p330, C2]
Serves good Thai food at

low prices considering the area. As a suggestion, try the DIY fresh spring rolls for starters, duck breast for main, sorbet for dessert and green tea to finish.

### The Stockpot

273 King's Rd, SW3 ☎ 7823 3175 ◐ L & D daily. £ [p330, C3]
Simple but filling dishes. Good for late meals (last orders 11.30pm).

## *Pubs, Bars and Cafés*

The King's Road has several good watering holes. There is the **Chelsea Potter** (119 King's Rd) or **Henry J Beans** (195–7), an American bar and grill with the lure of a beer garden. But head off its well-trodden track to unearth some of the area's best pubs. These include the **Pig's Ear** (35 Old Church St), lacking in authenticity after a continental-style refit, but with a fine real ale to its name; the **Cooper's Arms** (87 Flood St), upholding the Campaign for Real Food; the **Cross Keys** (1 Lawrence St), dating from 1708 and worth a visit for its gorgeous rooms; and the **Lots Road Pub and Dining Room** (114 Lots Rd), a good gastropub.

Closer to Belgravia, the **Orange Brewery** (37–9 Pimlico Rd) retains remnants of its former brewery and the tiny **Fox and Hounds** (29 Passmore St) has armchairs and classic tomes aplenty. There's also the historic **Grenadier** (18 Wilton Row), and **Thomas Cubitt** (44 Elizabeth St), another fine gastro-pub.

If cocktails or whiskies are your thing, the **Blue Bar** at The Berkeley Hotel (Wilton Place) does them in great style. Also try **Bardo** (196–8 Fulham Rd), **Apartment 195** (195 King's Rd) which has the feel of a private club, the New-Age Indian **Mokssh** (222 Fulham Rd) and the basement **606 Club** (90 Lots Rd) for live jazz.

Brompton Cross is the preserve of a more select class of bar, among them **Eclipse** (111–3 Walton St) serving a watermelon Martini, and **The Collection** (264 Brompton Rd). Pub-wise, the **Admiral Codrington** (17 Mossop St) attracts a smart-casual set, and does a popular line in fish and chips.

# Village London

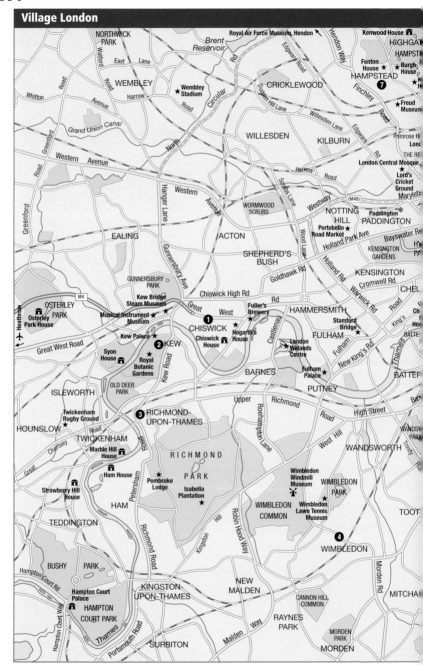

NORTHWICK PARK

Royal Air Force Museum, Hendon

Kenwood House 🏠

HIGHGA

Watford

East Lane

Brent Reservoir

Hendon Way

Fenton House ★ ★ Burgh House

HAMPST

WEMBLEY

Harrow Road

Wembley ★ Stadium

CRICKLEWOOD

Dudden Hill Lane

Finchley

HAMPSTEAD

K Hi

Whitton

Avenue

Circular

Harrow

Road

Freud ★ Museum

Grand Union Canal

North

Willesden Lane

WILLESDEN

KILBURN

Edgware

Primrose Hi
Lond

Greenford

Western Avenue

Harrow Road

THE RE

London Central Mosque

Lord's ★ Cricket Ground

Greenford Road

Hanger Lane

Western Avenue

Scrubs Lane

Westway

(M40)

Maryleb

WORMWOOD SCRUBS

NOTTING HILL

Paddington

PADDINGTON

EALING

Gunnersbury Ave

ACTON

SHEPHERD'S BUSH

Wood Lane

Holland Park Ave

Portobello ★ Road Market

Bayswater R

KENSINGTON GARDENS

H
PA

Holland Rd

Goldhawk Rd

Warwick Rd

Cromwell Rd

KENSINGTON

CHEL

GUNNERSBURY PARK

Chiswick High Rd

Rd

Great West

Fuller's Brewery

HAMMERSMITH

Castlenau

King's

Ch
Ho

OSTERLEY PARK

M4

Kew Bridge Steam Museum

Musical Instrument ★ Museum

❶

CHISWICK

Hogarth's ★ House

Stamford Bridge ★

BATTE

Heathrow ✈

Osterley 🏠 Park House

Kew Palace ★

❷ KEW

Chiswick 🏠 House

FULHAM

New King's Rd

Thames

Great West Road

Syon 🏠 House

Royal Botanic Gardens

Fulham

London ★ Wetlands Centre

BATTER

ISLEWORTH

OLD DEER PARK

Kew Road

BARNES

Fulham ★ Palace

PUTNEY

Upper Richmond Road

High Street

Ba

HOUNSLOW

Twickenham ★ Rugby Ground

❸ RICHMOND-UPON-THAMES

Roehampton Lane

West Hill

WANDSWORTH

WANDS
PAR

Chertsey Road

TWICKENHAM

Marble Hill 🏠 House

RICHMOND PARK

Trinity R

Great

Ham House 🏠

Pembroke ★ Lodge

Isabella ★ Plantation

Wimbledon Windmill Museum

WIMBLEDON PARK

Strawberry Hill 🏠 House

Petersham Road

WIMBLEDON COMMON

Wimbledon Lawn Tennis Museum

TOOT

TEDDINGTON

HAM

Richmond Road

Kingston Hill

Robin Hood Way

❹ WIMBLEDON

Morden Rd

BUSHY PARK

Hampton Court Rd

Hampton Court 🏠 Palace

KINGSTON-UPON-THAMES

NEW MALDEN

CANNON HILL COMMON

MITCHA

Hampton Court Way

HAMPTON COURT PARK

Thames

Portsmouth Road

Malden Way

RAYNES PARK

MORDEN PARK

SURBITON

MORDEN

❼

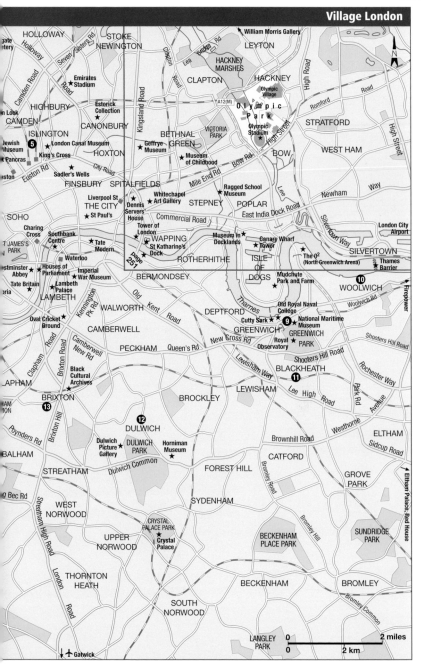

# VILLAGE LONDON

London grew by swallowing up surrounding villages. But many are still there in spirit, each with its own distinctive character. Here we explore them by the four points of the compass

**A**t its widest point, from South Croydon to Potter's Bar, the metropolis is nearly 60 miles (100km) from top to bottom, and London remains one of the world's most populous and multicultural cities. Perhaps because it is so big, many of those who live within its confines hardly think of it as a unified city at all, but as a collection of largely independent villages or communities. While Londoners may commute many miles to work, they are likely to do their shopping in their local high streets and build their social lives on their home patch.

The River Thames cuts through London, forming an effective physical and psychological block to free movement. While south Londoners stream across London Bridge to work in the City every day, they are more likely to go shopping in Croydon or Bromley than in the West End, and north Londoners will head further north to such shopping citadels as Brent Cross. Many people born within the metropolis rarely move more than a few miles from their home, and would not dream of relocating to the other side of the river.

## Where to go

While most visitors are busy with the tourist haunts of the West End and the City, those who go further afield are rewarded with a glimpse of what the locals call "real London". Head west to Kew for Kew Gardens and river walks at Chiswick and Richmond. Venture north to Islington and Camden for good shopping, nightlife, restaurants and Regent's Canal, or to Highgate and Hampstead for historic pubs and Hampstead Heath. Travel east of the centre to see high-rise Docklands, historic Spitalfields and the main 2012 Olympic site. In the southern suburbs are Greenwich, famous for its observatory and naval museum, Blackheath and Brixton.

All can be reached by public transport, using either the Tube, Docklands Light Railway, buses or, in the case of the southern suburbs, overground railway from London Bridge, Victoria or Charing Cross stations. ❑

**LEFT:** a slice of old London in Spitalfields. **ABOVE:** Artillery Passage, Spitalfields.

# WEST LONDON

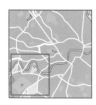

**West London offers 18th-century mansions, magnificent parks and walks along the River Thames. To the southwest is Henry VIII's great palace, Hampton Court, and Wimbledon, home of the famous tennis championship**

**Main attractions**
CHISWICK HOUSE
HOGARTH'S HOUSE
ROYAL BOTANIC GARDENS, KEW
KEW BRIDGE STEAM MUSEUM
SYON HOUSE AND PARK
OSTERLEY PARK HOUSE
RICHMOND PARK
HAM HOUSE
HAMPTON COURT PALACE
WIMBLEDON LAWN TENNIS MUSEUM
WIMBLEDON WINDMILL MUSEUM

Heading west out of London you can choose between grand riverside mansions, built as country retreats for royals and landed gentry, and wide-open spaces such as Richmond Park and Kew Gardens, the world renowned botanic gardens.

## CHISWICK ❶

Although it accommodates the main artery to the M4 and Heathrow Airport, Chiswick has the feel of a small town, with its independent shops, flower stalls, fashionable restaurants and pretty terraces. Near the fragrant Fuller's Brewery *(see margin note, opposite page)*, off Hogarth roundabout, stands a hidden gem, much loved by locals and at last being given the attention it deserves.

### Chiswick House

✉ Burlington Lane; www.chgt.org.uk ☎ 8995 0508 ⏱ Apr–Oct Sun–Wed 10am–5pm, Nov–Mar pre-booked appointments for groups only; gardens daily, all year round ⑤ charge for house 🚆 train Waterloo to Chiswick 🚌 190

This romantic 18th-century villa was designed by Lord Burlington (1694–1753), a renowned architect and patron of the arts, who was inspired by classical Rome. Burlington's Palladian house launched a new taste in architecture which was to spread throughout Britain and North America.

The gardens are historically important too, for it was here that the idea of the "natural style" of gardening – one of England's main contributions to European culture – was conceived. Burlington brought in his friend William Kent to redesign the grounds; Kent broke from the rigid formality which had characterised gardens of the early 18th century and created a more natural landscape.

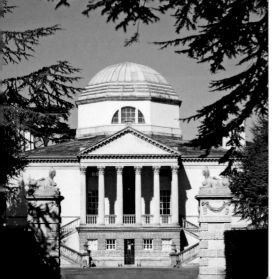

*Recommended Restaurants & Pubs on page 241*

Thus the English landscape movement was born. A £12 million project has recently restored the gardens, which include an abundance of statuary, a classical bridge, an Ionic temple, and a large conservatory.

Inside the house, the grand rooms are reserved for the first floor, which has a very unusual structure: in the centre is an octagonal room with a lavish domed ceiling – the tribune or saloon. This was the heart of the building and the setting for gatherings and *conversazioni*.

Amongst the celebrated guests welcomed here were Alexander Pope, Jonathan Swift, Handel and several crowned heads of state. The small scale and rounded edges of the rooms in the northern part of the house are intimate and sensual, with the overall symmetry heightened by framed views of the gardens through the doorways of the interconnected rooms. The most sumptuous of the Green, Red and Blue Velvet rooms, so-called because of their vivid wallpaper, is Lord Burlington's study, elegantly adorned in blue. The room's tiny dimensions and rich colours con-vey an impression of standing inside a jewel box, or inside a Fabergé egg.

## Hogarth's House

✉ Hogarth Lane, Great West Road
☎ 8994 6757 🕑 Tue–Sun and Bank Holiday Mon noon–5pm 🎫 free
🚆 train Waterloo to Chiswick 🚌 190

Not far from Chiswick House, sitting incongruously on the six-lane Great West Road, is Hogarth House, the modest residence of the father of political cartoons, William Hogarth (1697–1764). Hogarth highlighted the ills of society in a series of witty engravings that became bestsellers. Although the house is now looking rather neglected, the collection of drawings, including *The Rake's Progress* and *Marriage à la Mode*, is worth seeking out. (Free parking for Chiswick House and Hogarth's House can be found a short distance from the Hogarth roundabout along the A4.)

William Hogarth moved with his family to this three-storey house from busy Leicester Fields (now Leicester Square) in 1749. In a monstrous bit of irony that would not be lost on the

*To see how a pint of fine English ale is made, take a tour around Fuller's Griffin Brewery on the Hogarth roundabout. Pre-booking is essential (tel: 8996 2063).*

**LEFT:** Chiswick House. **BELOW LEFT AND RIGHT:** the beautifully-restored Gallery and Red Velvet room in Chiswick House.

*William Hogarth's grand tomb is in the cemetery of Chiswick parish church; take the underpass near Hogarth's house, then go down Church Street towards the river.*

**BELOW:** inside Kew's Palm House.
**BELOW RIGHT:** Kew's Chinese Pagoda.

satirist, this "little country box by the Thames" now lies by the A4 to Heathrow, its owner immortalised in the thundering Hogarth roundabout. The traffic noise is muted in the house though, and a small garden at the back attempts a pastoral charm. The mulberry tree here is said to date from Hogarth's day, one of the few to survive from a time when the trees were brought to England in a vain attempt to get silkworms to breed.

## KEW ❷

Downriver from Chiswick is Kew, home to the Royal Botanic Gardens, known as Kew Gardens. The village green gives the place a rural feel, particularly when cricket matches are played here. On the green is St Anne's Church, where the painter Thomas Gainsborough is buried.

### Royal Botanic Gardens

✉ Kew, Richmond; www.kew.org
📞 8332 5655  🄯 daily 9.30am–dusk
🄰 charge  🚇 tube from Waterloo to Kew Bridge

Kew Gardens, with 300 acres (120 hectares) of plants from all over the world, were first established in 1759 under the direction of Princess Augusta. In 1772, her son, George III put Kew in the hands of the botanist Sir Joseph Banks, who had just returned from a round-the-world expedition to collect plant specimens with Captain Cook. Other explorers and amateur enthusiasts added to the collection over the centuries, so that today Kew is not only a vast botanical garden but also a formidable repository and research centre. In 2003 Kew was added to Unesco's list of World Heritage Sites.

The gardens present a mix of landscaped lawns, wooded areas, formal gardens and glasshouses. Make the most of the map you receive on entering, as it features seasonal highlights and where to find them.

The most famous of Kew's nursery buildings is the Grade I-listed **Palm House**, built in 1844–8. The steamy warmth hits you as you enter this verdant tropical world, in which coconuts, bananas and coffee beans grow. Nearby, the **Waterlily House** (closed Nov–Apr) houses tropical

*Recommended Restaurants & Pubs on page 241*

aquatic plants. The **Temperate House** is the world's largest surviving Victorian glass structure.

In addition to the glasshouses there are various temples and other follies dating back to the period of royal ownership of the gardens in the 18th and early 19th centuries. The **Chinese pagoda**, built in 1762, reflects the fashion for chinoiserie in English garden design in the mid-18th century. The classically-styled, Grade I-listed Orangery dating from 1761, too dark to house citrus trees as was intended, is now a pleasant café-restaurant.

### Kew Palace

Built in 1631 for a Dutch merchant, **Kew Palace** (www.hrp.org.uk; Apr–Sept Tue–Sun 10am–5pm, Mon 11am–5pm; tel: 0844 482 7777; charge) was the country retreat of George III, Queen Charlotte and some of their children from 1801; the king came here during his bouts of supposed madness. The palace has been meticulously restored and brought back to life, revealing aspects of the original Georgian decor and architecture, and many of the family's treasures.

### SYON PARK AND MUSEUMS

Across Kew Bridge is the **Kew Bridge Steam Museum** (Green Dragon Lane; www.kbsm.org; Tue–Sun 11am–4pm; tel: 8568 4757; charge), whose original purpose was to supply London's water in the 19th century. It now houses the world's largest collection of steam-pumping engines and a steam railway, which you can ride (Sundays only Easter–Oct).

Further west along the high street is the **Musical Museum** (399 High Street, Brentford; www.musicalmuseum. co.uk; tel: 8560 8108; charge), which displays a large collection of automatic instruments, from clockwork music boxes to self-playing Wurlitzer organs.

## Syon House

✉ Syon Park, Isleworth; www.syonpark. co.uk ☏ 8560 0882 ⏱ Syon House: Apr–Sept Wed, Thur, Sun and bank holiday Mon 11am–5pm; gardens: Mar–Oct daily 10.30am–dusk 💲 charge

Syon House and its 200-acre (80-hectare) park is the London home of the Duke of Northumberland, whose family have lived here for over 400 years. Its 18th-century interior by Robert Adam is unsurpassed, celebrated as the architect's early English masterpiece. From the Long Gallery is a spectacular view over the last tidal water meadow on the Thames. The gardens were created by the great English landscape gardener Capability Brown in the mid-18th century.

Children are well catered for at Syon Park with Snakes and Ladders, a huge indoor play centre.

*In Evolution House at Kew Gardens you can take a walk through 3,500 million years of plant history.*

**ABOVE LEFT:** Xstrata treetop walkway, Kew Gardens. **BELOW:** 17th-century Kew Palace.

In Syon Park, Snakes and Ladders (daily 10am–6pm; charge) has slides, tunnels, rope climbs and electric motorbikes, as well as an outdoor adventure assault course.

Further west is another grand house built as a country retreat: **Osterley Park House** (Jersey Road, Isleworth; www.nationaltrust.org.uk; house: Mar–Oct Wed–Sun and bank hols noon–4.30pm; garden: Mar–Oct Wed–Sun and bank hols 11am–5pm; tel: 8232 5050; charge). This neoclassical mansion has fine interiors by Robert Adam, 18th-century gardens, and a large landscaped park.

## RICHMOND-UPON-THAMES ❸

Richmond makes for a pleasant day out, easily reached by District Line Underground or by overground trains from Waterloo. Richmond Green is lined with 17th- and 18th-century buildings, while the town centre is good for shopping. Richmond Bridge is the oldest on the river, and the waterfront is always lively, with boats available for hire.

The walk up Richmond Hill to the park leads past views over the Thames and London; in the foreground you may see cows grazing on Petersham Meadows. This view is the only one in England to be protected by an Act of Parliament, passed in 1902.

## Richmond Park

✉ Richmond; www.royalparks.gov.uk/parks/richmond_park 📞 8948 3209
🕐 daily 7.30am–dusk 💷 free
🚇 District Line to Richmond, then No. 371 or 65 bus to Petersham Gate

At 2,500 acres (1,000 hectares), Richmond Park is the largest of all the royal parks. The pastoral landscape of hills, ponds, gardens and grasslands is popular with walkers, cyclists and horse riders. Since 1625, when Charles I brought his court to Richmond Palace (now demolished) to escape the plague, there have been herds of wild red and fallow deer in the park.

The **Isabella Plantation**, an ornamental woodland garden in the southwest corner, has been designed to be interesting all year round, though a favourite time to visit is from April, when the azaleas and rhododendrons bloom. At **Pembroke Lodge**, a Georgian mansion on the western edge of the park, there are fabulous views over west London. There's also a car park here, and refreshments.

**BELOW:** soaking up the sun on Richmond Green.
**BELOW RIGHT:** the Great Conservatory in Syon Park.

*Recommended Restaurants & Pubs on page 241*

## Ham House

✉ Ham Street, Ham, Richmond; www.nationaltrust.org.uk ☎ 8940 1950 🕐 house: mid-Mar–Oct Mon–Thur and Sat–Sun noon–4pm, Nov Sat–Tue 11.30am–3pm; garden: all year Sat–Wed 11am–5pm 💲 charge 🚇 District Line to Richmond, then No. 371 bus

About a mile along the Thames Path from Richmond Hill is Ham House, built in 1610 with a sumptuous interior and important collections of textiles, furnishings and paintings. This Stuart mansion is also said to be one of the most haunted houses in the country. The formal garden is being restored to its former splendour.

Across the river is **Marble Hill House** (www.english-heritage.org.uk; Apr–Oct Sat 10am–2pm, Sun and bank hols 10am–5pm; tel: 8892 5115; charge), an elegant Palladian villa set in riverside parkland.

Intended as an Arcadian retreat, the house was built in 1724 for Henrietta Howard, mistress to King George II when he was Prince of Wales. It contains a fine collection of early Georgian paintings.

## Hampton Court Palace

✉ East Molesey, Surrey; http://hrp.org.uk/HamptonCourtPalace ☎ 0844 482 7799 🕐 daily 10am–6pm, Nov–Mar until 4.30pm 💲 charge 🚆 mainline train from Waterloo to Hampton Court

Surrounded by 60 acres (24 hectares) of magnificent gardens on the banks of the Thames, this vast palace, built to rival Versailles in

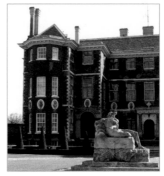

**TIP**

To visit Marble Hill House from the Richmond side of the river, take the Hammertons ferry, which runs between the riverbank outside Ham House in Richmond and Marble Hill Park in Twickenham (tel: 8892 9620; Mar–Oct Mon–Fri 10am–6pm, Sat–Sun 10am–6.30pm; Nov–Feb weekends only weather permitting).

**LEFT:** Ham House.
**BELOW:** late afternoon sunlight over tranquil Richmond Park.

## The Thames Path

Starting at the Thames Barrier in the east and ending at the river's source in the Cotswolds 180 miles (290km) away, the Thames Path provides some of the best views of the city and beyond. From Putney the path takes on a rural aspect, passing Barnes Wetland Centre, the grand riverside houses of Chiswick and the pretty cottages of Strand on the Green. After Kew Bridge, the path skirts round Kew Gardens, with Syon Park across the river. At Richmond, with Petersham Meadows on your left and a great sweep of the river ahead of you, it's hard to believe the city is in spitting distance. Along this stretch you'll see Marble Hill House and, a little further along, Ham House.

*The King's Staircase in the State Apartments of William III, Hampton Court Palace.*

**RIGHT:** Wimbledon's All England Lawn Tennis Club. **BELOW:** meeting an actor dressed as Henry VIII at Hampton Court Palace.

France, dates from the reign of Henry VIII (reigned 1509–47). In the late 1600s many of the Tudor apartments were rebuilt by Sir Christopher Wren, but the Great Hall and Chapel Royal – the most striking rooms – survive.

Start at the introductory exhibition behind the colonnade in Clock Court; here you can decide on your route and find out about activities for children. Costumed guides give entertaining tours of some parts of the palace, including Henry VIII's **State Apartments**.

These you enter through the **Great Hall**, the last of its kind to be built, and the largest room in the palace. The hammer-beam roof and richly carved decoration are original. In the **Tudor Kitchens**, you can feel the heat of the massive kitchen fires and smell the meat simmering in the boiling pot, as if in preparation for a feast in Henry VIII's time.

Allow time to visit the riverside gardens, and get lost in the famous maze, planted in 1702 and recently given sound effects such as whispers of conversation and a dog barking.

## WIMBLEDON ❹

This suburb hosts one of the world's top tennis tournaments in June/July and its history is brought to life in the **Wimbledon Lawn Tennis Museum** (Church Road, Wimbledon; www.wimbledon.com; daily 10am–5pm; tel: 8946 6131; charge). The Museum is closed to the public during the Championships.

On the edge of Wimbledon Common, a partly wooded expanse with nature trails, is the **Wimbledon Windmill Museum** (www.wimbledonwindmill.org.uk; Apr–Oct Sat 2–5pm, Sun 11am–5pm; tel: 8947 2825), in a disused windmill. Displays illustrate the milling process, with hands-on milling for children. ❑

# BEST RESTAURANTS AND PUBS

## Restaurants

Prices for a three-course dinner per person with a half-bottle of house wine:

**£** = under £20
**££** = £20–30
**£££** = £30–50
**££££** = over £50

## Chiswick

### Giraffe
270 Chiswick High Rd, W4
**℡** 8995 2100; www.giraffe.
net **℃** B, L & D daily. **£**
Bright decor and varied dishes – burgers, stir fries, enchiladas – make this chain member a popular choice for families.

### High Road Brasserie
162–4 Chiswick High Rd, W4 **℡** 8742 7474;
www.highroadhouse.co.uk
**℃** B, L & D daily. **££**
Located underneath the High Road House hotel, it attracts Chiswick's boho-chic crowd with its classic brasserie fare.

### La Trompette
5–7 Devonshire Rd, W4
**℡** 8747 1836; www.la
trompette.co.uk **℃** L & D
daily, **£££**
Award-winning French country menu with mix of simple classics, such as *côte de boeuf*, and more sophisticated offerings.

### Sam's
Barley Mow Centre, 11
Barley Mow Passage, W4

**℡** 8987 0555; www.sams
brasserie.co.uk **℃** L & D
daily. **£££** (set lunch **£**)
Excellent local restaurant which will suit all moods and appetites. Brunch Sat–Sun.

## Kew

### The Glasshouse
14 Station Parade, Kew, TW9
**℡** 8940 6777; www.glass
houserestaurant.co.uk
**℃** L & D daily. **££££** (set lunch **££**)
In a pleasant location, this is one of southwest London's culinary hotspots, with modern French-inspired cuisine.

### The Orangery
Kew Gardens, TW9 **℡** 8332
5655 **℃** 10am–1 hr before
Gardens close. **£**
Enjoy coffee, lunch or afternoon tea in this elegant former hothouse.

## Richmond

### Chez Lindsay
11 Hill Rise, TW10 **℡** 8948
7473; www.chez-lindsay.
co.uk **℃** L & D daily. **££**
(set lunch **£**)
Breton fishing village atmosphere, with superb fish, shellfish, *galettes*, *crêpes* and *steak-frites*.
Try a galette with goats' cheese and spinach, or a casserole of red gurnard, sea bream and lobster.

### Cote
24 Hill St, TW9
**℡** 8948 5971; www.cote-
restaurants.co.uk
**℃** B, L & D daily. **££**
This bistro, one of a small chain, serves classic French dishes such as moules marinières and tuna Niçoise alongside more contemporary choices.

### Petersham Nurseries
Off Petersham Rd, TW10
**℡** 8605 3627; www.peter
shamnurseries.com **℃** L
Tue–Sun noon–3pm. **£££**
An enchanting Michelin-starred café run by chef Skye Gyngell, with tables arranged around the greenhouse of a nursery. Seasonal produce features. Book in advance.

## Pubs

**Chiswick**
Have a drink on the river at Strand on the Green: pubs include **City Barge** (at No. 27) and the **Bell and Crown** *(11 Thames Road)*.

**Hammersmith**
Riverside pubs include **The Old Ship** *(25 Upper Mall)* and **The Dove** (19 Upper Mall), a pretty 17th-century pub.

**Kew**
The pubs around the green are appealing, especially when

there's a cricket match. **The Inn**, a former coaching inn, at Kew Gardens Hotel *(292 Sandycombe Road)* serves food.

**Richmond**
Pubs include **The Cricketers** *(The Green)*, at its best in the summer.

**Wimbledon**
Popular pub **Fox and Grapes** *(9 Camp Road)* offers a rural experience, with the Common on three sides.

**RIGHT:** The Cricketers pub, located on Richmond Green.

# NORTH LONDON

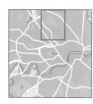

**For centuries north Londoners did their best to consign brothels, jails and polluting industries to the south side of the river. The well-to-do preferred to live in areas such as Islington, Hampstead and Highgate, which still retain a distinct, and often resented, air of superiority**

### Main attractions
ARSENAL EMIRATES STADIUM
CAMDEN LOCK MARKET
REGENT'S CANAL
HAMPSTEAD HEATH
KEATS HOUSE
FREUD MUSEUM
HIGHGATE CEMETERY

**BELOW:** the antiques village Camden Passage, in Islington.

I f you have time, there are several interesting areas to visit in north London, all of them most animated at weekends when they are a magnet for Londoners themselves. Choose between Islington with its vibrant eating and shopping scene, Camden with its canal and market, Hampstead with its famous heath, handsome period properties and museums, or Highgate with its overgrown Victorian cemetery containing the remains of many famous figures. They can all be reached on the Northern Line.

## ISLINGTON ⑤

North of the City of London, City Road rises to the Angel, named after a long-gone coaching inn, marking the start of Islington. In the first half of the 20th century this was a poor and even dangerous area of London. Its once handsome properties were in deep decline, their buddleia-sprouting facades hiding slum conditions and multi-family occupancy.

But as London's Georgian and Victorian dwellings were refurbished in the 1970s, Islington rose phoenix-like from the ashes. It came to epitomise gentrification, and by the 1980s a popular stereotype portrayed it as the happy hunting ground of liberal-minded *bien pensants*. This is where Tony and Cherie Blair lived before moving to 10 Downing Street.

### Place of entertainment

In the 18th and 19th centuries Islington was a place of entertainment. It remains a lively area, thronged with visitors both day and night. There are a vast number of restaurants and café-bars on Upper Street alone, a mile-long corridor of consumerism linking Angel Tube station with Highbury and Islington Tube station.

The area also has several theatres, most notably the **Almeida Theatre** in Almeida Street, one of London's most innovative small theatres, and,

*Recommended Restaurants, Bars, Pubs & Cafés on pages 248–9*

just around the corner, the **King's Head**, which is the best of several pub-theatres. At the southern end of Islington on Rosebery Avenue, **Sadler's Wells** is one of London's principal dance venues.

## Shopping

Near **Angel**, the crossroads at the top of Islington, the Angel Centre is a small mall of mainstream chain stores. More interesting for visitors is **Chapel Market**, a traditional London street market that retains its working-class character, and **Camden Passage** (off the other side of Islington High Street), whose elegant buildings and arcades have become a treasure trove of antiques shops, ranging from simple stalls to grand shops.

For offbeat individual shops, seek out Cross Street and environs, near the Almeida Theatre halfway along Upper Street.

## Islington's classic terraces

Prime examples of these can be found in **Gibson Square** and also **Canonbury Square**, where authors George Orwell and Evelyn Waugh

once lived. At 39A Canonbury Square is the **Estorick Collection** (Wed–Sat 11am–6pm, Sun noon–5pm; tel: 7704 9522; charge), a collection of Italian Futurist and figurative art in an elegant Georgian house, complete with bookshop.

Last, but to many minds by no means least, Islington is also the home of premier league **Arsenal Football Club**, which in 2006 moved to the new Emirates stadium.

**TIP**

Tickets for the better Arsenal fixtures are virtually impossible to obtain unless you are a club member. But anyone can take a stadium tour (which includes a visit to the museum) or a "Legends Tour" in which you can meet one of five Arsenal "legends", including Charlie George and John Radford. For further information about these, consult the website www.arsenal.com, or tel: 7619 5000.

**BELOW LEFT AND RIGHT:** shopping, and drinking at the Slug and Lettuce pub, on Islington's Upper Street.

**KIDS**

You can take a 90-minute narrowboat trip from Camden (on the *Jenny Wren*, tel: 7485 4433; www.walkers quay.com). The boat cruises from Camden Town to Little Venice and back daily from Apr–Oct, and at weekends in March.

Although it is virtually impossible for non-members to obtain tickets for a game, you can take a tour of the stadium and visit the museum (*see the margin tip on page 243*).

## CAMDEN ⑥

It's **Camden Market** that attracts the crowds to Camden, though like Islington it also has many fine period terraces and squares, and a hip pub and club scene. The main market (Camden High Street, Thur–Sun 9am–5.30pm) has cheap clothes. **Camden Lock Market** (off Chalk Farm Road, outdoor stalls Sat–Sun 10am–6pm, indoor stalls Tue–Sun) focuses on crafts (*also see pages 54–5*). The quality of goods has fallen in recent years, even if the size of the crowds hasn't.

One of the delights of Camden is Camden Lock. A sequence of two locks and a bridge in quick succession, it is one of the most attractive stretches of **Regent's Canal**. From here the towpath, busy with cyclists (including bicycling commuters during the weekday rush hours), walkers and fishermen, heads west to Little Venice and east to Hackney (*see box below*) and beyond. The last horse-drawn cargo passed along the canal in 1956.

### The Jewish Museum

✉ 128–129 Albert Street; www. jewishmuseum.org.uk  📞 7284 7384  🕒 Mon–Thur 10am–4pm, Fri 10am–2pm, Sun until 5pm  💲 charge  🚇 Camden Town

The Camden branch of the Jewish Museum (there is another one at 80 East End Road, Finchley, tel: 8349 1143) occupies an elegant early Victorian building but the interior is modern with sophisticated dis-

**RIGHT:** narrowboats on Regent's Canal.
**BELOW:** Camden Lock.

### Regent's Canal

This 8½-mile (14km) stretch of water running from Little Venice near Paddington in west London to Limehouse in Docklands was dug between 1812 and 1820 and drops 86ft (25 metres) through 12 locks beneath 57 bridges. The canal has some delightfully rural stretches and also passes through London Zoo. The stretch between Camden and Victoria Park in Hackney takes around a morning to complete (the towpath is interrupted in Islington, where the canal passes through a ¾ mile (1.5km) tunnel, but can be picked up again close to Angel). To learn more about the history of the canal visit the Canal Museum at 12–13 New Wharf Road, King's Cross (*see page 141*).

*Recommended Restaurants, Bars, Pubs & Cafés on pages 248–9*

plays, including an interactive map showing centres of Jewish population in different periods. There is a gallery devoted to Judaica, illustrating religious rituals as passed down the centuries, and exhibitions include the Holocaust Gallery and the story of the Jews in Britain.

## HAMPSTEAD ❼

Hampstead has long been a desirable address and attracts a literary set. Open spaces predominate. The 3-sq-mile (8-sq-km) **Heath** leads down to **Parliament Hill** which gives splendid views across London, as does the 112-acre (45-hectare) **Primrose Hill** overlooking Regent's Park. These are all welcome acres over which locals stride, walk dogs, fly kites, skate and swim in the bathing ponds. History-laden pubs near the heath include the **Spaniards Inn** and the congenial **Old Bull and Bush**.

## Keats House

✉ Keats Grove; www.keatshouse. cityoflondon.gov.uk  ☏ 7332 3868
🕐 Easter–Oct Tue–Sun 1–5pm, Nov–Easter Fri–Sun 1–5pm  💷 charge
🚇 Hampstead

The poet John Keats (1795–1821) wrote much of his work, including *Ode to a Nightingale*, during the two years he lived in Hampstead. It was here that he met and fell in love with Fanny Brawne, the daughter of his next door neighbour. His house-museum contains memorabilia such as facsimiles of his letters, a lock of his hair and Fanny Brawne's engagement ring. The Regency-style garden is free to visit.

## The Freud Museum

✉ 20 Maresfield Gardens; www.freud.org.uk  ☏ 7435 2002
🕐 Wed–Sun noon–5pm  💷 charge
🚇 Finchley Road

Sigmund Freud, fleeing the Nazis in 1938, moved from Vienna to this house in Hampstead. He died just a year later, but his daughter Anna, also a psychoanalyst, looked after it until her own death in 1982.

The museum preserves the house as they left it, and includes many pieces of furniture and other possessions brought over from Vienna. Freud's study on the ground floor includes the couch on which his Viennese patients free-associated, oriental rugs, books and pictures, plus his prize collection

*Keats lived in Hampstead between 1818 and 1820. In the winter of 1820 he was advised by his physician to leave England for the warmer climate of Italy. He never returned, dying in Rome in 1821, aged 25.*

**LEFT:** Freud's famous couch at the Freud Museum in Hampstead.
**BELOW:** views from Primrose Hill.

*Hampstead's elevation gave it a sense of safety. When a great flood that would wipe out London was forecast for 1 February 1524, crowds climbed the hill to observe it. In 1736, the end of the world was predicted and it was here many came to await their doom.*

of antiquities, including framed Roman frescoes and Greek vases.

## Kenwood House

✉ Hampstead Lane; www.english-heritage.org.uk 📞 8348 1286 🕐 daily 11.30am–4pm 💷 free 🚇 Archway or Highgate

Looking like a great wedding cake, Kenwood House was remodelled in 1764–79 by Robert Adam and overlooks Hampstead Heath. Its beautifully maintained rooms showcase the **Iveagh Bequest**, a major collection with works by Rembrandt, Vermeer, Reynolds, J.M.W. Turner and Gainsborough. The first floor contains many family portraits, and items such as silver tableware and fine furniture. The house is also a backdrop for picnic concerts held during the summer.

## Other grand houses

Hampstead has several other notable houses open to the public. On Windmill Hill, parallel to Heath Street, **Fenton House** (www.nationaltrust.org.uk; Mar–Oct Wed–Sun 11am–5pm; tel:

7435 3471; charge) is a 17th-century mansion containing collections of harpsichords and ceramics. Noted for its snowdrops in early spring.

Tucked away among the lanes is **Burgh House** (New End Square; www.burghhouse.org.uk; Wed–Fri and Sun noon–5pm, Sat ground floor gallery only; tel: 7431 0144) which has a fine music room and library and an award-winning garden. One of London's finest Queen Anne-style houses, it doubles as **Hampstead Museum**, which has a display on the landscape painter John Constable (1776–1837), a one-time local.

## HIGHGATE ❽

Neighbouring Highgate, a hill-top suburb built round a pretty square, contains London's grandest cemetery. **Highgate Cemetery** (www.highgate-cemetery.org; tel: 8340 1834; charge) comprises two sections *(see box)*. The eastern cemetery (Mon–Fri 10am–4.30pm, weekends 11am–4.30pm) can be visited independently, though guided tours are available. The western section, across Swain's Lane, is more atmospheric

**BELOW LEFT:** the memorial to Karl Marx.
**BELOW RIGHT:** Highgate Cemetery is full of elaborate memorials and statues, including plenty of weeping angels.

## Highgate Cemetery

**A**s London expanded in the early 19th century, the matter of where to bury the dead became a pressing problem. A number of new cemeteries were therefore built on the city's outskirts, including, in 1839, the western section of Highgate Cemetery. In 1854 the cemetery was expanded when another section was opened on the eastern side of Swain's Lane.

These quintessentially Victorian cemeteries are noted for their grandiose mausoleums (many listed structures) and statues, artfully covered in creepers and set amidst wild flowers. One of the chief attractions is the rather grim bust of Karl Marx, who was buried in the eastern section in 1883. There are some 850 notable people buried in the two cemeteries, among them the novelist George Eliot, members of the Rossetti family, and the scientist Michael Faraday. It is well worth taking one of the guided tours *(see contact details in the main text).*

but can only be visited on a one-hour guided tour (at weekends tours are conducted hourly between 11am and 4.30pm; the weekday tour at 1.45pm should be booked). The cemetery is administered as a museum, with charges for taking photographs.

## NORTHERN OUTPOSTS

Also worth highlighting are a couple of attractions in suburbs further north. Hendon is reached by the Northern Line.

### Hendon

The main reason to visit this northern suburb is the **Royal Air Force Museum** (Grahame Park Way; www.rafmuseum.org.uk; daily 10am–6pm; tel: 8205 2266; free). It has a large array of bombers and fighter jets, plus flight simulators and a Battle of Britain Hall with tableaux of scenes from World War II. You can wander among some of the most famous aeroplanes in history.

### Walthamstow

An outpost at the far end of the Tube's Victoria line, Walthamstow is not an

KIDS

Though rather a long trek by Tube to Colindale, plus a 15-minute walk from there, the Royal Air Force Museum is a huge hit with most children, especially boys. It is also free, as is the Tube journey for children under the age of 11.

obvious tourist attraction, but admirers of the British Arts and Crafts movement may like to visit the **William Morris Gallery** (Lloyd Park, Forest Road, Walthamstow, E17; www.walthamforest.gov.uk; Wed–Sun 10am–5pm; tel: 8496 4390; charge). It contains an outstanding collection of fabrics, rugs, wallpapers, furniture, glass and tiles, designed by Morris and members of his circle. ❑

**ABOVE LEFT:** characteristic William Morris fabric at the William Morris Gallery. **BELOW:** the Royal Air Force Museum, Hendon.

# BEST RESTAURANTS, BARS, PUBS AND CAFÉS

## Restaurants

Prices for a three-course dinner per person with a half-bottle of house wine:
**£** = under £20
**££** = £20–30
**£££** = £30–50
**££££** = over £50

## Islington

### Afghan Kitchen

35 Islington Green, N1
🕾 7359 8019 Ⓒ L & D
Tue–Sat. **£–££** [p323, D1]
A favourite of many Islingtonians, this tiny restaurant offers a small choice of delicately spiced, melt-in-the-mouth dishes such as chicken in yoghurt and lamb with spinach. One large table downstairs. Best to book. Cash only.

### Almeida

30 Almeida St, N1 🕾 7354
4777; www.almeida-restaurant.co.uk Ⓒ L & D
daily. **£££** (set lunch **£**)
An ex-Conran restaurant specialising in modern French cuisine, with dishes such as red wine braised beef and pan fried salmon. Bang opposite the Almeida Theatre. Also offers a petits plats menu for those who only want a light dish.

### Antepliler

139 Upper St, N1 🕾 7226
5441; www.antepliler restaurant.com Ⓒ L & D
daily. **£**
Serving cuisine from the Antep area of Turkey, this restaurant offers dishes such as spiced lentil koftes or diced lamb.

### The Draper's Arms

44 Barnsbury St, N1
🕾 7619 0348; www.the drapersarms.com Ⓒ L
Mon–Sat, D daily. **£££**
In a leafy residential street, this is one of the area's top gastropubs. Robust flavours include braised Welsh lamb with fennel and barley. Has a patio garden.

### Isarn

119 Upper St, N1 🕾 7424
5153; www.isarn.co.uk
Ⓒ L & D daily. **££**
Long and slender Thai restaurant with a few tables on the deck at the back. Well-prepared dishes range from simple green curries and stir-fries to lobster in tamarind sauce.

### Ottolenghi

287 Upper St, N1 🕾 7288
1454; www.ottolenghi.co.uk
Ⓒ L & D daily. **£–££**
Stylish, with one long white table stretching down the centre of the restaurant. Great for breakfasts, light lunches (including inventive salads), savoury pastries and divine cakes and tarts. They sell items on a take-away basis too.

### Pasha

301 Upper St, N1 🕾 7226
1454; www.pashaislington.
co.uk Ⓒ L & D daily. **££**
Upper Street has several inexpensive Turkish restaurants, but this one is a cut above the rest. It offers a sophisticated interior, good service and modern European food with a Turkish twist. The good-value meze is a great option for lunch.

## Camden

### Camden Brasserie

9 Jamestown Rd, NW1
🕾 7482 2114; www.camden brasserie.co.uk Ⓒ L & D
daily. **££–£££**
Still going strong after 29 years, this popular place appeals to celebrities and locals alike. The space is elegantly decorated and the grills, in particular, are recommended.

### Cottons

55 Chalk Farm Rd, NW1
🕾 7485 8388; www.cottons-restaurant.co.uk Ⓒ L Sat–
Sun, D daily (until 1am on
Fri). **££** (set menu **£££**)
Inspiring Caribbean restaurant with inventive options as well as firm favourites such as jerk chicken and roasted goat. A party atmosphere prevails on Friday and Saturday evenings.

**LEFT:** Almeida restaurant, Islington.
**ABOVE RIGHT:** Ottolenghi, Islington.

## Gilgamesh

The Stables Market, Chalk Farm Rd, NW1 ☎ 7428 4922; www.gilgameshbar. com ⊙ L & D daily. £££ (dim sum lunch £)

This glamorous pan-Asian restaurant, lounge, tea house and bar may have extravagant decor but this adds to its fun element. Food includes sushi, dim sum, and mains such as wagyu beef and Thai chicken curry.

## Lemonia

89 Regents Park Rd, NW1 ☎ 7586 7454 ⊙ L Mon–Fri and Sun, D Mon–Sat. ££ (set lunch £)

Long-established local serving tasty meze and Greek chargrills. A bona fide family restaurant.

## Odette's

130 Regent's Park Rd, NW1 ☎ 7586 8569; www.odettes primrosehill.com ⊙ L Tue–Sun, D Tue–Sat. £££ (set lunch ££)

Primrose Hill restaurant where Oasis frontman Liam Gallagher proposed to Patsy Kensit in the 1990s. Fussy over-the-top interior but good modern European food.

## Sardo Canale

42 Gloucester Ave, NW1 ☎ 7722 2800; www.sardo canale.com ⊙ L Fri–Sun, D daily. ££

Sardinian restaurant with a bustling Mediterranean atmosphere, superb fish and seafood. The canal-side patio is a great spot for a summer lunch.

## *Hampstead*

## The Wells

30 Well Walk, NW3 ☎ 7794 3785; www.thewells hampstead.co.uk ⊙ L & D daily. £££

Gastro-pub with discreet corners and pretty views from its upstairs restaurant. Dishes might include grilled plaice with garlic crust and red-wine lentils, or mint and feta gnocchi.

## Woodlands

102 Heath St, NW3 ☎ 7794 3080; www.woodlands restaurant.co.uk ⊙ L Tue–Sun, D daily. £

Sophisticated setting for authentically spiced vegetarian dishes from southern India. Part of a global chain that began in India over 70 years ago.

## Zara

11 South End Rd, NW3 ☎ 7794 5498; www.zara restaurant.co.uk ⊙ L & D daily. ££

Friendly Turkish place serving Anatolian specialities. Ottoman rugs and cushions abound.

## Bars, Pubs and Cafés

### Islington

Bars include the enjoyable, canal-facing **Canal 125** *(125 Caledonian Rd)*, the quirky **The Winchester** *(2 Essex Rd)*, the intimate, slightly louche **Embassy** *(119 Essex Rd)* and the music-oriented **Social** *(Arlington Square)*. Traditional pubs include the ornate **Camden Head** *(2 Camden Walk)* and the **King's Head** *(115 Upper St)* which pioneered pub theatre.

Islington has a host of lively cafés, but for possibly the best almond croissants in town visit **Patisserie Bliss** at 426 St John's St, a tiny café just south of Angel. **Ottolenghi** *(see main listings)* is also great for mid–morning or afternoon treats.

### Camden

Bars include the hip **Bar Vinyl** *(6 Inverness St)* and the bar in **Proud Galleries** *(The Horse Hospital, Chalk Farm Rd)* where the cool people hang out. **The Engineer** *(65 Gloucester Avenue)* is a grandiose gastro-pub with good but pricey food. **The Lord Stanley** *(51 Camden Park Road)* is a fantastic, spacious gastro-pub with Mediterranean-inspired food and a walled garden. The menu changes frequently. Attracts everyone from students to retired folk.

### Hampstead

One bar to try is the newly relaunched **The Hill** *(94 Haverstock Hill)*, while celebrated pubs include the Victorian **Flask** *(14 Flask Walk)*, the **Holly Bush** *(22 Holly Mount)*, and **Spaniards Inn** *(Spaniards Rd)*, a 16th-century coaching inn with garden and summer barbecues.

# EAST LONDON

**For centuries, waves of immigrants settled in areas such as Bethnal Green and Spitalfields, often in slum conditions. Today, museums recall their struggles to succeed, and the docklands which once provided them with jobs have given way to canyons of office blocks**

**Main attractions**
COLUMBIA ROAD FLOWER MARKET
MUSEUM OF CHILDHOOD
BRICK LANE CURRY HOUSES
TRUMAN BREWERY
SUNDAY UPMARKET
CHRIST CHURCH
SPITALFIELDS MARKET
WHITECHAPEL ART GALLERY
MUSEUM OF DOCKLANDS

**BELOW:** Columbia Road Market.

East London was the first stop for many of the immigrants whose labour helped fuel the Industrial Revolution and build the docks through which much of the British Empire's trade passed. Poverty and overcrowding were endemic.

Today, many areas remain poor, but others have been gentrified.

## HOXTON

Hoxton, north of Old Street, first became fashionable when young artists such as Damien Hirst and Tracey Emin moved here, creating studios in redundant warehouses. As they became successful, art dealers and web designers followed and urban desolation became urban chic.

Commercial galleries radiate from **Hoxton Square**, the location of Jay Jopling's White Cube gallery. Café-bars and clothes shops line the streets around Curtain Road, and the area is one of London's most popular places for a night out. On Sundays Hoxton's **Columbia Road Market** (8am–2pm) specialises in flowers, plants and garden accessories *(see pages 54–5)*.

### The Geffrye Museum Ⓐ

✉ 136 Kingsland Rd; www.geffrye-museum.org.uk ☎ 7739 9893 ⓒ Tue–Sat 10am–5pm, Sun noon–5pm ⓔ free; charge for special exhibitions ⓡ Old Street

This museum charts the interior decorating tastes of the urban middle classes from 1600 to the present day. Housed in a square of former almshouses, it was intended to inspire workers in the East End furniture trade. The rooms – all of which are "sitting" or "living" rooms – are arranged chronologically from 1620 to 1990. Behind the buildings the museum's gardens comprise period and walled herb gardens (Apr–Oct), overlooked by a pleasant restaurant.

## BETHNAL GREEN

Although this is one of the poorest areas of London, it has two excellent museums focusing on childhood.

### Museum of Childhood **B**

✉ Cambridge Heath Rd;
www.vam.ac.uk/moc ☎ 8983 5200
🕑 daily 10am–5.45pm 💷 free
🚇 Bethnal Green

Displays in this outpost of the V&A Museum *(see pages 216–7)* range from classic children's toys to the development of nappies and the root of adolescent rebellion. There's

much to appeal to children: a magnificent rocking horse can be ridden, the model railways can be activated, a dressing-up box can be rifled through, and an activity corner encourages learning through play. There are also some sobering facts to be learnt about childcare and health.

Less than a mile away, the **Ragged School Museum C** (46–50 Copperfield Road; www.raggedschoolmuseum. org.uk; Wed–Thur 10am–5pm, first Sun of month 2–5pm; tel: 8980 6405; free) has a reconstructed kitchen and classroom to show how life was once

*A Regency period room, 1800–30, at the Geffrye Museum.*

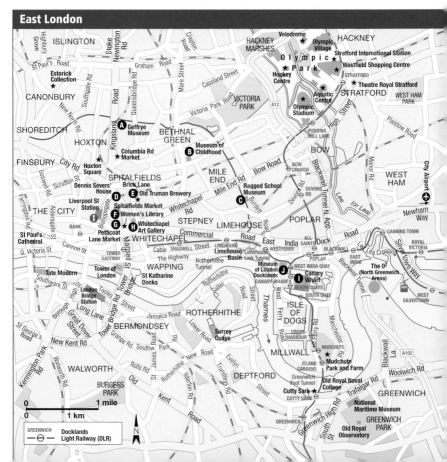

### East London

*[Map of East London with areas including ISLINGTON, CANONBURY, SHOREDITCH, HOXTON, FINSBURY, THE CITY, BETHNAL GREEN, SPITALFIELDS, WHITECHAPEL, MILE END, BOW, STRATFForD, WEST HAM, STEPNEY, LIMEHOUSE, POPLAR, WAPPING, BERMONDSEY, ROTHERHITHE, ISLE OF DOGS, MILLWALL, DEPTFORD, GREENWICH, and labelled landmarks such as Geffrye Museum, Museum of Childhood, Ragged School Museum, Olympic Park, Tower of London, Tate Modern, Canary Wharf, etc.]*

0 — 1 mile
0 — 1 km

GREENWICH
⊖ — Docklands
Light Railway (DLR)

# The 2012 Olympics

With London set to host the Olympic Games for a third time in 2012, a huge regeneration project is underway in east London, where most of the events will take place

**F**ollowing a closely fought contest between London and Paris in 2005, the International Olympic Committee announced that London would host the 2012 Olympics and Paralympics. One of the strengths of the London bid, which was led by former Olympic gold medallist Sebastian Coe, was the opportunity for urban development in east London.

The construction of a new Olympic Park in Stratford has brought much-needed investment to the area. Situated in the Lower Lea Valley, the 500-acre (200-hectare) site houses purpose-built sporting venues, a media centre and an Olympic Village providing accommodation for the athletes. The centrepiece of the park is the 80,000-seat athletics stadium which will also be the setting for the opening and closing ceremonies. There is a stunning velodrome, new arenas for basketball and handball, and a state-of-the-art Aquatics Centre with two 50m pools and a dive pool. Canoeing will be held at the new Lee Valley White Water Centre in Hertfordshire.

Existing sports venues in other parts of London will also be used for the games, with football matches at Wembley Stadium, tennis at Wimbledon and archery at Lord's Cricket Ground. Some of London's many parks have been incorporated into the extensive network of venues. Greenwich Park will provide a picturesque backdrop for equestrian events, while the triathlon will take place in Hyde Park. Horse Guards Parade, a parade ground usually reserved for royal occasions, will be transformed into a beach volleyball pitch.

London's ailing transport network is being extended and improved in order to accommodate the 500,000 spectators expected to travel to the Olympic Park each day. Many of these visitors are expected to travel on the Javelin, a high-speed shuttle which will whizz passengers from St Pancras International station to the Olympic Park in just seven minutes. Spectators travelling on Eurostar will also be able to catch a Javelin from Ebbsfleet, in Kent. Extensions to the East London line and the Docklands Light Railway are under construction.

The redevelopment has not been without controversy, however. Budgets have rocketed and the total bill is expected to be around £9.3 billion, far exceeding original estimates.

Perhaps with this in mind, much emphasis has been placed on the legacy of the games. The Olympic Park will become the largest urban public park in Europe, complete with waterways and wildlife areas, while the Olympic Village will be converted into apartments. Most of the sports venues in the park will become available for public use, as well as for potential future Olympians.  ❑

**ABOVE AND LEFT:** computer-generated impressions of the main stadium.

lived by London's indomitable East Enders. Children can sit at school desks and climb in the tin bath to get a taste of Victorian life.

## SPITALFIELDS

Spitalfields contains several streets of fine 18th-century houses that were originally the homes of Huguenot silk weavers.

## Dennis Severs' House ❶

✉ 18 Folgate St; www.dennissevers house.co.uk ☎ 7247 4013 ☉ every Mon evening (candlelit tours – booking required); Sun noon–4pm; Mon following the 1st and 3rd Sun of the month noon–2pm ⓖ charge ☒ Liverpool St

Among the 18th-century properties is this four-storey town house still lit only by gaslight. The late Dennis Severs, an American, laid out the 10 rooms as if they were still occupied by an 18th-century family.

## Markets

Successive waves of immigrants have left their mark on **Brick Lane** ❶. French Huguenots sought refuge here at the end of the 17th century, Jews fleeing the Russian pogroms arrived in the late-19th century and today the area has a large Bangladeshi community. Famous for its

curry houses, it also has some of East London's best bars and nightclubs, most of which are within the Old Truman Brewery, the self-styled "creative hub" of the East End. Also here is the Sunday UpMarket (Ely's Yard, Sun 10am–5pm), selling clothes from independent designers and gastronomic treats.

**Spitalfields Market** ❶ (Commercial Street; Mon–Fri 10am–4pm, Sun 9am–5pm), once a wholesale fruit and vegetable market, now sells mainly clothes and crafts, as well as antiques on Thursdays. To the south, centring on Middlesex Street is **Petticoat Lane Market** ❶, packed on Sundays with dozens of stalls flogging cheap clothes.

## WHITECHAPEL

On Old Castle Street, parallel to Middlesex Street, a Victorian bathhouse has been converted into **The Women's Library** (www.londonmet.ac.uk/thewomenslibrary; tel: 7320 2222), a collection of suffragette memorabilia, plus publications produced over the years by the women's movement. Proof of identification is

*At the end of Fournier Street, one of Spitalfields' finest streets, is Christ Church (1729), the greatest of Nicholas Hawksmoor's churches.*

**LEFT:** Spitalfields Market. **BELOW:** the Museum of Childhood in Bethnal Green.

**KIDS**

An incongruous attraction in this over-concreted part of Docklands (known as the Isle of Dogs) is the 35-acre (14-hectare) **Mudchute Park and Farm** (www.mudchute. org; park daily 9am–4.30pm, farm Tue–Sun 9am–5pm; tel: 7515 5901; free) on Pier Street. As well as farm animals, it has llamas, a pets' corner and a riding centre.

**RIGHT:** ground level in Docklands. **BELOW:** the Docklands Light Railway is being upgraded for the 2012 Olympics.

required to access the library. A space on the ground floor hosts exhibitions exploring all aspects of women's lives.

To the east is the **Whitechapel Art Gallery** N (80–82 Whitechapel High Street; www.whitechapelgallery.org; Tue–Sun 11am–6pm, Thur until 9pm; tel: 7522 7888; free), founded by a local vicar and his wife in 1897. Lacking a permanent collection, it mounts high-profile exhibitions. *Guernica*, by Picasso, was on display here in 1939.

## DOCKLANDS

London's docks, made derelict by heavy World War II bombing and rendered obsolete by new container ports to the east, were transformed in the 1990s. Their proximity to the financial institutions of the City made them an attractive location for developments such as **Canary Wharf** N, whose main tower, One Canada Square, is one of Britain's highest buildings, at 800ft (244 metres). Several national newspapers are based here.

It's worth taking a ride through the area on the **Docklands Light**

Railway (from Bank to Greenwich) to see how property developers turned the place into an architect's adventure playground.

The **Museum of London Docklands** N (No 1 Warehouse, West India Quay; www.museumoflondon.org.uk; daily 10am–6pm; tel: 7001 9844; free) recounts 2,000 years of history. It includes a 20ft (6-metre) model of Old London Bridge, an evocative reconstruction of the 19th-century Sailortown district, and a gallery on London, Sugar and Slavery, revealing the complexities of the city's involvement in the slave trade. ❑

# BEST RESTAURANTS, BARS, PUBS AND CAFÉS

## Restaurants

Prices for a three-course dinner per person with a half-bottle of house wine:
£ = under £20
££ = £20–30
£££ = £30–50
££££ = over £50

## Hoxton

### The Real Greek
14–15 Hoxton Market, N1
7739 8212; www.thereal greek.com L & D daily. ££
Authentic and award-winning taverna, serving delicious meze platters ideal for sharing, *souvlaki* and meat dishes cooked on a charcoal grill.

## Spitalfields

### Canteen
2 Crispin Place, E1 0845 686 1122; www.canteen. co.uk B, L & D daily. ££
Down-to-earth restaurant serving modern British food made with seasonal ingredients.

### Eyre Brothers Restaurant
70 Leonard St, EC2 7613 5346; www.eyrebrothers. co.uk L Mon–Fri, D Mon–Sat. £££–££££
Adventurous fusion of Iberian-influenced meat and vegetable dishes. Simple, distinct flavours. Tapas menu available.

### Great Eastern Dining Room
54–56 Great Eastern St, EC2
7613 4545; www.ricker restaurants.com L Mon–Fri, D Mon–Sat. £££
Contemporary pan-Asian food, from dim sum and Korean barbecue chicken to prawn *pad thai*. Chic but cramped interior. Attracts a young crowd.

### Les Trois Garçons
1 Club Row, E1 7613 1924; www.loungelover.co. uk D only Mon–Sat. ££££
(set dinner £££)
Extravagantly decorated (stuffed tigers, etc) ex-pub with French food. The nearby Loungelover cocktail bar run by the same people is the perfect place for a pre- or post-dinner drink.

## Docklands

### Browns Restaurant & Bar
Hertsmere Rd, E14 7987 9777; www.browns-restaurant.co.uk L & D daily. £££
Traditional British atmosphere and classics such as salmon fishcakes. Sunday roasts are popular, with dishes such as rib of beef or pork loin served with vegetables and roast potatoes.

## Bars, Pubs and Cafés

From classic East End pubs to trendy bars, there is no shortage of places to go drinking in east London. With its "shantytown" interior, **Favela Chic** (*Great Eastern St*) offers good food and even better music. At **Hoxton Square Bar and Kitchen** you can catch live music, sip cocktails or enjoy a tasty steak from their flame grill. Just the other side of Old Street, Curtain Road is lined with bars, including **The Elbow Room Pool Lounge and Bar**, a lively bar-cum-pool-hall. Around the corner on Shoreditch High Street, **Bar Kick** is a laid-back place with a good food and drinks menu and table football. Just off Brick Lane, the Old Truman Brewery houses **Café 1001**, a coffee shop and DJ bar, and **The Big Chill Bar** which lives up to its name with comfy sofas and cool tunes. The **Vibe Bar** is a buzzing venue with DJs every night of the week. Another Brick Lane institution, **93 Feet East**, has two bars, a large courtyard area and a main hall which plays host to a variety of gigs, DJs and film screenings. There are plenty of East End pubs around Spitalfields Market, including the **Ten Bells**, where one of Jack the Ripper's victims was allegedly last sighted.

**ABOVE RIGHT:** 93 Feet East is the place to go for gigs and DJs. **RIGHT:** Old Truman Brewery on Brick Lane.

# SOUTH LONDON

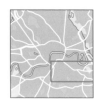

South London's suburban "villages" include Greenwich and Woolwich, with their distinguished naval and military heritage, historic Blackheath, leafy Dulwich and, in the southwest, vibrant Brixton

**Main attractions**
CUTTY SARK
NATIONAL MARITIME
   MUSEUM
GREENWICH PARK
ROYAL OBSERVATORY
OLD ROYAL NAVAL COLLEGE
GREENWICH MARKET
THAMES BARRIER
DULWICH PICTURE GALLERY
HORNIMAN MUSEUM
BRIXTON MARKET

**BELOW:** the Docklands from Greenwich.

Neighbourhoods and communities on the southern bank of the Thames offer parkland, museums, art galleries and great places to eat out. They are connected by a spaghetti of overground railway lines emanating from London Bridge and Charing Cross railway stations.

## GREENWICH ❾

A good way of getting to Greenwich is the time-honoured tradition of arriving at this maritime centre by water. Boats leave Westminster Pier daily from 10am (10.20am in winter) and take about 60 minutes. The best alternative is via the Docklands Light Railway.

### Cutty Sark

✉ King William Walk; www.cuttysark.org.uk ⏰ due to reopen spring 2012 ☎ 8858 2698 🚆 DLR

On the waterfront at Greenwich the *Cutty Sark* usually stands proudly in dry dock. However, the sailing ship from the great days of the 19th-

century tea clippers, now a museum, has been undergoing restoration, a process lengthened by a serious fire at the site in 2007 *(see box)*.

Built at a Dumbarton shipyard in 1869 the vessel was only expected to last about 30 years. But it has outlived its builders and crews. It opened as a museum in 1957 and was a popular London icon until old age began to show. The world's last tea clipper, the ship was named after one of the witches in Robert Burns' poem, *Tam O'Shanter*: "she wore a short petticoat, a 'cutty sark'".

## National Maritime Museum

✉ Park Row; www.nmm.ac.uk
🕒 daily 10am–5pm ☎ 8858 4422
🎫 free 🚆 DLR

Located in Greenwich Royal Park, the **National Maritime Museum** displays an unrivalled collection of maritime art and artefacts, with its many galleries set around the Neptune Courtyard. The museum is going through a process of redevelopment, due to last until 2018.

### Ground Floor

The Explorers Gallery looks at the history of sea exploration, covering early explorers such as the Vikings, Magellan's first circumnavigation of the earth, and the Europeans who sailed to America. The Maritime London gallery explores the city's naval heritage. Star item is the uniform coat worn by Admiral Horatio Nelson on HMS *Victory* during the Battle of Trafalgar. The fatal bullet hole at the shoulder is clearly visible.

In the new Sammy Ofer wing, visitors will find the Voyagers gallery, which looks at Britons and the sea. Focussing on the personal stories of this maritime nation, items on display include a letter from Nelson to Emma Hamilton, a sword and scabbard that belonged to Captain Bligh, and a watch worn by a passenger on the *Titanic*. This new wing also houses hi-tech exhibitions and a café.

### First Floor

The new Traders gallery explores Britain's maritime trade with Asia, looking at the mighty East India Company and the tea trade. Arte-

*A statue of the explorer Captain James Cook (1728–79) looks out to the Royal Observatory.*

**BELOW LEFT:** Greenwich Park. **BELOW:** the *Cutty Sark* will eventually be returned to its former glory.

## Restoration and Devastation

The *Cutty Sark* is the last ship of its kind in the world and for that reason the old tea clipper was made the subject of a £25 million restoration project in 2006. It was temporarily dismantled so that the hull and other valuable parts could be restored by a specialist team.

Then, in May 2007, midway through the project, there was a devastating early-morning fire at the site. The flames took two hours to contain. Although many sections of the ship were in safe storage at the time, including the masts, the stern, considered too fragile to move, suffered acute damage, and about 50 percent of the hull's ironwork and timber were destroyed.

However, the blaze was a setback rather than a death blow, and restoration was resumed. When the ship eventually reopens, the plan is that it will be suspended 3 metres (10ft) above ground, with elevators transporting visitors from the dry berth to all decks.

**TIP**

An alternative way to reach central London from Greenwich is to walk through a foot tunnel under the Thames and board a Docklands Light Railway train at Island Gardens. The 1,217ft (365-metre) -long tunnel, built in 1897–1902, enabled local workers to reach the West India Docks on the north bank of the river.

**ABOVE RIGHT:** entrance to the foot tunnel under the Thames. **BELOW LEFT:** Royal Observatory in Greenwich Park. **BELOW RIGHT:** the Queen's House.

facts on display include journals kept by sailors and a portrait of Robert Knox – the man said to have been the inspiration for Robinson Crusoe.

The Atlantic Worlds gallery deals with issues of trade and slavery, looking at the movement of people, goods and ideas across the Atlantic between the 17th and 19th centuries.

### Second Floor

The Navigators gallery looks at how maps were developed, the use of scientific instruments in sea voyages, underwater exploration, and the discovery of the polar regions. There are also interactive galleries aimed at

children, one with a simulator allowing visitors to take the helm of a ship and steer it into port.

### The Queen's House

Completed in 1637, the Queen's House, showcasing the museum's art collections, was designed as a summer palace for Queen Anne of Denmark, the wife of James I. Designed by Inigo Jones, it was England's first classical Renaissance building.

## Royal Observatory

✉ Greenwich Park, Blackheath Avenue; www.nmm.ac.uk 📞 8858 4422 🕐 daily 10am–5pm 🎫 free; charge for Flamsteed House and Meridian Courtyard 🚉 DLR Greenwich

It's a steep climb through the park – but worth it – to the **Royal Observatory**. Greenwich Mean Time was established here in 1884, and the observatory has Britain's largest refracting telescope. A brass rule on the ground marks the line between the Eastern and Western hemispheres.

Flamsteed House, designed by Sir Christopher Wren (himself a keen

*Recommended Restaurants, Pubs, Bars & Cafés on page 263*

astronomer), contains exhibits tracing the history of astronomy from its earliest origins in the ancient civilisations of Sumeria and Egypt. Valuable items on display include a Chinese sundial and a lodestone, an ore used for magnetising compass needles.

The *pièce de résistance* is a complete collection of John Harrison's ornate sea clocks, designed to remain accurate through the heat and cold, humidity and constant motion experienced on a ship at sea. They allowed mariners to determine their position east or west – an achievement chronicled in Dava Sobel's 1995 non-fiction bestseller *Longitude*.

A short distance from the main complex is the state-of-the-art **Peter Harrison Planetarium** (times of shows vary, tel: 8312 6608; charge). It includes interactive exhibits and an education centre, and offers a variety of shows.

## Old Royal Naval College

✉ 2 Cutty Sark Gardens;
www.oldroyalnavalcollege.org
☎ 8269 4747  ⏰ daily 10am–5pm
💲 free  🚉 DLR Greenwich

The **Old Royal Naval College** begun by Sir Christopher Wren in 1696 was built in two halves to preserve the view from Queen's House to the river. Originally a royal palace, it was given over to the training of naval officers in 1873. The chapel, where regular Sunday services are held, is full of decorative touches, and the ceiling of the Painted Hall, originally a sailors' dining room, displays a celebrated painting of William and Mary (who reigned 1689–1702) handing Liberty and Peace to Europe.

In 2006, during routine maintenance work, Tudor brickwork was unearthed in the grounds. Subsequent excavations revealed the remains of the palace chapel and vestry. The Discover Greenwich visitor centre has exhibitions, a shop and brewery café.

## Greenwich centre

The heart of Greenwich lies just to the west of the park. The town centre has interesting restaurants and shops, as well as **Greenwich Market** around Greenwich Church Street *(see margin)*. On the same street is **St Alfege's Church**, built in 1712–18 by

**SHOP**

Greenwich Market (Wed–Sun) spreads out from Greenwich Church Street. Here clothes, crafts created by local artisans, books and antiques are on sale, and there are numerous stalls selling tempting snacks and produce.

**BELOW:** the Old Royal Naval College.

**TIP**

There are excellent views of the Thames Barrier from a small urban park on the northern bank of the river. Thames Barrier Park on North Woolwich Road has a visitor café, a children's playground and paths lined with shrubs and flowers. Transport: Pontoon Dock DLR.

Nicholas Hawksmoor to replace an earlier church in which Henry VIII had been baptised. It was restored in 1952 after being badly bombed during World War II.

In an elegant period house is the **Fan Museum** (12 Croom's Hill; www. thefanmuseum.org.uk; Tue–Sat 11am–5pm, Sun noon–5pm; tel: 8305 1441; charge) displaying an unusual collection of hand-held fans from the worlds of fashion and the stage.

## WOOLWICH ⑩

River trips continue downriver from Greenwich, sweeping back up the eastern side of the Isle of Dogs to **Blackwall Reach**, around the O₂, an exhibition arena built for the year 2000, and once known as the Millennium Dome (www.theo2.co.uk). It is now a venue hosting everything from comedy and music gigs to ballet and the tennis ATP World Tour Finals.

Access to Woolwich is by overground train from Waterloo East, Charing Cross, London Bridge and Cannon Street, or by riverboat, the Woolwich ferry, and the Docklands Light Railway.

## Thames Barrier

✉ 1 Unit Way; www.environment-agency.gov.uk 📞 8305 4188
🕐 Thur–Sun 10.30am–5pm
💷 charge for information centre

Beyond the Dome is the massive **Thames Barrier**, which protects 45 sq miles (117 sq km) of London, including the Houses of Parliament, from the very real danger of flooding. In 1953, 300 people died in floods and the threat of tidal surges remains. The giant gates of the £435 million barrier, finished in 1982, can rise to 60ft (21m) high. The barrier has been closed 119 times in defence (as of May 2011) since its completion, and is raised once a month for tests (phone for times). You can reach the visitor centre on the south side by boat or bus from Greenwich.

Beyond is **Woolwich,** once the Royal Navy's dockyards and arsenal. The main attraction at the Royal Arsenal is **Firepower** (www.firepower. org.uk; Wed–Sun 10.30am–5pm, daily during school hols; tel: 8855 7755; admission charge), also known as the Royal Artillery Museum.

The centrepiece of this military museum is the ground-shaking "Field of Fire", which puts viewers in the midst of battle. Bombs and shells whizz overhead, guns roar and smoke fills the room. There is also a large two-level gunnery gallery which has an impressive display of artillery and "have a go" simulator.

## BLACKHEATH ⑪

A few miles south of Greenwich is **Blackheath**, one of London's neat middle-class villages. The windy heath is where Henry V was welcomed home after beating the French at Agincourt in 1415. Overlooking the heath is the Paragon, a crescent of colonnaded houses. **St Michael's Church** (1829) has a severely tapering spire known as "the needle of Kent".

**BELOW:** interesting places to eat and shop at Greenwich Market.

*Recommended Restaurants, Pubs, Bars & Cafés on page 263*

## DULWICH ⑫

With leafy streets, elegant houses and a spacious park, Dulwich is an oasis of calm. It is largely the creation of one man, Edward Alleyn, an Elizabethan actor-manager who bought land in the area in 1605 and established an estate to administer a chapel, almshouses and a school for the sons of the poor.

Today, the estate has more than 15,000 homes, Dulwich College, Alleyn's School and James Allen's Girls' School.

### Dulwich Picture Gallery

✉ Gallery Road; www.dulwichpicture gallery.org.uk ☎ 8693 5254
🕐 Tue–Fri 10am–5pm, Sat–Sun 11am–5pm ⓔ charge

**Dulwich College**, which schooled the writers P.G. Wodehouse and Raymond Chandler, spawned the **Dulwich Picture Gallery** by combining Edward Alleyn's collection with a bequest of paintings intended for a Polish National Gallery but diverted when the King of Poland was forced to abdicate.

The magnificent building, designed by Sir John Soane, opened in 1811 as the country's first major public art gallery. It contains 300 works by Rembrandt, Rubens, Van Dyck, Gainsborough and Murillo. A highlight is seven paintings by Poussin, including *The Roman Road*.

### Horniman Museum

✉ 100 London Road; www.horniman.ac.uk ☎ 8699 1872
🕐 daily 10.30am–5.30pm ⓔ free
🚆 take the train to Forest Hill from London Bridge

A mile to the east of the gallery is the **Horniman Museum**, one of south London's unsung treasures. Combining rich collections of ethnography and natural history, it was founded in 1901 by a wealthy tea merchant, Frederick Horniman, and is set in 16 acres (6.5 hectares) of parkland.

Highlights include a spectacular collection of African masks, bronze plaques from Benin, a large aquarium and a reptiles area. There are also over 7,000 unusual and historical musical instruments.

*An 18th-century toll road still operates alongside Dulwich College boys' school. Just up the road from the school is Dulwich Park with a dense wooded area. It was created in 1890 and Queen Mary visited the park regularly.*

**BELOW:** view from the Thames Barrier to the O₂ and Docklands.

### BRIXTON ⓫

It's not the architecture but the people who give **Brixton** its character. The population is around 60 percent white, and the balance includes Cypriots, Vietnamese, Chinese, Africans and Caribbeans. Its laid-back attitude to recreational drugs gets it

**RIGHT:** African Worlds exhibition in the Horniman Museum.
**BELOW:** Brixton Market.

a bad press, but the area also attracts affluent young professionals keen to own their own homes.

**Brixton Market** (Mon–Sat 8am–6pm, Wed until 3pm), running from Electric Avenue to shabby Brixton Station Road, mixes Caribbean produce with fruit, vegetables and fish, plus stalls of second-hand clothes, music and junk. There's a community buzz, but keep valuables out of sight.

Nightlife is lively here. The five-screen **Ritzy** cinema in Coldharbour Lane is popular, as are edgy dance clubs such as **Electric Brixton** (1 Town Hall Parade), and bars/clubs such as **Dogstar** (389 Coldharbour Lane).

Good restaurants and bars line the high street of nearby Clapham.

### THE SOUTHEAST

The National Trust-owned **Red House** (Red House Lane; www.nationaltrust.org.uk; Mar–mid-Nov Wed–Sun 11am–4.45pm; book a guided tour if you wish to visit 11am–1pm, unguided from 1.30pm; tel: 8304 9878; charge) is the only house commissioned by William Morris and is a temple to the Arts and Crafts movement. Built in 1859 by his friend Philip Webb, it contains furniture by Morris and Webb, and paintings and stained glass by Burne-Jones. Morris lived here for five years and the house was central to the lives of many of the Pre-Raphaelites. Trains depart from Charing Cross to Bexleyheath.

**Eltham Palace** (Off Court Road; www.english-heritage.org.uk; Apr–Oct Mon–Wed and Sun 10am–5pm, Nov–Mar Sun 10am–4pm; tel: 8294 2548; charge) is a stunning Art Deco mansion. It was built in the 1930s for the Courtaulds, onto the existing Great Hall of the medieval palace (built for Edward IV in the 1470s). The lavish rooms include a bathroom with gold plated taps, and a centrally heated area for the Courtaulds' pet ring-tailed lemur. ❏

# BEST RESTAURANTS, PUBS, BARS AND CAFÉS

## Restaurants

Prices for a three-course dinner per person with a half-bottle of house wine:
£ = under £20
££ = £20–30
£££ = £30–50
££££ = over £50

## Blackheath

### Chapters

43–45 Montpelier Vale, SE3
● 8333 2666; www.
chaptersrestaurants.com
◎ B Sat–Sun, L & D daily.
£££
Eclectic menu (roast belly of pork; pan-fried sea bream with cous cous) and a range of excellent desserts.

### Laicram

1 Blackheath Grove, SE3
● 8852 4710 ◎ L & D
Tue–Sun. ££
Friendly low-key Thai restaurant offering the standard satay, *pad thai* and green curry formula, but well executed.

## Brixton

### Asmara

386 Coldharbour Lane, SW9
● 7737 4144 ◎ D daily. ££
This quirky little Eritrean place offers a traditional Messob dinner, a "royal feast" of pancakes topped with stews and vegetable concoctions.

### Lisboa Grill

256a Brixton Hill, SW2
● 8671 8311 ◎ L Sat and

Sun, D daily. ££
No-frills Portuguese restaurant behind a take-away. Hearty fish and meat dishes.

### The Satay Bar

447–455 Coldharbour Lane, SW9 ● 0844 474 6080; www.sataybar.co.uk ◎ L & D daily. £
Round the corner from the Ritzy cinema. Offers cheap Indonesian rice and noodle dishes.

## Dulwich

### Dulwich Gallery Café

College Rd, SE21 ● 8693 5244 ◎ Tue–Fri 9am–5pm, Sat–Sun 10am–5pm £
Enjoy lunch or afternoon tea in a pastoral setting.

### Franklins

157 Lordship Lane, SE22
● 8299 9598; www.franklins restaurant.com ◎ L & D daily. £££ (set lunch ££)
A little off the beaten track, this offers unfussy modern British dishes.

## Greenwich

### Davy's Wine Vaults

159–161 Greenwich High Rd, SE10 ● 8858 7204; www.davy.co.uk ◎ L daily, D Mon–Sat. ££ [p335, C3]
Informed wine list, and good food. Sunday's lunch is served until 4pm.

### Inside

19 Greenwich South St, SE10 ● 8265 5060; www.

insiderestaurant.co.uk
◎ Brunch Sat, L Tue–Sun, D Tue–Sat. £££ (set menu ££)
Excellent, reliable local serving modern European dishes, such as pan-fried sea bass and barbary duck.

### North Pole Bar and Restaurant

131 Greenwich High Rd, SE10 ● 8853 3020; www.northpolegreenwich.com ◎ L & D daily. £££ (set menu ££) [p335, C3]
Resident pianist and

modern European cuisine. Dishes might include Scottish sirloin steak or cannelloni with spinach and ricotta, with treacle pudding or green tea and blueberry crème brûlée for dessert.

### The Spread Eagle

1–2 Stockwell St, SE10
◎ 8853 2333; www.spread eaglerestaurant.co.uk ◎ L & D daily. £££ [p335, D2]
French restaurant occupying a 17th-century coaching inn. Strong wine list.

## Pubs, Bars and Cafés

**Blackheath**
Traditional pubs in Blackheath include the **Hare & Billet** (*1a Eliot Cottages*) by the heath, and the **Princess of Wales** (*1a Montpelier Row*), where drinkers spill out onto the grass in summer.

**Brixton**
**Dogstar** (*389 Cold-harbour Lane*) is a legendary dance-bar, **Electric Brixton** (*1 Town Hall Parade, Brixton Hill*) is a club/live music venue and **Club 414** (*414 Coldharbour Lane*) is a techno/house music venue.
Convivial pubs in Brixton include the **Grand Union** (*123 Acre Lane*) and **Trinity Arms** (*45 Trinity Gardens*).

**Clapham**
An alternative to nearby Brixton, try the **Belle Vue** (*1 Clapham Common, South Side*), a friendly pub, or **Esca** (*160 Clapham High St*) a café/deli.

**Dulwich**
The **Crown and Grey-hound** (*73 Dulwich Village*), a decorative Victorian pub, is handy for the Dulwich Picture Gallery and has a pleasant beer garden.

**Greenwich**
The **Trafalgar Tavern** (*Park Row*), a traditional Thames-side pub. A less touristy riverside pub is the **Cutty Sark** (*Ballast Quay, off Lassell Street*). The **Green-wich Union** (*56 Royal Hill*) has unusual beers.

*Recommended Restaurants and Cafés on page 273*

# DAY TRIPS

Within striking distance of the capital is a vast range of places to visit, from castles to country houses, from theme parks to seaside resorts. Bath, Oxford, Cambridge and Canterbury are within reach, too

The roads around the capital are as busy as any European city's and, unless you are following a complex itinerary, it is best to travel by train or coach. For directions on how to reach places in this chapter, see the Transport section of Travel Tips, pages 276–80.

## WINDSOR

Just 25 miles (40km) from central London is **Windsor Castle ❶** (www. royalcollection.co.uk; daily Mar–Oct 10am–5.15pm, Nov–Feb 10am–4pm, last admission one hour before closing; tel: 01753 831118; charge), still a favourite residence of the Royal Family. William the Conqueror began fortification here in 1066, immediately after defeating King Harold at the Battle of Hastings.

The present stone castle was started 100 years later by Henry II. Queen Victoria had a special love for Windsor and is buried, along with her husband, Albert, at **Frogmore** (limited opening times; wwwroyalresidences.com), a former royal residence, set among sweeping lawns and exotic trees, about a mile (1.6km) away.

Though overshadowed by its vast castle, **Windsor** is a pleasant town,

with lovely walks among deer and ancient trees in Windsor Great Park, which spreads south from the castle, and along the River Thames.

A great draw for children is **Legoland Windsor ❷** (2 miles/3km from the town centre on the B3022 Bracknell/Ascot road; www.legoland.co.uk; daily Apr–Oct, closed selected weekdays in Apr, May, Sept and Oct; tel: 0871 2222 001). This theme park is based on the children's building blocks – in this case, millions of them. Its 150

| Main attractions |
| --- |
| WINDSOR CASTLE |
| LEGOLAND WINDSOR |
| BLENHEIM PALACE |
| SISSINGHURST CASTLE |
| CHARTWELL |
| ROCHESTER |
| WINCHESTER |
| CANTERBURY |
| BRIGHTON |
| BATH |
| CAMBRIDGE |
| OXFORD |
| STRATFORD-UPON-AVON |

**PRECEDING PAGES:** Brighton Pavilion.
**LEFT:** Winchester Cathedral. **RIGHT:** changing the guard, Windsor Castle.

*Blenheim Palace, one of England's finest stately homes, built in the early 18th century by John Vanbrugh is the birthplace of Winston Churchill.*

acres (60 hectares) of wooded landscape has rides for all age groups, ranging from white-knuckle roller-coasters for teenagers to gentle jaunts for toddlers.

More sedate, but also very popular with children, is **Bekonscot Model Village and Railway** (www.bekonscot. co.uk; Apr–Oct daily 10am–5pm; tel: 01494 672919; charge), near Beaconsfield, a stone's throw north of the

M40 (junction 2). This delightful attraction, rich in detail, has been expanding since 1929.

Six miles east of Windsor, on the other side of the river, is **Runnymede** (summer 8.30am–7pm, winter until 5pm; tel: National Trust 01784 432 891). This riverside meadow is where King John signed the Magna Carta in 1215.

## GREAT HOUSES AND GARDENS

The largest private house in England, **Blenheim Palace** ❸ (www. blenheimpalace.com; mid-Feb–Oct daily 10.30am–4.45pm, Nov–early Dec Wed–Sun only; tel: 0800 849 6500; charge) is just outside the Oxfordshire village of Woodstock (8 miles/ 13km north of Oxford on the A44 Evesham Road).

The palace was built by John Vanbrugh for the first Duke of Marlborough as a reward for his victory over the French at the Battle of Blenheim (1704). Winston Churchill

Day Trips

*Recommended Restaurants and Cafés on page 273*

was born here in 1874. He is buried in the church at nearby Bladon, on the edge of the Blenheim estate.

One of the country's most popular gardens is in Kent. **Sissinghurst Castle** ❹ (www.nationaltrust.org.uk; mid-Mar–Oct Fri–Tue 10.30am–5pm; tel: 015 80 710701; charge) has the famous garden created in the 1930s by the English aristocrats Vita Sackville-West and her husband, Harold Nicolson.

Winston Churchill's country home at **Chartwell** ❺ (www.national trust.org.uk; Mar–Oct, Wed–Sun and bank hol Mon 11am–5pm; entry by timed ticket; tel: 01732 868381; charge) at Westerham, close to the M25, has a water garden, rose garden and stunning views, and you can visit Churchill's studio.

## CATHEDRALS AND DICKENS

**Rochester** ❻ has a lovely Norman cathedral, and its huge castle, a gaunt ruin, stands brooding over the River Medway, 30 miles (48km) east of London. For many years the town was home to Charles Dickens, and in nearby Chatham is **Dickens World** (www.dickensworld.co.uk; daily 10am–

4.30pm, closes 5.30pm Sat–Sun; tel: 01634 890421; charge), a re-creation of Victorian London complete with Dickensian characters and an atmospheric boat ride.

**Winchester** ❼, a refined country town 66 miles (106km) from London, was the capital of England in Saxon times. Its cathedral has a fine English Perpendicular interior.

**KIDS**

Brighton, easily reached by train, is a great day out for families. As well as the beach and the promenade with their many attractions (sandpits, paddling pools, crazy golf and the Volk's Railway to name a few), Palace Pier is packed with fairground attractions, from state-of-the-art terrifiers to a traditional helter-skelter. Also worth visiting, near the pier, is the Sea Life Centre, a modern walk-through aquarium.

**ABOVE LEFT:**
Canterbury Cathedral.
**BELOW:** busker in Brighton's Royal Pavilion Gardens.

Canterbury **❽**, 62 miles (100km) from London, is also famous for its cathedral, where Thomas à Becket was martyred in 1170.

### SEASIDE EXCURSION

**ABOVE:** the Bridge of Sighs, Hertford College, Oxford. **BELOW:** the restaurant in the Pump Room, Bath.

Brighton **❾**, 59 miles (95km) from London, is a perennially popular spot. The old-fashioned pedestrianised streets known as The Lanes are a maze of antiques shops, book-sellers and souvenir stores, and much of the enjoyment to be had is in wandering. The jewel of Brighton is the exotic **Royal Pavilion** (www.brighton-hove-rpml.org.uk; Apr–Sept daily 9.30am–5pm, Oct–Mar 10am–4.30pm; tel: 03000 290900; charge), built in the architectural style of Mughal India by Henry Holland and John Nash for the Prince Regent at the end of the 18th century. The brilliant oriental interiors are decorated with golden dragons, chinoiserie, burnished palms and coloured glass.

### ROMAN BATH

Bath **❿**, with its beautifully integrated crescents, squares and terraces, is a Georgian masterpiece and well worth making a special effort to visit. Although 116 miles (187km) from London, it can be reached in 80 minutes by fast train from Paddington. At its elegant heart are the impressive **Roman Baths** (www.romanbaths.co.uk; daily 9.30am–5pm, until 9pm July–Aug, until 4.30pm Nov–Feb; tel: 01225 477 785; charge) to which has been added a new complex utilising the

*Recommended Restaurants and Cafés on page 273*

mineral-rich, soothing hot springs *(see margin tip)*.

The adjacent **Pump Room** was built in the 1790s as an elegant antechamber to the baths where visitors could sample the water, promenade and listen to musical entertainment. Today it is a restaurant and a lovely spot to have lunch or tea. You can still try the spa water, too.

Other architectural highlights of the city include the sweeping **Royal Crescent**, **Queen Square**, the **Circus**, the **Assembly Rooms** (which contain an excellent Museum of Costume) and pretty **Pulteney Bridge**, which is lined, like the Pontevecchio in Florence, with tiny shops.

## UNIVERSITY TOWNS

Within easy reach of the capital are the UK's finest university towns, each of which offers tours around the historic colleges, a pleasant city centre and that quintessentially Oxbridge pastime, punting on the river Cam or Isis.

**Cambridge** ⓫, 61 miles (98km) from London is compact and best explored on foot. It gained its first college, Peterhouse, in 1284, but undoubtedly the finest of all the college buildings is **King's College Chapel**, which boasts magnificent fan vaulting, 16th-century stained-glass windows and Rubens' *Adoration of the Magi*.

The college is also famous for the King's College Choir, whose carol performance is broadcast live across the world on Christmas Eve.

Among the other historic colleges, Sidney Sussex College in Sidney Street is remarkable for being the last resting place of the head of Oliver Cromwell, leader of the Roundheads in the English Civil War (1642–49), who had briefly been a student here.

Like Cambridge, **Oxford** ⓬, 56 miles (90km) from London, is also easily explored on foot. There's something about the light in Oxford, reflecting off the ancient stones, that gives the town a unique allure. Indeed, it was regarded by the poet John Keats as "the finest city in the world".

Coach-loads of tourists come to check, trooping respectfully round the university's three dozen colleges,

**TIP**

After many aborted attempts, Bath finally reopened its spa facilities in the form of Thermae Bath Spa, a luxurious and architecturally inspiring complex utilising two of the historic spa buildings. It offers an extensive range of pampering treatments to both men and women, and incorporates a rooftop pool with lovely views (tel: 01225 331234 or 0844 888 0844 from the UK; www.thermae bathspa.com).

**BELOW LEFT:** punting on the River Cam.
**BELOW:** Trinity College fountain, Cambridge.

**TIP**

The RSC (Royal Shakespeare Company) presents a varied programme of Shakespeare and other plays at its venues in Stratford (the Royal Shakespeare Theatre and the Elizabethan-style Swan Theatre). Check its website for details: www.rsc.org.uk.

a few of which have been centres of learning for up to seven centuries.

The best place to start a tour is Carfax, where the four main streets – Cornmarket, High Street, Queen Street and St Aldate's – meet. On St Aldate's is **Christ Church**, the grandest of Oxford's colleges, founded in 1525 by Cardinal Wolsey, Henry VIII's chancellor, on the site of an earlier priory.

For drivers, the Cotswolds to the west of Oxford beckon, their quaint showpiece villages seeming to grow out of the earth, so perfect is their relationship with the landscape. Tourism is intensive here, though it is possible to get off the beaten track with your own transport. Among the prettiest villages are Lechlade, Stow-on-the-Wold, Broadway and Chipping Camden.

To the northeast of Oxford, at Bletchley around 40 miles (64km) away, is a place that was once the best-kept secret in Britain. **Bletchley Park** (www.bletchleypark.org; daily Mar–Oct 9.30am–5pm, Nov–Feb 9.30am–4pm; tel: 01908 640404; charge) was a rambling country estate that became the heart of Britain's codebreaking operations in WWII. It was here that Germany's seemingly impenetrable Enigma code was broken, and here that the genius Alan Turing worked to build the Bombe, the machine that helped to crack it. You can see operational rebuilds of the Bombe, and the Colossus, the first semi-programmable electronic computer, built by the Post Office engineer Tommy Flowers to break another German cipher. Many of the original huts are still standing. If travelling from London, you may reach Bletchley by direct train from Euston in 40 minutes.

## SHAKESPEARE COUNTRY

**Stratford-upon-Avon ⑬**, birthplace of Shakespeare, is 40 miles (64km) north of Oxford. The **Shakespeare Centre** (www.shakespeare.org.uk; tel: 01789 204 016) in Henley Street is the headquarters of The Shakespeare Birthplace Trust, which administers five properties associated with the Shakespeare family (each with its own opening times, check website for details; money-saving multi-house tickets available).

**Shakespeare's Birthplace**, adjacent to the centre, was the Shakespeare family home and business premises – his father was a glove maker, wool merchant and moneylender, and became mayor in 1568. Like the other period properties run by the Trust, it has been authentically restored and furnished.

**Ann Hathaway's Cottage**, the childhood home of Shakespeare's wife, is in Shottery, about 1 mile (1.6km) west of town. It is an idyllic timber-framed thatched cottage with a pretty garden rather than the working farmyard it would have been in Shakespeare's day. The other properties are Mary Arden's Farm, Hall's Croft, and Nash's House and New Place. ❑

**BELOW:** the beautiful village of Broadway in the Cotswolds.

# BEST RESTAURANTS AND CAFÉS

## Restaurants

Prices for a three-course
dinner per person with a
half-bottle of house wine:

**£** = under £20
**££** = £20–30
**£££** = £30–50
**££££** = over £50

## Bath

### Demuths

2 North Parade Passage
☎ 01225 446059; www.
demuths.co.uk ◎ L & D
daily. **£–££**
Terrific vegetarian
restaurant near the
Roman Baths. Sample
dishes include a Middle
Eastern platter.

### The Hole in the Wall

16 George St ☎ 01225
425242; www.theholeinthe
wall.co.uk ◎ L & D daily. **££**
Long-established restau-
rant serving seasonal,
modern European food in
a period property. All
food is prepared onsite.
Good-value set lunches
and pre-theatre menus.
Log fires in winter.

### The Moon & Sixpence

27 Milsom Place ☎ 01225
320088; www.moonandsix
pence.co.uk ◎ L & D daily.
**££**
Restaurant in the
centre of town. British
favourites are given
an imaginative twist.
Smart but casual
ambience.

## Brighton

### Food for Friends

17–18 Prince Albert St, The
Lanes ☎ 01273 202 310;
www.foodforfriends.com
◎ L & D daily. **£**
This vegetarian restau-
rant is highly rated.

### The Gingerman

21a Norfolk Sq ☎ 01273
326688; www.gingerman
restaurants.com ◎ L & D
Tue–Sun. **££** (set menu **£**)
Modern European dishes
incorporating best qual-
ity ingredients.

### The Regency

131 King's Rd ☎ 01273
325014; www.theregency
restaurant.co.uk ◎ L & D
daily. **£–££**
Old-fashioned and bust-
ling fish restaurant on the
seafront. Serves every-
thing from fish and chips
to mussels and sea bass.
Some meat choices too.

### Terre à Terre

71 East St ☎ 01273
729051; www.terreaterre.
co.uk ◎ L & D daily. **££**
Busy café with innovative
vegetarian menu. Just
off the seafront.

## Cambridge

### Midsummer House

Midsummer Common
☎ 01223 369299; www.
midsummerhouse.co.uk
◎ L & D Tue–Sat. **£££**

Modern European cuisine
in stylish surroundings
beside the River Cam.

### Three Horseshoes

High St, Madingley
☎ 01954 210221;
www.threehorseshoes
madingley.co.uk ◎ L & D
daily. **£££**
Thatched inn in a pretty
village 2 miles (3km)
from Cambridge. Modern
Mediterranean food.

## Oxford

### Browns

5–11 Woodstock Rd
☎ 01865 511995; www.
browns-restaurant.co.uk
◎ B, L & D daily. **££**
This well-established
restaurant combines
classic British food with
a relaxed atmosphere.

### Brasserie Blanc

71–2 Walton St; www.
brasserieblanc.com
☎ 01865 510999 ◎ L & D
daily. **££–£££**

Member in a small chain
of Raymond Blanc
restaurants that provide
quality French food at
reasonable prices.

## Stratford

### Bensons

4 Bard's Walk ☎ 01789
261116; www.bensons
restaurant.co.uk ◎ B & L
daily. **£**
Come here for a cham-
pagne breakfast of eggs
and smoked salmon,
a light lunch or a first-
rate afternoon tea.
Booking is advisable
for tea.

## Windsor

### Oakley Court

Windsor Rd, Water Oakley
☎ 01753 609988 ◎ L & D
daily. **£££**
An elegant, formal
restaurant with high ceilings, set in magnificent
grounds. Excellent mod-
ern European cuisine.

**ABOVE RIGHT:** The Moon & Sixpence, Bath.

Insight Guides

# LONDON
## Travel Tips

# TRANSPORT

# GETTING THERE AND GETTING AROUND

London's size, and its knots of semi-static traffic, can make getting around slow. But things are getting better: thanks to the Congestion Charge traffic moves more freely in the city centre, bus services have improved, and even fares – so long as you make the most of Travelcards and Oyster cards *(see page 278)* – are now more reasonable. Information on all London's transport, including fares, is available from Transport for London, tel: 7222 1234, www.tfl.gov.uk.

**Note:** London telephone numbers are shown as 8-digit numbers. If dialling from elsewhere in the UK, precede these with the code 020. If outside the UK, dial +44 20 and then the 8 digits.

## GETTING THERE

### By Air

London is served by two major international airports: Heathrow, 15 miles (24km) to the west (mainly scheduled flights); and Gatwick, 28 miles (45km) to the south (scheduled, charter and low-cost flights). The smaller airports of Stansted and Luton, both to the north of London, are used by many European low-cost airlines, but have some long-haul flights. The tiny London City Airport in Docklands is used by small aircraft connecting London with some European cities.

### Heathrow Airport

Heathrow can be a daunting place in which to arrive, and it's important to plan how you'll get into central London. For further information on all airport services, see www.heathrowairport.com.
**Train** The fastest route is the **Heathrow Express** to Paddington Station, which runs every 15 minutes and takes 20 minutes. Paddington connects with several Underground (Tube) lines *(see map inside back cover)*. The fare is £16.50 single (£32 return) –

### FLIGHT INFORMATION

● Heathrow Airport,
  tel: 0844 335 1801
● Gatwick Airport,
  tel: 0844 335 1802
● Luton Airport,
  tel: 01582 405 100
● Stansted Airport,
  tel: 0844 335 1803
● London City Airport,
  tel: 020 7646 0000

perhaps the world's costliest rail ticket per mile. A cheaper option is the 25-minute **Heathrow Connect** service, which stops at several stations en route to Paddington, and costs £8.50.
**Underground** There is also a direct Tube route on the Piccadilly Line, which reaches the West End in around one hour. It goes directly to Kensington, Park Lane (Hyde Park Corner), Piccadilly, Covent Garden and King's Cross, and operates from 5am (6am on Sunday) until 11.49pm daily. A single ticket to central London will cost £5; keep your ticket, as you need it to exit the system. Heathrow Terminals 1, 2 (currently closed) and 3 all connect to the same Tube station, but there are separate ones for Terminals 4 and 5.
**Bus** National Express runs coaches from Heathrow to Victoria Coach Station; the journey takes between 45 and 80 min-

utes, depending on traffic, and the single fare is £5. The bus station is at Terminals 1, 2 and 3; from Terminals 4 and 5, take the free Heathrow Connect train to the bus station. For information, tel: 08717 818178; www. nationalexpress.com.

**Taxis** Heathrow is well-served by taxis. A ride into town in a London "black cab" will cost from £40–70 plus 10 percent tip, depending on destination.

**Car Hire** Heathrow offices of major car rental firms are:
**Alamo**, tel: 0871 384 1086; www.alamo.co.uk.
**Avis**, tel: 0844 544 6000; www.avis.co.uk.
**Budget**, tel: 0844 544 4600; www.budget.co.uk.
**Hertz**, tel: 0843 309 3009; www.hertz.co.uk.

### Gatwick Airport

Gatwick airport, 28 miles (45km) from the city centre, isn't on the Underground network, but trains and buses run to and from Victoria rail and coach stations. For further information, see www. gatwickairport.com.

The **Gatwick Express** train leaves every 15 minutes from 5am to 12.35am; it takes 30 minutes and costs £17.90 one-way. Children under five travel free; children aged 5–15 travel for half the adult fare. For more details see www.gatwickexpress.co.uk or tel: 0845 850 1530.

Southern Trains also runs services from Gatwick to Victoria, with stops en route: journey time is 30–40 minutes, and the fare £12.50. First Capital Connect has trains to King's Cross in London, via Blackfriars and London Bridge. Journey time is 45 minutes; the fare from £9.40.

easyBus (www.easybus.co.uk) run services from Gatwick to West London while National Express bus services (tel: 08717 818 181) operate the 32-mile (51km) journey between Heathrow and Gatwick (£24.50 single), taking between 60 and 90 minutes.

**Car Hire** from Gatwick:
**Alamo**, tel: 01293 567 790
**Avis**, tel: 0844 544 6001
**Enterprise**, tel: 0800 800 227; www.enterprise.com.
**Hertz**, tel: 0843 309 3030.

### Luton Airport

Luton is linked by First Capital Connect rail services with London King's Cross; some trains continue to Gatwick via Blackfriars. There is a shuttle bus between the airport and Luton train station. The journey to King's Cross takes about 40 minutes, and trains run every 20 minutes. Green Line buses (route 757) run to Victoria in London, and take about 90 minutes (tel: 0844 801 7261, www.greenline.co.uk).

### Stansted Airport

**Stansted Express** trains run to Liverpool Street Station in London every 15 minutes; journey time is 45 minutes, and a single ticket is £20. Buses run from Stansted to several destinations in London, notably the A50 bus direct to Victoria. It runs every 30 minutes, and tickets cost £9.

### London City Airport

London City Airport is mainly used by business travellers. The

---

**COACH CONNECTIONS**

National Express coach (long-distance bus) services connect Heathrow, Gatwick, Stansted and Luton airports with one another and with Victoria coach station. There are also direct bus services from all the main airports and destinations around Britain. For details and bookings, tel: 0871 781 8181, www.nationalexpress.com.

---

airport has its own station on the Docklands Light Railway (DLR), which connects with the Underground network at Bank station. For airport and flight enquiries, tel: 7646 0088; www.londoncityairport.com.

**By Channel Tunnel**

In 2007 the London terminus for **Eurostar** passenger trains from Paris and Brussels moved from Waterloo to St Pancras International/King's Cross. Journey times are about 2 hours 15 minutes from Paris, or 1 hour 50 minutes from Brussels. For information and reservations, tel: 08432 186 186 (UK) or 00 44 1233 617 575 (from outside the UK), or check www.eurostar.com.

Vehicles are also carried by **Le Shuttle** trains through the tunnel between Folkestone in Kent and Sangatte in France. There are two to five departures each hour, and the trip takes 35 minutes. Bookings are not essential, but advisable at peak times. Fares vary according to the time of travel: late at night or early morning are cheaper. Taking a car (with any number of passengers) through the tunnel costs from about £149 return, depending on availability. For information and reservations, tel: 08443 353 535 (UK), or see www.eurotunnel.com.

**By Ferry**

Ferries operate between many British and Continental ports. Calais–Dover is the shortest crossing (75–90 minutes). Some of the main companies are:
**Brittany Ferries**, tel: 0871 244 0744 (UK), www.brittany-ferries.co.uk. Sail from Portsmouth to Caen, Cherbourg and St-Malo, Poole–Cherbourg and Plymouth–Roscoff.
**Norfolk Line**, tel: 0871 574 7235 (UK), www.norfolkline.com. Dover–Dunkirk.
**P&O Ferries**, tel: 08716 642 121 (UK), 0825 12 01 56

TRANSPORT

ACCOMMODATION

SHOPPING

ACTIVITIES

A – Z

**ABOVE:** Docklands Light Railway.

(France), www.poferries.com.
Dover–Calais.
**SeaFrance**, tel: 0871 423 7119
(UK), www.seafrance.com. Frequent
sailings from Dover to Calais.

## GETTING AROUND

### Public Transport

### The Tube

The Underground (known as the
Tube, *see map on the inside back
cover*) is the quickest way across
town, but it badly needs more
investment. In rush hours (8am–
9.30am and 5–7pm) every station is packed with commuters.
Trains run from 5.30am to around
midnight. If you're heading for the
end of a line, the last train may
leave closer to 11pm.

Make sure you have a valid
ticket and keep hold of it after you
have passed through the electronic barrier – you will need it to
exit at your destination. If you have
an Oyster card *(see box)*, be sure
to touch in on entry and on exit, or
you will be charged the maximum
fare for the line. Stations are
divided into one of six zones,
spreading out from the centre; the
minimum adult fare for a single
ticket in zones 1–2 is £4, but only
£1.90 with an Oyster card. A single ticket from Heathrow to the
centre will cost £5.

It is illegal to smoke within the
Tube system or on buses.

You can print out itineraries
from the website www.thetube.com.

### Docklands Light Railway

Known as the DLR, this is a fully
automated railway that runs
through redeveloped areas of
east London and to Greenwich,
and connects with the Tube network at Bank, Tower Hill, Stratford and a few other stations.
Tickets and fares are the same
as for the Tube.

### Buses

Bus routes run throughout the
city. The flat fare in central
London is £2.20, but only £1.30
for Oyster card holders. On several routes, if you do not have a

**BELOW:** licensed taxis are reliable.

## FARES & TRAVELCARDS

Single tickets on London's
transport networks are very
expensive, so it's best to buy
one of several multi-journey
passes. **Travelcards** give
unlimited travel on the Tube,
buses, DLR and valid rail services. London is divided into
six fare zones, with zones 1–2
covering all of central London.
A one-day Travelcard for zones
1 and 2 and off-peak (valid
after 9.30am) costs £6.60
(£8 peak time, children aged
11–15 pay £2 each if an
accompanying adult has a
travelcard). You can also buy
three-day or seven-day cards.

**Oyster cards** are smart
cards that you charge up with
however much you wish to pay,
then touch in on card readers
at Tube and rail stations and
on buses, so that an amount
is deducted each time you use
it. They are cheaper than
Travelcards if you only travel a
few times daily.

Cards and Oysters can be
bought from Tube or DLR stations. Visitors can order them
from www.visitbritainshop.com.
Children under 16 travel free
on buses, and under-11s
travel free on the Tube and
DLR at off-peak times provided they are with an adult.

Travel- or Oyster card, you must buy single tickets before boarding, from machines at the bus stops. Several bus routes run 24 hours a day, and on others Night Buses (identified by an N before the number) run about every 30 minutes from midnight to 6am. Most Night Bus routes run through Trafalgar Square. A full bus route map is available from London's six Travel Information Centres.

## Taxis

Licensed **taxis** ("black cabs", the famous, squat London taxis, even though many are now multicoloured, being moving advertisements) are licensed and display the regulated charges on a meter. If you have a complaint, note down the driver's licence number and contact the Carriage Office, tel: 020 7491 7800.

If you telephone for a taxi you will be charged for the time and miles it takes to pick you up as well. **Minicabs** are cheaper than black cabs, but can only be hired by telephoning for one, as they're not allowed to pick up passengers on the street. Use minicabs with caution, particularly if travelling alone, and do not use any of the unlicensed cabs that tout for business on the street late-night in central London. Only call for a cab from a reputable company.

## Coaches

Coach (long-distance bus) travel is generally cheaper than travelling by train. National Express runs services throughout the

### PHONE CABS

To arrange for a licensed black cab by phone, call:
**Radio Taxis**
Tel: 7272 0272
**MINICAB COMPANIES**
**Addison Lee**
Tel: 0844 800 6677
**Lancaster Private Hire**
Tel: 7262 7282

### RAILWAY STATION TERMINALS

Britain's rail services are run by a variety of private companies. These are the principal mainline stations, with the areas they serve:
**Charing Cross Station**. Services to south London and southeast England: Canterbury, Folkestone, Hastings, Dover Priory.
**Euston Station**. Services to northwest London and beyond to Birmingham and the northwest: Liverpool, Manchester, Glasgow.
**King's Cross Station**. Services to north London and beyond to the northeast: Leeds, York, Newcastle, Edinburgh and Aberdeen.
**St Pancras Station**. Points not quite so far north, such as Nottingham, Derby and Sheffield, plus the Eurostar terminal for trains from Paris and Brussels.
**Liverpool Street Station** and **Fenchurch Street**. To east and northeast London, Cambridge and East Anglia.

**Paddington Station**. Services to west London and to Oxford, Bath, Bristol, the west, and South Wales.
**Victoria Station**. Services to south London and southeast England, including Gatwick airport, Brighton, Newhaven and Dover.
**Waterloo Station**. To southwest London, Southampton, and southern England as far as Exeter, including Richmond, Windsor and Ascot.
Other terminals, such as **Marylebone**, **London Bridge**, **Cannon Street** and **Blackfriars**, are mainly commuter stations, used for destinations around London.
For information on **train times**, tel: 0845 748 4950.

country from Victoria Coach Station on Buckingham Palace Road, tel: 08717 818 181, www.nationalexpress.com.

### Driving

Central London is a nightmare to drive in, with its web of one-way streets, bad signposting, and impatient drivers (taxi drivers hate hesitation). Drive on the left and observe speed limits (police detection cameras proliferate). Do not drive in bus lanes at the hours signposted. There are heavy penalties for driving after drinking over the limit. Drivers and passengers (front and back) must use seat belts.

### Parking

Meters are slightly cheaper than car parks, but only allow parking for a maximum of two or four

hours. Wardens are unforgiving. Some meter parking is free after 6.30pm each evening, after 1.30pm in many areas on Saturday afternoons and all day Sunday. However, always check the details given on the meter. Penalty tickets cost £80 or £130 and reclaiming your vehicle once it has been towed away can set you back over £200.

## Congestion Charge

Cars driving into a clearly marked Congestion Zone in inner and west London between 7am and 6pm Mon–Fri are filmed and their owners fined if a £10 payment is not made by 10pm the same day. You can pay at many small shops (newsagents, off licences/liquor stores) or by telephoning 0845 900 1234. Cars with non-UK plates usually escape a fine.

TRANSPORT

ACCOMMODATION

SHOPPING

ACTIVITIES

A – Z

## CYCLING

Cycling in London can be intimidating, but a bike is often the quickest means of getting around the city. Extensive information on cycling in London can be found on the Transport for London website, www.tfl.gov.uk, which has information on the Barclays cycle hire scheme. You can pay at docking stations with a credit or debit card. More information is available from the London Cycle Network (www.londoncyclenetwork.org.uk) and the London Cycling Campaign (www.lcc.org.uk).

**CYCLE HIRE**
**Veloruation**
tel: 7637 4004
www.velorution.biz
18 Great Titchfield Street, W1.
**London Bicycle Tour Company**
tel: 7928 6838
www.londonbicycle.com

## Car Hire

To rent a car you must be over 21 years old and have held a full driving licence for more than a year. The cost usually includes insurance and unlimited mileage.
**Alamo**, tel: 0871 384 1086
**Avis**, tel: 0844 581 0147
**Budget**, tel: 0844 544 3470
**Hertz**, tel: 0843 309 3049
(Marble Arch branch)

### Trips Out of London

This section details how to reach the day-trip destinations described on pages 267–72.
**Windsor**
Either take the train from Paddington, journey time 30–50 minutes, or from Waterloo, journey time about 45 minutes. Green Line coaches (tel: 0844 801 7261; www.greenline.co.uk) depart from Victoria approx. every hour, journey time about 1 hour.
**Blenheim Palace**
Trains from Paddington to Oxford, journey time 1 hour

(see also under Oxford). Bus No. 53 from Oxford to Woodstock at approx. 30-minute intervals.
**Sissinghurst Castle**
Trains from Charing Cross to Staplehurst Station, journey time 1 hour. A bus link from Staplehurst to the castle runs Tue and Sun only from May (tel: 01580 710 700). Or take Arriva bus No. 5 Maidstone–Hastings alighting at Sissinghurst.
By road, it is 2 miles/3km north-east of Cranbrook, 1 mile/1.6km east of Sissinghurst village.
**Chartwell**
Take a train from Victoria to Bromley South, then take bus 246. Alternatively, catch trains from Charing Cross or London Bridge to Sevenoaks, then take bus 238.
By road, it is 2 miles/3km south of Westerham, fork left off B2026.
**Rochester**
Trains from Victoria, journey time 40 minutes–1 hour.
**Winchester**
Trains from Waterloo, journey time 1 hour.
National Express coaches from Victoria, journey approx. 2 hours.
**Canterbury**
Trains from Victoria and Charing Cross, journey time

BELOW: beating the traffic.

90–105 minutes.
National Express coaches depart from Victoria, journey time 110 minutes.
**Brighton**
Trains from Victoria or London Bridge, journey time 50 minutes–1 hour.
National Express coaches from Victoria stopping at Gatwick and elsewhere, journey time 2 hours.
**Bath**
Trains from Paddington, journey time 80 minutes.
National Express coaches from Victoria; direct-service journey time 3¼–3¾ hours.
**Cambridge**
Trains from King's Cross, journey time 45–80 minutes; a slower service runs from Liverpool Street Station.
National Express coaches from Victoria, journey time 2 hours.
**Oxford**
Trains from Paddington, journey time 1 hour.
Two competing bus lines, Oxford Tube and Oxford Bus Company, run from Victoria bus station; they have services every 12 or 20 minutes.
**Stratford-upon-Avon**
Trains from Marylebone station, direct-service journey time 2¼ hours.
National Express coaches from Victoria: three services a day.

# **A** CCOMMODATION

## SOME THINGS TO CONSIDER
## BEFORE YOU BOOK THE ROOM

L ondon's hotels are famously expensive, and foreign visitors
can be disappointed by the standard provided for the high
rates charged. But fortunately, this is less true than it used
to be. New hotels offering affordable accommodation in a central
location, many belonging to mid-range chains, have sprung up in
areas such as the South Bank and the City, and even top-end
hotels offer special deals. And in addition to hotels, you will find
family-run guesthouses, self-catering flats and youth hostels.

### Choosing a Hotel

London has everything from
grand hotels of international
renown to family-run hotels,
guesthouses, self-catering flats
and youth hostels. The choice of
accommodation can make or
break a visit to the capital, and
the flip-side of the massive
choice is the equally massive
prices often charged.

However, there are bargains to
be had. As with most things, you
need to shop around. If a clean
room and a hot breakfast are all
you ask, a small hotel may offer
them for about a sixth of the
price of a top hotel. The smaller
hotels are often more friendly,
making up in the welcome what
they may lack in facilities. Just
don't expect a lot of space – the
cheaper rooms really are cell-like.

### Hotel Areas

There are hotels everywhere in
London, but some areas have

more than others. Don't necessarily expect to find a bargain two
minutes walk from Piccadilly Circus, though the main concentra-
tions tend to be around Victoria,
Earl's Court/Kensington, the
West End and Bayswater. SW1 is
London's traditional hotel district. There are some delightfully
old-fashioned hotels in Victoria,
in most price brackets, and the
streets close to Victoria Station
are full of terraced bed-and-
breakfast accommodation. There
are also streets full of terraced
(or rather town houses, for this is
Kensington) hotels in the second
big hotel area of SW5 and SW7.
This zone, around Kensington
High Street, Earl's Court and
Gloucester Road, is another
major centre for medium-range
hotels of dependable comfort.

The West End is the third area
and the best-known zone. You'll
pay more for budget or moderate
accommodation here than you
will in SW1 or SW5. W1 hotels at
the bottom end of the price

range can be very humble. WC1
is a clever choice: it's central
and has reasonable prices, and
there is still some dignity, even
romance, in Bloomsbury (don't
expect to find either quality in
Oxford Street).

Bayswater, or at least the
area between Edgware Road,
Bayswater Road, Paddington
and Queensway, is full of
hotels. It does have a few large
expensive hotels on its fringes
but has a greater concentration
of moderate and budget accommodation. Quality and prices
vary enormously but the area is
convenient for the West End.

### Budget Chains

**Premier Inn** is Britain's biggest
budget hotel chain, with several
outposts in central London, including County Hall (by Westminster
Bridge), Euston, Kensington,

Southwark and Tower Bridge. There are also branches close to Gatwick and Heathrow. They are clean, modern and cost between £80 and £99 per night. Central reservations: 0871 527 8000, www.premierinn.com.

The expanding **Travelodge** chain does a similar job at similar prices; book early for good deals: www.travelodge.co.uk. Other reputable chains include **Best Western** (tel: 08457 767 676; www.bestwestern.co.uk), **Holiday Inn** (tel: 0871 423 4896; www. holidayinn.com) and **Thistle** (tel: 0871 423 4896; www.thistle.com) which often have hotels in prime locations.

### Prices and Booking

The following listings are organised according to price brackets. The categories are based on one night's accommodation in a double room, exclusive of breakfast. Generally you can get whatever your heart desires in expensive hotels. In budget accommodation, you're not buying a view; if you get one it's a bonus. Almost all hotels offer special deals that are cheaper than the published "rack rate", particularly at weekends, so it is always worth checking.

Book ahead. London fills up in the summer months (May and September are also crowded because of conference traffic), but if you arrive without a reservation, you can call **Visit London**'s telephone accommodation booking service on 08456 443 010 and book by credit card.

Hotel bills usually include service and no extra tip is needed, but if you wish to repay good service, 10 percent split between the deserving is the custom. Equally, you can insist that service be deducted if you feel you've been treated poorly.

Check when booking that the price quoted is inclusive of VAT, whether it includes breakfast and if the price is per room or per person. If you reserve in advance, you may be asked for a deposit.

Reservations made, whether in writing or by phone, can be regarded as binding contracts, and you could be prosecuted for breaching that contract by not turning up on the day. Rooms must usually be vacated by midday on the day of departure.

### Youth Hostels

English Youth Hostels tend to be extremely basic. You get a single bed in a dormitory with basic washing and cooking facilities. Most hostels also have restaurants. The price is low, especially if you book reasonably far in advance or for several nights; it will often include breakfast.

The **Youth Hostelling Association** (YHA) has six London locations, including St Paul's (36 Carter Lane, EC4V 5AB, tel: 0845 371 9012), Earl's Court (38 Bolton Gardens, SW5 0AQ, tel: 0845 371 9114) and Kensington (Holland Walk, W8 7QU, tel: 0800 019 1700).

Prices for members are about £20–25; non-members pay slightly more. To join, write to the YHA: Trevelyan House, Matlock, Derbyshire, DE4 3YH, or visit www.yha.org.uk.

Another popular choice is **Piccadilly Backpackers Hostel** (12 Sherwood Street, W1F 7BR, tel: 7434 9009, www.piccadillyhotel.net), which has 700 beds, online booking prices starting from £12–15 per night, and a lively location just off Piccadilly Circus.

Details of other student and budget accommodation are free from the **Tourist Information Centre** (TIC) at 1 Regent Street, Piccadilly Circus, SW1, or online at www.visitlondon.com.

### Bed and Breakfasts

Staying in a private home ensures that you meet at least one London family. The **London Bed & Breakfast Agency** specialises in such accommodation, with prices from £37–55 per person per night double occupancy,

or £50–90 single occupancy, depending on the area. Tel: 7586 2768; www.londonbb.com.

### A Place of Your Own

There's no shortage of agents and private companies offering London apartments, many of them luxurious, others basic and frankly, overpriced. Many holiday letting agencies ask for a deposit which is also to cover against cancellation. Avoid agents who charge a fee for finding your accommodation (such a fee is chargeable only when you have agreed to take a property).

Rental in the following apartments includes all bills excluding the telephone:

**Allen House**, 8 Allen Street, W8. Tel: 7938 1346; www.allenhouse. co.uk. 42 Kensington flats, 1–3 beds. From £1,400–2,345 a week.

**Apartment Services**, 2 Sandwich Street, WC1H 9PL. Tel: 7388 3558; www.apartment-services.co.uk. Sixty flats in central London, particularly Bloomsbury. From £600–1,200 a week.

**Holiday Serviced Apartments**, P.O.Box 226, Northwood, HA6 2ZJ. Tel: 0845 470 4477; www.holidayapartments.co.uk. Have a large number of serviced flats in Greater London from £630–1,400. Brochure available.

**Kensgate House**, 38 Emperor's Gate, SW7 4HJ. Tel: 7370 1040. Three Victorian houses split into studios and 1-bed apartments in Kensington and Victoria. From £180–450 a week.

### Halls of Residence

University halls of residence offer some of the best value for money accommodation in central London during the summer (mid-June to the end of September). The **London School of Economics** (LSE) for example, has a number of residences that are centrally situated. Tel: 7955 7676; www.lsevacations.co.uk.

# WESTMINSTER AND VICTORIA

### Luxury

**41**
41 Buckingham Palace Rd,
SW1W 0PS
Tel: 7300 0041
[p332, A1]
www.41hotel.com
You can't sleep closer to Buckingham Palace than in this posh 30-room boutique hotel with full amenities and club-like atmosphere.

**Berkeley Hotel**
Wilton Place, SW1X 7RL
Tel: 7235 6000
[p325, D4]
www.the-berkeley.co.uk
Many regular guests consider the Berkeley to be the best hotel in London. It's low-key, seldom advertised, with a comfortable country-house atmosphere. Facilities include a pool. Attracts a lot of British customers.

**Goring Hotel**
15 Beeston Place, Grosvenor Gardens, SW1W 0JW
Tel: 7396 9000
[p332, A1]
www.thegoring.com
This is a family-owned, traditional hotel not far from Buckingham Palace. Kate Middleton spent the night here before her wedding.

**Halkin Hotel**
5–6 Halkin St, SW1X 7DJ
Tel: 7333 1000
[p325, E4]
www.halkin.como.bz
The style is very contemporary and there's a first-class restaurant.

**The Rubens**
39–41 Buckingham Palace Rd, SW1W 0PS
Tel: 7834 6600
[p332, A1]
www.rubenshotel.com
Traditional hotel with a smart location near the Royal Mews, but also

conveniently close to Victoria station. Ten suites, 143 rooms, and eight "royal" rooms named (and themed) after British monarchs.

### Moderate

**Mint Hotel**
30 John Islip St,
SW14 4DD
Tel: 7630 1000
[p332–3, C2]
www.minthotel.com
Many rooms have stunning views at this 460-room modern hotel. Free Wi-fi and Skype. Only a short walk from Big Ben and the Houses of Parliament.

**Sanctuary House Hotel**
33 Tothill St, SW1H 9LA
Tel: 7799 4044
[p332, B1]
www.fullershotels.co.uk
Handy for St James's Park, but even handier

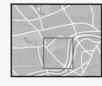

for the Fullers pub underneath the hotel's 34 rooms.

**Tophams**
24–32 Ebury St,
SW1W 0LU
Tel: 7730 3313
[p333, E2]
www.tophamshotellondon.co.uk
This luxury boutique hotel in Belgravia occupies five period houses and is very popular. Friendly and welcoming.

### Inexpensive

**Georgian House Hotel**
35 St George's Drive,
SW1V 4DG
Tel: 7834 1438
[p332, A2]
www.georgianhousehotel.co.uk
Friendly and well-run bed and breakfast hotel close to Victoria station. 53 rooms.

**Royal Westminster Thistle Hotel**
49 Buckingham Palace Rd,
SW1W 0QT
Tel: 0871 376 9039
[p332, A1]
www.thistle.com

### PRICE CATEGORIES

Price categories are for a double room without breakfast:
**Budget**: under £110
**Inexpensive**: £110–180
**Moderate**: £180–280
**Luxury**: more than £280

**BELOW:** clean minimalism at Halkin Hotel.

TRANSPORT

ACCOMMODATION

SHOPPING

ACTIVITIES

A – Z

Close to Buckingham Palace and St James's Park, with 134 rooms.
**Victoria Park Plaza**
239 Vauxhall Bridge Rd, SW1V 1EQ
Tel: 7769 9999
[p332, A2]
www.parkplaza.com
Four-star hotel close to Victoria station, with full amenities. 287 rooms.

### Budget

**Airways Hotel**
29–31 St George's Drive, SW1V 4DG
Tel: 7834 0205

[p332, A2]
www.airways-hotel.com
A pleasant hotel close to Buckingham Place and Westminster Abbey. 40 en-suite rooms.
**Blair Victoria Hotel**
78–84 Warwick Way, SW1V 1RZ
Tel: 7828 8603
[p332, A2]
www.blairvictoria.com
Attractive period hotel close to the train and bus stations. 48 rooms.
**Dover Hotel**
44 Belgrave Rd, SW1V 1RG
Tel: 7821 9085
[p332, A2]
www.dover-hotel.co.uk

Friendly B&B hotel three minutes' walk from Victoria station. 13 rooms.
**Grapevine Hotel**
117 Warwick Way, SW1V 4HT
Tel: 7834 0134
[p332, A2]
www.grapevinehotel.com
Friendly family-run B&B in Victoria. English breakfast provided.
**Hanover**
32 St George's Drive, SW1V 4BN
Tel: 7834 0367
[p332, A2]
www.hanoverhotel.co.uk
Good hotel close to Victoria station and situated between two

garden squares. 42 compact rooms.
**Sidney Hotel**
68–76 Belgrave Rd, SW1V 2BP
Tel: 7834 2738
[p332, B3]
www.sidneyhotel.com
Informal no-smoking hotel situated near Victoria station.
**Victoria Inn**
65 Belgrave Rd, SW1V 2BG
Tel: 7834 6721
[p332, B2]
www.victoriainn.co.uk
Popular, brightly furnished, 43-room hotel. Conveniently situated. Breakfast is included.

## SOHO AND COVENT GARDEN

### Luxury

**One Aldwych**
1 Aldwych, WC2B 4RH
Tel: 7300 1000
[p319, E3 also p336, D2]
www.onealdwych.com
Smart and stylish, One Aldwych has an excellent location a stone's throw from theatreland and Covent Garden. This

hotel is a showcase of modernity throughout with high-profile guests to match. 105 rooms, each with a minimum 6ft (2-metre) -wide bed, and television in the bathroom. Has a chlorine-free swimming pool.
**Hazlitt's**
6 Frith St, W1D 3JA
Tel: 7434 1771

[p318, C2 also p326, B1]
www.hazlittshotel.com
Named after the great English literary critic, Hazlitt's occupies one of London's oldest houses (built in 1718), in the heart of Soho. 23 rooms, all furnished with antiques.
**St Martin's Lane**
45 St Martin's Lane, WC2N 4HX

Tel: 7300 5500
[p319, D3 also p326, C2]
www.stmartinslane.com
Designed by Phillippe Starck, and still the most fashionable hotel in London. Outlandish lighting, good if expensive food and 204 blindingly white bedrooms. Very well placed for West End theatres and Trafalgar Square.
**The Savoy**
Strand, WC2R 0EU
Tel: 7836 4343
[p319, E3 also p327, D2]

**BELOW:** The Waldorf Hilton on Aldwych, well placed for Covent Garden.

### PRICE CATEGORIES

Price categories are for a double room without breakfast:
**Budget:** under £110
**Inexpensive:** £110–180
**Moderate:** £180–280
**Luxury:** more than £280

www.fairmont.com/savoy
This classic London hotel has a reputation for comfort and personal service. A massive and long-awaited £220m refurbishment has restored its reputation as one of London's very best hotels. 268 rooms and suites.

**W Hotel**
10 Wardour St, W1D 6QF
Tel: 7758 1000
[p318, C3 also p326, B2]
www.wlondon.co.uk
This newly opened Soho hotel radiates an urban hip vibe. A luxurious

base with 192 rooms, spa and gym.

**The Waldorf Hilton**
Aldwych, WC2B 4DD
Tel: 7836 2400
[p319, E2]
www.hilton.co.uk/waldorf
Renowned Edwardian hotel with 292 rooms. Modernised and with a superb location, close to Covent Garden and theatreland. Rooms come with plasma TVs and original Edwardian washstands. Restaurant, patisserie, bar, gym, sauna and swimming pool all onsite.

### Moderate

**Charing Cross Hotel**
The Strand, WC2N 5HX
Tel: 0871 376 9012
[p319, D4 also p326–7, C3]
www.guoman.com
Comfortable and reliable, this hotel occupies a Grade II listed building in a busy location by Charing Cross station.

### Inexpensive

**Holiday Inn**
57–59 Welbeck St,
W1G 9BL
Tel: 7935 4442

[p325, E1]
www.holidayinn.com
Very central but also a quiet hotel, modern behind its Edwardian facade. Family rooms available alongside those with twin, double and queen-size beds.

**Thistle Marble Arch**
Bryanston St, W1H 7EH
Tel: 0871 376 9027
www.thistlehotels.com
[p325, D2]
A huge, Art Deco hotel with 692 rooms. Very central, overlooking Oxford Street and across from Hyde Park.

# ST JAMES'S AND MAYFAIR

### Luxury

**Brown's Hotel**
30 Albemarle St, W1S 4BP
Tel: 7493 6020
[p318, A4 also p326, A3]
www.brownshotel.com
A distinguished, very British hotel with 117 rooms and a smart Mayfair location.

**Claridge's**
Brook St, W1K 4HR
Tel: 7629 8860
[p324, E2]
www.claridges.co.uk
Has long had a reputation for dignity and graciousness. The film stars' favourite.

**The Connaught**
16 Carlos Place, W1K 2AL
Tel: 7499 7070
[p325, E2]
www.the-connaught.co.uk
One of the best hotels in London, and very popular with British visitors. Discreet but immaculate service, and a restaurant with one Michelin star. Only 90 rooms.

**The Dorchester**
Park Lane, W1K 1QA
Tel: 7629 8888

[p325, E3]
www.thedorchester.com
This is one of the most expensive hotels in London, owned by the Sultan of Brunei. Lovely views over Hyde Park.

**Dukes Hotel**
35 St James's Place,
SW1A 1NY
Tel: 7491 4840
[p326, A3]
www.dukeshotel.com
90 rooms and suites, all with complimentary Wi-fi. Health club with marble steam room and beauty treatments.

**The Four Seasons**
Hamilton Place, Park Lane,
W1J 7DR
Tel: 7499 0888
[p325, E4]
www.fourseasons.com/london
This is a temple of modern opulence overlooking Hyde Park. Friendly and efficient service. Luxury spa.

**The Lanesborough**
1 Lanesborough Place,
SW1X 7TA
Tel: 020 7259 5599
[p325, E4]
www.lanesborough.com

Deluxe hotel overlooking Hyde Park Corner. The stately neoclassical facade of the former St George's hospital complements the opulent Regency-style interior. Despite being a relative newcomer this is one of London's finest hotels.

**London Hilton on Park Lane**
22 Park Lane, W1K 1BE
Tel: 7493 8000
[p325, E4]
www.hilton.co.uk

The more expensive rooms are on the higher floors, and the Michelin-starred restaurant on the 28th floor has stunning views of Hyde Park. Additional charge for internet access.

**BELOW:** Brown's Hotel is sophisticated and discreet.

**ABOVE:** The Dorchester on exclusive Park Lane.

**London InterContinental Hotel**
1 Hamilton Place, Hyde Park Corner, W1J 7QY
Tel: 7409 3131
[p325, E3]
www.ichotelsgroup.com
Perhaps the most opulent hotel on Park Lane's "millionaire's row". Modern and well equipped, with an Elemis spa and a fitness centre. Superb park views.

**Metropolitan**
19 Old Park Lane, W1K 1LB
Tel: 7447 1000
[p325, E3]
www.metropolitan.london.como.bz
Christina Ong's attempt to create a New York ambience. Home to the Michelin-starred, celebrity favourite, Japanese restaurant Nobu.

**No. 5 Maddox Street**
5 Maddox St, W1S 2QD
Tel: 7647 0200

[p318, A2 also p326, A2]
www.no5maddoxsreet.com
A stylish range of suites with minimalist decor and full facilities including a kitchen.

**The Ritz**
150 Piccadilly, W1J 9BR
Tel: 7493 8181
[p318, A4 also p326, A3]
www.theritzlondon.com
This is one of the most famous hotel names in the world. Not quite what it was, despite refurbishment, but it endeavours to keep up standards. Jackets and ties must be worn. Tea at the Ritz is an institution. 136 rooms.

**Stafford Hotel**
16 St James's Place, SW1A 1NJ
Tel: 7493 0111
[p326, A3]
www.kempinski.com
Beautifully located just minutes away from Piccadilly near Green Park. Three townhouses converted into a characterful hotel, with 105 rooms and suites.

**Moderate**

**Durrants Hotel**
George St, W1H 5BJ
Tel: 7935 8131

[p325, E1]
www.durrantshotel.co.uk
Period hotel in a Georgian terrace, 200 years old and oozing graciousness.

**Montagu House Hotel**
2 Montagu Place, W1H 2ER
Tel: 7467 2777
[p320, C4 also p325, D1]
www.montagu-place.co.uk
Well-equipped bed and breakfast hotel. The 16 rooms in this Georgian townhouse are graded "comfy", "fancy" and "swanky". All the stylishly designed rooms have TV, phones, free bottled water and high-speed internet. Has a bar and lounge.

**Montcalm Hotel**
34–40 Great Cumberland Place, W1H 7TW
Tel: 7958 3200
[p325, D1]
www.montcalm.co.uk
Quiet and rather plush hotel integrated into an elegant Georgian crescent. 153 rooms.

**Sherlock Holmes Hotel**
108 Baker St, W1U 6LJ
Tel: 7486 6161
[p320, C4]
www.parkplazasherlockholmes.com
Handy for Oxford Street shopping and close to Regent's Park. Contemporary furnishings strive for a boutique feel.

**Inexpensive**

**Cumberland Hotel**
Gt Cumberland Place, W1A 4RF
Tel: 0871 376 9014
[p325, D2]
www.guoman.com
Over 1,000 hi-tech designer rooms, each with individual works of art. Near Marble Arch.

**St George's Hotel**
Langham Place, Regent St, W1B 2QS
Tel: 7580 0111
[p318, A1 also p326, A1]
www.saintgeorgeshotel.com
Close to the BBC and Oxford Street, with 92 rooms. Impressive views from its public rooms and restaurant.

**BELOW:** The Lanesborough *(see previous page)*.

## Budget

**Beverley House Hotel**
142 Sussex Gardens, W2 1UB
Tel: 7723 3380
[p324, C1]
www.naylandhotel.co.uk/beverley
Well-equipped hotel in a Victorian building between Oxford Street and Hyde Park, with 23 rooms.

**Lincoln House Hotel**
33 Gloucester Place, W1U 8HY
Tel: 7486 7630
[p325, D1]
www.lincoln-house-hotel.co.uk
Georgian-style bed-and-breakfast hotel, with well-equipped rooms.

**Marble Arch Inn**
49–50 Upper Berkeley St, W1H 5QR
Tel: 7723 7888

[p325, D1]
www.marblearch-inn.co.uk
Convenient for Oxford Street and Hyde Park. 29 rooms.

**The Regency Hotel**
19 Nottingham Place, W1U 5LQ
Tel: 7486 5347
[p321, C4]
www.regencyhotelwestend.co.uk
An elegantly converted mansion in the heart of

the West End close to Regent, Oxford and Harley streets. Just 20 comfortable rooms.

**Wyndham Hotel**
20 Wyndham St, W1H 1DD
Tel: 7723 7204
[p320, B4]
www.wyndhamhotel.co.uk
Family-run hotel in period property on a quiet street. Small courtyard.

# MARYLEBONE, BLOOMSBURY AND HOLBORN

## Luxury

**Landmark London**
222 Marylebone Rd, NW1 6JQ
Tel: 7631 8000
[p320, B4]
www.landmarklondon.co.uk
This modern eight-storey building with a glass domed, palm tree filled atrium has good-sized rooms and all facilities.

**The Langham**
1 Portland Place, Regent St, W1B 1JA
Tel: 7636 1000
[p326, A1]
http://london.langhamhotels.com
Elegant and efficient hotel with 380 rooms, two bars and a restaurant. The attractive fountain room is an ideal place for taking afternoon tea. A short walk from Oxford Circus.

**St Pancras Renaissance Hotel**
Euston Rd, NW1 2AR
Tel: 7841 3540
[p322, A2]
www.marriott.co.uk
Stunning public areas at this restored hotel, originally designed by Sir George Gilbert Scott. There are 38 suites in the original building, and 207 in a new annexe. Right beside St Pancras Station.

**Sanderson Hotel**
50 Berners St, W1T 3NG
Tel: 7300 1400
[p326, B1]
www.sandersonlondon.com
A surrealist ultra-chic hotel, restaurant and bar with modern sex appeal, just north of Soho. A good retreat from the bustle of the city. 150 rooms.

## Moderate

**Montague on the Gardens**
15 Montague St, WC1 5BJ
Tel: 7637 1001
[p322, A4]
www.montaguehotel.com
A pretty period property with a garden at the rear. Flamboyant decor.

**Thistle Euston**
43 Cardington St, NW1 2LP
Tel: 0871 376 9017
[p321, E2]
www.thistlehotels.com
Modern hotel next to Euston station. 362 rooms with private bath.

## Inexpensive

**Academy Hotel**
21 Gower St, WC1E 6HG
Tel: 7631 4115
[p322, A4]
www.theetoncollection.com
A small and welcoming Bloomsbury hotel cre-

ated from five townhouses, with 49 rooms.

**Holiday Inn Bloomsbury**
Coram St, WC1N 1HT
Tel: 0871 942 9222
[p322, A3]
www.holidayinn.com
Modern, pleasant hotel with small indoor pool and leisure club. 284 rooms with private bath.

**Hotel Russell**
Russell Square, WC1B 5BE
Tel: 7837 6470
[p322, A4]
www.londonrussellhotel.co.uk
Landmark building in the heart of Bloomsbury with 373 rooms, all en suite.

**No Ten Manchester Street**
10 Manchester St, W14 4DG
Tel: 7317 5900
[p325, E1] www.tenmanchesterstreethotel.com
Comfortable Edwardian townhouse with just 45 bedrooms and an "all weather" cigar terrace, with a range of hand rolled Havanas. A lounge bar serves food all day.

## Budget

**Crescent Hotel**
49–50 Cartwright Gardens, WC1H 9EL
Tel: 7387 1515
[p322, A3]

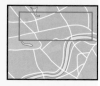

www.CrescentHotelofLondon.com
Situated in a quiet Bloomsbury crescent, with private gardens, tennis courts and 27 rooms.

**Gower House Hotel**
57 Gower St, WC1E 6HJ
Tel: 7636 4685
[p322, A4]
www.gowerhousehotel.co.uk
Pleasant bed-and-breakfast hotel near the British Museum.

**Lonsdale Hotel**
9–10 Bedford Place, WC1B 5JA
Tel: 8166 0990
[p322, B4]
www.lonsdalehotellondon.com
Long-established bed-and-breakfast hotel with real character. Over 40 rooms.

**Norfolk Towers Hotel**
34 Norfolk Place, W2 1QW
Tel: 8166 0990
[p324, C1]
www.starcrown.com
An elegant hotel with cocktail bar and restaurant. Has 85 rooms and is convenient for the West End.

# THE CITY AND CANARY WHARF

### Luxury

**Grange City**
8–14 Cooper's Row,
EC3N 2BO
Tel: 7863 3700
[p329, D2]
www.grangehotels.com
This 5-star hotel is a
member of a small well-
run chain, and is close
to the Tower of London
with views of the City.
Has excellent business
facilities plus a pool.

### Moderate

**Apex City of London**
1 Seething Lane, EC3 4AX
Tel: 0845 365 0000
[p329, C2]
www.apexhotels.co.uk
A modern medium-size
hotel near the Tower of
London. The 179 rooms
have good views of the
City, walk-in power show-
ers and widescreen TVs.

**Crowne Plaza London
Shoreditch**
100 Shoreditch High St,
E1 6JO
Tel: 7613 9800
[p329, C1]
www.ichotelsgroup.com
Situated in the heart of
the City, a few minutes'
walk from Liverpool
Street Station and
Spitalfields Market. Has
200 rooms and a roof-
top restaurant. Like
many City hotels, week-
end rates are consider-
ably cheaper than
weekday rates.

**Novotel Tower Bridge**
10 Pepys St, EC3N 2NR
Tel: 7265 6000
[p329, D2]
www.novotel.com
Overlooks the Tower of
London and London
Bridge. 203 light, well-
equipped rooms. Full
range of business
facilities. Good rates

available at weekends.
**The Tower**
St Katharine's Way, E1W 1LD
Tel: 0871 376 9036
[p329, D3]
www.guoman.com
Not the most attractive
building, but modern and
comfortable with wonder-
ful views, being right next
to Tower Bridge.
**West India Quay
Marriott**
22 Hartsmere Rd,

Canary Wharf, E14 46D
Tel: 7093 1000
[329, E1]
www.marriott.co.uk
This branch of the Mar-
riott offers particularly
good weekend rates.

**BELOW:** St Katharine's Dock, Tower Bridge.

# SOUTHWARK AND THE SOUTH BANK

### Luxury

**Marriott London
County Hall**
County Hall, SE1 7PB
Tel: 7928 5200
[p327, D4]
www.marriott.co.uk
Luxurious setting, with
many of the 200 rooms
facing the river at West-
minster Bridge. Full-size
indoor pool plus health
centre.

### Moderate

**London Bridge Hotel**
8–18 London Bridge St,
SE1 9SG
Tel: 7855 2200
[p328, B3]

www.londonbridgehotel.com
Independent four-star
hotel in an efficient
location for Bankside's
attractions. Has 138
rooms, a gym, two
restaurants and a bar.
**Mercure London City
Bankside**
75–79 Southwark St,
SE1 0JA
Tel: 7902 0800
[p328, A3]
www.mercure.com
A French chain hotel
close to Tate Modern
and the Globe Theatre.
**Park Plaza County Hall**
1 Addington St, SE1 7RY
Tel: 7021 1810
[p327, D4]
www.parkplaza.com

Sleek hotel convenient
for the London Eye. 398
rooms, each with kitch-
enette equipped with
fridge and microwave.
**Park Plaza Riverbank**
18 Albert Embankment, SE1
Tel: 7958 8000
[p333, D2]
www.parkplaza.com
Within walking distance
of many attractions,
394 rooms and views
over the Houses of Par-
liament and London Eye.

### Inexpensive

**Mad Hatter**
3–7 Stamford St, SE1 9NY
Tel: 7401 9222
[p327, E3]

www.fullershotels.com
30 rooms above a
Fullers pub. Just a short
stroll from Tate Modern
and other attractions on
the South Bank.
**Novotel City South**
53–61 Southwark Bridge Rd,
SE1 9HH
Tel: 7089 0400
[p328, B3]
www.novotel.com
Close to Shakespeare's
Globe and Tate Modern.
Clean, modern rooms.

# KNIGHTSBRIDGE, KENSINGTON AND CHELSEA

## Luxury

**Blakes Hotel**
33 Roland Gardens, SW7 3PF
Tel: 7370 6701
[p330, B2]
www.blakeshotel.com
Very trendy and up-to-the-minute hotel which is popular with theatrical and media folk. Cosmopolitan, tolerant, laid-back in style. 51 rooms.

**Cadogan Hotel**
75 Sloane St, SW1X 9SG
Tel: 7235 7141
[p325, D4 also p331, D1]
www.cadogan.com
Another 19th-century style hotel. Interesting position between Knightsbridge and Chelsea. Lily Langtry once lived in what is now the bar, and Oscar Wilde was arrested in room 118.

**Capital Hotel**
22 Basil St, SW3 1AT
Tel: 7589 5171
[p331, D1]
www.capitalhotel.co.uk
Luxurious little hotel (50 rooms) in the heart of Knightsbridge. Restrained in style, with tasteful decor, and rooms in the country-

house style of interior design. Friendly service.

**The Gore**
190 Queen's Gate, SW7 5EX
Tel: 7584 6601
[p324, B4]
www.gorehotel.com
This idiosyncratic Kensington hotel is close to the Royal Albert Hall. Every inch of the walls is covered in paintings and prints, and it attracts a lively, fashionable crowd. There are 50 individually themed rooms, some with four-poster beds.

**Mandarin Oriental Hyde Park**
66 Knightsbridge, SW1X 7LA
Tel: 7235 2000
[p325, D4]
www.mandarinoriental.com
A hotel of character (185 rooms), right on Knightsbridge and close to Harrods. Sumptuous in a Victorian marble-and-chandeliers style.

**Royal Garden Hotel**
2–24 Kensington High St, W8 4PT
Tel: 7937 8000
[p324, A4]
www.royalgardenhotel.co.uk
Refurbished from top to bottom, this is now

a 5-star hotel. Decorated throughout in a luxurious contemporary style, it has a health club and one of London's finest views over Kensington Gardens from the top-floor Min Jiang restaurant.

**Wyndham Grand**
Chelsea Harbour,
Off Lots Rd, SW10 0XG
Tel: 7823 3000
www.wyndhamgrandlondon.co.uk
Luxury hotel within the exclusive Chelsea Harbour complex by the Thames. Many of the 154 suites have private balconies. The spa has a 17m indoor swimming pool, and a range of spa treatments are offered.

## Moderate

**Aster House**
3 Sumner Place,
South Kensington, SW7 3EE
Tel: 7581 5888
[p330, B2]
www.asterhouse.com
Victorian townhouse B&B, well located for the famous museums. The rooms have chintzy fabrics, Wi-fi and power showers in the bathrooms. Guests can obtain a free loan of a mobile phone during their stay.

**Knightsbridge Green Hotel**
159 Knightsbridge, SW1X 7PD
Tel: 7584 6274
[p325, D4]
www.knightsbridgegreenhotel.com
This hotel is very good value for the location and is unusual in that it consists mostly of suites, double and family-sized rooms.

Thirty rooms, all of which are non-smoking.

## Inexpensive

**Abbey Court**
20 Pembridge Gardens,
W2 4DU
Tel: 7221 7518
[p334, B2]
www.abbeycourthotel.co.uk
Beautifully restored Notting Hill town house, with the atmosphere of a private home. The 22 rooms have Italian marble bathrooms with whirlpool baths.

**Abcone Hotel**
10 Ashburn Gardens,
SW7 4DG
Tel: 7460 3400
[p330, A2]
www.abcone.co.uk
Located not far from Kensington High Street in a pleasant, rather old-fashioned hotel district. 38 en-suite rooms.

**Barkston Gardens Hotel**
34–48 Barkston Gardens,
SW5 0EW
Tel: 7373 7851
[p330, A2]
www.barkstongardens.com
Set in a quiet tree-lined street in a Victorian

**BELOW:** a fashionable choice in South Kensington.

terrace, but close to the bustle of Earl's Court and the world-class museums of South Kensington. Meals available. 93 rooms, all with private bath.

**Bayswater Inn**
8–16 Princes Sq, W2 4NT
Tel: 7727 8621
[p334, C2]
www.bayswaterinn.co.uk
Situated in a quiet residential square, close to Portobello Road Market, and handy for the Tube. 139 rooms, all en suite.

**Garden Court Hotel**
30–31 Kensington Gardens Sq, W2 4BG
Tel: 7229 2553

[p334, C2]
www.gardencourthotel.co.uk
Friendly, family-run 32-room bed and breakfast set in a traditional English garden square.

**My Place Hotel**
1–3 Trebovir Rd, SW5 9LS
Tel: 7373 0833
[p330, A2]
www.myplacehotel.co.uk
Modern amenities with Victorian ambience in Earl's Court area. 50 en suite rooms, bar, lounge and Wi-fi.

### Budget

**easyHotel**
14 Lexham Gardens, Kensington, W8 5JE

[p330, A1]
www.easyhotel.com
Some of the cheapest rooms in London. No frills – some rooms don't even have a window – but great for budget travellers. There are other locations in London as well. Internet bookings only.

**Enterprise Hotel**
15–25 Hogarth Rd, SW5 0QJ
Tel: 7373 4502
[p330, A2]
www.enterprisehotel.co.uk
Good location close to Kensington High Street and Earl's Court tube station. 100 small but functional en suite rooms.

**London House Hotel**
81 Kensington Gardens Sq, W2 4DJ
Tel: 7243 1810
[p334, C1]
www.londonhousehotels.com
Friendly and stylish, in a pleasant location, and with 102 newly refurbished rooms. Extremely good value for money.

**Oliver Plaza Hotel**
33 Trebovir Rd, SW5 9NF
Tel: 7373 7183
[p331, A2]
www.hoteloliverplaza.co.uk
Bed-and-breakfast hotel providing good, friendly service and comfortable rooms, all 46 of which have en suite bathrooms.

# OUTSIDE THE CENTRE

### Luxury

**Cannizaro House**
Wimbledon Common, SW19
Tel: 8879 1464
www.cannizarohouse.com
Named after a Sicilian Duke this 18th-century country house hotel is in as rural a setting as London can offer. The more interesting rooms lie in the original building.

**BELOW:** Cannizaro House, Wimbledon.

### Moderate

**Hendon Hall**
Ashley Lane, Hendon, NW4 1HF
Tel: 0845 072 7448
www.handpickedhotels.co.uk
An historic mansion with its own grounds, giving a country atmosphere in the middle of north London. Fully modernised kitchen and

opulent dining room means meals are available. 57 rooms.

**The Petersham Hotel**
Nightingale Lane, Richmond, Surrey, TW10 6UZ
Tel: 8940 7471
www.petershamhotel.co.uk
Unspoilt views over parkland and the River Thames. Richmond train or Tube allow for easy ride into London (20 mins). 60 rooms.

**Town Hall Hotel**
Patriot Square, E2 9NF
Tel: 7871 0460
www.townhallhotel.com
The former Town Hall in Bethnal Green has been converted into guest rooms and apartments. Free Wi-fi, crisp styling and a pool in the basement.

**The Zetter Townhouse**
49–50 St John's Square, EC1V 4JJ
Tel: 7324 4567
www.thezettertownhouse.com
A 13-bedroom Georgian townhouse hotel in

Clerkenwell, with a cool cocktail lounge. Rooms range in size from "crash pad" to a large suite. Contemporary style and comfort.

### Inexpensive

**Hampstead Britannia Hotel**
Primrose Hill Rd, Hampstead, NW3 3NA
Tel: 0871 222 0043
www.britanniahotels.com
Near affluent and fashionable Primrose Hill, this hotel has a relaxed atmosphere, 121 rooms, a restaurant and a bar.

**Hotel Orlando**
83 Shepherd's Bush Rd, W6 7LR
Tel: 7603 4890
www.hotelorlando.co.uk
Family-run hotel with 14 rooms in Hammersmith, near the Tube.

**Kingston Lodge Hotel**
94 Kingston Hill, Kingston upon Thames, KT2 7NP

Tel: 8541 4481
www.brook-hotels.co.uk
Country-house hotel in
a pretty location to the
west of London. Close
to Richmond Park,
Hampton Court Palace,
and Kingston shopping
centre.
**Richmond Hill Hotel**
146-150 Richmond Hill,

Richmond, Surrey TW10 6RW
Tel: 8940 2247
www.richmondhill-hotel.co.uk
Four star, traditional
English hotel with a
friendly atmosphere and
spectacular views over
the Thames. Close to
Kew Gardens, Rich-
mond Park and Hamp-
ton Court Palace.

**The York and Albany**
127–129 Parkway, NW1 7PS
Tel: 7387 5700
www.gordonramsey.com
This townhouse hotel,
owned by Gordon Ram-
sey, has 10 rooms all
individually designed
with antiques and mod-
ern amenities. Located
in Camden Town.

**Budget**

**Andrews House Hotel**
12 Westbourne St, W2 2TZ
Tel: 7723 4514
www.andrewshousehotel.co.uk
Family-run, in a busy
area close to Padding-
ton and Oxford Street.
Has 17 rooms, most
with showers.

# EXCURSIONS

**ABOVE:** The Royal Crescent hotel, Bath

**Bath**

**Apsley House Hotel**
(Inexpensive)
141 Newbridge Hill, BA1 3PT
Tel: (01225) 336966
www.apsley-house.co.uk
Georgian country
house set in its own
grounds, with 12
individually decorated
rooms.
**The Royal Crescent**
(Luxury)
16 Royal Crescent, BA1 2LS
Tel: (01225) 823 333
www.royalcrescent.co.uk
Exclusive hotel in the
centre of the splendid
Royal Crescent. Tradi-
tional furnishings, and
every comfort.

**Brighton**

**The George Inn**
(Budget/Inexpensive)

High St, Alfriston
BN26 5SY
Tel: (01323) 870 319
www.thegeorge-alfriston.com
14th-century pub/
hotel in a village 18
miles (29km) from
Brighton. It has oak
beamed rooms and
the restaurant spe-
cialises in local fish.
**The Grand**
(Luxury)
Kings Rd, BN1 2FW
Tel: (01273) 224300
www.devere.co.uk
Victorian grandeur
and friendly service,
with indoor pool.
Overlooks beach.
**Hotel Pelirocco**
(Inexpensive)
10 Regency Sq, BN1 2FG
Tel: (01273) 327055
www.hotelpelirocco.co.uk
Cheap but chic hotel
in the best pre-

served Regency
square in town.

**Cambridge**

**Arundel House Hotel**
(Budget)
53 Chesterton Rd, CB4 3AN
Tel: (01223) 367701
www.arundelhousehotels.co.uk
A privately owned ter-
raced hotel near the
town centre that over-
looks the River Cam.
**Hilton Hotel Cambridge**
(Luxury)
Granta Place, Mill Lane
CB2 1RT
Tel: (01223) 259988
www.doubletreebyhilton.co.uk
Modern Moat House by
the river, in a conve-
nient central location.
Has its own punts and
rowing boats.

**Oxford**

**Bath Place Hotel**
(Inexpensive)
4-5 Bath Place, OX1 3SU
Tel: (01865) 791 812
www.bathplace.co.uk
Family-run, 15-room
licensed hotel in the
heart of Oxford that
occupies a group of
restored 17th-
century cottages.
**Le Manoir aux Quat'
Saisons**
(Luxury)
Church Rd, Great Milton, near

Oxford, OX44 7PD
Tel: (01844) 278881
www.manoir.com
The chef Raymond
Blanc's renowned
restaurant and hotel.
Stunning gardens
and luxurious rooms,
some with a terrace.

**Stratford**

**Mercure Shakespeare**
(Moderate)
Chapel St, CV37 6ER
Tel: (01789) 294 997
www.mercure.com
A 17th-century, half-
timbered hotel next
to the Town Hall.

**Windsor**

**Oakley Court**
(Moderate)
Windsor Rd, Water Oakley
SL4 5UR
Tel: (01753) 609988
www.principal-hayley.com
Victorian Gothic
house with 118
rooms and extensive
landscaped grounds.

**PRICE CATEGORIES**

Price categories are for
a double room without
breakfast:
**Budget**: under £110
**Inexpensive**: £110–180
**Moderate**: £180–280
**Luxury**: more than £280

# SHOPPING

## BEST BUYS

L ondon is a great place to shop. Whether you prefer to spend hours roaming around one of its grand department stores – Harrods, Liberty, Selfridges and Harvey Nichols are four of the best – or rummaging among the bargains of its many and diverse markets, there are retail opportunities to suit all budgets and tastes. The city is also known for its terrific end-of-season sales, especially after Christmas until the end of January and throughout July.

### WHERE TO BUY

#### Antiques

London has an enormous selection of antiques shops and markets. Many of the most elite dealers are in Mayfair, centring around Old Bond Street, many at **Grays Antique Market** at 58 Davies Street, W1, with valuable collections of silver, fine art, jewellery, porcelain, carpets, furniture and antiquities.

**Chelsea** and **Knightsbridge** have a large share of fine dealers. **Fulham Road** is excellent for period furniture and decorative items, as is the **King's Road**, with indoor markets such as **Antiquarius** housing a wide variety of artefacts.

**Westbourne Grove** in W11 has many interesting dealers. The whole area comes to life on Friday and Saturday mornings when hordes of tourists descend on the antique arcades and stalls

of Portobello Road market.
**Kensington Church Street** in W8 is filled with a great variety of expensive antiques shops dealing in everything from fine art to porcelain. **Alfie's Antique Market** in Church Street, NW8, is

**BELOW:** successful shopping.

London's largest indoor antiques bazaar and has a lively atmosphere. Many former dealers have now set up shops along the same road.

**Bermondsey**'s early-morning Friday antiques market at Bermondsey Square, SE1, is a major trading event. The best items change hands by 10am. **Islington**, N1, is also a popular but more expensive area with more than 100 dealers. Of particular interest is the **Mall Antiques Arcade** at 359 Upper Street and the adjacent **Camden Passage**.

Further advice and information on buying antiques in Britain as a whole can be obtained from: **London and Provincial Antique Dealers' Association (LAPADA)**, 535 King's Road, SW10. Tel: 7823 3511; www.lapada.org. They run an up-to-date online information service on auctions, specific items and antiques offerings throughout the country.

## Art

Commercial galleries are subject to the dictates of rent and market prospects, and their geographic centres shift accordingly. Bond Street and Cork Street in London's West End are as upmarket as E.57th Street in New York and have been the high streets of the art trade since the late 19th century. Leases expire though, and the galleries there are being replaced by fashion outlets; the presence, nearby, of the Sotheby's and Christie's auction houses is reason enough for some to remain, however. They include **Agnews** and **Colnaghi's**, specialising in the traditional, which includes the Old Masters.

Gallery-going technique is a matter of nonchalance and confidence. You are not expected to buy: galleries are shop windows and the selling takes place behind the scenes, usually before an exhibition opens: nothing is expected of you beyond your willingness to take a look.

A stroll from Oxford Circus to Green Park should be by way of Dering Street (**Annely Juda**), Bond Street (the **Fine Art Society**), Cork Street (**Bernard Jacobson**, **Flowers Central**, **Waddington**, **Mayor**, **Browse** and **Darby**) and, in adjacent streets, **Sadie Coles HQ**, **Stephen Friedman** and **Marlborough Fine Art**. The **Frith Street Gallery** can be found on Golden Square in Soho.

**Flowers East** at 82 Kingsland Road, E2 is worth the trek to see young British talent in a vast white space.

Many of the "Young British Artists" who leapt to fame in the 1990s rented studios in Hoxton, north of Old Street, N1. Commercial galleries followed them. In Hoxton Square, the dealer Jay Jopling has **White Cube**, a larger and more conventional version of his original premises in Mason's Yard, off Duke Street. Others to note include **Lux** in Hoxton Square, **Maureen Paley/Interim Art** in Herald Street, E2, **Matt's**

**ABOVE:** Edwardian bookshop Daunt Books.

**Gallery** (for large installations) in Copperfield Road, E2, **The Gallery** in Redchurch Street, E2, **Victoria Miro** in Wharf Road, N1, **The Agency** in Cremer Street, EC2, and **The Approach** in Approach Road, E2.

## Books

Charing Cross Road is traditionally the home of book selling. Cecil Court is its old-fashioned heart, selling second-hand and rare books of all kinds. **Foyles** on Charing Cross Road is still among the largest, and its traditional eccentricities have given way to greater efficiency. It also incorporates the foreign language bookshop **Grant & Cutler**.

**Waterstone's** is now the only major high street chain of booksellers still standing after the recession. A well-stocked chain with a good travel section, its superstores (421 Oxford Street and 203 Piccadilly) have the usual coffee bars, sofas and events. Waterstone's in Piccadilly also has the cocktail bar 5th View, which has great views. **Blackwell's** (100 Charing Cross Road) is the London flagship of the Oxford bookseller. The **W.H.**

Smith chain has a smaller, more general selection.

Book shops in W1 project an up-market image: **Hatchard's** on Piccadilly, London's oldest book shop, features a huge variety of biographies and fiction. Of the second-hand and rare book sellers in W1, **Quaritch** in South Audley Street is the best known.

Specialist book shops abound. **Bertram Rota** at 31 Long Acre, Covent Garden, is good for modern first editions. **Stanfords** on Long Acre is the best map and travel book shop. **Daunt Books**, at 83 Marylebone High Street, has a great mix of travel-oriented books and guidebooks and now has a branch on Cheapside in the City. **French's**, the theatre book shop, is at Fitzroy Street, W1. Close to Portobello market is **The Travel Bookshop** at 13 Blenheim Crescent, W11, made famous by Hugh Grant in the 1999 film *Notting Hill*.

## China and Glass

All of the big department stores have excellent china and glass departments. For more up-market English goods, try **Thomas Goode** at 19 South Audley Street, W1.

**BELOW:** the finishing touches.

**ABOVE:** four floors of fashion.

## Clothing and Footwear

**Agent Provocateur**, 16 Pont Street, SW1 and 6 Broadwick Street, W1. The place to go for decadently sexy lingerie.

**Alexander McQueen**, 4–5 Old Bond Street, W1. McQueen was one of Britain's most famous designers, known for his imaginative, cutting-edge fashions. His label has continued after his premature death, led by Sarah Burton who designed Kate Middleton's wedding dress.

**Anya Hindmarch**, 15–17 Pont Street, SW1 and 118 New Bond Street, W1. London's bag queen sells lines ranging from the classic and bespoke leather to totes with pictures or environmental slogans printed on.

**Aquascutum**, 100 Regent Street, W1. This venerable British luxe label has recently had a contemporary overhaul, but you can still find their classic traditional pieces and smart raincoats.

**Austin Reed**, 103–113 Regent Street, W1. Good-quality gentlemen's suits, casual menswear and women's separates, aimed at professionals.

**Browns**, 25 South Molton Street, W1. With over 100 leading labels stocked in Browns' five interconnecting shops, this is a very popular one-stop fashion boutique. Browns Labels for Less and the directional Browns Focus are alternatives on the same street.

**Burberry**, 21–23 New Bond Street, W1. Traditional trench-coats and accessories in the famous plaid are sold alongside the stylish Prorsum range, which offers a fresh, contemporary take on a classic British aesthetic.

**The Cross**, 141 Portland Road, W11. An eclectic mix of designers, both home-grown and imported, alongside own-brand cashmere at this trendy shop.

**Dover Street Market**, 17–18 Dover Street, W1. At the height of cutting-edge cool is this fashion baazar, with lines by directional designers displayed in conceptual spaces.

**Jaeger**, 204 Regent Street, W1. Tailored classic English clothes for men and women with formal, business and casual ranges.

**Jimmy Choo**, 27 New Bond Street, W1 and 32 Sloane Street, SW1. Footwear of choice for many celebrities and girls-about-town. Glamorous, vertiginous stilettos abound.

**Joseph**, 77–79 Fulham Road, SW3. Sexy trousers and sleek classics make up the basis of this label's success; stores also stock a smattering of other designers such as Gucci and Diane von Furstenberg.

**Koh Samui**, 65 Monmouth Street, WC2. A cornucopia of the hottest British and European designers. Chic clothes in a variety of styles, arranged by colour.

**Kurt Geiger**, 198 Regent Street, W1. Incorporates a number of lines, ranging from affordable diffusion to luxe lines, providing a huge variety of footwear choices.

**Lulu Guinness**, 3 Ellis Street, SW1. Fun, retro bags and other pieces, stylistically positioned between ladylike and kitsch.

**Matthew Williamson**, 28 Bruton Street, W1. Brightly coloured and patterned womenswear, often intricately embellished and ethnic-inspired.

**Mulberry**, 41 New Bond Street. Modern clothes along classic British lines, but most renowned for the leather pieces. Their range of handbags is enormously popular and the men's accessories are interesting too.

**Myla**, 77 Lonsdale Road, W11. Sensual, gorgeous lingerie boutique. Also sells swimwear.

**Nicole Farhi**, 158 New Bond Street, W1. Smart, yet comfortably casual, classic separates in soft fabrics.

**Paul Smith**, 40 Floral Street, W1. Designer famous for his quirky take on classic tailoring and use of colourful patterns. Men's and women's clothing is found here.

**Rellik**, 8 Golbourne Road, W10. Probably the most fashionable of London's many vintage emporiums, specialising in retro pieces from the 1920s to 1980s, many by iconic designers.

**Size?**, 33–34 Carnaby Street, W1. Trainers specialist, stocking a good range of technical sports shoes as well as classic and old-school trainers.

**Stella McCartney**, 30 Bruton Street, W1. Femininity with an edge and "vegetarian" (non-leather) shoes is the house style of this high-profile British designer.

**Ted Baker**, 9–10 Floral Street, WC2. Trendy, casual and sophisticated clothing, often with a quirky edge, for men and women.

**BELOW:** vintage clothes at Rellik.

**ABOVE:** Paul Smith's store in Covent Garden.

**Temperley**, 6–10 Colville Mews, W11. Romantic, slightly bohemian dresses and daywear, popular with fashionistas.

**Topshop**, 216 Oxford Street, W1. No shopping trip in London would be complete without scouring for a bang-on-trend bargain. The largest fashion store in the world, this flagship branch is fast becoming iconic.

**Urban Outfitters**, 36–38 Kensington High Street, W8 and 200 Oxford Street. A boutique featuring many hot young designers.

**Vivienne Westwood**, 6 Davies Street, W1. This is formal compared to Westwood's eccentric World's End boutique on the King's Road, and is the outlet for her more tailored collections. Her menswear collection is available at 18 Conduit Street, W1.

**Westfield** Shopping Centre, (www.westfield.com). Europe's largest shopping centre, by Shepherd's Bush and Wood Lane tube stations, is a hub for fashionistas. High street names rub shoulders with Armarni, Louis Vuitton, Ted Baker and Ugg. There is a second branch by the Olympic Stadium in Stratford,

**Whistles**, 20 The Market, Covent Garden. One of the best places to shop for good clothing with an individualistic take on trends.

## Men's Clothes

London is well served for men's clothes shops. Covent Garden is full of them: the fashion-conscious man is catered for with quality designers such as **Paul Smith** and **Michiko Koshino**, as well as the reasonably priced **Reiss**, **All Saints** and **Ted Baker**.

What really distinguishes London's menswear is the city's traditional gentlemen's outfitters. Savile Row is the best-known street for tailor-made suits.

**Gieves & Hawkes** at No. 1 is synonymous with handmade and off-the-peg classic English tailoring and has a long and noble history. As does the prestigious **Anderson and Sheppard** at Old Burlington Street, who have discreetly tailored suits for Marlene Dietrich and Prince Charles, amongst other notables. **Ozwald Boateng**, at No. 30, is known for his flamboyant colours and fashion and media clients. A relative newcomer to the street (1994), he was creative director of Givenchy menswear for four years. **Huntsman & Sons**, like many tailors in the Row, has been established since the 18th century.

The St James's area, which is littered with gentlemen's clubs,

is full of shops selling expensive well-made clothes, toiletries and shoes. In St James's Street is **John Lobb**, considered to make some of the finest handmade shoes in the world, and the fine hat maker **James Lock**. In Jermyn Street are **Turnbull & Asser**, famed for their made-to-measure and striped shirts; **Bates** hat shop and **Geo Trumpers** traditional toiletry shop are here too. Dover Street and Burlington Gardens are also worth a visit.

If you want the look without paying the price, second-hand and period clothes shops are an option and can yield up great finds; for instance, vintage tailoring and second-hand Savile Row suits can be found at **Old Hat** at 66 Fulham High Street, SW6.

## Department Stores

**Conran Shop**, Michelin Building, 81 Fulham Road, SW3. Tel: 7589 7401. Sir Terence Conran's unique and stylish shop sells designer furniture and household accessories, and in many ways resembles a design museum. Set within the beautiful Art Nouveau tiled Michelin Building, it is

**BELOW:** find directional designer pieces at Dover Street Market.

**ABOVE:** Selfridges, Oxford Street.

worth a visit just to browse.
**Fortnum & Mason**, 181 Piccadilly, W1. Tel: 7734 8040. Fortnum & Mason opened their store in the 18th century with the grocery needs of the Palace in mind. They began importing exotic and unusual foodstuffs which have long been the basis of the shop's success. The Queen's grocer also stocks fine clothes and household goods. At Christmas the window displays are a joy to behold and many hanker after one of their famous hampers. A fashionable place to have tea.

**Harrods**, 87–135 Brompton Road, SW1. Tel: 7730 1234. One of the world's largest and most famous department stores owned, until recently, by Egypt's Al-Fayed family. Since the 19th century Harrods has maintained a reputation for quality and service, priding itself on stocking the best of everything. No one should miss the fabulous displays in the Edwardian tiled food halls. Harrods sales are major events with those prepared to queue a long time to be first through the door.

**Harvey Nichols**, 109–125 Knightsbridge SW1. Tel: 7235 5000. London's leading fashion department store, with an excel-

lent range of women's designer fashions and footwear. Men and children are also well catered for.

**Liberty**, Regent Street, W1. Tel: 7734 1234. The goods on sale in this distinctive store are still largely based along the same lines as the Oriental, Art Nouveau and Arts and Crafts furniture, wallpaper, silver, jewellery and fabrics Liberty began selling in the late 19th century. There is a particularly fine fashion-accessory department and an exotic bazaar in the basement.

**Marks & Spencer**, 458 Oxford Street, W1. Tel: 7935 7954. The venerable chain has triumphantly revitalised over the past few years, with strong advertising and a big push to update its clothes collections. Its food department, with its gourmet ready-cooked meals, remains fantastic, as does the underwear range.

**Peter Jones**, Sloane Square, SW1. Tel: 7730 3434. This King's Road branch of John Lewis promises customers that its prices cannot be beaten and assures to refund the difference if you can prove otherwise. Stocks a variety of quality goods, most notably household furnishings and appliances.

**BELOW:** speciality teas in Harrods' food hall.

**Selfridges**, 400 Oxford Street, W1. Tel: 0800 123 400. For sheer variety of quality goods, this 100-year-old institution has cornered the market, in a massive one-stop shop. Home furnishings, china, stationery, beauty products, food and a vast selection of fashions are just some of what's on offer. Selfridges is also the most fashionable of the department stores, managing to combine a sense of its history with contemporary style.

## Food and Drink

**Berry Bros**, 3 St James's Street, SW1. Dating back to the 17th century, Berry Bros has a superb range of wines and spirits, with prices ranging from £5 to £5,000.

**Degustibus**, 4 Southwark Street, SE1 and 53 Carter Lane, EC4. Artisan bakers.

**Fresh & Wild**, 69–75 Brewer Street, W1. Organic, healthy food store that also comprises a juice bar, deli and café.

**Justerini & Brooks**, 61 St James's Street, SW1. Top range of fine wines and whiskies.

**Konditor & Cook**, 10 Stoney Street, SE1. Delicious cakes plus hot and cold lunches.

**Ladurée**, Burlington Arcade, W1. Mouthwatering and colourful displays of this Parisian company's famous macaroons.

**Natural Kitchen**, 77 Marylebone High Street, W1. Well stocked deli/café.

**Paxton & Whitfield**, 93 Jermyn Street, SW1. Traditional cheesemongers.

**Rococo**, 321 King's Road, SW3. Gourmet chocolates.

**Vinopolis**, 1 Bank End, SE1. A large branch of Majestic Wines and the well-stocked Whiskey Exchange, attached to the winetasting and dining complex.

## Gifts and Souvenirs

**Asprey & Garrard**, 167 New Bond Street, W1. Seriously expensive sterling silver and jewellery. Favourite for wedding gifts.

TRANSPORT

**ABOVE:** Burlington Arcade in Mayfair.

ACCOMMODATION

**Cath Kidston**, 51 Marylebone High Street, W1. Homeware, bags and gifts all in Kidston's unmistakeable patterns: flowers, strawberries and stars.

**Octopus**, 28 Carnaby Street, W1. Bright, often witty designs in bags, watches, jewellery, umbrellas, ties and much more.

**Oliver Bonas**, 801 Fulham Road, SW6. Small chain of lifestyle shops selling homeware, fashion and beauty accessories.

**Smythson**, 40 New Bond Street, W1. Luxurious, expensive stationery, as well as diaries and gifts in vibrantly coloured or classic leather.

### Jewellery

For innovative modern jewellery, head for Fulham Road and check out **Theo Fennell** at No. 169. For period or Art Deco jewellery try **Cobra & Bellamy** at 149 Sloane Street; at the other end is **Boodle & Dunthorne** for classic and modern designs at No. 1. Stylish and innovative pieces in gold and silver can be found at **Links of London**, at 16 Sloane Square. This is also a good place to find gifts. The finest costume jewellery can be found at **Butler & Wilson**, 20 South Molton Street or **Agatha**, at No. 4.

If you want to spend serious money on serious rocks or simply gawp at gems, then head for New Bond Street (**Asprey & Garrard, Cartier, Bulgari and Graff**).

The other main centre is Hatton Garden EC1, a street of jewellery retailers and wholesalers. A lively area and home to the London Diamond Bourse.

### Specialist Shops

**The Button Queen**, 19 Marylebone Lane, W1. Lots of antique and modern buttons.

**Ellis Brigham**, 30–32 Southampton Street, WC2. The ideal store for stocking up on outdoor equipment, for camping, climbing and sports. They also sell a good range of rucksacks and their staff are very knowledgable.

**Legends Boardriders**, 119–21 Oxford Street, W1. Heaven for skaters and surfboarders.

**Neal's Yard Remedies**, 15 Neal's Yard, WC2. Alternative health shop which also sells aromatherapy blends, shampoos, skin protection and gift boxes.

**Vintage Magazine Shop**, 39–43 Brewer Street, Soho, W1. A cardboard cutout of Harrison Ford or Marilyn Monroe? They've got it, as well as a huge collection of vintage mags.

### Markets

**Camden Market**, NW1. Hugely popular at the weekends, this sprawling market near Camden Lock sells clothes, jewellery, arts and crafts, food and antiques amongst other things.

**Columbia Road Flower Market**, E2. All kinds of cut flowers and houseplants are sold here at wholesale prices on Sundays, 8am–2pm. Other specialist shops on Columbia Road open to coincide with the market.

**Petticoat Lane**, Middlesex Street, E1. London's oldest market is so-named for the undergarments and lace once sold here by French Huguenots. Cheap clothes, fabrics and leather goods are still sold here, on some of the 1,000 stalls.

**Portobello Road**, W11. Renowned for its antiques, this is also a good place to pick up fashionable and vintage clothing, art and general bric-a-brac. It gets very crowded on Saturdays.

**Spitalfields**, Commercial Street, E1. This historic covered market has been gentrified with cafés and boutiques, but remains a great place to spot new talent, as many young fashion and jewellery designers sell their wares here.

**BELOW:** Spitalfields market.

SHOPPING

ACTIVITIES

A – Z

# **A**CTIVITIES

# THE ARTS, NIGHTLIFE, FESTIVALS, SPORT AND TOURS

I n the famous words of Samuel Johnson, "If a man is tired of London he is tired of life." The city has long offered a wealth of activities and entertainments to choose from, but never more so than in the 21st century. Whether your taste runs to high-energy nights out dancing or more refined evenings at the opera, London has it all. The ever-expanding range of options caters to all manner of passions, and although the cost of a great day (or night) out can be expensive, there are many excellent museums, festivals and spectacles that are free.

## THE ARTS

### Museums & Art Galleries

A public lottery funded the British Museum's foundation in 1759 and fittingly it was lottery money released in the late 1990s to celebrate the new millennium that helped finance its spectacular Great Court. The same millennial largesse aided many of London's museums and galleries and the government decreed that the great national collections should abolish entrance fees.

Alongside the rejuvenation of the star attractions came a rash of specialist new museums. There are more than 130 museums and galleries worth a visit.

### *Money-saving Passes*

Although national museums and galleries are free, most others have entrance charges. Energetic visitors will benefit from the London Pass, which allows free entry

to several dozen attractions. Free travel on the Tube and buses is also included. At press time, prices ranged from £52 for a one-day pass to £135.50 for a six-day pass (children £32–86.20). For details tel: 01664 485 020 or check www.londonpass.com.

Joining the Art Fund costs £40 a year and provides free admission to more than 200 museums, galleries and historic houses around the country, plus discounts on some exhibitions. Details on 0844 415 4100 or from www.artfund.org.

### Theatre

The only way to get a ticket at face value is to buy it from the theatre box office. Most open 10am–mid-evening. You can pay by credit card over the phone for most theatres, or reserve seats three days in advance before paying. A ticket booth (tkts) on the south side of Leicester Square offers unsold seats at half price or three-quarter price

**ABOVE:** performance at the Globe.

(plus booking fee) on the day of performance (open Mon–Sat 10am–7pm, Sun noon–3pm). There are booking agents throughout London (and quite a few unofficial kiosks around Leicester Square), but beware: some charge high fees. It's sensible to ask what the face value of a ticket is before parting with your money. Two reputable 24-hour agents are **Keith Prowse** on 0845 125 4880 and **Ticket-master** at www.ticketmaster.co.uk.

Ignore ticket touts unless you're prepared to pay several times a ticket's face value for sell-out performances.

● *For further information see Theatreland chapter, page 42. For West End theatre locations, see the map on page 353.*

**Holland Park Open Air Theatre**, Holland Park, W8.

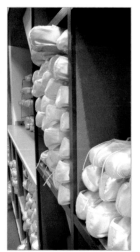

**ABOVE:** backstage at the ROH.

www.operahollandpark.com or
www.ohp.rbkc.gov.uk.
During the warm summer months
opera, dance and theatre performances are staged here in the
semi-open air. Tube: Holland
Park/High Street Kensington.
**National Theatre**, South
Bank, SE1. Tel: 7452 3000;
www.nationaltheatre.org.uk.
Three repertory theatres are
housed within the National's
concrete mass. They always
provide a good and varied
selection of plays. Tube:
Waterloo/Embankment.
**Open Air Theatre, Regent's Park**
Tel: 0844 826 4242;
http://openairtheatre.org.
With a 15-week summer season,
this not-for-profit charity hosts a
variety of plays, including Shakespeare. Tube: Baker Street.
**Shakespeare's Globe Theatre**,
Bankside, SE1. Tel: 7401 9919;
www.shakespeares-globe.org.
May–Sept season in a
re-creation of the Tudor original.
Tube: Southwark/London Bridge.

### Ballet

**Coliseum**, St Martin's Lane,
WC2. Tel: 0871 911 0200;

www.eno.org.
Hosts performances of ballet in
the summer months by the Royal
Festival Ballet and visiting
companies. Is particularly popular
with visiting Russian ballets.
Tube: Leicester Square.
**Royal Opera House**, Covent
Garden Piazza, WC2E. Tel: 7304
4000; www.roh.org.uk.
Home to the Royal Ballet and the
Royal Opera. Was extensively
refurbished for the millennium.
Backstage tours are available.
Tube: Covent Garden.
**Sadlers Wells Theatre**, Rosebery
Avenue EC1. Tel: 0844 412
4300; www.sadlerswells.com.
A flexible, state-of-the-art perfor-
mance space that offers an exciting and innovative programme of
dance and opera. London's lead-
ing venue for contemporary and
classical dance. Tube: Angel.

### Opera

**Coliseum**, St Martin's Lane,
WC2. Tel: 0871 911 0200;
www.eno.org.
This elegant Edwardian theatre is
easily distinguished on London's
skyline by the illuminated golden

globe on its roof. Home to the
English National Opera (ENO),
this is where English-language
operas are performed. Productions tend to be more theatrical
than those of the Royal Opera.
Tube: Leicester Square.
**Royal Opera House**, Covent
Garden piazza, WC2E. Tel: 7304
4000; www.roh.org.uk.
More traditional than the Coliseum, this theatre attracts the
crème de la crème of the opera
world. Operas are performed in
their original language and tickets are very expensive. Dressy
affair. Tube: Covent Garden.

### Classical Music

**Barbican Arts Centre**, Silk
Street, EC2. Tel: 7638 8891;
www.barbican.org.uk.
Home to the London Symphony
Orchestra and the English Chamber Orchestra. This huge concrete complex built for the arts is
one of London's major classical-
concert venues. Tube: Barbican.
**The Royal Albert Hall**, Kensington Gore, SW7. Tel: 0845 401
5045; www.royalalberthall.com.
This circular hall comes alive

**BELOW:** the plush interior of the Royal Opera House in Covent Garden.

**ABOVE:** the Royal Festival Hall on the South Bank.

every summer for the Henry Wood Promenade Concerts, known simply as The Proms. Also hosts occasional comedians and indie bands. Tubes: Kensington High Street/South Kensington.
**Royal Festival Hall**, South Bank, Belvedere Road, SE1. Tel: 0844 875 0073; www.southbankcentre. co.uk.
London's premier classical music venue was built as part of the Festival of Britain of 1951. The exterior of this hall appears somewhat dated and arouses mixed public comment on its appearance. However, it is an excellent concert hall with space for large-scale performances. Next door is the Queen Elizabeth Hall where chamber concerts and solos are performed. There is also the small Purcell Room for more intimate music. Tube: Waterloo/ Embankment.
**Wigmore Hall**, 36 Wigmore Street, W1. Tel: 7935 2141; www.wigmore-hall.org.uk.
Delightful intimate hall with seating for 550. It has a pleasant atmosphere and excellent acoustics and is most renowned for chamber recitals. Also hosts Sunday morning coffee concerts. Tube: Bond Street.

### Churches

Many of London's historic churches also offer superb, and in some cases free, music. Three of the best are:
**St John's, Smith Square**, Westminster, SW1. Tel: 7222 1061. This church has been converted into a concert hall hosting chamber music and BBC lunch time concerts. Tube: Westminster.
**St Martin-in-the-Fields**, Trafalgar Square, WC2. Tel: 7766 1100; www.smitf.org.
Concerts are held at lunch times and evenings in this church. Tube: Charing Cross.
**St Mary-le-Bow**, Cheapside, EC2. Tel: 7248 5139.
Lunch time recitals most Thursdays (www.stmarylebow.co.uk has details). Home to the famous Bow bells. Tube: St Paul's/ Mansion House/Bank.

# NIGHTLIFE

## Late Spots

If you're under 30 and believe the hype, London is one of the best places to party in the world. It certainly has built a solid reputa-

tion as one of the great international clubbing centres. But not all nightlife is dance-till-dawn. Other nightlife options range from dinner dances to cocktail bars, comedy gigs to smart nightclubs.
Despite its reputation, and despite a relaxation of licensing laws in recent years, London is not an especially late city. Most restaurants, pubs and even bars have wound down by 1am, leaving just a few determined establishments to stagger on until the city awakes.

## Jazz Clubs

**Jazz Café**, 5 Parkway, Camden NW1. Tel: 0844 847 2514 (tickets) or 7688 8899 (for a table). Intimate jazz club in Camden Town that attracts some top names. Tube: Camden.
**Jazz@Pizza Express**, 10 Dean Street, W1. Tel: 0845 602 7017. This Soho branch of the pizza chain has a high standard of performers. Tube: Leicester Square/Piccadilly Circus/ Tottenham Court Road.
**Ronnie Scott's**, 47 Frith Street, W1. Tel: 7439 0747.
Scott, who died in 1996, had eclectic taste, and this is still reflected in this legendary Soho venue, which has hosted some of the biggest names in jazz since 1959. Very relaxed. Tube: Leicester Square/Piccadilly Circus/ Tottenham Court Road.

## Dance Clubs

**Café de Paris**, 3–4 Coventry Street, SW1. Tel: 7734 7700. Posh old dancehall attracts an older sophisticated crowd. Trendy/smart. Tube: Piccadilly Circus/Leicester Square.
**Cargo**, 83 Rivington Street, EC2. Tel: 7749 7840.
This venue under the railway arches offers a variety of live line-ups. Tube: Old Street.
**EGG**, 200 York Way, N7. Tel: 78 71 7111.
Spacious venue with three dance floors. Fashionable gay nights.

**ABOVE:** for reliably good jazz visit Ronnie Scott's on Frith Street.

Tube: Caledonian Road.
**Electric Ballroom**, 184 Camden High Street, NW1. Tel: 7485 9006.
This old dancehall has a huge main dance floor where on Saturday nights Shake plays hits of the 1970s, '80s and '90s, attracting a mixed crowd. Upstairs it's R&B and hip-hop. Casual. Tube: Camden.
**Fabric**, 77A Charterhouse Street, EC1. Tel: 7336 8898.
Celebrated club that mixes big names (generally on Fridays), with top DJs (Saturdays) and new talent. Big on techo and electronica. Open until 3am. Tube: Farringdon.
**Heaven**, The Arches, Villiers Street, WC2. Tel: 7930 2020.
Submerged beneath the Charing Cross development is one of the best dance clubs in town. Gay nights are Tuesday, Wednesday, Friday and Saturday. Very casual dress code. Tube: Charing Cross/Embankment.
**Koko**, 1A Camden High Street, NW1. Tel: 0870 432 5527. Venue for club nights and gigs by some of the biggest names in rock and pop. Tube: Mornington Crescent.
**Mass**, St Matthew's Peace Garden SW2. Tel: 7738 7875.

Atmospheric Brixton venue in the bowels of a converted church. Wide range of music, with great R&B on the Friday Nite Mass. Tube: Brixton.
**Ministry of Sound**, 103 Gaunt Street, SE1. Tel: 0870 060 0010.
This renowned dance club is London's top house-music venue. Open until 7am Sat. Tube: Elephant & Castle/Borough.
**Neighbourhood**, 12 Acklam Road, W10. Tel: 0871 971 3995.

**BELOW:** the cocktail hour can last a lot longer.

West London's main club with its well-designed modern interior hewn out of the concrete structure of the Westway. Trendy/hip. Tube: Westbourne Park.
**Salsa**
96 Charing Cross Road, WC2. Tel: 7379 3277.
A good Latin venue in the heart of the West End. Lots of fun, very busy and a good place to practise your moves with regular dance classes. Casual. Tube: Charing Cross/Leicester Square.
**The Telegraph**, 228 Brixton Hill, SW2. Tel: 8678 0777.
A former home of punk, this long-established venue combines a club and a Thai restaurant, has fair bar prices and a cheerful atmosphere. Tube: Brixton.
**333**, 333 Old Street, EC1. Tel: 7739 5949.
Hip club with a good drinking lounge upstairs and pounding dance music in the basement. Tube: Old Street.

### Comedy/Cabaret

**Comedy Store**, 1a Oxendon Street, SW1. Tel: 0844 871 7699 (tickets).
A night at this well-established venue for stand-up comedians will remind you that comedy need not always be accompanied by

## GAY VENUES

**Candy Bar**, 4 Carlisle Street, Soho, W1. Tel: 7287 5041.
www.candybarsoho.com
Claiming to be the most prolific lesbian bar in the world, Candy offers everything from hip-hop and R&B to acoustic sets and poetry, striptease in the basement and its very own pole dancing candy girls all set in retro pink. Tube: Tottenham Court Road.

**G-A-Y Bar**, 30 Old Compton Street, Soho. Tel: 7494 2756; www.g-a-y.co.uk
Although its crowd of screeching 18-year-olds might not be to everyone's taste, the fun never stops at the legendary club night's sister bar, where giant video screens blare out the latest hits across three floors. At closing, the party continues round the corner at **G-A-Y Late** (5 Goslett Yard, Soho; tel: 7734 9858) until 3am.
Tube: Tottenham Court Road
**Ghetto**, 58 Old Street, EC1V. Tel: 7287 3726.

www.ghetto-london.co.uk
Week-long fun at a noted gay venue, with a packed dance floor downstairs and sister bar Trash Palace above. Wig Out (Sat 10.30pm–5am) is the raucous weekend blowout, playing Blondie, Britney and everything in-between. Drinks from £2. Tube: Old Street.

**Heaven**, under the arches, Villiers Street, WC2. Tel: 7930 2020; www.heaven-london.com
Famous beyond these shores and still a good night out, even if it is a bit worn around the edges. There is generally plenty of flesh on show and a good range of music, and since 2008 it's been home to legendary cheese-fest G-A-Y club nights (www.g-a-y.co.uk; Thur–Sat). Tube: Charing Cross/ Embankment.

**XXL**, 53 Southwark Street, SE1. Tel: 7403 4001. www.xxl-london. com. There are two beer gardens, two bars and a range of DJs. Tube: London Bridge.

across to Brick Lane after a night out to stock up on freshly baked bagels filled with smoked salmon and cream or hot salt beef with lashings of mustard and gherkin. Open 24 hours. Tube: Shoreditch.
**El Burrito**, 5 Charlotte Place, W1. Tel: 7580 5048.
Mexican food to eat in or take away. Come for nachos, taco salad or burritos. Mon–Fri 11am–4pm. Tube: Goodge Street.
**Paul Rothe & Son**, 35 Marylebone Lane, W1. Tel: 7935 6783.
Historic café/greengrocers' shop offering imaginative sandwiches, bagels and hearty soups. Mon–Fri 8am–6pm, Sat 11am–5.30pm. Tube: Bond Street.

### Coffee/Breakfast

**Bar Italia**, 22 Frith Street, W1. Tel: 7437 4520.
A piece of real Italy located in the centre of Soho. No matter what the hour, this family-run bar is always buzzing. Can be expensive but reputed to have the best coffee in London. Open 24 hours Mon–Sat, until 4am Sun (Mon morning). Tube: Leicester Square.
**Chelsea Bridge Snack Kiosk**.
A kiosk is reputed to have been doing hot food and teas at this location since the 1920s. Ever popular with early-morning truck drivers, cabbies and their passengers. Open all night.

canned laughter. Avoid sitting in the front row unless you want to become part of the show. Tube: Piccadilly Circus/Leicester Square.
**Jongleurs**, Middle Yard (Camden Lock), Chalk Farm Road, NW1. Also at Battersea and Bow. Tel: 0844 499 4064.
Leading stand-up comedy club. Camden venue attracts the best acts. Tube: Chalk Farm/Camden.
**Madame Jo Jo's**, 8 Brewer Street, W1. Tel: 7734 3040.
Ultra-camp transvestite revue bar popular for hen or stag nights. Lacking in the sleaze and daring associated with Soho's sometimes unsavoury past, Madame Jo Jo's still offers one of the best late-night outings in London with captivating cabaret shows. Closes 3am. Tube: Piccadilly Circus.
**Stringfellow's**, 16 Upper St Martin's Lane, WC2. Tel: 7240 5534.

This slightly tongue-in-cheek lapdancing joint is strong on tacky glamour. Tube: Covent Garden/ Leicester Square.

### Dinner Dance

Some of the best and most romantic dine and dance places are at the luxury hotels. The glamorous restaurant at The Ritz (Piccadilly, W1; tel: 7493 8181) holds traditional dinner dances on Friday and Saturday nights. A four course meal is followed by dancing to a four piece band. Dress is formal so ties for men and no jeans. Booking required.

### Quick Bites

#### Takeaways

**Beigel Bake**, 159 Brick Lane, E1. Tel: 7729 0616.
Join Londoners who ritually pile

## CALENDAR OF EVENTS

### January

**New Year's Day Parade** from Berkeley Square to Parliament Square.
**London International Boat Show**, ExCel, Docklands. This is the world's largest exhibition of its kind. DLR: Custom House.
**Charles I Commemoration** (last Sunday). English Civil War Society dress up as Royalists from the King's army and make their way from Charles I's statue in Whitehall to his place of execution outside Banqueting House.

## February

**Chinese New Year**. Colourful Chinese celebrations centred around Gerrard Street in Chinatown, Soho. Tube: Leicester Square/Piccadilly Circus.
**Great Spitalfields Pancake Day Race** (Shrove Tuesday). Old Truman Brewery, Brick Lane, E1. Teams run along Dray Walk tossing pancakes. Musicians and jesters accompany them. Tube: Aldgate East/Shoreditch.

## March

**Ideal Home Exhibition**. Earl's Court. Exhibition of new ideas and products for the home. Tube: West Brompton/ Earl's Court.
**Easter Parade**, Battersea Park. Carnival with floats and fancy-dress costumes.

**ABOVE:** for fantastic fireworks head to the Thames on New Year's Eve.

## April

**London Marathon**. One of the world's biggest runs, beginning at Blackheath and ending at Buckingham Palace a gruelling 26.2 miles (42km) later.
**Queen's Birthday** (21st). The Queen's real birthday (as opposed to her official one in June) is celebrated with a gun salute in Hyde Park and at the Tower of London.
**The Boat Race** Two teams from Oxford and Cambridge universities row from Putney to Mortlake in a fiercely-fought contest.

**BELOW:** the Chelsea Flower Show in late May.

## May

**Chelsea Flower Show**, Royal Hospital, SW3. Tel: 7834 4333. Major horticultural show, featuring spectacular displays, and social event in the fine grounds of the Chelsea Royal Hospital. Tube: Sloane Square.
**FA Cup Final**, Wembley. The final of the nation's main football competition. Tube: Wembley Park/Wembley Central.
**Coin Street Festival**, Oxo Tower Wharf, South Bank. Starts on Spring Bank Holiday (last Monday in May) and continues most weekends until the end of August. Free music and street performances from around the world. Tube: Blackfriars/Waterloo.

## June

**Beating Retreat**, Horse Guards Parade, Whitehall. Annual ceremonial display of military bands on two successive evenings. Tube: Charing Cross/Westminster.
**City of London Festival** (www.colf.org). Venues in the city host a range of artistic events, from concerts in St Paul's to swing bands in the Guildhall Yard.
**Derby Day**, Epsom Racecourse. Tel: 01372 726 311. Famous flat race for 3-year-old colts and fillies. Train: from Vauxhall or Victoria to Epsom, or Victoria to Tattenham Corner.
**Flower Festival** (last week). Exhibition on the history of Covent Garden's fruit and vegetable market, and demonstrations on garden design and flower arranging. Tube: Covent Garden.
**Greenwich & Docklands International Festival**. Three-week festival beginning at the end of June, with music, dance, theatre and spectacular firework displays. Various venues.
**London 2012 Festival** (www.london 2012.com). The cultural Olympiad

TRANSPORT

ACCOMMODATION

SHOPPING

ACTIVITIES

A – Z

**ABOVE:** The Puppini Sisters performing at the City of London Festival.

will run from 21 June to 9 September. Events in film, visual arts, theatre, opera and fashion will bring together artists from all over the world.

**Oak Apple Day**, Chelsea Royal Hospital. Parade of the Chelsea Pensioners in memory of their founder, Charles II. Tube: Sloane Square.

**Queen's Diamond Jubilee**, In 2012 the Queen's 60th year of reigning will be celebrated with events from 2–5 June. The highlight will be a pageant on the Thames, when a 1,000-strong flotilla will sail along the river.

**Royal Academy Summer Exhibition**, Burlington House, Piccadilly. Tel: 7300 8000. Large exhibition of work by professional and amateur artists running until August. All works for sale. Tube: Piccadilly/Green Park.

**Royal Ascot**, Ascot Racecourse. Tel: 0870 722 7227. Elegant and dressy race meeting attended by royalty. Train: Vauxhall to Ascot.

**Trooping the Colour.** Apply in writing for seats, details at www.royal.gov.uk. The Queen's official birthday celebrations, with a royal procession along the Mall to Horse Guards Parade for the ceremonial parade of regimental colours. Followed by the presence of the Royal Family on Buckingham Palace's balcony. Tube: Green

Park/St James's Park.

**Wimbledon Lawn Tennis Championships**, All England Club. Tel: 8944 1066 (or 8971 2473 for tickets). World-famous fortnight of tennis on grass courts. Tube: Southfields.

## July

**Doggett's Coat and Badge Race.** Race for single-scull boats between London Bridge and Chelsea that has been a tradition since 1715.

**Hampton Court Palace Flower Show.** The world's largest flower show held in the stunning setting of the Palace grounds.

**Henley Royal Regatta**, Henley-on-Thames. Historic rowing regatta – picnic by the Thames and watch the fun. Train: Paddington to Henley-on-Thames.

**Henry Wood Promenade Concerts**, Royal Albert Hall. Tel: 0845 401 5034. Series of classical concerts known as The Proms, culminating in the rumbustious Last Night which spills out into Hyde Park. Tube: South Kensington/High Street Kensington.

**Swan Upping** on the Thames. All the swans on the Thames belong to the Queen, the Vintners and the Dyers and for five days every year officials can be seen rowing on the river registering them.

## August

**London Riding Horse Parade**, Rotten Row, Hyde Park. Elegant competition for best turned-out horse and rider. Tube: Hyde Park Corner/Knightsbridge/Lancaster Gate/Marble Arch.

**Notting Hill Carnival**, Ladbroke Grove (last weekend). Colourful and lively West Indian street carnival (Europe's largest) with exciting and imaginative costumes, live steel bands and reggae music. The streets can get extremely crowded. Tube: Notting Hill Gate.

## September

**Chelsea Antiques Fair**, Old Town Hall, King's Road, SW3. Tel: 7361 2220. Wide range of antiques on sale. Tube: Sloane Square.

**Horseman's Sunday**, St John's Church, Hyde Park, W2. Morning service dedicated to the horse with mounted vicar and congregation. Followed by procession through Hyde Park. Tube: Paddington/Edgware Road.

**Open House London**, Hundreds of great buildings not usually open to the public open for one weekend, free of charge. Check tourist board for dates.

**Thames Festival**, between Waterloo Bridge and Blackfriars Bridge. Fanfare, river displays, face painting, craft and food stalls.

## October

**Costermongers' Pearly Harvest Festival** (1st Sunday or last Sun in September), St Martin-in-the-Fields, Trafalgar Square. Pearly Kings and Queens (street traders) attend a service in their traditional attire, which is elaborately adorned with pearl buttons. Tube: Charing Cross.

**Judges' Service** marks the beginning of the legal year in Britain with a procession of judges in full attire from Westminster Abbey to the Houses of Parliament. Tube: Westminster.

**Trafalgar Day Parade** (21st). Commemorates Nelson's victory over the French and Spanish at Trafalgar. Tube: Charing Cross.

## November

**Christmas Lights** switched on in Oxford and Regent streets. Tube: Oxford Circus/Piccadilly Circus.
**Guy Fawkes Day** (5th). Traditional firework celebration of the failure to blow up the Houses of Parliament by Guy Fawkes in 1605. Bonfires and organised firework displays all over London.
**London to Brighton Veteran Car Run** (1st Sunday). Hundreds of immaculately preserved veteran cars and their proud owners start out from Hyde Park and make their way sedately to Brighton. Tube: Hyde Park Corner.
**Lord Mayor's Show**. Grand procession from the Guildhall in the City to the Royal Courts of Justice, celebrating the annual election of the Lord Mayor. Tube: Bank.
**Remembrance Sunday** (nearest the 11th). Commemorates those who have died in war since WWI while serving their country. Main wreath-laying service is at the Cenotaph. Tube: Westminster.
**State Opening of Parliament**, House of Lords, Westminster. Official re-opening of Parliament (following the summer recess) by the Queen, who travels down the Mall in a state coach. Tube: Westminster.

## December

**Christmas Carol Services**, Trafalgar Square. Carols (Christmas hymns) are sung in the evenings beneath the giant tree which is presented each year by Norway. Tube: Charing Cross. Carol services are also held in many churches all over London.
**London International Horse Show**, Olympia. Tel: 0871 230 5580 (tickets). Major international show-jumping championships that attracts all the big names. Dog agility and Shetland pony Grand National included. Tube: Kensington (Olympia).
**New Year's Eve**. River Thames fireworks display at midnight around the London Eye. Thousands gather on the Embankment to watch.

# SPORT

## Spectator Sports

### Football (Soccer)

The football season runs from August to May, with matches usually held Saturday 3pm, but also sometimes on Sundays, and Tuesday evenings. The top football clubs in London are Arsenal (Emirates Stadium, Drayton Park, N5, www.arsenal. com), Chelsea (Stamford Bridge, Fulham Road, SW6, www.chelsea fc.com) and Tottenham Hotspur (White Hart Lane, 748 High Road, N17, www.tottenhamhotspur. com).

### Rugby

This is played Sept–April/May. Top Rugby Union games are played at Twickenham Rugby Football Ground (Whitton Road, Twickenham, Middlesex, tel: 0870 405 2000; www.rfu.com/ TwickenhamStadium). The Rugby League holds its cup final matches at Wembley Stadium (tel: 0844 980 8001; www. wembleystadium.com).

# SPAS

Whether you want a simple pedicure, a cleansing facial or hot stone treatment, you'll be able to find a spa to suit your needs. Some of the best are: Bliss (tel: 7590 6146), The Refinery (tel: 7409 2001) and The Porchester (7792 3980), the latter for men.

### Cricket

The game is played in summer only, at the Oval (Kennington, SE11, tel: Surrey County Cricket Club 7820 5700, or 0844 847 9866 for tickets; www.kiaoval.com), or at Lord's Cricket Ground (St John's Wood, NW8, tel: 7432 1000 for tickets; www.lords.org). You should buy tickets well in advance for Test matches but there's generally less competition for seats for one-day internationals and Twenty20 games.

### Tennis

Wimbledon, on the District line of the Underground (Southfields), is the venue for the famous two-week tennis championship, which starts in the last week in June. Seats for the show courts

TRANSPORT

ACCOMMODATION

SHOPPING

ACTIVITIES

A – Z

**BELOW:** a summer game of croquet.

**ABOVE:** Wimbledon fortnight begins in the last week of June.

(Centre Court and Courts 1 and 2) are allocated by ballot and should be applied for before mid-December the preceding year by writing to the All England Tennis Club, P.O. Box 98, Wimbledon, SW19 5AE, enclosing a self-addressed envelope (or an international reply coupon if applying from overseas). However, apart from Centre Court action on the last four days, you can queue on the day for tickets (cash only, to speed things up), though for popular games this can mean queueing all night under the watchful eye of supervisors. For information contact the ticket office on 8971 2473 or check www.wimbledon.org. Buses for the championships leave Victoria and Marble Arch every 30 minutes, while trains from Waterloo are met by a shuttle bus at Wimbledon station.

### Horse Racing

The flat-racing season is March to November, while steeplechasing takes place virtually all year round. The nearest racecourses to London are: Ascot (tel: 0870 727 1234 for tickets; www.ascot.co.uk); Jockey Club Race Courses (Kempton Park, Epsom and Sandown Park, tel: 0844

579 3019 for tickets; www.jockey clubracecourses.com); and Windsor (tel: 01753 498 400; www.windsor-racecourse.co.uk).

### The Boat Race

Rowers from Oxford and Cambridge universities race down the Thames from Putney to Mortlake. This annual event (since 1856) in late March/early April is watched by around 250,000 cheering spectators lining the river banks.

## Participant Sports

### Golf

Contact the English Golf Union (tel: 01526 354 500; www.english golfunion.org) for details of courses.

Many golf courses in London's suburbs offer "pay and play" access, though booking is advisable at weekends. They include: **Beckenham Place Park**, Beckenham Hill Road, Beckenham, BR3 (tel: 8650 2292), a parkland course with an imposing 18th-century mansion for a clubhouse. **Lee Valley**, Lee Valley Leisure Complex, Picketts Lock Lane, Edmonton, N9 (tel: 8803 3611), an urban course built on reclaimed land. **Stockley Pines**, Uxbridge, UB11 (tel: 8813 5700), a championship-length course in 240 acres (97 hectares) of pleasantly undulating parkland.

### Horse Riding

Hyde Park Stables (tel: 7723 2813; www.hydeparkstables.com) arrange hacking in Hyde Park and lessons, and are approved by the British Horse Society (BHS). Wimbledon Village Stables (tel: 8946 8579; www.wvstables.com) are BHS- and ABRS-approved and offer hacking on Wimbledon Common and lessons.

### Tennis

Many local parks have bookable courts. The Lawn Tennis Association (tel: 8487 7000; www.lta.org.

## SWIMMING

In spite of the UK's reputation for cold, wet weather, summers in London have been very warm in recent years. Few hotels have swimming pools and most municipal pools are indoors. Outdoor pools include: **The Oasis**, 32 Endell Street, WC2. Tel: 7831 1804. Between Covent Garden and Tottenham Court Road, this heated outdoor pool is a hidden gem and open year-round (steamy in winter). It isn't smart but it is clean and well-loved by regulars. **Brockwell Lido**, Dulwich Road, SE24. Tel: 7274 3088; www.brockwelllido.com. Very popular amenity open during the summer months only. Barbecues held on hot days. Other pools include the **Serpentine** in Hyde Park and the Bathing Ponds on **Hampstead Heath**. The latter comprise three pools – a men's, a women's and a mixed one, open 7am–7pm year-round for the single-sex pools and summer only for the mixed.

uk) has a leaflet on grass courts and you can locate a court in a park or leisure area near you by checking www.londontennis.co.uk.

## TOURS

### Guided Tours – Bus

A guided tour of London by bus is the best way for visitors to familiarise themselves with the city. All tours that are registered with the London Tourist Board use Blue Badge Guides, whose ranks number around 1,000. **The Big Bus Company**, tel: 7233 9533; www.bigbustours.com. Open-top bus tours over a choice of two routes lasting 2½ to 3½ hours. You are free to hop on or hop off at any of the 70 stops. Buses run every 5–15 minutes. Tours have live commentary in English or recorded commentary in seven languages as well as English. Tickets are valid for 24 hours; buses operate 8.30am–8pm in the summer and until 6pm in the winter. Cost: £27 for adults and £12 for children.

**Evan Evans**, tel: 7950 1777; www.evanevanstours.co.uk. A variety of tours giving a comprehensive introduction to the city with emphasis on historic sites. Admittance to St Paul's Cathedral, the Royal Albert Hall and the Tower of London are part of some tours. Picks up from many hotels. Cost: £69 (£59 for children under 16) for a full day.

**Golden Tours**, tel: 0844 880 5050; www.goldentours.com. Various tours of the city in air-conditioned coaches accompanied by guides who hold the coveted Blue Badge. The London Experience full-day tour takes in major sights such as the Tower and St Paul's, and includes a Thames cruise and a London Eye ride. Cost: £89 (£79 for children).

**The Original London Sightseeing Tour**, tel: 8877 1722; www.theoriginaltour.com. A choice of three different tours in traditional red double-decker buses, some of which are open-top. The Original tour features live commentary in English; the other two have recorded commentary in a choice of seven languages. A unique feature is the recorded children's commentary – by kids for kids. Tours run from 9am approximately every 12 minutes and passengers can hop on and off at any of the 90 stops. Tickets cost £26 for adults and £13 for children under 16, and are valid for 24 hours. There are departure points throughout central London. A free river cruise from Embankment is included in the price.

## River Tours

**Bateaux London**, tel: 7695 1800. Romantic dinner cruises along the Thames with cabaret and dancing. From £47–67 for a Sunday lunch jazz cruise, £79–120 per person for a dinner cruise (including wine).

**Thames River Services**, tel: 7930 4097. Trips between Westminster and Greenwich piers every 30 minutes (£13 return, child £6.50). Tours go beyond Greenwich to the Millennium Dome and the Thames Flood Barrier.

## Guided Tours – Walks

Some walking tour operators use London Tourist Board-trained Blue Badge Guides – a guarantee of quality. Walks generally last one or two hours. *Time Out* magazine lists a selection of weekly walks in its Visitors section.

**City Walks**, www.walklondon-uk.com. Tailor-made tours of London and the City.

**Ghost Walk**, tel: 8530 8443, www.london-ghost-walk.co.uk. Explores the graveyards, nooks and crannies of the City of London. Cost: £8.

**Jack the Ripper Tours**, tel: 8530 8443, www.jack-the-ripper-tour.com. As the title suggests, a two-hour after dark tour which explores

London's more murky past and shady courtyards. Cost: £8.

**Original London Walks**, tel: 7624 3978; www.walks.com. More than 200 walks, including Along the Thames Pub Walk, Hidden London, Hampstead, Historic Westminster, Little Venice and Ghost walks. Adults £8, under 15s free with an adult.

## Theatrical Tours

**Royal National Theatre**, tel: 7452 3400. Daily tours and workshops. Up to five times a day (Mon–Sat), with each tour lasting 1¼ hours. Cost: £7.50.

**Shakespeare's Globe Theatre**, tel: 7902 1500. Daily (10am–5pm) 40-minute tours. Adults £12.50, children £8.

**Theatre Royal Drury Lane**, tel: 0870 890 1109. Tours (Mon–Sat) lasting about 1 hour. Cost: £9.

**Theatreland Walking Tour**, tel: 7557 6700; www.londontheatre.co.uk. Two-hour tours on Sunday, except during winter. Book in advance. Cost: £9.50.

**BBC Television Tours**, tel: 0370 901 1227; www.bbc.co.uk/tours. The BBC runs tours of its Television Centre at Wood Lane, W12 (Tube: White City). Pre-booking essential. Adults £9.95, children over nine £7.75.

**BELOW:** see the city from a different angle on board a tourist boat.

**A–Z**

## AN ALPHABETICAL SUMMARY OF PRACTICAL INFORMATION

**A** Accidents 308
**B** Budgeting for a Trip 308
**C** Car Breakdown 308
   Children 308
   Climate and Clothing 309
   Crime 309
   Customs Regulations 309
**D** Disabled Access 310
**E** Electricity 310
   Embassies 310
   Entry Requirements 310

**G** Gay and Lesbian 311
   Government 311
**H** Health & Medical Care 311
**I** Internet 311
**L** Left Luggage 312
   Lost Property 312
**M** Maps 312
   Money 312
**N** Newspapers 312
**P** Population and Size 313
   Postal Services 313

   Postcodes 313
   Public Holidays 313
**R** Radio Stations 313
**S** Student Travellers 314
**T** Telephones 314
   Television Stations 314
   Time 315
   Tipping 315
   Tour Operators 315
   Tourist Offices 315
**W** Websites 315

### A ccidents

In the event of a serious accident or emergency, dial 999. In the case of minor accidents, your hotel will know where to find the nearest hospital with a casualty department. If you're outside, hail a taxi – cabbies know even more than hotel receptionists.

### B udgeting for a Trip

London is a very expensive city. You'll be lucky to find a conveniently located double room for less than £100 a night and prices soar to well over £400. Breakfast is often included in the price, but if not, a full English will start at £6 and a Continental breakfast at £3. Expect to pay from £25 to £50 each for a three-course dinner, including a modest wine, at a reasonable restaurant. Most cinema tickets cost £6–12, and a good seat for a West End musical is about £40. Taxis aren't cheap, especially at night, but neither is the Underground, with a short Tube journey costing from £4 – check out the special passes listed on page 278.

### C ar Breakdown

The following organisations operate 24-hour breakdown assistance. Phone calls to these numbers are free, but the service is free only to members:
**AA**, tel: 0800 887 766

**RAC**, tel: 0800 828 282
**Green Flag**, tel: 0800 051 0636

### Children

For ideas on museums and other attractions suitable for children of various ages, see *Best of London, page 10*.
**Accommodation.** Some hotels do not accept children under a certain age, so be sure to check when you book. Most restaurants accept well-behaved children, but only those that want to encourage families have children's menus and nappy-changing facilities. Only pubs with a Children's Certificate can admit children, and even these will usually restrict the hours and areas open to them. Publicans, like restaurateurs,

reserve the right to refuse entry.

**Public transport.** Up to four children aged 11 or under can travel free on the Tube if accompanied by a ticket-holding adult. Eleven–15-year-olds can get unlimited free travel on buses, and child rates on the Tube, DLR and London Overground, providing they have a photo Oyster card (this can take up to two weeks to obtain).

Buses are free for all children under 16, but those over 10 years need an Oyster photocard if unaccompanied. Buses can take up to two unfolded pushchairs (buggies) at one time (they must be parked in a special area halfway down the bus). Any further pushchairs must be folded. Visit www.tfl.gov.uk.

**Supplies.** Infant formula and nappies (diapers) can be found in chemists (pharmacies) and supermarkets.

**Hospitals.** In a medical emergency, take your child to the Accident & Emergency department of the nearest hospital. If you require over-the-counter medications such as Calpol (liquid paracetamol) late at night, Bliss Pharmacy (5 Marble Arch; tel: 7723 6116) is open until midnight every day.

## Climate and Clothing

The climate in London is mild, with the warming effects of the city itself keeping off the worst of the cold in winter. Snow and temperatures below freezing are unusual, with January temperatures averaging 43°F/6°C. Consequently, if it does snow hard, London is unprepared. Temperatures in the summer months average 64°F/18°C, but they can soar, causing the city to become airlessly hot (air conditioning is not universal). Rainfall is unpredictable, and it's wise, even in summer, to keep a fold-up umbrella close by.

### What to Wear

Between the stuffy Tube and often damp weather, it's best to

**ABOVE:** posing with police officers outside Buckingham Palace.

dress in layers. A cool, rainy day can turn beautiful unexpectedly and vice versa. In general, short sleeves and a jacket are recommended for summer and a warm coat and woollens for winter.

While a few of the traditional restaurants retain a dress code, smart-casual is generally the norm for restaurants and theatres. In general, Londoners are quite style-conscious but also practical; most getting around will be on foot or via public transport, so wearing comfortable shoes is wise.

## Crime

Serious crime is low for a city of this size, but the Dickensian

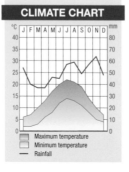

**CLIMATE CHART**

tradition of pickpocketing is alive and well. Hold on tightly to purses, do not put wallets in back pockets, and do not place handbags on the ground in busy restaurants. Gangs of professional thieves target the Tube.

In a genuine emergency, dial 999 from any telephone (no cash required). Report routine thefts to a police station (address found under Police in a telephone directory). The threat of terrorism has led to an increase in police patrols, so don't hesitate to report any suspicious packages.

## Customs Regulations

There are no official restrictions on the movement of goods within the European Union, provided those goods were purchased within the EU. However, British Customs have set the following personal-use "guide levels".
**Tobacco** 3,200 cigarettes or 400 cigarillos or 200 cigars or 3kg tobacco. (Limits are 200 cigarettes or 250g of smoking tobacco if coming from Bulgaria, Czech Republic, Estonia, Hungary, Latvia, Lithuania, Poland, Romania, Slovakia and Slovenia.)
**Alcohol** 10 litres spirits, 20 litres fortified wines, 90 litres wine, 110 litres beer.

Those entering from a non-EU state are subject to these limits:
**Tobacco** 200 cigarettes or 100 cigarillos or 50 cigars or 250g of tobacco are permitted.
**Alcohol** 1 litre of spirits, or 2 litres of fortified or sparkling wine, or 2 litres of table wine (an additional 2 litres of still wine allowed if no spirits are bought). £390-worth of other goods, such as perfume, are also permitted.
**Animals** Cats and dogs may enter Britain from EU countries providing they have the appropriate documentation. All other pets are placed in quarantine for six months at the owner's expense. For further details, log on to www.defra.gov.uk.
The following are prohibited entry into the United Kingdon:
**Plants** and **perishable foods** such as meats and meat products, eggs, fruit; some drugs (check with your doctor if you need to carry strong medication. You may need to carry a letter from them).
**Firearms** and ammunition (without special arrangement).
**Obscene** film or written material.
There are no restrictions on the amount of currency you can bring into the country.

**ABOVE:** entry requirements depend on where you are coming from.

# D isabled Access

**Venues.** Artsline, London's information and advice service on access to the arts and entertainment for disabled people, provides detailed access information for venues across London, including theatres, cinemas, museums, arts centres, tourist attractions, comedy and music venues, and selected restaurants. Tel: 7388 2227, www.artsline.org.uk.
**Advice.** William Forrester is a museum lecturer, co-author of *Access in London*, a trained guide and wheelchair user. He offers tailor-made tours of the city for chair users utilising accessible taxis, and arranges special visits to the Houses of Parliament, Westminster Abbey

and the British Museum. He operates a telephone advice service for anyone planning to visit the UK in a wheelchair. Tel: +44 (0)1483 575401.
**Toilets.** Britain has a system of keys to open many of the public toilets available for disabled people. To obtain a key, contact RADAR on 7250 3222; www.radar.org.uk. There is a charge of £3.50 (plus value-added tax – VAT) for the key and £10.25 (including post and packing) for the guidebook detailing their locations.
**Public transport.** Wheelchair-friendly buses have been progressively introduced across the network; almost all are accessible via low-floor vehicles or retractable ramps. Tubes are more difficult as entry is mainly by steps; the exception is the Jubilee Line, which has lifts. Ticket offices can provide a free leaflet on *Access to the Underground* or alternatively call 7222 1234 for help planning an accessible route.
**River cruises.** Step-free access is available from most major piers and newer boats have designated wheelchair spaces. Mobility-impaired groups can obtain information and advice by telephoning London River Services on 7941 2400.

# E lectricity

230 volts. Square, three-pin plugs are used, and virtually all visitors will need to bring or buy adaptors if planning to plug in their own equipment.

## Embassies

**Australia** Australia House, Strand, WC2B 4LA. Tel: 7379 4334
**Canada** Macdonald House, 1 Grosvenor Square, W1X 4AB. Tel: 7258 6600
**India** India House, Aldwych, WC2B 4NA. Tel: 7836 8484
**Ireland** 17 Grosvenor Place, SW1X 7HR. Tel: 7235 2171
**Jamaica** 1–2 Prince Consort Road, SW7 2BZ. Tel: 7823 9911
**New Zealand** 80 Haymarket, SW1Y 4TQ. Tel: 7930 8422
**South Africa** South Africa House, Trafalgar Square, WC2N 5DP. Tel: 7451 7299
**United States** 24 Grosvenor Square, W1A 1AE. Tel: 7499 9000.

## Entry Requirements

To enter Britain you need a valid passport (or any form of official identification if you are an EU citizen). Visas are not needed if you are from the USA, are a Commonwealth citizen or an EU national (or from most other European or South American countries). Health certificates are not required unless you have arrived from Asia, Africa or South America. If you wish to stay for a protracted period or apply for work, contact the Border and Immigration Agency after looking at the website www.ind.homeoffice.gov.uk. London's nearest Public Enquiry Office (PEO) is at Lunar House, 40 Wellesley Road, Croydon, CR9 2BY, tel: 0870 606 7766.

## G ay and Lesbian

With Europe's largest gay and lesbian population, London has an abundance of bars, restaurants and clubs to cater for most tastes. Many of them will make space for one or more of London's free gay weekly magazines, *Boyz*, the *Pink Paper*, and *QX*. Monthly magazines on sale at newsstands include *Gay Times*, *Diva* and *Attitude*.

Two established websites for meeting other gay people in London are www.gaydar.co.uk and the female version, www.gaydargirls.com. Other websites reflecting the gay scene include www.rainbownetwork.com and www.outuk.com.

Useful telephone contacts for advice and counselling include **London Lesbian and Gay Switchboard** (tel: 7837 7324) and **London Friend** (7.30–10pm, tel: 7837 3337). Support and advice about legal issues concerning HIV and Aids is available from the **National Aids Helpline** (tel: 0800 567 123).

## Government

When people refer to London, they mean the county of Greater London. When they speak of the City of London, they generally mean the financial district, the historic square mile between St Paul's Cathedral and the Tower of London, governed by the Corporation of London and headed by the Lord Mayor, which even has its own police force. The rest of the metropolis is run by 12 inner boroughs and 20 outer boroughs, each of which is responsible for local services.

In 1986 Margaret Thatcher's Conservative government, tiring of the left-wing policies of the Greater London Council and its leader, Ken Livingstone, abolished it. This decision left London's government balkanised between the existing 32 local boroughs. The most conspicuous victim of this lack of central planning was transport: traffic congestion slowed down bus services and the Underground's infrastructure and rolling stock deteriorated because of lack of investment.

Tony Blair's first Labour government, elected in 1997, restored a measure of local government by creating a Greater London Authority under the direction of a mayor – a new post for London and distinct from the centuries-old post of Lord Mayor who presides over the Corporation of London's administration. Four bodies eat up most of the GLA's budget: the Metropolitan Police Authority, the London Fire and Emergency Planning Authority, the London Development Agency and Transport for London.

Local services such as refuse disposal, housing grants and parking control are still run by the 32 boroughs: Barking, Barnet, Bexley, Brent, Bromley, Camden, Croydon, Ealing, Enfield, Greenwich, Hackney, Hammersmith and Fulham, Haringey, Harrow, Havering, Hillingdon, Hounslow, Islington, Kensington and Chelsea, Kingston-upon-Thames, Lambeth, Lewisham, Merton, Newham, Redbridge, Richmond-upon-Thames, Southwark, Sutton, Tower Hamlets, Waltham Forest, Wandsworth, and Westminster.

## H ealth & Medical Care

If you fall ill and are a national of the European Union, you are entitled to free emergency medical treatment for illnesses arising while in the UK. Many other countries also have reciprocal arrangements for free treatment. However, most visitors will be liable for medical and dental treatment so will have to pay for any non-emergency treatment. They should ensure they have adequate health insurance.

**Major hospitals** include Charing Cross Hospital (Fulham Palace Road, W6, tel: 8846 1234), St Mary's Hospital (Praed Street, W2, tel: 7886 6666), and St Thomas's (Lambeth Palace Road, SE1, tel: 7188 7188).

**Emergency dental treatment** is available on weekdays 9am–5pm (queuing begins at 8am) at Guy's Hospital, St Thomas Street, SE1, tel: 7188 7188.

**Chemists (pharmacists)**. Boots is a large chain of pharmacies with branches throughout London that will make up prescriptions. The branch at 114 Queensway, W2 is open until 10pm daily, whilst Bliss Chemist at 5 Marble Arch is open until midnight daily.

**Accidents**: in the case of an emergency, dial **999**.

## I nternet

London has many internet cafés. The most widespread is the easyEverything chain which has mega cafés in Oxford Street, Trafalgar Square, Tottenham Court Road and Kensington High Street, all open 24 hours a day: www.easyinternetcafe.com. You can also surf at Waterstone's bookshop at 203–206 Piccadilly.

# **L**eft Luggage

Most of the main railway stations have left luggage departments where you can leave your suitcases on a short-term basis, although all are very sensitive to potential terrorist bombs. Left luggage offices close at 11pm.

## Lost Property

If you can't find a policeman, dial directory enquiries (118 500 or 118 888 or 118 118) and ask for the number of the nearest police station. Don't call the emergency number 999 unless there has been a serious crime or accident. For non-emergencies, the Metropolitan Police number is 101. If your passport has been lost, let your embassy know as well.

For possessions lost on public transport or in taxis, contact Transport for London's central Lost Property (200 Baker Street, NW1 5RZ, tel: 0845 330 9882; www.tfl.gov.uk) Mon–Fri 8.30am–4pm, or fill in an enquiry form, available from any London Underground station or bus garage. It can take two to four days for items left on a Tube train or bus to reach the office and more

than a week for items a taxi driver has handed in at a police station. It is therefore advisable to wait several days before visiting or phoning the office, which can search for your property while you are on the phone. It can also post your property back to you for a fee. The office receives 600 items a day.

# **M**aps

Insight Guides' *FlexiMap London* is laminated for durability and easy folding. For detailed exploration of the city centre and suburbs, the *London A–Z* books come in various formats. Free Tube maps are available at Underground stations. Map lovers should head for Stanford's flagship shop (12–14 Long Acre, Covent Garden), one of the world's top map and guidebook stores.

## Money

The pound sterling (divided into 100 pence) is the currency, though many large London stores will accept euros.

Most **banks** open Mon–Fri 9.30am–5pm (or even later), with Saturday morning banking com-

mon in shopping areas. Major British banks tend to offer similar exchange rates; it's only worth shopping around if you have large amounts of money to change. Banks charge no commission on sterling traveller's cheques. If a London bank is affiliated to your own bank, it may make no charge for cheques in other currencies either. However, there will be a charge for changing cash into another currency.

Some High Street travel agents, such as Thomas Cook, operate **bureaux de change** at comparable rates. There are also private bureaux de change (some are open 24 hours) where rates can be very low and commissions high. Chequepoint (www. chequepoint.com) is a reputable chain with branches at 222 Earl's Court, 71 Gloucester Road, 2 Queensway and 550 Oxford Circus.

International **credit cards** are almost universally accepted. However, a few stores and restaurants do not accept them, so check for signs at the entrance first.

**Tax refunds** enable visitors from outside the European Union to reclaim the 17.5 percent value-added tax when spending over a certain amount. Stores can supply VAT refund forms which should be presented to Customs officials when leaving the country.

# **N**ewspapers

Politically speaking, the *Daily Telegraph* and *The Times* are on the right, *The Guardian* is on the left and *The Independent* has a liberal, international slant. To appeal to commuters, some are printed in a compact (tabloid) format rather than the traditional full-size broadsheet. On Sunday *The Observer* is more liberal than the *Sunday Times*, *Independent on Sunday* and *Sunday Telegraph*. The *Financial Times* is renowned for the clearest, most unslanted

**BELOW:** newsstands abound, but free newspapers are also plentiful.

headlines in its general news pages (plus, of course, its financial coverage).

Among the mass-market tabloids, *The Sun* and *The Star* are traditionally on the right (and obsessed with royalty, soap operas and sex), and the *Daily Mirror* and *Sunday Mirror* are on the left, as is the *Sunday People*. The *Daily Mail* and *Mail on Sunday* are more up-market and right-wing equivalents of the politically eclectic *Express*.

Editions of the free, London-only *Evening Standard* come out Mon–Fri mid-morning and are good for London news, cinema and theatre listings. The free tabloid *Metro* can be picked up at stations in the morning from Mon–Fri. Both of these contain useful but not comprehensive listings sections.

**Listings magazines.** Supreme in this field is the long-established weekly *Time Out*.

**Foreign newspapers and magazines** can be found at many street newsstands, at mainline stations, and at these outlets:
A Moroni & Son: 68 Old Compton Street, W1.
Compton News: 48 Old Compton Street, W1.
Eman's: 123 Queensway, W2.
Selfridges: Oxford Street, W1.
Victoria Place Shopping Centre: Victoria Station, SW1.

## P opulation and Size

After decades of decline, London's population has increased since the mid-1980s to its present 7.5 million and forecasts show it surging to almost 8 million by 2016. More than a quarter of residents are from a minority ethnic group, and around 300 languages are spoken (from Abem, a language of the Ivory Coast, to Zulu, from South Africa).

Officially, London's area is 610 sq miles (1,580 sq km), but the urban sprawl around the capital makes it hard to know where to stop measuring.

**ABOVE:** a familiar red post box.

## Postal Services

Post offices open Mon–Fri 9am–5pm, Sat 9am–noon. Stamps are available from post offices and selected shops, usually newsagents, and from machines outside some post offices. There is a two-tier service within the UK: first class is supposed to reach a UK destination the next day, second class will take at least a day or two longer. London's main post office is at Trafalgar Square, behind the church of St Martin-in-the-Fields. It stays open until 6.30pm Mon–Fri.

The cost of sending a letter or parcel depends on weight as well as size. Queues tend to be long over the lunch period.

## Postcodes

The first half of London postcodes indicates the general area (WC = West Central, SE = South East) and the second half, used only for mail, identifies the exact block. Here is a key to some of the more common codes:

**W1** Mayfair, Marylebone, Soho; **W2** Bayswater; **W4** Chiswick; **W8** Kensington; **W11** Notting Hill; **WC1** Bloomsbury; **WC2** Covent Garden, Strand; **E1** Whitechapel; **EC1** Clerkenwell; **EC2** Bank, Barbican; **EC4** St Paul's, Blackfriars; **SW1** St James's, Belgravia; **SW3** Chelsea; **SW7** Knightsbridge, South Kensington; **SW19** Wimbledon; **SE1** Lambeth, Southwark; **SE10** Greenwich; **SE21** Dulwich; **N1** Hoxton, Islington; **N6** Highgate; **NW3** Hampstead.

## Public Holidays

Compared to most European countries, the UK has few public holidays:
**January** New Year's Day (1st)
**March/April** Good Friday, Easter Monday
**May** May Day (first Monday of the month), Spring Bank Holiday (last Monday)
**August** Summer Bank Holiday (last Monday)
**December** Christmas Day (25th), Boxing Day (26th).

## R adio Stations

You can receive national stations as well as many targeted specifically at London. A selection:

### Commercial Stations
**Capital FM** – 95.8FM, 24-hour pop music.
**Classic FM** – 100.9FM, 24-hour light classical music.
**Choice FM** – 96.9FM, soul music.
**Heart** – 106.2FM, classic rock.
**Kiss FM** – 100FM, 24-hour dance music.
**LBC** – 97.3FM, 24-hour chat, showbiz, opinion, news.
**Smooth FM** – 102.2FM, bland playlist of jazz, soul and blues and middle-of-the-road.
**Virgin** – 105.8FM, adult-oriented rock.

### BBC Stations
**Radio 1** – 98.8FM, mainstream pop.

**Radio 2** – 89.2FM, easy-listening music, chat shows.
**Radio 3** – 91.3FM, 24-hour classical music, plus drama and serious talks.
**Radio 4** – 93.5FM, heavyweight news, current affairs, plays.
**Radio Five Live** – 909MW, rolling news, sport.
**BBC Radio London** – 94.9FM, London-oriented music, chat and sports station.
**BBC World Service** – 648 kHz, international news.

## S moking

In July 2007 England imposed a ban on smoking in all enclosed public spaces, including pubs, clubs and bars (though not in outside beer gardens). This extends to railway platforms.

### Student Travellers

International students can obtain various discounts at attractions, on travel services (including Eurostar) and in some shops by showing a valid ISIC card. Visit www.isiccard.com.

**BELOW:** a British icon, sadly becoming less common.

## T elephones

Despite the ubiquity of mobile phones (cellphones), London still has an adequate number of public kiosks and public phones in pubs. It is cheaper to use a public phone than one in your hotel as many hotels still make an outrageous charge for calls from your room.

British Telecom (BT) is the main telephone operating company. The smallest coin accepted is 20p. Most kiosks will also accept phone cards, which are widely available from post offices and newsagents in varying amounts between £5 and £20. Credit card phones can be found at major transport terminals and on busy streets.

### Phoning Abroad

You can telephone abroad directly from any phone. Dial 00 followed by the international code for the country you want, and then the number. Some country codes:
**Australia** (61); **Hong Kong** (852); **Ireland** (353); **New Zealand** (64); **Singapore** (65); **South Africa**

(27); **US and Canada** (1).

If you are using a US credit phone card, first dial the company's access number as follows:
**Sprint**, tel: 0800-890877
**MCI**, tel: 0800-279 5088
**AT&T**, tel: 0800-890011.

### Useful Numbers

**Emergency** – police, fire, ambulance: 999
**Operator** (for difficulties in getting through): 100
**International Operator**: 155
**Directory Enquiries (UK)**: 118 500 or 118 888 or 118 118
**International Directory Enquiries** 118 505 or 118 866 or 118 899
**London Regional Transport** 24-hour information: 7222 1234
**Rail information** for all London stations: 0845 748 4950.
**Accommodation bookings**: 0870 156 6366 or call Visit London on 08701 566 366.

### Television Stations

The BBC (British Broadcasting Corporation) is financed by compulsory annual television licences and is advertising-free. The independent channels (ITV1, C4 and Five) are funded by commercials.

In recent years the choice of channels has expanded exponentially as cable, satellite and digital channels have joined the small number of terrestrial channels. The BBC has several digital channels, including the round-the-clock BBC News 24, the youth-oriented BBC3, and the arts-oriented BBC4. By the end of 2012 the terrestrial broadcasting network will cease to exist, and even BBC1, BBC2 and the terrestrial commercial channels will only be available through digital technology.

**Teletext**. A vast range of information (news, business, sport and entertainment) is available on the teletext services transmitted by all the terrestrial

channels. This is accessed via the TV set's remote control.

## Time

British Summer Time (one hour ahead of Greenwich Mean Time) operates from the last Sunday in March until the last Sunday in October. Greenwich Mean Time is 8 hours in front of Los Angeles, 5 hours in front of New York and Montreal, and 10 hours behind Sydney.

## Tipping

Most hotels and many restaurants automatically add 10–15 percent service charge to your bill. It's your right to deduct it if you're not happy with the service. If you pay by chip and PIN, the machine will often require you to add or decline to add a tip before you insert your PIN number, which feels rather cheeky when the waitress or waiter is standing in front of you. If a service charge has already been included in the bill, you certainly shouldn't feel obliged to add anything extra.

It is not customary to tip in pubs, cinemas, theatres or elevators, but you should tip sightseeing guides (about ten percent) and railway porters. It is also usual to tip cab drivers if they've been particularly helpful or assisted with your bags.

## Tour Operators

**The Original Tour** is the first and biggest London sightseeing operator. Hop-on and hop-off at over 90 different stops, with commentary in a wide choice of languages and a Kids' Club for 5–12 year olds. Buy tickets on the bus or in advance. Operates year round. Tel: 8877 1722; www.theoriginaltour.com.

**Big Bus Company** operates three routes of hop-on hop-off services. Tel: 7233 9533; www.bigbustours.com.

**Duck Tours** use World War II amphibious vehicles which drive past famous London landmarks before taking to the water. Great for children. Departure from County Hall. Tel: 7928 3132; www.london ducktours.co.uk.

## Tourist Offices

The offical tourist board maintains a website at www.visitlondon. com. It contains a huge amount of information on attractions, upcoming events and festivals, as well as practical information and a hotel booking service.

Personal enquires can be made at **Britain and London Visitor Centre**, 1 Regent Street, Piccadilly Circus, SW1Y 4XT. The office is open Mon 9.30am–6.30pm, Tue–Fri 9am–6.30pm, Sat–Sun 10am–4pm (June–Sept, Sat 9am–5pm). You can email BLVCenquiry@visitbritain.org, or tel: 08701 566 366.

Other tourist information centres are located at:

**City of London Information Centre**, St. Paul's Churchyard, EC4M 8BX. Tel: +44 (0) 20 7332 1456. Open Mon–Sat 9.30am–5.30pm, Sun 10am–4pm.

**Greenwich TIC**, Pepys House, 2 Cutty Sark Gardens, Greenwich SE10 9LW. Tel: +44 (0)870 608 2000. Open daily 10am–5pm. Email: tic@greenwich.gov.uk.

## Websites

**www.visitlondon.com** The official tourist board site, with lots of advice, listings and links.
**www.thisislondon.co.uk** Run by the *Evening Standard* newspaper; has detailed listings of events.
**www.london-se1.co.uk** has up-to-date coverage of the South Bank and Bankside.
**www.streetmap.co.uk** locates the address you type in.
**www.24hourmuseum.co.uk** has up-to-date information on what UK museums are exhibiting.
**www.bbc.co.uk** is a gigantic site with lots on London.

**BELOW:** getting one's bearings.

# FURTHER READING

## Good Companions

*A Literary Companion: London* by Peter Vansittart. A journey around the capital with the literary luminaries.
*Secret London* by Andrew Duncan. Uncovers London's hidden landscape from abandoned tube stations to the gentlemen's club.
*The London Blue Plaque Guide* by Nick Rennison. Details the lives of more than 700 individuals who have been commemorated with a blue plaque on their houses.
*A Literary Guide to London* by Ed Glinet. A very detailed, street-by-street guide to literary lives.
*London on Film* by Colin Sorensen. How the cinema has portrayed the city.

## History

*The Concise Pepys* by Samuel Pepys. Read a first-hand account of the Great Fire of London and find out about daily life in 17th-century England.
*Dr Johnson's London* by Liza Picard. Brings 18th-century London to life.
*London: The Biography* by Peter Ackroyd. Anecdotal and entertaining history.
*London: A Social History* by Roy Porter. Less quirky than Ackroyd but a telling account of how badly the capital has been governed over the centuries.
*The Story of the British Museum* by Marjorie Caygill. A fascinating tale, authoritatively told, featuring an astonishing variety of heroes and villains.
*London Villages* by John Wittich. A walker's notes on his travels through village London.

*Thames: Sacred River* by Peter Ackroyd. Social history of London's famous river.

## Memoirs

*The Shorter Pepys* by Samuel Pepys. A distillation of 11 volumes of diaries describing London life, including the Great Fire and the plague, from 1660 to 1669.

## FEEDBACK

We do our best to ensure the information in our books is as accurate and up-to-date as possible. The books are updated on a regular basis using local contacts, who painstakingly add, amend and correct as required. However, some details (such as telephone numbers and opening times) are liable to change, and we are ultimately reliant on our readers to put us in the picture.

We welcome your feedback, especially your experience of using the book "on the road". Maybe we recommended a hotel that you liked (or another that you didn't), or you came across a great bar or new attraction we missed.

We will acknowledge all contributions, and we'll offer an Insight Guide to the best letters received.

Please write to us at:
Insight Guides
PO Box 7910
London SE1 1WE
United Kingdom
Or send an email to:
insight@apaguide.co.uk

*84 Charing Cross Road* by Helene Hanff. Touching book-lover's correspondence with a London book seller.
*London Orbital* by Iain Sinclair. A walk round the M25, exploring little-known parts of London's periphery.
*The Oxford Book of London* edited by Paul Bailey. A bran-dip of observations by famous visitors over eight centuries.

## Art and Architecture

*A Guide to London's Contemporary Architecture* by Ken Allinson and Victoria Thornton. Covers buildings since the 1980s; black-and-white pictures.
*London Under London* by Richard Trench and Ellis Hillman. Traces the astonishing maze of railway lines, sewers and utilities that lies beneath the streets.

## Other Insight Guides

Other titles covering London in the Insight Guides range include **Insight Step by Step London**. This book details 20 self-guided walks and tours written by a local expert and designed to suit every interest and taste. Comes with a free pull-out map with street index.
**Insight Smart Guide London** provides a full run-down of London's sights in an easy-to-use A–Z format.
**Insight FlexiMap London** is a fold-out laminated map that is easy to use and long-lasting.

# LONDON STREET ATLAS

The key map shows the area of London covered by the atlas
section. An index of street names and places of interest
shown on the maps can be found on the following pages.
For each entry there is a page number and grid reference.

## Map Legend

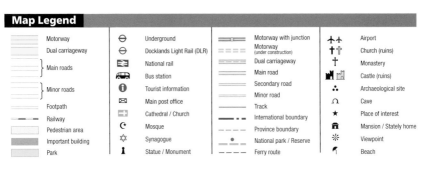

| | | | |
|---|---|---|---|
| Motorway | ⊖ Underground | Motorway with junction | ✈✈ Airport |
| Dual carriageway | ⊖ Docklands Light Rail (DLR) | Motorway (under construction) | ✝✝ Church (ruins) |
| Main roads | National rail | Dual carriageway | ✝ Monastery |
| | Bus station | Main road | Castle (ruins) |
| Minor roads | ❶ Tourist information | Secondary road | ⸫ Archaeological site |
| | ✉ Main post office | Minor road | Ω Cave |
| Footpath | Cathedral / Church | Track | ★ Place of interest |
| Railway | ☾ Mosque | International boundary | Mansion / Stately home |
| Pedestrian area | ✡ Synagogue | Province boundary | Viewpoint |
| Important building | 🛉 Statue / Monument | National park / Reserve | Beach |
| Park | | Ferry route | |

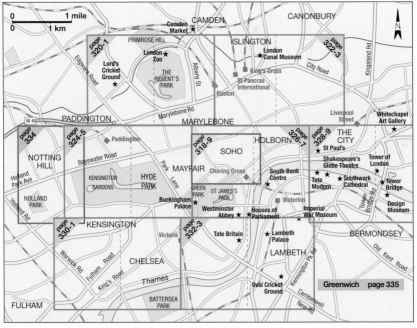

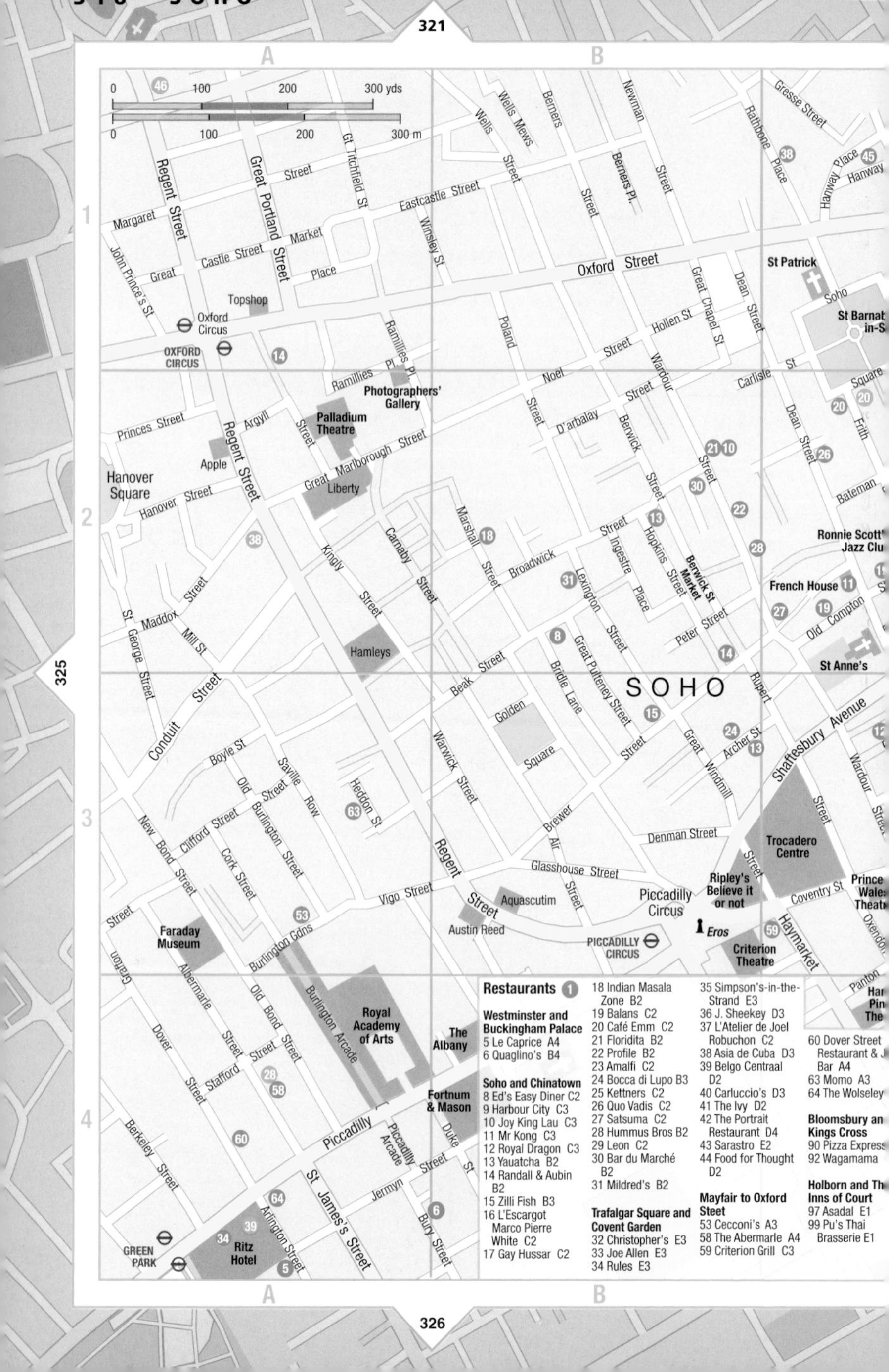

321

325

326

A        B

0     100     200     300 yds
0     100     200     300 m

**Streets and places (map labels):**

Regent Street, Great Portland Street, Margaret Street, John Prince's St, Castle Street, Great Portland Street, Market Place, Topshop, Oxford Circus, OXFORD CIRCUS, Princes Street, Argyll Street, Hanover Square, Apple, Hanover Street, Palladium Theatre, Great Marlborough Street, Liberty, Photographers' Gallery, Ramillies Pl, Ramillies St, St. George Street, Maddox Street, Regent Street, Mill St, Kingly, Carnaby Street, Broadwick, Hamleys, Conduit Street, Boyle St, Saville Row, Old Burlington Street, Beak Street, Golden Square, Warwick Street, Brewer, Air St, Heddon St, New Bond Street, Clifford Street, Cork Street, Burlington Gardens, Regent Street, Glasshouse Street, Vigo Street, Aquascutum, Austin Reed, Albemarle Street, Old Bond Street, Dover Street, Stafford Street, Berkeley Street, Faraday Museum, Royal Academy of Arts, The Albany, Fortnum & Mason, Piccadilly, Piccadilly Arcade, Burlington Arcade, Duke Street, Jermyn Street, Arlington Street, GREEN PARK, Ritz Hotel, St James's Street, Bury Street

Wells Mews, Walls Street, Berners Street, Berners Pl, Newman Street, Eastcastle Street, Winsley St, Oxford Street, Poland Street, Noel Street, D'arblay Street, Berwick Street, Wardour Street, Marshall Street, Lexington Street, Great Pulteney Street, Bridle Lane, Brewer Street, Great Windmill Street, Denman Street, Piccadilly Circus, PICCADILLY CIRCUS, Eros, Criterion Theatre, Ripley's Believe it or not, Trocadero Centre, Coventry St, Haymarket, Prince of Wales Theatre

Gresse Street, Rathbone Place, Hanway Place, Hanway, Great Chapel Street, Hollen St, Dean Street, Carlisle St, St Patrick, Soho, St Barnabas-in-S, Square, Frith Street, Dean Street, Bateman Street, Ronnie Scott's Jazz Club, French House, Old Compton Street, St Anne's, Peter Street, Rupert Street, Archer St, SOHO, Shaftesbury Avenue, Wardour Street, Panton Street

Berwick St Market, Indiaste St

### Restaurants ❶

**Westminster and Buckingham Palace**
5 Le Caprice  A4
6 Quaglino's  B4

**Soho and Chinatown**
8 Ed's Easy Diner  C2
9 Harbour City  C3
10 Joy King Lau  C3
11 Mr Kong  C3
12 Royal Dragon  C3
13 Yauatcha  B2
14 Randall & Aubin  B2
15 Zilli Fish  B3
16 L'Escargot Marco Pierre White  C2
17 Gay Hussar  C2
18 Indian Masala Zone  B2
19 Balans  C2
20 Café Emm  C2
21 Floridita  B2
22 Profile  B2
23 Amalfi  B2
24 Bocca di Lupo  B3
25 Kettners  C2
26 Quo Vadis  C2
27 Satsuma  C2
28 Hummus Bros  B2
29 Leon  C2
30 Bar du Marché  B2
31 Mildred's  B2

**Trafalgar Square and Covent Garden**
32 Christopher's  E3
33 Joe Allen  E3
34 Rules  E3
35 Simpson's-in-the-Strand  E3
36 J. Sheekey  D3
37 L'Atelier de Joel Robuchon  C2
38 Asia de Cuba  D3
39 Belgo Centraal  D2
40 Carluccio's  D3
41 The Ivy  D2
42 The Portrait Restaurant  D4
43 Sarastro  E2
44 Food for Thought  D2

**Mayfair to Oxford Steet**
53 Cecconi's  A3
58 The Abermarle  A4
59 Criterion Grill  C3
60 Dover Street Restaurant & Jazz Bar  A4
63 Momo  A3
64 The Wolseley

**Bloomsbury and Kings Cross**
90 Pizza Express
92 Wagamama

**Holborn and The Inns of Court**
97 Asadal  E1
99 Pu's Thai Brasserie  E1

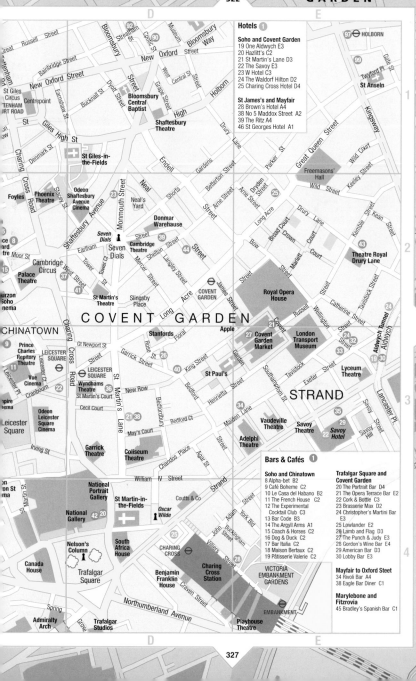

**Hotels ➊**

**Soho and Covent Garden**
19 One Aldwych E3
20 Hazlitt's C2
21 St Martin's Lane D3
22 The Savoy E3
23 W Hotel C3
24 The Waldorf Hilton D2
25 Charing Cross Hotel D4

**St James's and Mayfair**
28 Brown's Hotel A4
38 No 5 Maddox Street A2
39 The Ritz A4
46 St Georges Hotel A1

**Bars & Cafés ➊**

**Soho and Chinatown**
8 Alpha-bet B2
9 Café Boheme C2
10 Le Casa del Habano B2
11 The French House C2
12 The Experimental
   Cocktail Club C3
13 Bar Code B3
14 The Argyll Arms A1
15 Coach & Horses C2
16 Dog & Duck C2
17 Bar Italia C2
18 Maison Bertaux C2
19 Pâtisserie Valerie C2

**Trafalgar Square and
Covent Garden**
20 The Portrait Bar D4
21 The Opera Terrace Bar E2
22 Cork & Bottle C3
23 Brasserie Max D2
24 Christopher's Martini Bar
   E3
25 Lowlander E2
26 Lamb and Flag D3
27 The Punch & Judy E3
28 Gordon's Wine Bar E4
29 American Bar D3
30 Lobby Bar E3

**Mayfair to Oxford Steet**
34 Rivoli Bar A4
38 Eagle Bar Diner C1

**Marylebone and
Fitzrovia**
45 Bradley's Spanish Bar C1

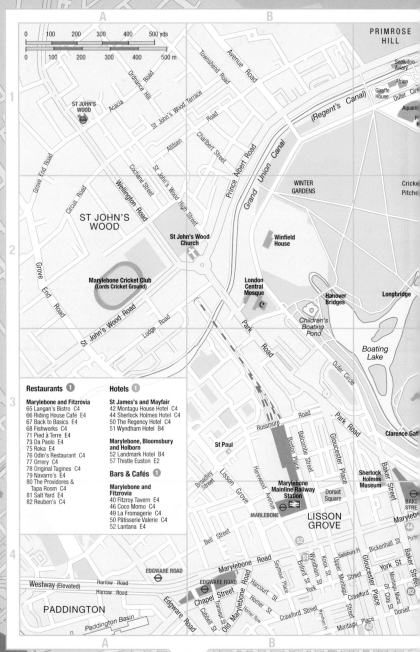

A | B

PRIMROSE HILL

0 100 200 300 400 500 yds
0 100 200 300 400 500 m

Snowdon Aviary
Africa
Giraffe House
Outer Cir
Aquariu

ST JOHN'S WOOD

Ordnance Hill
Acacia Road
Townshend Road
Avenue Road

(Regent's Canal)

Grove End Road
Circus Road
Wellington Road
Cochrane Street
St John's Wood Terrace
Allitsen Road
Charlbert Street
St John's Wood High Street
Prince Albert Road
Grand Union Canal

WINTER GARDENS

Cricke
Pitche

ST JOHN'S WOOD

St John's Wood Church

Winfield House

Grove End Road

Marylebone Cricket Club
(Lords Cricket Ground)

London Central Mosque

Hanover Bridges

Longbridge

St John's Wood Road
Lodge Road
Park Road

Children's Boating Pond

Outer Circle

Boating Lake

## Restaurants ①

### Marylebone and Fitzrovia
65 Langan's Bistro  C4
66 Riding House Café  E4
67 Back to Basics  E4
68 Fishworks  C4
71 Pied à Terre  E4
73 Da Paolo  E4
75 Roka  E4
76 Odin's Restaurant  C4
77 Orrery  C4
78 Original Tagines  C4
79 Navarro's  E4
80 The Providores & Tapa Room  C4
81 Salt Yard  E4
82 Reuben's  C4

## Hotels ①

### St James's and Mayfair
42 Montagu House Hotel  C4
44 Sherlock Holmes Hotel  C4
50 The Regency Hotel  C4
51 Wyndham Hotel  B4

### Marylebone, Bloomsbury and Holborn
52 Landmark Hotel  B4
57 Thistle Euston  E2

## Bars & Cafés ①

### Marylebone and Fitzrovia
40 Fitzroy Tavern  E4
46 Coco Momo  E4
49 La Fromagerie  C4
50 Pâtisserie Valerie  C4
52 Lantana  E4

Rossmore Road
Park Road
Clarence Gat

St Paul

Balcombe Street
Boston Place
Gloucester Place

Sherlock Holmes Museum

Broadley Street
Lisson Grove
Harewood Avenue

Marylebone Mainline Railway Station

Dorset Square

BAKE STRE

Bradley Street

MARYLEBONE

LISSON GROVE

Bell Street

Bickenhall St.
Baker Street

Maryleb

Porte

44

EDGWARE ROAD

Salisbury Pl
Knox St
Upper Montagu Street
York Street
Gloucester Place

York St.

Montagu Mans

Westway (Elevated)
Harrow Road
Harrow Road

EDGWARE ROAD
Chapel Street
Homer St.
Harcourt St
York
Enford St.
Wyndham St.
Crawford Place

Baker Street

92

PADDINGTON

Paddington Basin

Edgware Road
Cabbell St
Transept St
Old Marylebone Road
Homer Row
Crawford Street
Wyndham Place
Seymour Place
Crawford Street
Montagu Place
Clay St.
Dorset

42

A | B

325

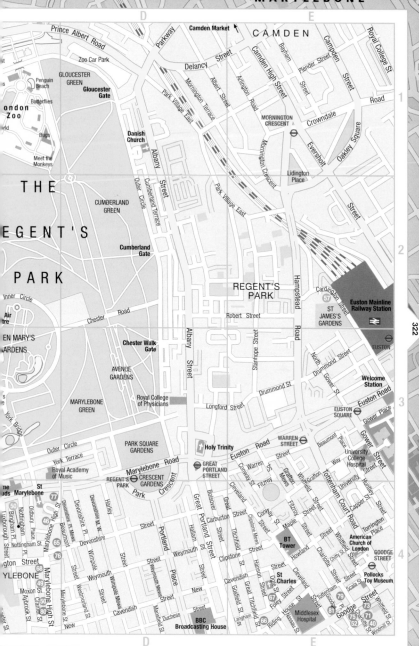

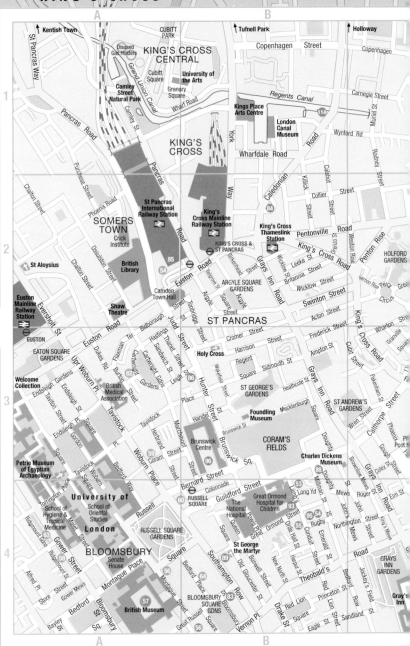

↑ Kentish Town

CUBITT
PARK

KING'S CROSS
CENTRAL

↑ Tufnell Park

↑ Holloway

Copenhagen    Street

Copenhagen

St Pancras Way

Disused
Gas Holders

Grand Union Canal

Cubitt
Square

University of
the Arts

Camley
Street
Natural Park

Granary
Square

Camley St

Regents    Canal

Kings Place
Arts Centre

114

Pancras    Road

KING'S
CROSS

Wharf Road

York

London
Canal
Museum

Road

Wynford Rd

Rodney Street

Carnegie Street

Purchese Street

Charlton Street

Phoenix Road

SOMERS
TOWN

St Pancras
International
Railway Station

King's
Cross Mainline
Railway Station

Way

Caledonian

Killick

Collier        Street

Street

84

Pentonville        Road

HOLFORD
GARDENS

Penton Rise

Crick
Institute

King's
Cross Thameslink
Station

King's Cross Rise

Weston Street

Percy

Vernon Rise

Grea

St Aloysius

Dessalain Street

British
Library

85

KING'S CROSS &
ST PANCRAS

Road

54

Euston

Belgrove Street

Birkenhead Street

Grays Inn Road

Wicklow Street

ARGYLE SQUARE
GARDENS

Leeke Street

Britannia Street

Swinton Street

Acton Street

Wicklow Street

King's Cross Road

Circus

Wharton

Granville

Euston
Mainline
Railway
Station

EUSTON

Eversholt St

Camden
Town Hall

Shaw
Theatre

Road

Argyle

Square

Tonbridge

Street

ST PANCRAS

Cromer    Street

Frederick    Street

Cubitt    Street

Pakenham St

Gough    St

EATON SQUARE
GARDENS

Euston

Road

Bidborough St

Flaxman Ter.

Dukes Rd.

Cartwright

Gardens

Burton St

Hastings

Thanet Street

Sandwich St

Cartwright Gdns

Leigh

65

Hunter

Street

Harrison

Regent

Square

Sidmouth St

ST GEORGE'S
GARDENS

Heathcote St

Ampton St.

Wren Street

ST ANDREWS
GARDENS

Cathorpe

Phoenix

Welcome
Collection

Endsleigh Gardens

Endsleigh Gardens

Endsleigh Pl.

Gordon

Square

Woburn

Tavistock

British
Medical
Association

Tavistock

Pl.

Herbrand

Marchmont

Place

Handel St

Wakefield Street

Brunswick St.

Mecklenburgh

Square

Foundling
Museum

Doughty

Brownlow Mews

Gough St

Colley St

Petrie Museum
of Egyptian
Archaeology

Tavistock Place

Taviton Street

Gordon

Square

Woburn
Place

59

Coram

Street

Brunswick
Centre

96

CORAM'S
FIELDS

Charles Dickens
Museum

88

John's

Mews

Roger St

Elm St

Torrington
Place

School of
Hygiene &
Tropical
Medicine

School of
Oriental
Studies

University of

Bernard    Street

Colonnade

60

RUSSELL
SQUARE

Brunswick Sq.

Guildford    Street

The
National
Hospital

Great Ormond
Hospital for
Children

53

Great Ormond

93

Long Yd

Millman    St

Lamb's

95

54

Conduit

St

Rugby

Emerald St

Northington    Street

Northington    Mews

Street

London

43

Ridgmount Gardens

Gower    Street

Malet Street

Ridgmount St

BLOOMSBURY

66

Senate
House

RUSSELL SQUARE
GARDENS

Bedford Way

Bedford

Russell

Square

Southampton    Row

89

St George
the Martyr

Old Gloucester    Street

Boswell    Street

New North St

Theobald's        Road

Red Lion    Square

Princeton St

Bedford

Jockey's Field

GRAYS
INN
GARDENS

Gray's
Inn

Alfred Pl.

Store    Street

Gower Mews

Bedford

Montague Place

Bloomsbury    St

Montague    Street

57

British Museum

Great Russell    Street

BLOOMSBURY
SQUARE GDNS

64

Bloomsbury    Square

56

Barter    St

Vernon Pl.

56

Drake St

Eagle    St

Red Lion    Street

Sandland    St

Gray's
Inn

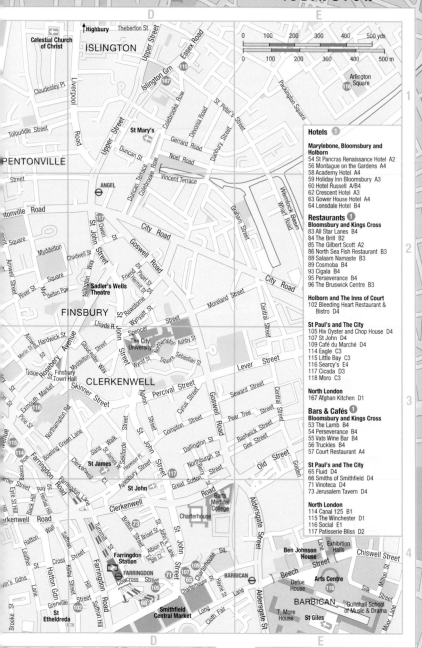

Celestial Church of Christ

ISLINGTON

PENTONVILLE

ANGEL

FINSBURY

CLERKENWELL

St Mary's

Sadler's Wells Theatre

Finsbury Town Hall

The City University

St James

St John

Farringdon Station

FARRINGDON Cowcross Street

Smithfield Central Market

St Etheldreda

Barts Medical College

Charterhouse

BARBICAN

Ben Johnson House

Exhibition Halls

Arts Centre

Defoe House

T. More House

St Giles

BARBICAN

Guildhall School of Music & Drama

Chiswell Street

Arlington Square

### Hotels ❶

**Marylebone, Bloomsbury and Holborn**
54 St Pancras Renaissance Hotel A2
56 Montague on the Gardens A4
58 Academy Hotel A4
59 Holiday Inn Bloomsbury A3
60 Hotel Russell A/B4
62 Crescent Hotel A3
63 Gower House Hotel A4
64 Lonsdale Hotel B4

### Restaurants ❶
**Bloomsbury and Kings Cross**
83 All Star Lanes B4
84 The Brill B2
85 The Gilbert Scott A2
86 North Sea Fish Restaurant B3
88 Salaam Namaste B3
89 Cosmoba B4
93 Cigala B4
95 Perseverance B4
96 The Bruswick Centre B3

**Holborn and The Inns of Court**
102 Bleeding Heart Restaurant & Bistro D4

**St Paul's and The City**
105 Hix Oyster and Chop House D4
107 St John D4
109 Café du Marché D4
114 Eagle C3
115 Little Bay C3
116 Searcy's E4
117 Cicada D3
118 Moro C3

**North London**
167 Afghan Kitchen D1

### Bars & Cafés ❶
**Bloomsbury and Kings Cross**
53 The Lamb B4
54 Perseverance B4
55 Vats Wine Bar B4
56 Truckles B4
57 Court Restaurant A4

**St Paul's and The City**
65 Fluid D4
66 Smiths of Smithfield D4
71 Vinoteca D4
73 Jerusalem Tavern D4

**North London**
114 Canal 125 B1
115 The Winchester D1
116 Social E1
117 Patisserie Bliss D2

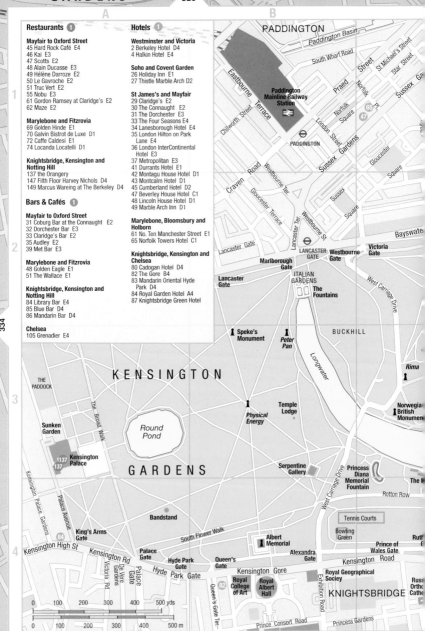

## Restaurants ●

**Mayfair to Oxford Street**
45 Hard Rock Café  E4
46 Kai  E3
47 Scotts  E2
48 Alain Ducasse  E3
49 Hélène Darroze  E2
50 Le Gavroche  E2
51 Truc Vert  E2
55 Nobu  E3
61 Gordon Ramsey at Claridge's  E2
62 Maze  E2

**Marylebone and Fitzrovia**
69 Golden Hinde  E1
70 Galvin Bistrot de Luxe  D1
72 Caffe Caldesi  E1
74 Locanda Locatelli  D1

**Knightsbridge, Kensington and Notting Hill**
137 the Orangery  E1
147 Fifth Floor Harvey Nichols  D4
149 Marcus Wareing at The Berkeley  D4

## Bars & Cafés ●

**Mayfair to Oxford Street**
31 Coburg Bar at the Connaught  E2
32 Dorchester Bar  E3
33 Claridge's Bar  E2
35 Audley  E2
39 Met Bar  E3

**Marylebone and Fitzrovia**
48 Golden Eagle  E1
51 The Wallace  E1

**Knightsbridge, Kensington and Notting Hill**
84 Library Bar  E4
85 Blue Bar  D4
86 Mandarin Bar  D4

**Chelsea**
105 Grenadier  E4

## Hotels ●

**Westminster and Victoria**
2 Berkeley Hotel  D4
4 Halkin Hotel  E4

**Soho and Covent Garden**
26 Holiday Inn  E1
27 Thistle Marble Arch  D2

**St James's and Mayfair**
29 Claridge's  E2
30 The Connaught  E2
31 The Dorchester  E3
33 The Four Seasons  E4
34 Lanesborough Hotel  E4
35 London Hilton on Park Lane  E4
36 London InterContinental Hotel  E3
37 Metropolitan  E3
41 Durrants Hotel  E1
42 Montagu House Hotel  D1
43 Montcalm Hotel  D1
45 Cumberland Hotel  D2
47 Beverley House Hotel  C1
48 Lincoln House Hotel  D1
49 Marble Arch Inn  D1

**Marylebone, Bloomsbury and Holborn**
61 No. Ten Manchester Street  E1
65 Norfolk Towers Hotel  C1

**Knightsbridge, Kensington and Chelsea**
80 Cadogan Hotel  D4
82 The Gore  B4
83 Mandarin Oriental Hyde Park  D4
84 Royal Garden Hotel  A4
87 Knightsbridge Green Hotel

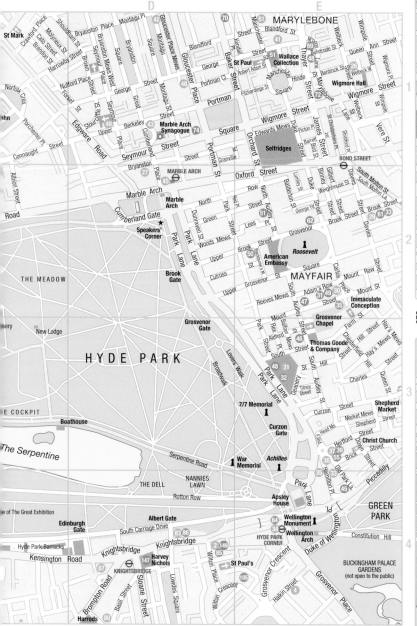

326

St Mark

MARYLEBONE

Crawford Place
Shouldham St
Bryanston Place
Montagu Pl.
Gloucester Place Mews
Manchester
Blandford St
Wimpole
70
61
Molyneux St
Cato Street
Bryanston
Montagu
Blandford
Kendal
41
M'ing La.
Welbeck
Queen Ann Street
Brendon St
Gloucester Place
Square
Square
Portman Cl.
Kendal
Thayer
Bulstrode St
St Bentinck St
Welbeck
Welbeck W.
Wigmore Street
Brown
Seymour Place
Bryanston
Montagu St
Baker Street
Wallace
Robert Adam St
Hinde
St Marylebone
Wimpole
Harrowby St
Street
George
Street
48
Portman
St Paul 51 Collection
Manchester
72
Wigmore Hall
26
Welbeck
Nutford Place
Norfolk Cres.
Great
Street
Seymour
Place
Fitzhardinge St
Square
Wigmore
Street
James Street
Vere St
Stourcliffe
Berkeley
43
74
Marble Arch
Synagogue
Street
Duke
Edwards Mews S.
St Christopher's Pl.
Gilbert
Picton Pl.
Stratford Pl.
Orchard St
Barret
Bird St
49
Upper
Cumberland
Selfridges
BOND STREET
Albion Street
Edgware
Seymour
Bryanston
Street
Granville
South Molton St
South Molton La.
Connaught
Road
Porchester Pl.
Street
27
Place
45
Oxford
Street
Duke
Binney
29
61
33
John
MARBLE ARCH
Davies
Brook Street
Row
North
Red
51
Weighhouse St
Street
Street
Brook
Marble Arch
Marble
Arch
North
Park
Street
Audley
George Yd
62
Street
Davies
Road
Cumberland Gate
Dunraven St
Street
Lees Pl.
Brook
★ Speakers'
Corner
Green
Roosevelt
Street
Woods Mews
Grosvenor
60
American
Carlos
Street
THE MEADOW
Park
Lane
Upper
Brook
Embassy
Square
Mount Row
Street
Brook
Gate
Culross
St.
MAYFAIR
Mount St
Upper
Grosvenor
St.
Adam's Row
31
49 50
Reeves Mews
47
Immaculate
35 Conception
New Lodge
Mount
Balfour
46
Grosvenor
Street
Chapel
Farm
St.
Grosvenor
Gate
Park
Aldford
St.
South
Thomas Goode
& Company
Lovers' Walk
St.
Hay's Mews
Hill
Street
Hay's Mews
Grosvenor
Chapel
HYDE PARK
Broadwalk
Street
Chesterfield
48 31
Audley
Hill
Queen St.
32
Street
Charles
Boathouse
E COCKPIT
7/7 Memorial
Park
South
St.
Shepherd
Market
Deanery
Tilney
Street
Curzon
Street
Shepherd
Street
Curzon
Gate
Market Mews
The Serpentine
Shepherd
Street
Hertford
Christ Church
37 39
Brick
St.
Achilles
Serpentine Road
Down St.
36
55
Street
35
Old Park La.
Piccadilly
THE DELL
NANNIES
LAWN
War
Memorial
45
Hamilton Pl.
GREEN
PARK
Rotton Row
Park
Lane
of The Great Exhibition
Apsley
House
Edinburgh
Gate
Albert Gate
South Carriage Drive
84
Wellington
Monument
Duke of Wellington
Constitution Hill
83 86
Hyde Park Barracks
Knightsbridge
34
Wellington
Arch
Kensington Road
Knightsbridge
HYDE PARK
CORNER
2 149
65
BUCKINGHAM PALACE
GARDENS
(not open to the public)
147 Harvey
Nichols
St Paul's
87
Brompton Road
KNIGHTSBRIDGE
Wilton Place
105
Grosvenor
Crescent
4
Basil St.
Sloane Street
Lowndes Square
Wilton Crescent
Halkin Street
Grosvenor
Place
Harrods
80

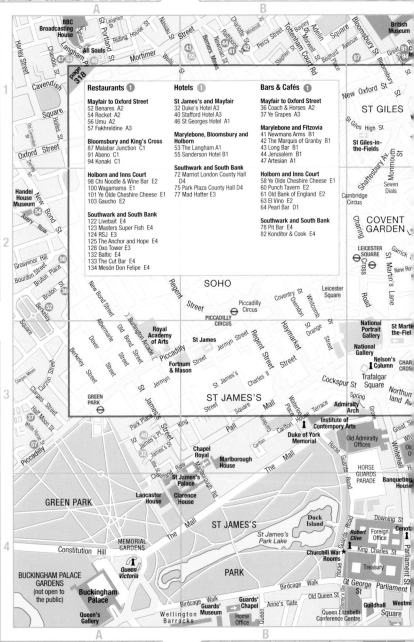

321

**Restaurants** ❶

**Mayfair to Oxford Street**
52 Benares A2
54 Rocket A2
56 Umu A2
57 Fakhreldine A3

**Bloomsbury and King's Cross**
87 Malabar Junction C1
91 Abeno C1
94 Konaki C1

**Holborn and Inns Court**
98 Chi Noodle & Wine Bar E2
100 Wagamama E1
101 Ye Olde Cheshire Cheese E1
103 Gaucho E2

**Southwark and South Bank**
122 Livebait E4
123 Masters Super Fish E4
124 RSJ E3
125 The Anchor and Hope E4
128 Oxo Tower E3
132 Baltic E4
133 The Cut Bar E4
134 Mesón Don Felipe E4

**Hotels** ❶

**St James's and Mayfair**
32 Duke's Hotel A3
40 Stafford Hotel A3
46 St Georges Hotel A1

**Marylebone, Bloomsbury and Holborn**
53 The Langham A1
55 Sanderson Hotel B1

**Southwark and South Bank**
72 Marriot London County Hall D4
75 Park Plaza County Hall D4
77 Mad Hatter E3

**Bars & Cafés** ❶

**Mayfair to Oxford Street**
36 Coach & Horses A2
37 Ye Grapes A3

**Marylebone and Fitzovia**
41 Newmans Arms B1
42 The Marquis of Granby B1
43 Long Bar B1
44 Jerusalem B1
47 Artesian A1

**Holborn and Inns Court**
58 Ye Olde Cheshire Cheese E1
60 Punch Tavern E2
61 Old Bank of England E2
63 El Vino E2
64 Pearl Bar D1

**Southwark and South Bank**
78 Pit Bar E4
82 Konditor & Cook E4

332

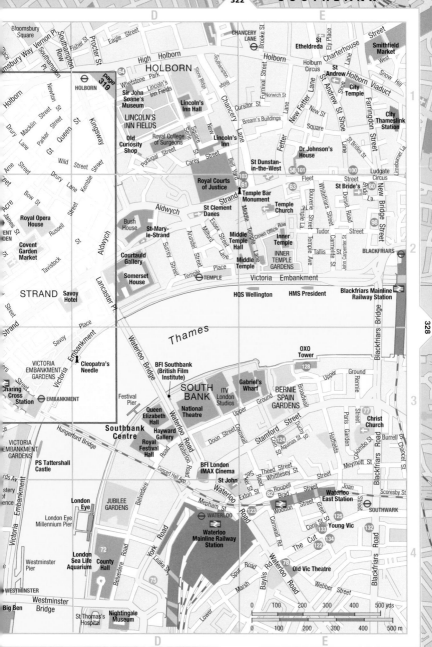

A

B

Smithfield
Central Market
110
West  Cloth Fair
Smithfield St
Thomas More
House
St Giles
BARBICAN
Aldersgate
MOORGATE
Moorfields
Moorgate
Old Street
Eldon Street
Finsbury
Hosier Lane  Smithfield
West  St
Snow  Hill
Cock Lane
Holborn Viaduct
Barts
Hospital
Little
Bartholomew
Monkwell
Sq
Fore
Street
London Wall
Moor La.
Circus
Blomfield Street
Liverpool
London Wall
Museum
of London
Britain
St Anne
& St
Agnes
Basinghall La.
City
Thameslink
Station
St Botolph-
without-
Aldersgate
Grand
Oat
Lane
Gresham
Street
Aldermanbury
Moorgate
Coleman Street
Coleman
Copthall Avenue
Winchester St
London Wall
Newgate
Street
St Martin's
Angel St
Foster
Lane
Wood
Street
Friars
Great
Swan
Central
Criminal Court
(Old Bailey)
St Martin's
Le
Gresham Street
Guildhall
King's Arms Yd
Throgmorton St
Tower 42
70
Stock
Exchange
62
ST PAUL'S
St Vedast
Cheapside
Trump St
St Mary-
le-Bow
King
Street
Prince's Street
Lothbury
Bank
of
England
Threadneedle
Bishop
City
Thameslink
Station
Ludgate
Hill
St Paul's
Cathedral
106
One New
Change
104
Bow La.
Poultry
BANK
Royal
Exchange
77
Cornhill
The Pinnacle
(u/c)
112
St Michael
74
Leadenhall
Market
New Bridge Street
St Andrew-
by-the-
Wardrobe
Paternoster
Square
St Paul's Churchyard
Carter Lane
Knightrider St
St Benet's
69
Watling St
Queen Victoria
108
St Stephen
Walbrook
Mansion
House
BANK
66
Lombard
Street
Gracechurch
Fenchurch
BLACKFRIARS
Queen
Victoria
Street
Distaff
Cannon
Street
MANSION
HOUSE
Cloak
Lane
Cannon St
113
CANNON
STREET
Cannon
St
Swithin's La
St Clements La.
MONUMENT
Puddle
Dock
Queen Victoria
Street
St James's
College
Street
Dowgate Hill
Cannon Street
Station
Upper Thames St
Arthur St
Eastcheap
Monument
Lower
Blackfriars Mainline
Railway Station
Trig La.
Upper
Thames
Street
Queen St Pl
Cousin La
Allhallows La
Swan La.
Fish St
Bot'olph La.
Mon. St
Thames St
Old
Billingsgate
Market
Millennium Bridge
Bankside
Pier
Shakespeare's
Globe Theatre
& Exhibition
Southwark
Bridge
Swan Lane
Pier
London Bridge
St Magnus
the Martyr
Thames
Bankside
Gallery
Bankside
Beer C'dns
Clink
Prison
Museum
Golden
Hinde
Southwark
Cathedral
London Bridge
Experience
London
Bridge
City Pier
131
Tate
Modern
SOUTHWARK
Park
Rose
Theatre
Exhibition
Park Street
The
Archer
80 126
Clink St.
130
LONDON
BRIDGE
Tooley St
Hay's
Galleria
Holland Street
Hopton Street
Sumner
Street
Great Guildford
Street
Southwark Bridge Road
Vinopolis
78
Borough
Market
121
120
London Bridge St
Railway App.
London
Dungeon
Burrell
St
Price's St
74
Southwark
Street
Lavington Street
Thrale St
Maiden La.
61
76
135
Southwark
Street
LONDON
BRIDGE
Old Operating
Theatre &
Herb Garret
London Bridge
Mainline
Station
75
Tooley
Street
Shard
Winston
Church
Britain at
War Museum
Great Suffolk St
Zoar
Street
Scoresby Street
America St
77
THE
BOROUGH
Guy's
Hospital
St Thomas Street
Weston Street
Union  Street
Most
Precious
Blood
Union Street
83
Copperfield  Street
Borough High Street
Newcomen Street
Surrey Row
Pocock Street
Marshalsea  Road
Redcross Way
Tennis Street
St George
the Martyr
St Hughs
Snowsfields
Snowsfields
Kipling Street
Lant  Street
Borough High St
BOROUGH
Gt Dover St
Long
Lane
Leathermarket
Elephant
and Castle
0   100   200   300   400   500 yds
0   100   200   300   400   500 m

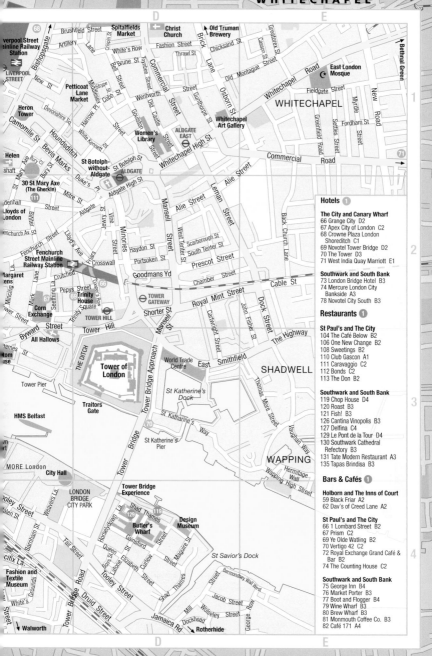

**Liverpool Street mainline Railway Station**

**LIVERPOOL STREET**

Heron Tower

Helen

30 St Mary Axe (The Gherkin)

shaft

Lloyds of London

Fenchurch Street Mainline Railway Station

Margaret ens

Corn Exchange

All Hallows

om se

Tower Pier

HMS Belfast

MORE London

City Hall

Walworth

Rotherhide

Spitalfields Market

Christ Church

Old Truman Brewery

East London Mosque

WHITECHAPEL

Petticoat Lane Market

Women's Library

St Botolph-without-Aldgate

ALDGATE

ALDGATE EAST

Whitechapel Art Gallery

Commercial Road

Trinity House Square

TOWER GATEWAY

TOWER HILL

Tower Hill

Tower of London

World Trade Centre

East Smithfield

SHADWELL

Traitors Gate

St Katherine's Dock

St Katherine's Way

St Katherine's Pier

WAPPING

Wapping High Street

Hermitage Wall

LONDON BRIDGE CITY PARK

Tower Bridge Experience

Butler's Wharf

Design Museum

Shad Thames

St Savior's Dock

Fashion and Textile Museum

Bermondsey Wall West

Tooley Street

Jamaica Rd

Dockhead

## Hotels ⓘ

**The City and Canary Wharf**
66 Grange City  D2
67 Apex City of London  C2
68 Crowne Plaza London
   Shoreditch  C1
69 Novotel Tower Bridge  D2
70 The Tower  D3
71 West India Quay Marriott  E1

**Southwark and South Bank**
73 London Bridge Hotel  B3
74 Mercure London City
   Bankside  A3
78 Novotel City South  B3

## Restaurants ⓘ

**St Paul's and The City**
104 The Café Below  B2
106 One New Change  B2
108 Sweetings  B2
110 Club Gascon  A1
111 Caravaggio  C2
112 Bonds  C2
113 The Don  B2

**Southwark and South Bank**
119 Chop House  D4
120 Roast  B3
121 Fish!  B3
126 Cantina Vinopolis  B3
127 Delfina  C4
129 Le Pont de la Tour  D4
130 Southwark Cathedral
    Refectory  B3
131 Tate Modern Restaurant  A3
135 Tapas Brindisa  B3

## Bars & Cafés ⓘ

**Holborn and The Inns of Court**
59 Black Friar  A2
62 Dav's of Creed Lane  A2

**St Paul's and The City**
66 1 Lombard Street  B2
67 Prism  C2
69 Ye Olde Watling  B2
70 Vertigo 42  C2
72 Royal Exchange Grand Café &
   Bar  B2
74 The Counting House  C2

**Southwark and South Bank**
75 George Inn  B4
76 Market Porter  B3
77 Boot and Flogger  B4
79 Wine Wharf  B3
80 Brew Wharf  B3
81 Monmouth Coffee Co.  B3
82 Café 171  A4

KENSINGTON

Royal College of Music

Imperial College

Princes Gdns

Elvaston Place

Imperial College Road

Science Museum

Queen's Gate Gardens

Cornwall Gardens

Cornwall Gardens

Queen's Gdns

Natural History Museum

Victoria & Alber Museum

Cromwell Road

St Stephen

Cromwell Road

Thurloe Place

Thurloe Square

Cromwell Road

GLOUCESTER ROAD

Thurloe Street

SOUTH KENSINGTON

St Jude's

Courtfield Road

Stanhope Gdns

SOUTH KENSINGTON

Harrington Road

Pelham Stree

Courtfield Gdns

EARL'S COURT

Harrington Gardens

Wetherby Gardens

Old Brompton Road

Cranley Pl

Onslow Square

Onslow Place

Onslow Gardens

Laverton Place

Sumner

EARL'S COURT

Bramham Gdns

Bolton Gardens

Old Brompton Road

Onslow Gdns

Fraser's Terrace

Neville St

St Paul

Fulham Road

Chel Farm Ma

Sydney

Old Brompton Rd

Drayton Gardens

Roland Gardens

Selwood Terrace

Redcliffe Square

The Little Boltons

The Boltons

St Yeghiche

Dovehouse Stre

Chelsea Square

Finborough Road

Coleherne Road

Redcliffe Gardens

Hardcourt Terrace

Tregunter Road

Drayton Gardens

Evelyn Gardens

Elm Park Gdns

Old Church Street

St Luke's

Carlyle Square

WEST BROMPTON

Cathcart Road

Hollywood Road

Gliston Road

Redcliffe Road

Fulham Road

Elm Park Gdns

Elm Park Road

Beaufort Street

King's Road

Manressa

Finborough Road

Ifield Road

Park Walk

Pultons Square

Chelsea Old Church

BROMPTON CEMETERY

Cemetery Chapel

Edith Grove

Hortensia Road

WORLD'S END

Milman's Square

Beaufort Road

Old Church Street

Danvers Street

Chelse

Cheyne Walk

Battersea Bridge

Stamford Bridge (Chelsea Football Club)

Fulham,

Gunter Grove

King's

**Hotels** 1

**Westminster and Victoria**
8 Tophams E2

**Knightsbridge, Kensington and Chelsea**
79 Blakes Hotel B2
80 Cadogan Hotel D1
81 Capital Hotel A1
85 Wyndham Grand A4
86 Aster House B2
89 Abcone Hotel A2
90 Barkston Gardens Hotel A2
93 My Place Hotel A2
94 easyHotel A1
95 Enterprise Hotel A2
97 Oliver Plaza Hotel A2

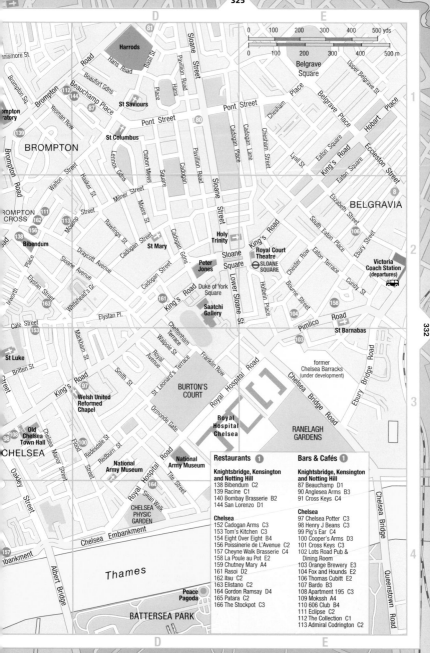

A · B

Grosvenor Place
Queen's Gallery
Wellington Barracks
France
ST JAMES'S PARK
Tothill Street
St Margar Chu
Buckingham Road
Stafford Pl.
The Place Street
Wilfred Street
Petty
Palmer St
St James's
Westminster Abbey
The Royal Mews
Royal Mews
Buckingham Palace
Castle Lane
Westminster Chapel
160
Caxton Street
Broadway
Dacre St
Victoria Street
Dean's
Yard
Lwr Grosvenor Pl.
Bressenden Place
War
Spenser St
6
Gate
New Scotland Yard
Great
Hobart Pl.
Grosvenor
Victoria Sq
Allington
Westminster City Hall
Old
Pye
Street
St Ann St
St Matthew
WESTMINSTER
Grosvenor Gdns
Beeston
Eaton La.
10
Buckingham
Victoria Street
Howick
Place
Artillery Row
St Mathew
St Mathew St
Peter Street
Great
Tufton
Romney
BELGRAVIA
Victoria Bus Station
VICTORIA
Victoria Palace Theatre
Ashley Pl.
Ambrosden
Westminster Roman Catholic Cathedral
Morpeth
Carlisle Place
Thirleby
Francis St
Emery Hill
Greycoat Pl.
Chadwick
Moreton
Peter Street
Monck
Marsham
Street
Street
Ebury
155
Eccleston St
Apollo Victoria Theatre
Victoria Mainline Railway Station
Francis
New Royal Horticultural Society Hall
Medway St
Road
Horsefe
Eccleston Bridge
Victoria Place Shopping Centre
King's Scholars Passage
Willow St
Stillington St
Greencoat
Rochester
Vincent
Page Street
Victoria Coach Station (arrivals)
Bridge Place
11
Vauxhall
Francis
Street
Row
WESTMINSTER SCHOOL PLAYING FIELD
Vincent Street
Marsham Street
Erasmus Street
Tate Britai
Victoria Coach Station (departures)
Buckingham
High Street
Eccleston
Gillingham St.
Wilton Road
Belgrave Road
Warwick Way
Bridge
Road
Square
Regency Street
John Islip
Atterbur
Eccleston Square
14
13
Warwick Way
Warwick
Square
St George's
St James the Less
Tachbrook Street
Belgrave Road
Vauxhall Bridge Road
Bessborough Gdns
Millbank
RIVERSI GARDEN
St George's Pl.
15
16
St George's Drive
12
9
17
18
St George's Sq
PIMLICO
PIMLICO
Clarendon Street
Alderney Street
Winchester Street
St Gabriel
Gloucester
St George's Drive
Lupus Street
Sutherland Street
Chichester Street
PIMLICO GARDENS
St George's Square
Grosvenor Road
Thames
Battersea Power Station (disused)
Nine Elms Road
New Covent Garden Flower Market (North)
future American Embassy Site
NINE ELMS
Nine Elms Road
Portland Road
Wandsworth
Battersea, Wandsworth

## Hotels 🅗

**Westminster and Victoria**
1 41 A1
3 Goring Hotel A1
5 The Rubens A1
6 Mint Hotel C2
7 Sanctuary House Hotel B1
9 Georgian House Hotel A2
10 Royal Westminster
   Thistle Hotel A1
11 Victoria Park Plaza A2
12 Airways Hotel A2
13 Blair Victoria Hotel A2
14 Dover Hotel A2
15 Grapevine Hotel A2
16 Hanover A2
17 Sidney Hotel B3
18 Victoria Inn B2

## Restaurants 🅡

**Westminster and Buckingham Palace**
1 Boisdale A1
2 Goring Dining Room A1
3 Smith Square Restaurant C1
4 Tate Britain Restaurant C2
7 The Cinnamon Club C1

**Chelsea**
155 Ken Lo's Memories of
    China A1
160 Quilon B1

## Bars & Cafés 🅑

**Westminster and Buckingham Palace**
3 Tapster B1
4 Balls Brothers A1
5 Cinnamon Club Bar C1
6 Zander B1
7 Millbank Lounge C2

Palace of
Westminster

Houses of
Parliament

St Thomas's
Hospital

LAMBETH
NORTH

Westminster Bridge Rd

St George's
Cathedral

Christ Church &
Upton Chapel

VICTORIA
TOWER
GARDENS

n's
ert Hall

ARCHBISHOP'S
PARK

Palace Road

Baylis Rd

Waterloo Rd

Lambeth
Bridge Road

Westminster Bridge

Kennington Road

Carlisle Lane

Hercules Road

St George's Road

GERALDINE MARY
HARMSWORTH
PARK

1

Lambeth Road

Lambeth
Palace

St Mary's

Imperial
War
Museum

Museum of
Garden History

Lambeth Road

Lambeth Bridge

Old Paradise St

Lambeth High Street

Lambeth Walk

Walnut Tree Walk

Fitzalan Street

Brook Drive

Millbank

Newport Street

LAMBETH
WALK

Wincott Street

Kennington Road

Gilbert Road

LAMBETH

2

Millbank
Millennium
Pier

Embankment

76

Black Prince Road

Tyers Street

Vauxhall Street

Chester Square

Lane

Kennington Lane

Albert

Vauxhall Walk

Vauxhall
Methodist
Church

Sancroft Street

Newburn Street

Cleaver
Square

KENNINGTON

Kennington Park Road

De Laune Street

3

Glass House Walk

MI6
Headquarters

SPRING
GARDENS

VAUXHALL

Tyers Street

Kennington Lane

Kennington Road

Kennington Park Pl.

Vauxhall Cross

VAUXHALL

Vauxhall
Station

Kennington Lane

Durham St

Harleyford Road

Vauxhall Street

KENNINGTON

Kennington Oval

Clayton Street

Bowling Green St

St Agnes Place

Kennington Park Road

KENNINGTON
PARK

4

arry Street

andsworth Rd

Lawn Lane

The Oval
Cricket
Ground

South Lambert Rd

es Street

VAUXHALL
PARK

Kennington Oval

Fentiman Road

OVAL

KENNINGTON
COMMON

Clapham

0    100    200    300    400    500 yds

0    100    200    300    400    500 m

0 100 200 300 400 500 yds
0 100 200 300 400 500 m

Cambridge Gardens
Westway (elevated)
LADBROKE GROVE
Lancaster Road
Tavistock Road
St All Saints Road
St Luke's Road
Basing St
Leamington Rd Villas
Aldridge Rd Villas
St Luke's Mews
Westbourne Park Villas
Westbourne Park Road
95
Westbourne Park Road
Porchester Road
ROYAL OAK

St Marks Road
Cornwall Crescent
Ladbroke Grove
Blenheim Crescent
Westbourne Park Road
Talbot Road
Elgin Cres.
Portobello Road Market
Portobello Road
Park
Colville
Powis Terrace
Powis Square
Colville Terrace
Lonsdale Rd
Colville Road
Talbot Road
Powis Square
Ledbury Rd
Moorhouse Rd
Artesian Mews
Sutherland Pl
Chepstow Road
Shrewsbury Road
Northumberland Road
Talbot Road
Bridstow Place
Hereford Road
Newton Rd
Queensway
Westbourne Grove
Whiteley's Shopping Centre
150
Westbourne Grove
89
Kensington Gardens Square
92
96
Redan Place
Queensway

Walmer Road
Clarendon Road
Elgin Crescent
Lansdowne Road
Arundel Gdns
Ladbroke Gdns
Stanley Crescent
Westbourne Grove
Denbeh Rd
Chepstow Villas
NOTTING HILL
Pembridge Villas
Pembridge Pl
Chepstow Pl
Dawson Place
Hereford Road
Leinster Square
Princes Square
91
Greek Orthodox
Moscow Road
Place Court
Ossington Street
St Petersburgh Place
Palace Court
BAYSWATER
QUEENSWAY

Portland Road
Clarendon Road
Lansdowne Rise
St John's Gdns
Lansdowne Walk
Lansdowne Crescent
Ladbroke Grove
Kensington Park Gardens
Ladbroke
Ladbroke Square
Kensington Park Road
Pembridge Cres.
Portobello Road
Pembridge Square
Pembridge Gdns
Pembridge Rd
88
NOTTING HILL GATE
Bayswater Road
Diana Memorial Playground
Elfin Oak

Ladbroke Road
Ladbroke Walk
Ladbroke Ter.
Ladbroke Road
Notting Hill Gate
141
148
136
HOLLAND PARK
Holland Park Avenue
Aubrey Road
Campden Hill Square
Hillsleigh Road
Campden Hill Road
Kensington Place
Peel Street
Campden Street
94
Bedford Gardens
93
Kensington Church Street
146
Brunswick Gardens
Palace Gardens Ter.
Kensington Palace Gardens
KENSINGTON GARDENS
Sunken Garden
Kensington Palace

Holland Park Mews
Holland Park
Aubrey Walk
Tennis Courts
Sheffield Terrace
Gloucester Walk
Campden Gr.
Campden Hill
St Luke's La.
Royal Garden Hotel

Abbotsbury Road
HOLLAND PARK
Holland House
Youth Hostel
Open Air Theatre
Holland Walk
Hornton
Pitt St
Duchess of Bedford's Walk
Holland Street
Campden Hill Road
KENSINGTON
St Mary Abbots
91
Kensington Road
142

## Hotels 1

**Knightsbridge, Kensington and Chelsea**
88 Abbey Court B2
91 Bayswater Inn C2
92 Garden Court Hotel C2
96 London House Hotel C1

## Restaurants 1

**Knightsbridge, Kensington and Chelsea**
136 Geales B3
141 Malabar B2
142 Zaika C4
143 Osteria Basilico A1
145 Babylon C4
146 Clarke's B3
148 Kensington Place B2
150 Ottolenghi B1
151 The Terrace B3

## Bars & Cafés 1

**Knightsbridge, Kensington and Chelsea**
88 Montgomery Place A1
89 The Elbow Room B1
92 The Abingdon B4
93 Churchill Arms B3
94 Windsor Castle B3
95 The Cow B1
96 The Fat Badger A1

Addison Road
Oakwood Court
Ilchester Place
Tennis Courts
Cricket Pitch
former Commonwealth Institute (proposed Design Museum)
Upr Phillimore Gdns
Phillimore Pl
Essex Villas
Stafford Ter.
Phillimore Gdns
Phillimore Walk
Argyll Road
Campden Hill Road
Holland Street
Kensington Town Hall
145
HIGH STREET KENSINGTON
Wright's Lane
Young St
Kensington Square
Kensington Road

KENSINGTON (OLYMPIA)
Kensington (Olympia) Mainline Railway Station
Olympia Exhibition Halls
Russell Road
Holland Road
Addison Road
Melbury Road
Holland Park Road
Leighton House
St Edwardes Square
Kensington High Street
Earls Court Road
92
Allen Street
Abingdon Road
Scarsdale Villas
Abingdon Villas
Iverna Gdns
Marloes Road
Stanford Road
Hammersmith

Restaurants ①

outh London
8 Davy's Wine Vault C3
9 North Pole Bar & Restaurant C3
0 The Spread Eagle D2

ars & Cafés ①

outh London
8 Trafalgar Tavern E1
9 Cutty Sark E1
20 Greenwich Union D3

Thames

Greenwich Foot Tunnel

119

118

Crane St

Eastney

Park Row

Prime Meridian Line

Old Woolwich Road

Greenwich Pier

Queen Anne Court

Trafalgar     Road

Street

Trafalgar Gr.

Greenwich Pk St.

Greenwich Foot Tunnel
Southern Entrance

Trinity College
of Music

Queen Mary
College

Cutty
Sark

University of Greenwich

Thames Street

Thames Street
CUTTY
SARK

College
Approach

King William Walk

Old
Royal Naval
College

Romney    Road

Park Row

Feathers Pl.

Park Vista

Covered
Market

Dreadnought
Library

Queen's
House

Park Row
Gate

Boating
Lake

Creek    Road

Bardsley Lane

Walland St

Gipsy Moth

Nelson Rd

St Mary's
Gate

National
Maritime Museum

ONE TREE
HILL

GREENWICH

Church   Street

Cooper
Building

St Alfege's
Church

Roan    Street

Stockwell St

Nevada St

170

HERB
GARDEN

GREENWICH
PARK

Randall Place

Straightsmouth

Burney   Street

Circus Gate

The Avenue

Prime Meridian Line

THE
GARDENS

Croom's Hill

Greenwich Mainline
Railway Station

GREENWICH

Greenwich High Rd

Royal Hill

Gloucester Circus

George   Street

King George
Street Gate

Old Royal
Observatory

Blackheath Ave.

69

Circus Street

King

120

Our Ladye
Star of the Sea

Croom's Hill

Planetarium

Royal
Observatory

Brand Street

Prior Street

Greenwich South Street

Blissett Street

Winforton Street

Point Hill

Hyde Vale

Diamond Terrace

Croom's Hill
Gate

Charlton Way

Hill

Maidenstone

BLACKHEATH
THE POINT

West Grove

BLACKHEATH

Cade Road

Great Wolfe Road

Rangers House

0      100       200 yds
0      100       200 m

lackheath

Hill

Shooters  Hill  Road

D

E

## Sights of Interest

30 St Mary Axe (The Gerkin) **329** C2
Achilles Statue **325** D3
Adelphi Theatre **319** E3
Admiralty Arch **319** C4
The Albany **318** B4
Albert Gate **325** D4
Albert Memorial **324** B4
Alexandra Gate **324** B4
All Hallows **329** C3
American Church of London **321** E4
American Embassy **325** E2
The Archer **328** B3
Apsley House **325** E4
Arts Centre **323** E4
The Avenue **335** E3
BBC Broadcasting House **321** D4
Bank of England **328** B2
Banqueting House **326** C4
Bar Italia **318** C2
Battersea Power Station (disused) **332** A4
BFI London IMAX Cinema **327** D3
BFI Southbank **327** D3
Big Ben **327** C4
Boathouse **325** C3
The Boltons **330** A3-B3
Borough Market **328** B3
Bream's Buildings **327** E1
British Library **322** A2
British Museum **322** A4
The Broad Walk **324** A3
Brompton Oratory **331** C1
Brunswick Shopping Centre **322** B3
BT Tower **321** E4
Buckingham Gate **332** B1
Buckingham Palace **326** A4
Burlington Arcade **318** A4
Bush House **327** D2
Butler's Wharf **329** D4
Cartoon Museum **326** C1
Celestial Church of Christ **323** C1
Cenotaph **326** C4
Central Criminal Court (Old Bailey) **328** A1
Chapel Royal **326** B3
Charles Dickens Museum **322** B3
Chelsea Farmer's Market **330** C3
Chelsea Old Church **330** C4
Christ Church **325** D3
Christ Church & Upton Chapel **333** E1
Churchill War Rooms **326** B4
City Temple **327** E1
Clarence Gate **320** C3
Clarence House **326** A4
Cleopatra's Needle **319** E4
Clink Prison Museum **328** B3
Clock Tower **324** A3
Commonwealth Institute

(former) **334** B4
Corn Exchange **329** C2
Courtauld Gallery **327** D2
Covent Garden Flower Market **332** C4
Covent Garden Market **319** E3
Criterion Theatre **318** B3
Cumberland Gate **321** D2
Curzon Gate **325** D3
Custom House **329** C3
The Cut **327** E4
Cutty Sark **335** D1
Danish Church **321** D1
Design Museum **329** D4
Diana Memorial Playground **324** A2
Donmar Warehause **319** D2
Dr Johnson's House **327** E1
Duke of York Memorial **326** B3
East London Mosque **329** E1
Edinburgh Gate **325** D4
Eros statue **318** B3
Exhibition Halls **323** E4
Faraday Museum **318** A3
Fashion and Textile Museum **329** C4
Fortnum & Mason **318** B4
Foundling Museum **322** B3
The Fountains **324** B2
French House **318** C2
GLA City Hall **329** C3
Gray's Inn **322** C4
Greek Orthodox **334** C3
Greenwich Foot Tunnel **335** D1
Greenwich Pier **335** D1
Grosvenor Gate **325** D3
Guards' Chapel **326** B4
Guards' Museum **326** B4
Guildhall **326** C4
HMS President **327** E2
HQS Wellington **327** E2
Hamleys **318** A2
Handel House Museum **326** A2
Hanover Bridges **320** B2
Harrods **325** D4
Harvey Nichols **325** D4
Hay's Galleria **328** C3
Hayward Gallery **327** D3
The Highway **329** E3
Heron Tower **329** C1
HMS Belfast **329** C3
Holland House **334** B4
Holy Cross **322** B3
Holy Trinity **321** D3
Houses of Parliament **333** C1
Immaculate Conception **325** E2
Imperial War Museum **333** E1
Inner Circle **321** C2
Inner Temple **327** E2
Institute of Contemporary Arts (ICA) **326** B3
Kennington Oval **333** D4
Kensington Palace **324** A3
Kensington Town Hall **334** B4
Kings Place Arts Centre **322** B1
Lambeth Palace **333** D1
Lancaster Gate **324** B2

Lancaster House **326** A4
Leadenhall Market **328** C2
Leighton House **334** A4
Liberty **318** A2
The Lido **324** C3
Lincoln's Inn **327** D1
Lincoln's Inn Hall **327** D1
The Little Boltons **330** A3
Lloyds of London **329** C2
London Bridge City Pier **328** C3
London Bridge Experience **328** B3
London Canal Museum **322** B1
London Central Mosque **320** B2
London Dungeon **328** C3
London Eye **327** D4
London Sea Life Aquarium **327** D4
London Transport Museum **319** E2-E3
London Zoo **321** C1
Lords Cricket Ground **320** A2
Lyceum Theatre **319** E3
Madame Tussauds **321** C3
Marble Arch **325** D2
Marble Arch Synagogue **325** D1
Marlborough Gate **324** B2
Marlborough House **326** B3
MI6 Headquarters **333** C3
Middle Temple **327** E2
Middle Temple Hall **327** E2
Millennium Bridge **328** A2
Millennium Pier **333** C2
Monument **328** C2
Museum of Garden History **333** D2
Museum of London **328** A1
National Army Museum **331** D3
National Gallery **319** C4
National Maritime Museum **335** D2-C2
National Portrait Gallery **319** D4
National Theatre **327** D3
Natural History Museum **330** B1
Nelson's Column **319** D4
New Scotland Yard **332** B1
Nightingale Museum **327** D4
Norwegian/British Monument **324** C3
Old Billingsgate Market **328** C3
Old Chelsea Town Hall **331** C3
Old Curiosity Shop **327** D1
Old Royal Observatory **335** E3
Old Vic Theatre **327** E4
Olympia Exhibition Halls **334** A4
One New Change **328** B2
Open Air Theatre **321** C2
Orme Square Gate **324** A2
Oval Cricket Ground **333** D4
PS Tattershall Castle **327** C3
Palace Gate **324** A4
Palace Theatre **319** C2
Palladium Theatre **318** A2
Percival David Foundation of Chinese Art **322** A3
Peter Jones **331** D2
Peter Pan statue **324** B3

Petrie Museum of Egyptian Archaeology **322** A3-A4
Petticoat Lane Market **329** D1
Petty France **332** B1
The Pinnacle **328** C2
Phoenix Theatre **319** C2
Physical Energy **324** B3
Planetarium **335** E3
Playhouse Theatre **319** E4
Portobello Road Market **334** A1-B2
Prince Charles Repitory Theatre **319** C3
Prince Edward Theatre **319** C2
Prince of Wales Gate **324** C4
Princess Diana Memorial Fountain **324** C3
Queen Anne's Gate **326** B4
Queen Elizabeth Conferenc Centre **326** C4
Queen Elizabeth Hall **327** D3
Queen Victoria Memorial **326** A4
Queen's Gallery **332** A1
Queen's House **334** E2
Rangers House **335** E4
Rima Statue **324** C3
Ripley's Believe it or not **318** B3
Robert Clive **326** C4
Ronnie Scott's Jazz Club **318** C2
Roosevelt Memorial **325** D2
Rose Theatre Exhibition **328** A3
Royal Academy of Arts **318** A4
Royal Academy of Music **321** C3
Royal Albert Hall **324** B4
Royal College of Art **324** B4
Royal Court Theatre **331** E2
Royal Courts of Justice **327** D1
Royal Exchange **328** C2
Royal Festival Hall **327** D3
Royal Garden Hotel **334** C3
Royal Geographical Sociey **324** B4
Royal Hospital Chelsea **331** D3-E3
The Royal Mews **332** A1
Royal Observatory **335** E3
Royal Opera House **319** E2
Russian Orthodox Cathedral **324** C4
Rutland Gate **325** C4
Saatchi Gallery **331** D2
Sadler's Wells Theatre **323** D2
Savoy Hotel **319** E3
Science Museum **330** B1
Selfridges **325** E1
Serpentine Gallery **324** B3
Shakespeare's Globe Theatre & Exhibition **328** A3
Shard **328** C4
Shaw Theatre **322** A2
Shepherd Market **325** D3
Sherlock Holmes Museum **320** C3
Sir John Soane's Museum **327** D1
Smithfield Central Market **323** D4
Somerset House **327** D2

South Africa House **319** D4
Southbank Centre **327** D3
Southwark Cathedral **328** B3
Speakers' Corner **325** D2
Speke's Monument **324** B3
St Alfege's Church **335** D2
St Andrew **327** E1
St Andrew-by-the-Wardrobe **328** A2
St Anne & St Agnes **328** A1
St Anne's **318** C2
St Barnabas **331** E2
St Barnabas-in-Soho **318** C1
St Benet's **328** A2
St Botolph Street **329** D1
St Botolph-without-Aldergate **328** A1
St Bride's **327** E2
St Charles **321** E4
St Clement Danes **327** D2
St Dunstan-in-the-West **327** E1
St Etheldreda **323** C4
St Gabriel **332** A3
St George the Martyr **322** B4
St George's Cathedral **333** E1
St Giles **323** E4
St Giles-in-the-Fields **319** D1
St Helen **329** C1
St James **318** B4
St James the Less **332** B2
St James's **328** B2
St James's Palace **326** B4
St John **323** D4
St John's Concert Hall **332** C1
St John's Wood Church **320** B2
St Luke **331** C3
St Magnus the Martyr **328** C2
St Mararet's Church **332** C1
St Margaret Pattens **329** C2
St Mark **325** C1
St Martin's **328** A1
St Martin-in-the-Fields **319** D4
St Mary **331** D2
St Mary Abbots **334** C3
St Mary at Hill **328** C2
St Mary's **323** D1
St Mary-le-Bow **328** B2
St Marylebone **321** C3
St Mathew **332** C1
St Michael **328** C2
St Patrick **318** C1
St Paul **320** B3
St Paul's **319** D3
St Paul's Cathedral **328** A2
St Vedast **328** B1
Stamford Bridge Football Ground (Chelsea F.C.) **330** A4
St-Mary-le-Strand **327** D2
Stock Exchange **328** A1
Swan Lane Pier **328** B3
Tate Britain **332** C2
Tate Modern **328** A3
Temple Bar Monument **327** E2
Temple Church **327** E2
Theatre Royal Drury Lane **319** E2
Thomas Goode & Company

**325** E3
Tower 42 **328** C1
Tower Bridge **329** D3
Tower Bridge Experience **329** D4
Tower of London **329** D3
Tower Pier **329** C3
Trafalgar Studios **319** D4
Traitors Gate **329** D3
Trinity House **329** D2
Trocadero Centre **318** C3
University of Greenwich **335** D1
University of London **322** A4
Vauxhall Methodist Church **333** D3
Victoria & Albert Museum **330** C1
Victoria Bus Station **332** A1
Victoria Coach Station **331** E2
Victoria Place Shopping Centre **332** A2
Vinipolis **328** B3
Wallace Collection **325** E1
Welcome Collection **322** A3
Wellington Arch **325** E4
Wellington Monument **325** E4
Welsh United Reformed Chapel **331** D3
Westbourne Gate **324** B2
Westminster Abbey **332** C1
Westminster Chapel **332** B1
Westminster Hall **326** C4
Westminster Pier **327** C4
Westminster Roman Catholic Cathedral **332** B1
Whitechapel Art Gallery **329** D1
Whiteley's Shopping Centre **334** C1
Wigmore Hall **325** E1
Winfield House **320** B2
Winston Churchill's Britain at War Museum **328** C4
Women's Library **329** D1
Young Vic **327** E4

## Rail and Tube Stations
Aldgate **329** D1
Aldgate East **329** D1
Angel **323** D2
Baker Street **320** C4
Bank **328** B2
Barbican **323** E4
Blackfriars **327** E2
Blackfriars Mainline Railway Station **327** E2
Bond Street **325** E1
Borough **328** B4
Cannon Street **328** B2
Cannon Street Mainline Railway Station **328** B2
Chancery Lane **327** E1
Charing Cross **319** D4
Charing Cross Mainline Railway Station **319** D4
City Thameslink Mainline Railway Station **327** E1
Covent Garden **319** D3

Cutty Sark **335** D2
Earl's Court **330** A2
Edgware Road **320** A4
Embankment **319** E4
Euston **322** A3
Euston Square **321** E3
Euston Mainline Railway Station **321** E2
Farringdon **323** D4
Farringdon Station **323** D4
Fenchurch Street Mainline Railway Station **329** C2
Gloucester Road **330** B2
Goodge Street **321** E4
Great Portland Street **321** D3
Green Park **318** A4
Greenwich DLR **335** C3
Greenwich Mainline Railway Station **335** C3
High Street Kensington **334** B4
Holland Park **334** A3
Hyde Park Corner **325** E1
Kennington **333** E3
Kensington (Olympia) **334** A4
King's Cross & St Pancras **322** B2
King's Cross Mainline Railway Station **322** B2
King's Cross Thameslink Mainline Railway Station **322** B2
Knightsbridge **325** D4
Ladbroke Grove **334** A1
Lambeth North **333** E1
Lancaster Gate **324** B2
Leicester Square **319** D3
Liverpool Street **329** C1
Liverpool Street Mainline Railway Station **329** C1
London Bridge **328** B3
London Bridge Mainline Railway Station **328** C3
Mansion House **328** B2
Marble Arch **325** D2
Marylebone **320** B4
Monument **328** C2
Moorgate **328** B1
Mornington Crescent **321** E1
Notting Hill Gate **334** B2
Oval **333** E4
Oxford Circus **318** A1
Paddington **324** B1
Paddington Mainline Railway Station **324** B1
Piccadilly Circus **318** B3
Pimlico **332** B3
Queensway **324** A2
Regent's Park **321** D3
Royal Park **334** C1
Russell Square **322** B4
Sloane Square **331** E2
South Kensington **330** C2
Southwark **327** D4
St James' Park **332** B1
St John's Wood **320** A1
St Pancras International Railway Station **322** A2
St Paul's **328** A1

Temple **327** D2
Tottenham Court Road **319** D1
Tower Gateway **329** D2
Tower Hill **329** B2
Vauxhall **333** C3
Vauxhall Mainline Railway Station **333** C3
Victoria **332** A1
Victoria Mainline Railway Station **332** A1
Warren Street **321** E3
Waterloo **327** D4
Waterloo East Mainline Railway Station **327** E4
Waterloo Mainline Railway Station **327** D4
Westminster **327** C4

## Parks
Abbey Garden **333** C1
Archbishop's Park **333** D1
Argyle Square Gardens **322** B2
Battersea Park **331** D4
Bernie Spain Gardens **327** E3
Blackheath The Point **334** D4
Bloomsbury Square Gardens **322** B4
Brompton Cemetery **330** A4
Burton's Court **331** D3
Chelsea Physic Garden **331** D4
Coram's Fields **322** B3
Crescent Gardens **321** D4
Eaton Square Gardens **322** A3
Geraldine Mary Harmsworth Park **333** E1
Grays Inn Gardens **322** C4
Green Park **326** A3
Greenwich Park **334** D2-E4
Holford Gardens **322** C2
Holford Gardens **323** C2
Holland Park **334** A3
Hyde Park **324-5** B2-E4
Inner Temple Gardens **327** E2
Jubilee Gardens **327** D4
Kennington Park **333** E4
Kensington Gardens **334** C3 **324** A2-B4
Lambeth Walk **333** E1
Lincoln's Inn Fields **327** D1
London Bridge City Park **329** D4
Park Square Gardens **321** D3
Pimlico Gardens **332** B3
Primrose Hill **320** C1
Queen Mary's Gardens **321** C3
Ranelagh Gardens **331** E4
Regent's Park, The **320-1** B1-D3
Riverside Gardens **332** C3
Russell Square Gardens **322** A4
Spring Gardens **333** D3
St Andrew's Gardens **322** C3
St George's Gardens **322** B3
St James's Gardens **321** E2
St James's Park **326** B4
Vauxhall Park **333** D4
Victoria Embankment Gardens **319** E4 **327** C3
Victoria Tower Gardens **333** C1

Westminster School
Playing Field **332** B2

## Streets

Abbotsbury Road
**334** A3-A4
Abchurch Lane **328** B2
Abingdon Road **334** B4
Abingdon Street **333** C1
Abingdon Villas **334** B4
Acacia Road **320** A1
Acton Street **322** B2
Adam Street **319** E3-E4
Adam's Row **325** E2
Addison Road **334** A3-A4
Adelin Place **326** B1
Agar Street **319** D3
Agdon Street **323** D3
Air Street **318** B3
Albany Street **321** D1-D3
Albermarle Street **318** A3
Albert Bridge **331** C4
Albert Embankment
**333** D2
Albert Street **321** D1
Albion Place **323** D4
Aldermanbury **328** B1
Alderney Street **332** A3
Aldersgate Street **328** A1
Aldersgate Street **323** E4
Aldridge Road Villas
**334** B1
Aldwych **319** E2-E3
Alexandra Gate **324** B4
Alfred Place **322** A4
Alie Street **329** D2-E1
All Saints Road **334** A1
Allen Street **334** B4
AllhallowsLane **328** B2
Allington Street **332** A1
Allitsen Road **320** A1-B1
Ambrosden Avenue
**332** B1
America Street **328** A4
Ampton Street **322** B3
Amwell Street **323** C2-C3
Angel Street **328** A1
Apsley House **325** E4
Aquinas Street **327** E3
Archer Street **318** B3
Argyle Square **322** B2
Argyle Street **322** B2
Argyll Road **334** B4
Argyll Street **318** A2
Arlington Road **321** E1
Arlington Square **323** E1
Arlington Street **318** A4
Arlington Way **323** D2
Arne Street **319** D2
Artesian Mews **334** B1
Arthur Street **328** B2
Artillery Lane **329** C1-D1
Artillery Row **332** B1
Arundel Gardens **334** A2
Arundel Street **327** D2
Ashby Street **323** D3
Ashley Place **332** A1

Atterbury Street
**332** C2-C3
Aubrey Road **334** A3-B3
Aubrey Walk **334** B3
Austin Friars **328** C1
Avenue Road **320** B1
Avery Row **326** A2
Aybrook Street **321** C3
Aylesbury Street
**323** D3-D4
Back Church Lane **329** E2
Back Hill **323** C4
Bainbridge Street
**319** C1-D1
Baker Street **320** C3-C4 1
Bakers Row **323** C3
Balcombe Street **320** B3
Balderton Street **325** E2
Baldwin's Gardens
**323** C4
Balfour Mews **325** D3
Bankside **328** A3
Banner Street **323** E3
Bardsley Lane **335** C2-D2
Bark Place **334** C3
Barkston Gardens **330** A2
Barnham Street **329** C4
Barnsbury Road **323** C1
Barrett Street **325** E1
Barter Street **327** C1
Bartholomew Close
**328** A1
Basil Street **325** D4
Basing Street **334** A1
Bastwick Street
**323** D3-E3
Bateman Street **318** C2
Bath Street **323** E3
Battersea Bridge **330** C4
Battle Lane **328** C3
Bayham Street **321** E1
Bayley Street **322** A4 **326**
B1 **326** B1
Baylis Road **333** E1
Bayswater Road
**324** A2-C2
**334** B2-C2
Beak Street **318** B2-B3
Bear Gdns **328** A3
Bear Lane **328** A3
Beauchamp Place **331** D1
Beaufort Road **330** B4-C4
Beaufort Street
**330** B3-B4
Beaumont Place **321** E3
Bedford Avenue **326** B1
Bedford Gardens **334** B3
Bedford Place **322** B4
Bedford Row **322** B4-C4
Bedford Square **322** A4
Bedford Street **319** D3
Bedford Way **322** A3-A4
Bedfordbury **319** D3
Beech Street **323** E4
Beeston Place **332** A1
Belgrave Road

**332** A2-B
Belgrave Square **331** E1
Belgrove Street **322** B2
Bell Street **320** B4 **329** D1
Bell Yard **327** D1-D2
Belvedere Road
**327** D3-D4
Ben Johnson House
**323** E4
Benjamin Franklin House
**319** D4
Bentinck Street **325** E1
Berkeley Square **326** A2
Berkeley Street **318** A4
Bermondsey Street
**329** C4
Bermondsey Wall West
**329** D4-E4
Bernard Street **322** B3-B4
Berners Place **318** B1
Berners Street **318** B1
Berry Street **323** D3-D4
Berwick Street **318** B2
Bessborough Gardens
**332** B3-C3
Betterton Street
**319** D2-E1
Bevis Marks **329** C1
Bickenhall Street **320** C3
Bidborough Street **322** A2
Billiter Street **329** C2
Bingham Place **321** C3
Binney Street **325** E2
Birchin Lane **328** C2
Bird Street **325** E1
Birdcage Walk **326** B4
Birkenhead Street **322** B2
Bishop's Bridge Road
**324** A1
Bishopsgate **329** C1-C2
Black Lion Gate **324** A2
Black Prince Road
**333** D2-D3
Blackburne's Mews
**325** E2
Blackfriars Bridge **327** E2
Blackfriars Lane **328** A2
Blackfriars Road **327** E3
Blackheath Ave **335** E3
Blackheath Hill
**335** C4-D4
Blandford Street
**325** D1-E1
Blenheim Crescent
**334** A1-A2
Blissett Street **335** C4
Blomfield Street **328** C1
Bloomsbury Square
**322** B4
Bloomsbury Street
**319** D1 **322** A4
Bloomsbury Way **319** D1
**327** C1
Bolsover Street **321** D4
Bolton Gardens **330** A3
Bolton Street **326** A3
Borough High Street

Boss Street **329** D4
Boston Place **320** B3
Boswell Street **322** B4
Botolph Lane **328** C2
Bourdon Street **326** A2
Bourne Street **331** E2
Bouverie Street **327** E2
Bow Lane **328** B2
Bow Street **319** E2
Bowling Green Lane
**323** C3-D3
Bowling Green Street
**333** D4
Boyle Street **318** A3
Brad Street **327** E4
Bramham Gardens **330** A2
Brand Street **335** D3
Bread Street **328** B2
Brendon Street **325** C1
Bressenden Place **332** A1
Brewer Street **318** B3
Brick Lane **329** D1
Brick Street **325** D3
Bride Lane **327** E2
Bridge Place **332** A2
Bridge Street **326** C4
Bridle Lane **318** B2-B3
Bridstow Place **334** B1
Briset Street **323** D4
Britannia Street **322** B2
Britten Street **331** C3
Britton Street **323** D4
Broadley Street
**320** A4-B4
Broadwall **327** E3
Broadway **332** B1
Broadwick Street **318** B2
Brompton Road **325** D4
**331** C1-C2
Brook Drive **333** E2
Brook Gate **325** D2
Brook Street **325** E2
Brooke Street **323** C4
**327** E1
Brown Street **325** D1
Brownlow Mews
**322** C3-C4
Brune Street **329** D1
Brunswick Gardens
**334** B3
Brunswick Square **322** B3
Brunswick Street **322** B3
Brushfield Street
**329** C1-D1
Bruton Place **326** A2
Bruton Street **326** A2
Bryanston Mews West
**325** D1
Bryanston Place **325** D1
Bryanston Square **325** D1
Bryanston Street **325** D1
Buckingham Palace Road
**332** A1
Bulstrode Street **325** E1
Burlington Gardens
**318** A3

Burlington Street **318** A3
Burney Street **335** D3
Burrell Street **327** E3
**328** A3
Burslem Street **329** E2
Burton Street **322** A3
Bury Ct **329** C1
Bury Place **327** C1
Bury Street **318** A4-B4
BushLane **328** B2
Cabbell Street **320** B4
Cable Street **329** E2
Cade Road **335** E4
Cadogan Gardens **331** D2
Cadogan Lane **331** E1
Cadogan Place **331** D1-E1
Cadogan Square
**331** D1-D2
Cale Street **331** C2-C3
Caledonian Road
**322** B1-B2
Calshot Street **322** B1-B2
Calthorpe Street **322** C3
Cambridge Circus **319** C2
Cambridge Gardens
**334** A1
Camden High Street
**321** E1
Camley Street **322** A1
Camomile Street **329** C1
Campden Grove **334** B3
Campden Hill Road
**334** B3-B4
Campden Hill Square
**334** B3
Campden Street **321** E1
**334** B3
Cannon Street **328** A2-B2
Cannon Street Road
**329** E2
Canon Row **326** C4
Capper Street **321** E4
Carburton Street **321** E4
Cardington Street **321** E2
Carey Street **327** D1
Carlisle Lane **333** D1
Carlisle Place **332** A1-B2
Carlisle Street **318** B2-C1
Carlos Place **325** E2
Carlton Gardens **326** B3
Carlton House Terrace
**326** B3
Carlyle Square **330** C3
Carmelite Street **327** E2
Carnaby Street
**318** A2-B2
Carnegie Street **322** C1
Carter Lane **328** A2
Carting Lane **319** E3
Cartwright Gardens
**322** A3
Cartwright Street
**329** D2-D3
Casson Street **329** E1
Castle Lane **332** B1
Cathcart Road **330** A3
Catherine Place **332** A1-

B1
Catherine Street **319** E2
Cato Street **325** C1
Cavendish Square **326** A1
Caxton Street **332** B1
Central Street **323** E2-E3
Chadwick Street **332** B1
Chalton Street **322** A2
Chamber Street **329** D2
Chancel Street **327** E3 **328** A3
Chancery Lane **327** D1-E1
Chandos Place **319** D3
Chandos Street **326** A1
Chapel Street **320** B4
Charlbert Street **320** B1
Charles II Street **318** B4-C4
Charles Street **325** D3
Charlotte Street **321** E4 **326** B1
Charlton Way **335** E3-E4
Charterhouse Sq. **323** D4
Charterhouse Street **323** D4
Cheapside **328** B2
Chelsea Bridge **331** E4
Chelsea Bridge Road **331** E3
Chelsea Embankment **331** C4-E3
Chelsea Manor Street **331** C3
Chelsea Square **330** C3
Chepstow Place **334** B1-B2
Chepstow Road **334** B1
Chepstow Villas **334** B2
Chesham Place **331** E1
Chesham Street **331** E1
Chester Road **321** D2
Chester Row **331** E2
Chesterfield Hill **325** D3
Chesterfield Street **332** B3
Chicksand Street **329** D1
Chiltern Street **320-1** C3
Chilworth Street **324** B1
Chiswell Street **323** E4
Chitty Street **321** E4
Church Street **320** A3 **335** D2
Churchill Gardens Road **332** A3
Circus Road **320** A2
Circus Street **335** D3
City Road **323** D2-E2
Claremont Square **323** C2
Clarence House **326** A4
Clarendon Street **332** A3
Clarges Mews **326** A3
Clarges Street **326** A3
Clay Street **320** C3
Clayton Street **333** D4
Clements Lane **328** C2
Clerkenwell Close **323** D3
Clerkenwell Road **323** C4-D4
Cleveland Row **326** A4
Cleveland Square **324** A1-A2
Cleveland Street **321** E4
Clifford Street **318** A3
Clink Street **328** B3
Clipstone Mews **321** E4
Cloak Lane **328** B2
Cloth Fair **323** D4 **328** A1
Cloudesley Place **323** C1
Cobb Street **329** D1

Cochane Street **320** A1-A2
Cock Lane **328** A1
Cockspur Street **319** C4
Coin Street **327** E3
Colebrooke Row **323** D1-D2
Coleherne Road **330** A3
Coleman Street **328** B1
Coley Street **322** C3
College Approach **335** D2
College Street **328** B2
Collier Street **322** B2-C2
Colligham Road **330** A2
Colombo Street **327** E3
Colonnade **322** B4
Colville Road **334** B1
Colville Terrace **334** A1-B1
Commercial Road **329** E1
Commercial Street **329** D1
Compton Street **323** D3
Concert Hall Approach **327** D3
Conduit Street **318** A2-A3
    **322** B4
Cons Street **327** E4
Constitution Hill **325** E4 **326** A4
Conway Street **321** E3
Cooper's Road **329** D2
Copenhagen Street **322** B1-C1
Copperfield Street **328** A4
Copthall Avenue **328** B1
Coram Street **322** A3
Cork Street **318** A3
Cornhill **328** B2
Cornwall Crescent **334** A1
Cornwall Gardens **330** A1
Cornwall Road **327** D3-E4
County Hall **327** D4
Courtfield Road **330** A2
Courtnell Street **334** B1
Cousin Lane **328** B2
Covent Garden **319** E2-E3
Coventry Street **318** C3
Cowcross Street **323** D4
Cramer Street **321** C3
Cranbourn Street **319** C3-D3
Crane Street **335** E1
Cranley Gardens **330** B2-B3
Craven Hill **324** A2-B2
Craven Road **324** B1-B2
Craven Street **319** D4
Crawford Place **325** C1
Crawford Street **320** B4-C4
Creek Road **335** C2-D2
Cromer Street **322** B3
Cromwell Gardens **330** C1
Cromwell Road **330** A2-C1
Croom's Hill **335** D3-E4
Crosswall **329** D2
Crowder Street **329** E2
Crown Office Row **327** E2
Crowndale Road **321** E1
CrucifixLane **329** C4
Cruiksank Street **323** C2
Crutched Frairs **329** C2-D2
Cubit Street **322** C3
Cullum Street **329** C2
Culross Street **325** D2-E2
Cundy Street **331** E2

Curlew Street **329** D4
Cursitor Street **327** E1
Curzon Street **325** D3 **326** A3
Cutty Sark **335** D1
Cutty Street **329** D4
D'arbalay Street **318** B2
Dacre Street **332** B1
Dallington Street **323** D3
Danbury Street **323** D1
Dawson Place **334** B2
De Laune Street **333** E3
De Vere Gardens **324** A4
Dean Street **318** B1-C2
Dean's Yard **332** C1
Deanery Street **325** D3
Delancy Street **321** D1-E1
Denbigh Road **334** B2
Denman Street **318** B3
Denmark Street **319** C1
Denvers Street **330** C4
Derby Gate **326** C4
Dering Street **326** A1
Devonia Road **323** D1
Devonshire Mews West **321** D4
Devonshire Place **321** D4
Devonshire Square **329** C1
Devonshire Street **321** D4
Diamond Terrace **335** D4
Distaff Lane **328** A2
Dock Street **329** E2
Dockhead **329** D4
Donegal Street **322-3** C2
Doon Street **327** D3
Dorset Road **327** E2
Dorset Street **320** C3
Doughty Mews **322** B3-B4
Doughty Street **322** B3-B4
Dovehouse Street **330** C3
Dover Street **318** A4
Dowgate Hill **328** B2
Down Street **325** D3
Downing Street **326** C4
Draycott Avenue **331** D2
Drayton Gardens **330** B3
Druid Street **329** D4
Drummond Street **321** E3
Drury Lane **319** D1-E2
Duchess of Bedford's Walk
    **334** B3
Duchess Street **321** D4
Duchy Street **327** E3
Dufferin Street **323** E4
Duke of Wellington Place **325** E4
Duke of York Street **318** B4
Duke Street Hill **328** B3-C3
Duke Street **318** B4
Duke Street **325** E1
Duke's Lane **334** B3
Dukes Road **322** A3
Dumford Street **335** D2
Duncan Street **323** D1
Duncan Terrace **323** D1-D2
Dunraven Street **325** D2
Durham Street **333** D3-D4
Dyott Street **319** D1
Eagle Close **323** D4
Eagle Street **322** B4
Eagle Wharf Road **323** E1

Earl's Court Road **330** A2
Earlham Street **319** D2
Earls Court Road **334** B4
Earnshaw Street **319** C1-D1
East Smithfield **329** D3-E3
Eastbourne Terrace **324** B1
Eastcastle Street **318** A1-B1
Eastcheap **328** C2
Eastney Street **335** E1
Easton Street **323** C3
EatonLane **332** A1
Eaton Square **331** E1
Eaton Terrace **331** E2
Ebury Bridge Road **331** E3
Ebury Street **331** E2
Eccleston Bridge **332** A2
Eccleston Square **332** A2
Eccleston Street **332** A2
Eccleston Street **331** E1
Edgware Road **320** A3-A4
Edith Grove **330** B4
Edward Street **328** A1
Edwards Mews **325** E1
Eldon Street **328** C1
Elfin Oak **334** C3
Elgin Crescent **334** A1-A2
Elizabeth Street **331** E2
Ellen Street **329** E2
Elm Park Gardens **330** B3
Elm Park Road **330** B3
Elm Street **322** C4
Elvaston Place **330** B1
Ely Place **327** E1
Elystan Place **331** D2
Elystan Street **331** C2
Emerald Street **322** B4
Emerson Street **328** A3
Endell Street **319** D1-D2
Endsleigh Gardens **322** A3
Endsleigh Street **322** A3
Enford Street **320** B4
Ennismore Street **331** C1
Erasmus Street **332** C2
Essex Road **323** D1
Essex Street **327** D2
Essex Villas **334** B4
Euston Road **321** E3 **322** A3-B2
Evelyn Gardens **330** B3
Eversholt Street **322** A2-A3
    **321** E1-E2
Ewer Street **328** A3-A4
Exeter Street **319** E3
Exhibition Road **324** B4 **330** C1
Exmouth Market **323** C3
Eyre Street Hill **323** C4
Fair Street **329** C4-D4
Fairclough Street **329** E2
Farm Street **325** E2-E3
Farringdon Lane **323** D4
Farringdon Road **323** C3-D4
Farringdon Street **327** E1
Fashion Street **329** D1
Feathers Place **335** E2
Fenchurch Avenue **329** C2
Fenchurch Street **328-9** C2
Fentiman Road **333** D4
Fetter Lane **327** E1

Finborough Road **330** A3-A4
Finch Lane **328** C2
Finsbury Circus **328** C1
Fish Street Hill **328** C2
Fisher Street **327** C1
Fitzalan Street **333** D2-E2
Fitzhardinge Street **325** E1
Fitzroy Square **321** E4
Fitzroy Street **321** E4
Flaxman Terrace **322** A3
Fleet Street **327** D2
Flood Street **331** D3
Floral Street **319** D2-E2
Foley Street **321** E4
Fordham Street **329** E1
Fore Street **328** B1
Forset Street **325** C1
Foster Lane **328** A1
Frampton Street **320** A3
Francis Street **332** B1-B2
Franklin Row **331** D3
Frederick Street **322** B2-B3
Friend Street **323** D2
Frith Street **318** C2
Fulham Road **330** A4-C2
Furnival Street **327** E1
Gainsford Street **329** D4
Galway Street **323** E3
Gambia Street **328** A4
Garrick Street **319** D3
Garway Road **334** C1-C2
Gate Street **319** E1
Gee Street **323** E3
George Row **329** E4
George Street **325** D1-E1
George Yard **325** E2
Gerrard Road **323** D1
Gerrard Street **318** C3
Gertrude Street **330** B4
Gilbert Road **333** E2
Gilbert Street **325** E2
Gillingham Street **332** A2
Gilston Road **330** B3
Giltspur Street **328** A1
Glass House Walk **333** D3
Glasshouse Street **318** B3
Gloucester Circus **335** D3
Gloucester Gate **321** D1
Gloucester Place **320** B3-B4
Gloucester Place Mews **325** D1
Gloucester Road **330** A1-B2
Gloucester Terrace **324** A1-B2
Gloucester Walk **334** B3
Gloucester Way **323** D3
Godliman Street **328** A2
Golden Lane **323** E3-E4
Golden Square **318** B3
Goodge Place **321** E4
Goodge Street **321** E4
Goodmans Yard **329** D2
Gordon Square **322** A3
Gosfield Street **321** E4
Goswell Road **323** D2-D3
Gough Street **322** C3
Goulston Street **329** D1
Gower Mews **322** A4
Gower Place **321** E3

Gower Street **321** E3
Gracechurch Street **328** C2
Grafton Mews **321** E3
Grafton Street **318** A3
Grafton Way **321** E3
Graham Street **323** D2-E2
Granville Place **325** D1
Granville Square **322** C3
Grape Street **319** D1
Grays Inn Road **322** B2-C4
Great Castle Street **318** A1
Great Chapel Street **318** B1
Great College Street **332**-3 C1
Great Cumberland Place **325** C1
Great Guildford Street
  **328** A3-A4
Great Marlborough Street
  **318** A2-B2
Great Maze Pond **328** B4
Great Ormond Street **322** B4
Great Percy Street **322**-3 C2
Great Peter Street **332** B1-C1
Great Portland Street **318** A1
  **321** D4
Great Pulteney Street **318** B2-B3
Great Queen Street **319** E1
Great Russell Street **319** C1
Great Scotland Yard **326** C3
  **322** B4
Great Smith Street **332** C1
Great Suffolk Street **328** A3-A4
Great Sutton Street **323** D3-D4
Great Titchfield Street **321** E4
Great Windmill Street **318** B3
Great Wolfe Road **335** E4
Greatorex Street **329** E1
Greek Street **318** C2
Green Street **325** D2-E2
Greencoat Place **332** B1-B2
Greenfield Road **329** E1
Greenwich High Road **335** C3
Greenwich Park Street **335** E1
Greenwich South Street
  **335** C3-C4
Greet Street **327** E4
Grenville Street **323** C4-D4
Gresham Street **328** B1
Gresse Street **318** C1
Greycoat Place **332** B1
Grosvenor Crescent **325** E4
Grosvenor Gardens **332** A1
Grosvenor Hill **326** A2
Grosvenor Place **325** E4 **332** A1
Grosvenor Road **332** A3-B3
Grosvenor Square **325** E2
Grove End Road **320** A1-A2
Great Dover Street **328** B4
Great George Street **326** C4
Great Titchfield Street **318** A1
Great Tower Street **329** C2
Great Winchester Street **328** C1
Guildford Street **322** B3-B4
Gunter Grove **330** A4
Gunthorpe Street **329** D1
Gutter Lane **328** B1
Half Moon Street **326** A3
Halkin Street **325** E4

Hallam Street **321** D4
Hamilton Place **325** D3-D4
Hampstead Road **321** E2-E3
Handel Street **322** B3
Hanover Square **318** A2
Hanover Street **318** A2
Hans Place **331** D1
Hans Road **331** D1
Hanson Street **321** E4
Hanway Place **318** C1
Hanway Street **318** C1
Harcourt Street **320** B4
Hardcourt Terrace **330** A3
Hardwick Street **323** C3
Harewood Avenue **320** B3-B4
Harley Street **321** D4
Harleyford Road **333** D3-D4
Harpur Street **322** B4
Harrington Gardens **330** A2
Harrington Road **330** B2
Harrison Street **322** B3
Harrow Place **329** D1
Harrow Road **320** A4
Harrowby Street **325** C1
Hasker Street **331** D2
Hatfields **327** E3
Hatton Garden **323** C4
Hatton Wall **323** C4
Hay's Mews **325** D3
Haydon Street **329** D2
Haymarket **318** C3-C4
Hayne Street **323** D4
Haywood Place **323** D3
Heathcote Street **322** B3
Heddon Street **318** A3
Heneage Street **329** D1
Henrietta Street **319** D3-E3
Herbal Hill **323** C4
Herbrand Street **322** A3
Hercules Road **333** D1-E1
Hereford Road **334** B1-B2
Hermit Street **323** D2
Hermitage Wall **329** E3
Hertford Street **325** D3
High Holborn **319** D1-E1
Hill Street **325** D3
Hillsleigh Road **334** B3
Hobart Place **331** E1
Holbein Place **331** E2 **332** A1
Holborn Viaduct **328** A1
Holland Park **334** A3
Holland Park Avenue **334** A3
Holland Park Mews **334** A3
Holland Park Road **334** A4-B4
Holland Road **334** A4
Holland Street **328** A3 **334** B3
Holland Walk **334** B3-B4
Hollen Street **318** B1
Holles Street **326** A1
Hollywood Road **330** A3-B3
Homer Row **320** B4
Homer Street **320** B4
Hopkins Street **318** B2
Hopton Street **334** A3
Hornton Street **334** B3-B4
Horse Guards Avenue **326**-7 C3
Horse Guards Road **326** B3-B4

Horseferry Road **332** B1-C2
Horselydown Lane **329** D4
Hortensia Road **330** A4
Hosier Lane **328** A1
Houndsditch **329** C1-D1
Howick Place **332** B1
Howland Street **321** E4
Hugh Street **332** A2
Hunter Street **322** B3
Huntley Street **321** E4
Hyde Park Cr. **324** C1
Hyde Park Gate **324** A4-B5
Hyde Park Street **325** C2
Hyde Vale **335** D4
Idol Lane **328** C2
Ifield Road **330** A4
Ilchester Place **334** A4-B4
Imperial College Road **330** B1
Ingestre Place **318** B2
Inverness Terrace **324** A1-A2
Inverness Terrace Gate **324** A2
Irving Street **319** C3
Islington Green **323** D1
Iverna Gdns **334** B4
Ixworth Place **331** C2
Jacob Street **329** D4-E4
Jamaica Road **329** D4
James Street **319** D2-E2 **325** E1
James's Street **326** A3
Jermyn Street **318** A4
Jewry Street **329** D2
Joan Street **327** E4
Jockey's Field **322** C4
John Adam Street **319** D4-E4
John Carpenter Street **327** E2
John Fisher Street **329** E2
John Islip Street **332** C2-C3
John Prince's Street **318** A1
John Street **322** C4
John's Mews **322** B4-C4
Judd Street **322** A2-B3
Kean Street **319** E2
Keeley Street **319** E1-E2
Kemble Street **319** E2
Kennet Street **329** E3
Kennington Lane **333** D3-E2
Kennington Park Place **333** E3
Kennington Park Road **333** E3
Kennington Road **333** E1
Kenrick Place **320** C3
Kensingston Gardens Square
  **334** C1
Kensington Church Street
  **334** B3
Kensington Gore **324** B4
Kensington High Street
  **334** A4-B4
Kensington Palace Gardens
  **324** A3-A4 **334** C3
Kensington Park Gardens
  **334** A2-B2
Kensington Park Road
  **334** A1-B2
Kensington Place **334** B3
Kensington Square **334** C4
King Charles Street **326** C4

King George Street **335** D3
King Street **319** D3 326 B3
King William Street **328** B2
King William Walk **335** D2
King's Arms Yard **328** B1
King's Cross Road **322** B2-C3
King's Mews **322** C4
King's Road **331** A1-E1
King's Scholars Passage
**332** A1-A2
Kingly Street **318** A2
King's Cross Central **322** A1
Kingsway **319** E1
Kipling Street **328** B4
Knightrider Street **328** A2
Knightsbridge **325** D4
Knox Street **320** B4
L. Pountney Lane **328** B2
Ladbroke Gardens **334** A2
Ladbroke Grove **334** A1-B2
Ladbroke Road **334** A3-B2
Ladbroke Square **334** A2-B2
Ladbroke Terrace **334** B2
Ladbroke Walk **334** A2-B2
Lafone Street **329** D4
Lambeth Bridge **333** C2-D2
Lambeth High Street **333** D2
Lambeth Palace Road **333** D1
Lambeth Road **333** D2-E1
Lambeth Walk **333** D2-E2
Lancaster Place **319** E3
Lancaster Road **334** A1
Lancaster Terrace **324** B2
Langham Place **326** A1
Langham Street **321** E4 326 A1
Langley Street **319** D2
Lansdowne Crescent **334** A2
Lansdowne Rise **334** A2
Lansdowne Road **334** A2
Lansdowne Walk **334** A2
Lant Street **328** A4
Launceston Place **330** A1
Laverton Place **330** A2
Lavington Street **328** A3
Lawn Lane **333** D4
Lawrence Street **330** C4
Layatall Street **322** C4
Leake Street **327** D4
Leamington Road Villas **334** B1
Leather Lane **323** C4
Leathermarket Street **328** C4
Ledbury Road **334** B1
Leeke Street **322** B2
Leicester Square **319** C3
Leicester Street **318** C3
Leigh Street **322** A3-B3
Leinster Square **334** B2
Leinster Terrace **324** A2
Leman Street **329** D2
Lennox Gardens **331** D1-D2
Lever Street **323** E3
Lexham Gardens **330** A1-A2
Lexington Street **318** B2
Limeburner Lane **327** E1 328 A1
Limerston Street **330** B4
Lincoln's Inn Fields **327** D1
Lincoln's Inn Hall **327** D1

Linden Gdns **334** B2
Lisle Street **318** C3
Lisson Grove **320** A3-B4
Little Britain **328** A1
Little Street **326** A3
Liverpool Road **323** D1
Liverpool Street **328-9** C1
Lloyd Baker Street **322** C3
Lloyd Square **323** C2
Lloyd Street **323** C2
Lloyd's Avenue **329** C2-D2
Lloyds Road **323** D2
Lodge Road **320** A2-A3
London Bridge **328** B3
London Bridge Street **328** B3
London Street **324** B1
London Wall **328** B1-C1
Long Acre **319** D2
Long Lane **323** D4-E4 328 B4
Long Yard **322** B4
Longbridge **320** C2
Longford Street **321** D3-E3
Lonsdale Road **334** B1
Lothbury **328** B1
Lowdes Square **325** D4
Lower Marsh **327** D4-E4
Lower Thames Street **328** C3
Ludgate Hill **328** A2
Lumley Street **325** E2
Lupus Street **332** A3-B3
Luxborough Street **321** C3
Lyall Street **331** E1
Macklin Street **319** E1
Maddox Street **318** A2
Maguire Street **329** D4
Maiden Lane **319** D3 328 B3
Maidenstone Hill **335** C4-D4
Malet Street **322** A4
Manchester Square **325** E1
Manchester Street **321** C3
**325** E1
Manresa Road **330** C3
Mansell Street **329** D2
Mansfield Street **321** D4
Mansion House **328** B2
Maple Street **321** E4
Marchmont Street **322** A3-B3
Margaret Street **333** C1
Margaret Street **318** A1
Margery Street **322-3** C3
Mark Lane **329** C2
Market Mews **325** D3
Market Place **318** A1
Markham Street **331** D3
**328** B1-B2
Marlborough Road **326** B3-B4
Marloes Road **334** B4
Marshall Street **318** B2
Marshalsea Road **328** B4
MartinLane **328** B2
Marylebone High Street **321** C3
Marylebone Lane **325** E1
Marylebone Road **320** B4-D3
Marylebone Street **321** D3-D4
Mecklenburgh Square **322** B3
Medway Street **332** B1
Melbury Road **334** A4

Mepham Street **327** D4
Mercer Street **319** D2
Merlin Street **323** C3
Meymott Street **327** E3
Micawber Street **323** E2
Middle Temple Lane **327** E2
Middlesex Street **329** D1
Miles Street **333** C4
Milford Lane **327** D2
Milk Street **328** B1
Mill Street **318** A2 329 D4
Millbank **333** C1-C3
Millman Street **322** B3-B4
Milner Street **331** D2
Milton Street **323** E4
Mincing Lane **329** C2
Minories **329** D2
Mitre Street **329** C2-D2
Molyneux Street **325** C1
Mon Street **328** C2
Monkwell Square **328** B1
Monmouth Street **319** D2
Montagu Mansions **320** C3
Montagu Place **320** B4-C4
Montagu Square **325** D1 325 D1
Montagu Street **325** D1
Montague Close **328** B3
Montague Place **322** A4
Montague Street **322** A4-B4
Moor Lane **323** E4 328 B1
Moor Street **319** C2
Moorfields **328** B1
Moorgate **328** B1
Moorhouse Road **334** B1
Moreland Street **323** D2-E2
Mornington Terrace **321** D1
Morpeth Terrace **332** A1-B2
Mortimer Street **326** A1-B1
Morwell Street **326** B1
Moscow Road **334** B2-C2
Mossop Street **331** C2-D2
Mount Pleasant **322-3** C3
Mount Row **325** E2
Mount Street **325** E2
Moxon Street **321** C3
Muriel Street **322** C1
Murry Grove **323** E2
Museum Street **319** D1
Myddelton Passage **323** C2
Myddelton Square **323** C2
Myddelton Street **323** D3
Myrdle Street **329** E1
Nassau Street **321** E4 326 A1
Neal Street **319** D2
Nelson Road **335** D2
Nevada Street **335** D2
New Bond Street **318** A3
New Bridge Street **327** E2
**328** A2
New Cavendish Street **321** D4
New Change **328** A2
New Fetter Lane **327** E1
New North Street **322** B4
New Oxford Street **319** C1-E1
New Road **329** E1
New Row **319** D3
New Square **327** D1

New Street **329** C1
New Street Square **327** E1
Newburn Street **333** D3
Newcomen Street **328** B4
Newgate Street **328** A1
Newman Street **318** B1
Newport Street **333** D2
Newton Road **334** B1-C1
Newton Street **319** E1
NicholasLane **328** B2
Nine Elms Road **332** B4-C4
Noble Street **328** A1-B1
Noel Road **323** D1
Noel Street **318** B1-B2
Norfolk Square **324** B1
North Audley Street **325** E2
North Gower Street **321** E3
North Row **325** D2-E2
Northampton Road **323** C3
Northampton Square **323** D3
Northington Street **322** B4-C4
Northumberland Avenue **319** D4
323 D3
Northumberland Place **334** B1
Norwich Street **327** E1
Notting Hill Gate **334** B2
Nottingham Place **321** C3
Nottingham Street **321** C3
Nutford Place **325** C1
Oakley Square **321** E1
Oakley Street **331** C3-C4
Oakwood Court **334** A4
Oat Lane **328** B1
Ogle Street **321** E4
Old Bailey **328** A1
Old Bond Street **318** A4
Old Broad Street **328** C1
Old Brompton Road **330** B2
Old Castle Street **329** D1
Old Cavendish Street **326** A1
Old Church Street **330** B3-C4
Old Compton Street **318** C2
Old Gloucester Street **322** B4
Old Montague Street **329** D1-E1
Old Paradise Street **333** D2
Old ParkLane **325** D3-D4
Old Pye Street **332** B1-C1
Old Queen Street **326** B4
Old Street **318** A3 323 E3
Old Woolwich Road **335** E1
Oldbury Place **321** C3
Onlow Square **330** C2
Onslow Gardens **330** B2
Onslow Square **330** C2
Orange Street **318** C4
Orchard Street **325** E1
Orde Hall Street **322** B4
Ordnance Hill **320** A1
Orenzo Street **322** B2
Osborn Street **329** D1
Ossington Street **334** B2
Ossulston Street **322** A2
Outer Circle **320** B1-D3
Owen Street **323** D2
Oxendon Street **318** C3
Oxford Circus **318** A1
Oxford Street **318** A1-C1

Packington Square 323 E1
Paddington Street 321 C3
Page Street 332 B2-C2
Paget Street 323 D2
Pakenham Street 322 C3
Palace Gardens Terrace 334 B3
Palace Gate 324 A4
Palace Street 332 A1-B1
Palace Theatre 319 C2
Pall Mall 318 C4
Pall Mall East 319 C4
Palladium Theatre 318 A2
Palmer Street 332 B1
Pancras Road 322 A1-B2
Panton Street 318 C3-C4
Paris Garden 327 E3
Park Crescent 321 D4
Park Lane 325 D2-E4
Park Place 326 A3
Park Road 320 B2-C3
Park Row 335 E1-E2
Park Street 325 D2-E3
    328 A3-B3
Park Village East 321 D1
Park Vista 335 E2
Park Walk 330 B4
Parker Street 319 E1
Parkway 321 D1
Parliament Square 326 C4
Parliament Street 326 C4
Parry Street 333 C4
Paternoster Square 328 A1
Pavillion Road 331 D1-D2
Pear Tree Street 323 D3-E3
Peel Street 334 B3
Pelham Street 330-1 C2
Pembridge Crescent 334 B2
Pembridge Gardens 334 B2
Pembridge Place 334 B2
Pembridge Road 334 B2
Pembridge Square 334 B2
Pembridge Villas 334 B1-B2
Pennington Street 329 E3
Penton Rise 322 C2
Pentonville Road 322-3 B2-C2
Percy Circus 322 C2
Percy Street 326 B1
Perkins Rents 332 B1
Peter Street 318 B2
Phillimore Gardens 334 B4
Phillimore Place 334 B4
Phillimore Walk 334 B4
Philpot Lane 328 C2
Phoenix Place 322 C3
Piccadilly 318 A4-B3
    325 D3-D4
Piccadilly Circus 318 B3
Picton Place 325 E1
Pimlico Road 331 E2-E3
Pinchin Street 329 E2
Pine Street 323 C3
Pitt Street 334 B3
Pitt's Head Mews 325 D3
Place Court 334 B2-C2
Plender Street 321 E1
Pocock Street 328 A4

Point Hill 335 D4
Poland Street 318 B1-B2
Pont Street 331 D1-E1
Ponton Road 332 B4
Porchester Gate 324 A2
Porchester Road 334 C1
Porchester Terrace 324 A2
Porter Street 320 C3
Portland Place 334 A2
Portman Close 325 D1
Portman Square 325 D1
Portman Street 325 D1
Portobello Road 334 A1-B2
PortpoolLane 322-2 C4
Portsoken Street 329 D2
Portugal Street 327 D1
Poultry 328 B2
Powis Place 322 B4
Powis Square 334 B1
Powis Terrace 334 B1
Praed Street 324 B1-C1
Prescot Street 329 D2
Price's Street 328 A3
Prince Albert Road 320 B1-D1
Prince Consort Road 324 B4
Prince's Street 328 B1-B2
Princedale Road 334 A2-A3
Princes Gardens 330 C1
Princes Square 334 B2
Princes Street 318 A2
Princess Gardens 324 B4-C4
Princeton Street 322 B4
Procter Street 327 C1
Puddle Dock 328 A2
Pultons Square 330 C4
Purchese Street 322 A1-A2
Queen Ann Street 325 E1
Queen Elizabeth Street 329 D4
Queen Square 322 B4
Queen Street 325 D3
Queen Street Place 328 B2
Queen Street 328 B2
Queen Victoria Street 328 A2-B2
Queen's Gate 324 B4
Queen's Gate Gardens 330 B1
Queen's Gate Mews 330 B1
Queen's Gate Terrace 330 B1
Queen's Gardens 330 B1
Queensborough Terrace 324 A2
Queensdale Road 334 A3
Queenstown Road 331 E4
Queensway 324 A1-A2
    334 C1-C2
Radnor Street 323 E3
Railway Approach 328 B3
Ramillies Place 318 A1-A2
Randall Place 335 C2
Rathbone Place 318 B1-C1
Rathbone Street 326 B1
Rawlings Street 331 D2
Rawstorne Street 323 D2
Ray Street 323 C4
Red Lion Square 322 B4
Red Lion Street 322 B4
Redan Place 334 C1-C2
Redburn Street 331 D3
Redcliffe Gardens 330 A3-A4

Redcliffe Road 330 B3
Redcross Way 328 B4
Redesdale Street 331 D3
Reeves Mews 325 E2
Regency Street 332 B2
Regent Square 322 B3
Regent Street 318 A1-C4
Rennie Street 327 E3
Rex Place 325 D3
Ridgemount Street 322 A4
Ridgmount Gardens 322 A4
Riding House Street 321 E4
    326 A1
River Street 323 C2
Roan Street 335 C2-D2
Robert Adam Street 325 E1
Robert Street 321 D2-E2
Rochester Row 332 B1-B2
Rodney Street 322 C1-C2
Roger Street 322 C4
Roland Gardens 330 B2-B3
Romilly Street 318 C2
Romney Street 332 C1
Rood Lane 328 C2
Rose Street 319 D3
Rosebery Avenue 323 C3-D3
Rossmore Road 320 B3
Roupell Street 327 E3-E4
Royal College Street 321 E1
Royal Hill 335 D3
Royal Hospital Road 331 D4-E3
Royal Mint Street 329 D2
Rugby Street 322 B4
Rupert Street 318 B3-C3
Russell Road 334 A4
Russell Square 322 A4
Russell Street 319 E2
Saffron Hill 323 C4-D4
Salisbury Place 320 B4-C4
Sancroft Street 333 D3-E3
Sandwich Street 322 A3
Sans Walk 323 D3
Saville Row 318 A3
Savoy Hill 319 E3
Savoy Place 319 E3-E4
Savoy Street 319 E3
Sawyer Street 328 A4
Scala Street 321 E4
Scarborough Street 329 D2
Scarsdale Villas 334 B4
Scoresby Street 327 E4 328 A4
Sebastian Street 323 D3
Secker Street 327 E3-E4
Seething Lane 329 C2
Sekforde Street 323 D3
Serle Street 327 D1
Settles Street 329 E1
Seven Dials 319 D2
Seward Street 323 D3-E3
Seymour Place 320 B4 325 D1
Seymour Street 325 D1
Shad Thames 329 D4
Shaftesbury Avenue 318-9 B3-C2
Sheffield Terrace 334 B3
Shelton Street 319 D2
Shepherd Street 325 D3
Shepherdess Walk 323 E2

Shoe Lane 327 E1
Shorter Street 329 D2
Shorts Gardens 319 D2
Shouldham Street 325 C1-D1
Shrewsbury Road 334 B1
Sidmouth Street 322 B3
Silk Street 323 E4
Skinner Street 323 D3
Sloane Avenue 331 C2-D2
Sloane Square 331 D2
Sloane Street 325 D4 331 D1-D2
Smeaton Street 329 E3
Smith Square 332-3 C1
Smith Street 331 D3
Snow Hill 327 E1 328 A1
Snowsfields 328 B4-C4
Soho Square 318 C1-C2
South Audley Street 325 E2-E3
South Eaton Place 331 E2
South Lambert Road 333 C4
South Molton Lane 325 E2
South Molton Street 325 E2
South Square 322 C4
South Street 325 D3
South Tenter 329 D2
South Wharf Road 324 B1-C1
Southamptom Street 319 E3
Southampton Buildings 327 D1
Southampton Place 327 C1
Southampton Row 322 B4
Southwark Bridge 328 B3
Southwark Bridge Road 328 A4
Southwark Street 328 A3-B3
Spencer Street 323 D2-D3
Spenser Street 332 B1
Spring Grove 319 C4-D4
Spur Road 327 D4-E4
St Agnes Place 333 D4
St Alban's Street 318 C4
St Andrew Street 327 E1
St Ann's Street 332 C1
St Botolph Street 329 D1
St Brides Street 327 E1
St Christophers Place 325 E1
St Cross Street 323 C4-D4
St Edwardes Square 334 B4
St George Street 318 A2-A3
St George's Drive 332 A2-B2
St George's Road 333 E1
St George's Square 332 B3
St Giles Circus 319 C1
St Giles High Street 319 C1-D1
St James West 323 D3
St James's 328 B2
St James's Palace 326 B4
St James's Place 326 A3
St James's Square 318 B4
St James's Street 318 A4-B4
St John Street 323 D2
St John's Gardens 334 A2
St John's Lane 323 D4
St John's Wood High Street
    320 A1-B2
St John's Wood Road 320 A2-A3
St John's Wood Terrace
    320 A1-B1
St Katharine's Way 329 D3

St Leonard's Terrace **331** D3
St Luke's Mews **334** A1-B1
St Marks Road **334** A1
St Martin Street **319** C4
St Martin's **328** A1
St Martin's Lane **319** D3
St Mathew Street **332** B1
St Michael's Street **324** C1
St Pancras Way **322** A1
St Paul's Churchyard **328** A2
St Peter's Street **323** D1-E1
St Petersburgh Place **334** C3
St Stephen Walbrook **328** B2
St Swithin's Lane **328** B2
St Thomas Street **328** C4
Stacey Street **319** C2-D2
Stafford Place **332** A1
Stafford Street **318** A4
Stafford Terrace **334** B4
Stainer Street **328** C3-C4
Stanford Road **334** C4
Stanhope Gardens **330** B2
Stanhope Street **321** E2-E3
Stanley Crescent **334** A2
Star Street **324** C1
Stephen Street **326** B1
Stillington Street **332** B2
Stockwell Street **335** D2
Stone Buildings **327** D1
Stoney Street **328** B3
Store Street **322** A4
Storey's Gate **326** B4
Strand **319** D4-E3 **327** D2
Stratford Place **325** E1
Strype Street **329** D1
Stukeley Street **319** E1
Suffolk Street **319** C4
Sumner Place **330** B2-C2
Sumner Street **328** A3
Sunken Garden **334** C3
Surrey Row **328** A4
Surrey Street **327** D2
Sussex Gardens **324** B1-C1
Sussex Square **324** B2
Sutherland Place **334** B1
Sutherland Street **332** A3
Sutton Row **318** C1
Swallow Street **318** B3-B4
SwanLane **328** B2-B3
Swan Walk **331** D4
Swinton Street **322** B2
Sydney Street **331** C2-C3
Tachbrook Street **332** B2-B3
Talbot Road **334** A1-B1
Tallis Street **327** E2
Tavistock Place **322** A3-B3
Tavistock Road **334** A1
Tavistock Square **322** A3
Tavistock Street **319** E3
Taviton Street **322** A3
Temple Avenue **327** E2
Temple Lane **327** E2
Temple Lodge **324** B3
Temple Place **327** D2
Tench Street **329** E3-E4
Tennis Street **328** B4

Thames Street **329** C3 335 C2
Thanet Street **322** A3-B3
Thayer Street **325** E1
Theed Street **327** E3
Theobald's Road **322** B4-C4
Thirleby Road **332** B1
Thomas More Street **329** E3
Thrale Street **328** B3 329 D1
Threadneedle Street **328** B2-C2
Throgmorton Street **328** B1-C1
Thurloe Place **330** C1-C2
Thurloe Square **330** C1-C2
Thurloe Street **330** C2
Tilney Street **325** D3
Tite Street **331** D3
Tolpuddle Street **323** C1
Tonbridge Street **322** B2-B3
Tooley Street **328** B3-D4
Torrington Place **321** E4
Torrington Place **322** A4
Tothill Street **332** B1-C1
Tottenham Court Road **319** C1
    **321** E3-E4
Tottenham Street **321** E4
Tower Bridge Approach **329** D3
Tower Bridge Road **329** C4-D4
Tower Hill **329** D2-D3
Tower Street **319** D2
Townshend Road **320** B1
Toynbee Street **329** D1
Trafalgar Grove **335** E1
Trafalgar Road **335** E1
Trafalgar Square **319** D4
Transept Street **320** B4
Tregunter Road **330** A3
Trig Lane **328** A2
Trinity Square **329** C2-D2
Trump Street **328** B1
Tudor Street **327** E2
Tufton Street **332** C1
Turnmill Street **323** D4
Tyers Street **333** D3
Tysoe Street **323** C3
Union Street **328** A4-B4
University Street **321** E3-E4
Upper Belgrave Street **331** E1
Upper Berkeley Street **325** D1
Upper Brook Street **325** D2-E2
Upper Grosvenor Street
    **325** D2-E2
Upper Ground **327** D3-E3
Upper Montagu Street **320** B4
Upper Phillimore Gardens
    **334** B3-B4
Upper Street **323** D1
Upper Thames Street **328** B2
Upper Woburn Place **322** A3
Vaughan Way **329** E3
Vauxhall Bridge **332-3** C3
Vauxhall Bridge Road
    **332** A2-B3
Vauxhall Street **333** D3-D4
Vauxhall Walk **333** D3
Vere Street **325** E1
Vernon Place **322** B4 327 C1
Vernon Rise **322** C2
Victoria Embankment **319** E4

Victoria Gate **324** C2
Victoria Road **324** A4
Victoria Square **332** A1
Victoria Street **332** A1-C1
Vigo Street **318** A3
Villiers Street **319** D4-E4
Vincent Square **332** B2
Vincent Street **332** B2-C2
Vine Hill **323** C4
Vine Street **329** D2
Wakefield Street **322** B3
Walbrook **328** B2
Walmer Road **334** A2
Walnut Tree Walk **333** E2
Walton Street **331** C2-D1
Wandsworth Road **333** C3-C4
Wapping High Street **329** E4
Wardour Street **318** B1-C3
Warren Street **321** E3
Warwick Lane **328** A1-A2
Warwick Row **332** A1
Warwick Square **332** A2-A3
Warwick Street **318** B3
Warwick Way **332** A2-B2
Waterloo Bridge **327** D3
Waterloo Place **318** C4
Waterloo Road **327** D3-E4
Watling Lane **328** B2
Weavers Lane **329** C4
Webber Street **327** E4
Weighhouse Street **325** E2
Welbeck Street **325** E1
Welbeck West **325** E1
Wellington Road **320** A1-A2
Wellington Street **319** E2-E3
Wells Mews **318** B1
Wells Street **318** B1
Wemlock Street **323** E2
Wentworth Street **329** D1
West Grove **335** D4
West Smithfield **328** A1
West Street **319** D2
West Tenter Street **329** D2
Westbourne Grove **324** A1
    **334** A2-C1
Westbourne Park Road
    **334** A1-C1
Westbourne Park Villas
    **334** B1-C1
Westbourne Street **324** B2
Westbourne Terrace **324** B1
Westminster Bridge **327** C4
Westminster Bridge Road
    **333** D1-E1
Westmorland Street **321** D4
Weston Rise **322** C2
Weston Street **328** C3-C4
Westway **334** A1
Wetherby Gardens **330** A2
Weymouth Street **321** D4
Wharf Road **323** E2
Wharfdale Road **322** B1
Wharton Street **322** C2
Whetstone Park **327** D1
Whitcomb Street **318** C3-C4
White Horse Street **326** A3
White Kennett Street **329** D1

White's Grounds **329** C4
White's Row **329** D1
Whitechapel High Street **329** D1
Whitecross Street **323** E3-E4
Whitefriars Street **327** E2
Whitehall **326** C3
Whitehall Ct **327** C3
Whitehall Place **326-7** C3
Whitehead's Gr. **331** C2-D2
Whitfield Street **321** E3-E4
Whittlesey Street **327** E3
Wicklow Street **322** B2
Wigmore Place **325** E1
Wigmore Street **325** E1
Wild Court **319** E1
Wild Street **319** E2
William IV Street **319** D3
Willow Place **332** B2
Wilton Crescent **325** D4
Wilton Place **325** D4
Wilton Road **332** A2
Wimpole Mews **321** D4
Wimpole Street **321** D4 325 E1
Winchester Street **332** A3
Wincott Street **333** E2
Windmill Street **321** E4 326 B1
Winforton Street **335** C4-D4
Winsley Street **318** A1-B1
Woburn Place **322** A3-A4
Woburn Square **322** A3-A4
Wolseley Street **329** D4-E4
Wood Street **328** B1
Woods Mews **325** D2
Wootton Street **327** E4
Wren Street **322** C3
Wright's Lane **334** B4
Wyclif Street **323** D3
Wyndham Place **320** B4
Wyndham Street **320** B4
Wynford Road **322** B1-C1
Wynyatt Street **323** D2
Yardley Street **323** C3
York Bridge **321** C3
York Road **327** D4
York Street **320** B4-C4
York Terrace **321** C3-D3
York Way **322** B1-B2
Young Street **334** C4
Zoar Street **328** A3

# ART AND PHOTO CREDITS

**Jonathan Player/Rex Features**
49TL
**Scala Archives** 28TL, 29TR, 31TL
**Rex Features** 92B
**RHS Images** 303B
**The Ritz** 281T
**Royal Airforce Museum** 247B
**Royal Festival Hall** 298T
**Royal Opera House** 299T&B
**St Pancras Renaissance Hotel
London** 140T
**Grant Smith/OXO Restaurant** 11T
**Tom Smyth** 3, 70, 103B, 104BR,
118BR, 172C, 197C, 274, 292T
**Sir John Soane's Museum** 153
**Dorothy Stannard/APA** 25BR,
137BL, 140BR
**SuperStock** 18, 60/61
**Sarah Sweeney/APA** 125, 127BR
**TopFoto** 43
**Ray Tang/Rex Features** 44TR
**Ming Tang-Evans/APA** 6, 7T&B,
9TR&CR, 11CR, 12B, 14/15, 20,
21, 22TR, 23, 24, 25CL, 46,
49TR, 56L&R, 58B, 59, 62/63,
71, 73B, 79B, 83TR&B,
84BL&BR, 88, 89, 90, 91T&BR,
93B, 94T, 95B, 97, 98, 99,
100B, 101T&BR, 102L, 104BL,
105B, 112, 113, 115B, 116B,
117T&B, 118T, 119B, 126,
127TR, 129BL, 134, 135, 137BR,
139BR, 140BL, 141, 151T,
152BL&C, 154BL, 155T&C,
156TR&B, 158, 159, 161B,
164B, 165B, 168R, 170BL,
171(all), 172T&B, 173L&R, 182,
183, 187BL&BR, 188T&BR, 189T,
191B, 193B, 196, 202, 204,
205TL&B, 206BR, 209BR, 210TR,
211C, 221, 222, 226B, 228,
236BL&BR, 237TL, 238BL, 239B,
241, 242, 243BL&BR, 245B,

249, 250, 254B, 255B, 258BL,
259B, 260B, 278T&B, 279, 280,
292B, 293T, 294T&B, 295B,
296T&B, 297T&B, 307, 308, 309,
311, 312, 314, 315B
**Anthony Upton/Rex Features**
150
**The Waldorf** 284
**The William Morris Gallery** 247TR
**Roger Williams** 77TR
**Corrie Wingate** 10BL, 253B
**Corrie Wingate/APA** 267, 269T,
270T, 271R

**PHOTO FEATURES**

**Pages 52/53**: 52TR, 53CL Glyn
Genin, 52BR, 53BR, BL, CL& BCL
Britta Jaschinski, 52BL Lily Elms,
53TCL Getty Images, 52/3 TC
Ming Tang-Evans
**Pages 54/55**: 54TL, 55TR Glyn
Genin, 54BR, 54/5TC 55CL&BL
Ming Tang-Evans, 54BL, 55TCR
Corrie Wingate, 55BR Sian Lezard.
**Pages 86/87**: all pictures Dean
and Chapter of Westminster
except TC Ming Tang-Evans
**Pages 108/109**: all pictures
Scala Archives/National Gallery
**Pages 110/111**: all pictures
National Portrait Gallery except
111TR Corbis, 110/111T Alex
Segre/Rex Features
**Pages 122/123**: 123C Glyn
Genin, 123B Rex Features, 122T,
BL&BR, 123T
**Pages 132/133**: all pictures
Brian Bell except 133TR, CR&BR
courtesy Madame Tussauds,
133BL Tony Kyriacou/Rex
Features
**Pages 145/149**: 145, 146,

148CL,CR & TR all courtesy
British Museum, 147/48 all
TopFoto/HIP/British Museum
except 147CR APA, 147BR Werner
Forman Archive.
**Pages 178/181**: all pictures
Historic Royal Palaces, Crown
Copyright except 178/9TC Britain
on View, 179TR
Bridgeman/Guildhall Library/
Corporation of London, 180TR
Corbis, 181BR Getty Images.
**Pages 198/199**: all pictures
©Tate, London except 199BR APA,
198B Alex Lentati/Evening
Standard/Rex Features
**Pages 200/201**: all pictures
Imperial War Museum except
200BR Clare Peel, 201TR Glyn
Genin, 200/1TC Ming Tang-Evans
**Pages 214/215**: all pictures Glyn
Genin except 215BL Science &
Society Photo Library.
**Pages 216/217**: 216/7TC Derry
Moore/V&A, 217BR V&A,
216/7BC Bridgeman Art
Library/V&A, 216CR Ming Tang-
Evans. Rest Glyn Genin.
**Pages 218/219**: all pictures Glyn
Genin.

**Map Production:** Phoenix Mapping
and APA Cartography Department.
London original base map data
derived from OpenStreetMap
©OpenStreetMap and
Contributors, CC-BY-SA.

©2012 APA Publications (UK) Ltd.

**Production:** Linton Donaldson and
Rebeka Ellam

# GENERAL INDEX

### A

accommodation 281–91
activities 298–307
Adam, John 129
Adam, Robert 129, 203, 237, 238, 246
Adams, John 118
Admiralty Arch 83
African artefacts 148, 261
afternoon tea 51
Aikens, Tom 48
air travel 276–7
Al-Fayed, Mohamed 25, 205
Albert, Prince 32, **207**, 267
Albert Bridge 227
Albert Memorial 207
Alleyn, Edward 261
Anchor Inn 191
Angel 242, 243
Anglo-Saxons 27, 59
Angsterstein, John Julius 108
Ann Hathaway's Cottage (Stratford) 272
antiques 195, 208, 209, **292**
Apsley House 203–4
architecture 56–9
Arne, Thomas 105
Arsenal Football Club 243–4
art galleries *see* galleries
the arts 42–5, 298–300
Asian artefacts 149

### B

Bacon, Francis 91, 102, 129, 154
Baden-Powell House 206
Baird, John Logie 91
Baker, Robert 113
Baker Street 127
ballet 243, 299
Bank 169
Bank of England 169–70
Bankend 191
Banks, Joseph 236
Bankside 35, **189–91**
Bankside Power Station 189, 198

Banqueting House 30, 57, **72**
Barbican Centre 165
Barry, Charles 32, **59**, 76
bars
  best views 11
  *see also* eating out
Barts Hospital 162
Bath 270–1, 273, 291
Battersea Power Station 189, 227
Battlebridge Basin 141
Baylis, Lilian 188
Bazalgette, Joseph 33
Beadles 115
Beardsley, Aubrey 119
Beatles, The 115
Beauchamp Place 205
Bede 27
Bedford Square 59
Beefeaters 180
Bekonscot Model Village & Railway (Beaconsfield) 168
HMS *Belfast* 10, **194**
Belgrave Square 221
Belgravia 221
Bell, Steve 137
Bell, Vanessa 135
Belloc, Hilaire 226
Bennett, Alan 44
Berkeley Square 116–17
Bermondsey Street 194–5
Berwick Street 93
Bethnal Green 251–3
BFI Southbank 187–8
Big Ben 8, **75–6**
Birdcage Walk 80
Black Death 28
Black Friar 12, 156, 157
Blackfriars 156
Blackfriars Bridge 31
Blackheath 260
Blackwall Reach 260
Blade Rubber 136
Blair, Tony 242
Blake, William 30, 165
Bleeding Heart Yard 154
Blenheim Palace 268–9
Bletchley Park 272
Bligh, Capt. William 138, 184
Blitz, the **33–4**, 159, 253

Bloomsbury **135–40**
  accommodation 287
  eating out 142–3
Bloomsbury Set 135, 139
blue plaques 138
Boleyn, Anne 29, 178
Bond Street 115, 119
bookshops 105, 136, 209, **293**
Borough 193
Borough High Street 193
Botero, Fernando 172
Boudicca, Queen 27
Bow Street police station 105
bowling alleys 137
brass rubbings 101
Brawne, Fanny 245
Brick Lane 55
Brighton 269, **270**, 273, 291
British Empire 99
British Film Institute 187–8
British Library 141
British Museum 9, 32, 59, **135–6**
  plan & highlights **144–9**
Brixton 262
Broadcasting House 129
Broadgate Square 171–2
Broadgate Station 171
Brompton Cross 224
Brompton Road 204–5
Brook Street 115
Brunel, Isambard Kingdom 226
Brunswick Centre 139
Buckingham Palace 8, **80–2**
budgeting 13, 308
Bunhill Fields 30, **164–5**
Bunyan, John 30, 165
Burbage, James 42
bureaux de change 312
Burgh House 246
Burlington Arcade 115
Burlington House 113
Burlington, Lord 234–5
Burne-Jones, Edward 208, 262
bus travel 278–9
Bush House 151
Butlers Wharf 195
Byron, Lord 127, 138

### C

cabaret 302
Cabinet Offices 73
Cabinet War Rooms 75
Café Royal 119
Cambridge **271**, 273, 291
Camden 244–5
Camden Lock 128
Camden Passage 243
Camley Street 141
canal trips 128, 244
Canaletto, Antonio 91
Canary Wharf 35, 58, 59, **254**
Canonbury Square 243
Canterbury 270
car hire 280
Carlton House Terrace 83
Carlyle, Thomas 227
Carnaby Street 34, **93–4**
Caro, Anthony 190
Carrington, Dora 135
Casanova 91
cathedrals
  Canterbury 270
  Rochester 269
  St Paul's 9, 30, **159–60**, **176–7**
  Southwark 56, **192–3**
  Westminster 11, **79–80**
  Winchester 269
Catherine of Aragon 29
Caxton, William 78, 155–6
Celts 27
cemeteries
  Bunhill Fields 30, **164–5**
  Frogmore (Windsor) 267
  Highgate 246–7
Cenotaph 73
Central Criminal Court 156
Channel Tunnel 277
Chaplin, Charlie 94, 138
Charing Cross Pier 102–3
Charing Cross Road 105
Charing Cross Station 102, 279
Charles I, King 57, 72, 238
Charles II, King 91, 101, 224
Charles X of France 117

Charles, Prince 34
Charlotte Street 129
Charterhouse Square 164
Chartists 129, 164
Chartwell 269
Chatham 269
Chaucer, Geoffrey 28, 86
Chavot, Eric 49
Cheapside 163
Chelsea 221–7
  accommodation 289–90
  eating out 228–9
  Flower Show 12, 225
Chelsea Embankment
  226–7
Chelsea Hospital 58
Chelsea Pensioners 224,
  225
Cheyne Walk 226
Childhood, Museum of
  10, 251
children 308–9
  activities for 10, 116
china and glass 117, 293
Chinatown 22, 94, 95
Chinese Pagoda (Kew)
  237
Chiswick 234–6
Chiswick House 234–5
Chopin, Frederic 221
Christ Church (Oxford)
  272
Christie's 205
churches
  All Hallows-by-the-Tower
    56
  All Souls' 129
  American Chapel (St
    Paul's) 177
  Brompton Oratory 205
  Chelsea Old 227
  Christ Church 253
  concerts in 300
  French Protestant 93
  Guards' Chapel 80
  Henry VII's Chapel 57,
    59, 87
  King's College Chapel
    (Cambridge) 271
  Queen's Chapel of the
    Savoy 103
  St Alfege's 259–60
  St Andrew-by-the-
    Wardrobe 161
  St Anne's 93
  St Bartholomew the
    Great 163
  St Benet's 161
  St Bride's 155–6

St Clement Danes 151
St George 137
St George the Martyr
  183
St James Garlickhythe
  161–2
St John's Priory 164
St John's, Smith
  Square 78
St Katherine Cree 173
St Luke's 224
St Margaret's 78
St Martin-in-the-Fields
  101–2
St Mary (Lambeth) 183
St Mary Abbots 208
St Mary-le-Bow 173
St Mary le Strand 151
St Marylebone 127
St Michael Paternoster
  162
St Michael's 260
St Nicholas Cole Abbey
  161
St Pancras Old 141
St Patrick's (Soho) 23,
  93
St Paul's (Covent
  Garden) 57, 104–5
St Stephen Walbrook
  168
St-Barnabas-in-Soho 93
Temple 152
Wesley's Chapel 165
Westminster Abbey 27,
  56, 77–89, 86–7
Churchill, Winston 75,
  117, 119, 138
  Blenheim Palace 268–9
  Britain at War Museum
    194
  Chartwell 269
cinemas 187–8, 209,
  262
City Hall 58, 194
City of London 159–81
  accommodation 288
  eating out 174–5
Clarence House 83
Claridge's Hotel 116
Cleopatra's Needle 102,
  103
Clerkenwell 164–5
Clink Street 192
Clive, Robert 73, 116–17
Clive Steps 73
clothing
  shopping for 294–6
  what to wear 309

coach travel 277, 279
Cock Lane 162
Cockneys 21–2
Cole, Henry 205, 206
Coleridge, Samuel Taylor
  102
College of Arms 161
comedy 302
Commons Chamber 77
Commonwealth
  immigrants 24–5
Conan Doyle, Arthur 127
congestion charge 280
Conran, Terence 46–7,
  195, 296–7
Cook, Capt. James 257
Copley, John Singleton
  169
Coram, Thomas 139
Coram's Fields 139
Cork Street 115
Cotswolds 272
County Hall 194–5
Covent Garden 32, 57,
  103–5
  accommodation 284–5
  eating out 106–7
Crapper, Thomas 165
cricket 12, 128–9, 305
crime 309
Cromwell, Oliver 153
Crown Jewels 178, 181
Crystal Palace 32, 205
customs regulations
  309–10
Cutty Sark 256–7
cycling 280

D
Dainton, Roger 187
Dalí, Salvador 185
dance clubs 300–2
Darwin, Charles 86
day trips 267–73, 280,
  291
Defoe, Daniel 30, 164
Dekker, Thomas 42
Dench, Judi 44
department stores 52,
  295–6
Diana, Princess 205, 211
Diana Memorial
  Playground 10, 211
Dickens, Charles 33,
  138, 154, 193
  Dickens World
    (Chatham) 269
  House Museum 139–40

dictionary, Johnson's 155
disabled access 310
Disraeli, Benjamin 153
Docklands 254
  history 31–2, 33, 34–5
Dorchester Hotel 118
Downing Street 72–3
D'Oyly Carte 103
Drake, Francis 192
driving 279–80
Drury Lane 105
Duck Tours 10
Duke of York Square
  223
Duke of York Steps 84
Dulwich 261–2

E
Earl's Court 208
East End, history 31–2,
  33
East London 250–5
eating out 46–51
  Chelsea 228–9
  day trips 273
  East London 255
  Holborn and the Inns of
    Court 157
  Knightsbridge,
    Kensington and
    Notting Hill 212–13
  Marylebone and
    Fitzrovia 130–1
  Mayfair to Oxford Street
    120–1
  North London 248–9
  St Paul's and the City
    174–5
  Soho and Chinatown
    90, 95–7
  South London 263
  Southwark and the
    South Bank 196–7
  Trafalgar Square and
    Covent Garden 106–7
  West London 241
  Westminster 85
Eaton Square 221
Edward the Confessor
  27, 71
Edward I, King 102
Edward VII, King 169
Edward VIII, King 119
Egyptian artefacts 139,
  145, 147
Eisenhower, Dwight D.
  117, 118
Eleanor of Castile 102

**Elgin Marbles** 32, 59, **146–7**
**Eliot, George** 102, 226, 246
**Elizabeth I, Queen 29**, 57, 86, 117
**Elizabeth II, Queen** 24, 81–2
**Eltham Place** 262
**embassies** 310
**emergencies** 308
**English Civil War** 72, 80, 180
**English National Opera** 105
**entry requirements** 310–11
**Eros** 89
**ethnic mix** 21–5
**European Union** 25
**Euston Station** 141, 279
**Eyre, Richard** 188

**F**

**Faraday, Michael** 246
**Farrell, Terry** 79
**fashion** 294–6
**Fawkes, Guy** 29, 76
**Fenchurch Street** 172, 279
**ferries** 277–8
**festivals and events 303–5**
 Boat Race 303, 306
 Changing of the Guard 11, **82**
 Chelsea Flower Show 12, **225**, 303
 Chinese New Year 13, 22, 94, 303
 Frost Fair 190
 Guy Fawkes Day 29, 305
 Lord Mayor's Show 13, **168**, 305
 music and theatre in the park 123
 Notting Hill Carnival 12, 13, 305
 the Proms 13, 123, 207, 304
 Royal Academy Summer Exhibition 114, 304
 State Opening of Parliament 74, 82, 305
 summer 12

 Trooping the Colour 13, 24, 71–2, 304
**Finsbury Street** 172
**fish and chips** 48
**Fitzrovia 129**, 130–1
**Fitzroy Square** 129
**Flamsteed House** 258–9
**Flanagan, Barry** 153
**Fleet Prison** 156
**Fleet, River** 156
**Fleet Street** 154–6
**food and drink 46–51**
 afternoon tea 51
 fish and chips 48
 shopping for 296
**football** 243–4, 305
**Foreign Office** 73
**Forster, E.M.** 135
**Fortnum & Mason** 51, 53, **114**, **296**
**Foster, Norman** 172, 190
**Foyles** 105
**Frampton, George** 211
**Franklin, Benjamin** 102, 138
**Frederick, Duke of York** 84
**Freemasons' Hall** 105
**French House** 91
**Freud, Lucian** 91
**Freud, Sigmund** 245
**Fry, Roger** 135
**Funland** 90

**G**

**Gabriel's Wharf** 188
**Gainsborough, Thomas** 91
**galleries** 13, 100, 298
 see also **museums**
 Bankside 189
 Courtauld Institute 150
 Dalí Universe 185
 Dulwich Picture 261
 Estorick Collection 243
 Guildhall 168–9
 Hayward 186–7
 Iveagh Bequest 246
 Mall 83
 National 100–1, **108–9**
 National Portrait 101, **110–11**
 Percival David Foundation of Chinese Art 137
 Queen's 81–2
 Queen's House (Greenwich) 258

 Royal Academy of Arts 113–14
 Saatchi 223
 Serpentine 211
 Tate Britain 78–9
 Tate Modern 9, 35, **189–90**, **198–9**
 Wallace Collection 126
 Whitechapel 254
 William Morris 247
**Galvin, Chris** 48
**Gambon, Michael** 44
**garden parties,**
 **Buckingham Palace** 81
**gardens** see **parks & gardens**
**Gatwick Airport** 276, 277
**gays and lesbians 311**
 venues 91, 92, **302**
**George I, King** 137
**George II, King** 27, 239
**George III, King** 81, 237
**George IV, King** 58, 81, 99
**George VI, King** 119
**George Inn** 12, 193, **197**
**Georgian architecture** 58–9
**Gerrard Street** 94
**the Gherkin** 58, 59, **172**
**Gibbons, Grinling** 105, 210
**Gibbs, James** 101, 151
**Gibson Square** 243
**gifts and souvenirs** 297–8
**Giltspur Street** 162
**Gladstone, William** 151, 153
**Golden Hinde** 10, **192**
**Goldsmiths Hall** 167
**Gormley, Antony** 100
**Gothic architecture** 56–7
**Gothic Revival** 59
**Gough Square** 155
**government** 311
**Graham, Dan** 187
**Grant, Duncan** 135
**Gray, Rose** 46
**Gray's Inn** 152, **154**
**Great Exhibition (1851)** 32, 205
**Great Fire** 30, 57, 159, 166
 Monument 172–3
**Greek artefacts** 145, **146–7**
**Greek community** 24
**Greenwich** 256–60

**Greenwich Hospital** 58
**Grosholtz, Marie** 133
**Grosvenor House Hotel** 118
**Grosvenor Square** 117–18
**Guildhall** 168
**guilds** 167
**Gunpowder Plot** 29
**Gwynne, Nell** 101, 105

**H**

**Hall, Peter** 188
**halls of residence** 282
**Ham House** 239
**Hamilton, Emma** 101, 111
**Hamleys** 10, 119
**Hammermith Bridge** 32
**Hampstead** 245–6
**Hampstead** 245–6, 290–1
**Hampstead Heath** 11, 122, **245**
**Hampton Court Palace** 29, 57, **239–40**
**Handel, George Frederic** 104, 139
 House Museum 115–16
**Harley Street** 125
**Harrison, John** 259
**Harrods** 11, 25, 52, **204–5**, **296**
**Harry, Prince** 24
**Hartnett, Angela** 48
**Harvard, John** 193
**Harvey Nichols** 52, 204
**Hatton Garden** 154
**Havelock, Maj. Gen. Henry** 99
**Hawksmoor, Nicholas** 137, 210, 253, 259
**Hay's Galleria** 194
**Hazlitt's Hotel** 12
**health** 311
**Heathrow Airport** 276–7
**Henderson, Fergus** 49
**Hendon 247**, 290
**Hendrix, Jimi** 116
**Henry VII, King** 57, 87
**Henry VIII, King** 28–9, 57, 178, 227, 240
**Herland, Hugh** 56
**Hess, Rudolph** 178
**Highgate** 246–7
**Hilton Hotel** 118
**history** 27–39
**Hockney, David** 207
**Hoffman, Dustin** 44

Hogarth, William 127, 137, 139, 153, 162
House 235–6
tomb 236
Holbein, Hans 173
Holborn 150–6
accommodation 287
eating out 157
Holland, Henry 270
Holland House 123
Hop Exchange 193
Horse Guards 71
Horse Guards Parade 71
horse racing 306
horse riding 306
hotels 281–91
distinctive 12
Houses of Parliament 8, 74, 75–7
history 29, 32, 59
visiting 76
Howard, Catherine 178
Howard, Henrietta 239
Hoxton 250
Huguenots 93
Hulanicki, Barbara 34
Hungerford Footbridge 187
Hyde Park 11, 29, 122, 123, **211**
Hyde Park Corner 203
Hytner, Nicholas 45, 188

**I**

ice-skating 10, 150, 171
immigration 21, **22–5**
Imperial War Museum 184, **200–1**
Industrial Revolution 31
Inner Temple 152
Inns of Court 152–4
Institute of Contemporary Arts 83
internet access 311
Irish community 23
Isle of Dogs 31, **254**
Islington 242–4
Italian community 23

**J**

James I, King **29**, 57
James, Henry 19, 138
Jenner, Edward 210
Jewel Tower 56, **77**
Jewish community 23, 244–5
John, King 268

John, Augustus 129
John Street 140
Johnson, Boris **34**, 58
Johnson, Samuel 155
Jones, Inigo 29–30, 57
Banqueting House 72
Covent Garden 104–5
Queen's House 258
Jonson, Ben 29, 163

**K**

Keats, John 245, 271
Kemp, David 194
Kensington 205–11
accommodation 289–90
eating out 212–13
museums 32, **214–19**
Kensington Church Street 208
Kensington Gardens 11, 122, 123, **210–11**
Kensington High Street 208–9
Kensington Palace 210–11
Kensington Square 208
Kenwood House 123, **246**
Kew 236–7
Keynes, Maynard 135
Kidman, Nicole 44
Kidston, Cath 53
King's Cross 35, 140–1, 279
King's Road **34**, 222–3
Kingsway 151
Kipling, Rudyard 102
Knights of St John 164
Knightsbridge 203–5
accommodation 289–90
eating out 212–13
Knott, Ralph 184

**L**

Ladbroke Grove 209
Lambeth Bridge 183
Lambeth Palace 57, **183**
Lamb's Conduit Street 139
Lancaster House 83
Landseer, Edwin 99
Langham Place 129
Lapper, Alison 100
Lasdun, Denys 188
Leadenhall 171
Leather Lane 154
Legoland Windsor 267–8

Leicester Square 94
Lenin, V.I. 164
Lewis, Wyndham 129
Liberty 52, **94**, **296**
Lincoln's Inn 152, **153**
Lincoln's Inn Fields 153
Lisle Street 94
Little, Alastair 49
Little Venice 128, 244
Liverpool Street 171, 279
livery companies 167–8
Livingstone, David 86
Livingstone, Ken **34**, 58, 311
Lloyd Webber, Andrew 42–3
Lloyd's of London 59, **170–1**
Lombard Street 169
London Bridge 32, 194, 254
London Bridge Tower 58
London Charterhouse 164
London City Airport 276, 277
London Dungeon 10, **194**
London Eye 8, 11, 35, **186**
London Library 84
London Review Bookshop 136
London Transport Museum 10, **105**
Long Acre 105
Lord Mayor **34**, 162, 168
Lord's Cricket Ground 12, **128–9**
Lubetkin, Berthold 128
Ludgate Hill 156
Lutine Bell 171
Luton Airport 276, 277
Lutyens, Edwin 73, 155, 169

**M**

McCartney, Stella 53
McCulloch, Robert P. 194
McEwan, Ian 129
McGill, Donald 137
McKellen, Ian 44
McLaren, Malcolm 223
Maclaren-Ross, Julian 129
Madame Tussauds 10, **127**, **132–3**
The Mall 82–3
Mansion House 168
maps 312

Marble Arch 118
Marble Hill House 239
markets 54–5, **297**
Bermondsey Antiques 195
Berwick Street 93
Borough 54, **193**
Brick Lane 55, **253**
Brixton 262
Broadway 54
Camden 55, **244**, 297
Chapel 243
Chelsea Framers' 224
Chinatown 94
Columbia Road 54, **250**, 297
Covent Garden 104
Greenwich 55, **260**
Leadenhall 55
Moxon Street Farmer's 126–7
Petticoat Lane 253, 297
Portobello Road 55, **209**, 297
Smithfield 163–4
Spitalfields 54, **253**, 297
Marks & Spencer 52, 119, **296**
Marlborough House 83
Marx, Karl 25, 91, 136, 138, 246
Marx Memorial Library 164
Mary I, Queen 86, 162
Mary, Queen consort 83
Mary, Queen of Scots 86
Marylebone **125–9**
accommodation 287
eating out 130–1
Marylebone High Street 126–7
Marylebone Lane 127
Marylebone Road 127
Mayfair **115–18**
accommodation 285–7
eating out 120–1
Mayflower 12, **195**
Mayhew, Henry 33
Mazzini, Giuseppe 164
medical care 311
Menier Chocolate Factory 193
Meunier, Morgan 49
Middle Temple 152
Mill, John Stuart 208
Millennium Bridge 35, 190
money 312

Monument 11, **172–3**
Moore, Henry 168, 207
More, Thomas 178, 227
Morris, William 247, 262
mosques 24, **129**
Mount Street 117
Mozart, Wolfgang 91
museums 13, 100, 298
  see also **galleries**
Bank of England 170
Bart's Hospital 162
Benjamin Franklin
  House 102
British 9, 32, 59,
  **135–6**, **144–9**
Cabinet War Rooms 75
Carlyle House 227
Cartoon 137
Childhood 10, **251**
Churchill 75
Clink Prison 192
*Cutty Sark* 256–7
Denis Severs' House
  253
Design 195
Dickens House 139–40
Dr Johnson's House 155
Fan 260
Fashion and Textile 195
Firepower 260
Florence Nightingale 184
Foundling 139
Freud 245–6
Garden **183**, 184
Geffrye 250
Guards' 80
Hampstead 246
Handel House 115–16
Hogarth's House 235–6
Horniman 261–2
Imperial War 184,
  **200–1**
Instruments 207
Jewish 244–5
Keats House 245
Kew Bridge Steam 237
Leighton House 208
London Canal **141**, 244
London Docklands 254
London Dungeon 10,
  **194**
London Transport 10,
  **105**
Lord's 128
Madame Tussauds 10,
  **127**, **132–3**
Museum of London
  165–7
Musical 237

National Army 225–6
National Maritime 257–8
Natural History 10,
  206, **218–19**
Old Operating Theatre &
  Herb Garret 193–4
Petrie Museum of
  Egyptian Archaeology
  139
Pollock's Toy 129
Ragged School 251–3
Ripley's Believe It Or
  Not 89
Royal Air Force 247
Royal Fusiliers 181
St John's Priory 164
Science 10, 206,
  **214–15**
Shakespeare's Globe
  Exhibition 191
Sherlock Holmes 127
Sir John Soane's 153
Tower Bridge Experience
  195
Undercroft 87
Victoria & Albert 11,
  206, **216–17**
Vinopolis, City of Wine
  191–2
Wellcome Collection 141
Wesley's House 165
Wimbledon Lawn Tennis
  240
Winston Churchill's
  Britain at War 194
music
classical 101–2, 125,
  127, 156, 186, 193,
  207, **299–300**
jazz 91, 188, **300**
museums 207, 237
opera 104, 105, 299
in the park 123
**musicals** 42–3

**N**

Naipaul, V.S. 25
Namco Station 185
Napier, Gen. Charles 99
Nash, John 58, 80, 81,
  128, 129, 270
National Gallery 100–1,
  **108–9**
National Portrait Gallery
  101, **110–11**
National Theatre 44–5,
  59, **188**

**Natural History Museum**
  10, 206, **218–19**
Nelson, Horatio 99, **101**,
  127, 177, 257
Nelson's Column 32, **99**,
  101
Neon Tower 187
New Hall (Lincoln's Inn)
  59
Newgate Prison 156
newspapers 312–13
Nicolson, Harold 269
Nightingale, Florence 184
nightlife 92, 300–2
Normans 28, 56
North London 242–9
Notting Hill **209**, 290
Carnival 12, 13, 209
  eating out 212–13
Nunn, Trevor 43, 45, 188

**O**

*1 America Square* 172
**Old Bailey** 156
**Old Chelsea Town Hall**
  223
**Old Compton Street** 91–2
**Old Curiosity Shop** 29,
  **154**
Olivier, Laurence 188
Olympia 209
Olympic Park 59, **252**
Olympics (2012) 35, **252**
One Canada Square 35,
  58, **254**
Open House 57
Orwell, George 129, 243
Osterley Park House 238
Ove Arup & Partners 190
Oxford 271–2, 273, 291
Oxford Street 52, 118–21
Oxo Tower 11, **189**

**P**

Paddington Station 279
Pall Mall 83–4
Palladio, Andrea 104
Pankhurst, Emmeline 77
Park Lane 118
parking 280
parks and gardens
  **122–3**
Bushy Park 122
Chelsea Physic Garden
  226
Dulwich Park 262
Green Park 122, 123

Greenwich Park 122,
  123
Hampstead Heath 122
Holland Park 123, 208,
  **209**
Hyde Park 11, 29, 122,
  123, **211**
Isabella Plantation 238
Italian Garden 210
Kensington Gardens 11,
  122, 123, **210–11**
Postman's Park 167
Regent's Park 58, 122,
  123, **127–9**
Richmond Park 122,
  123, **238–9**
Roof Gardens 208
Rose Garden (Regent's
  Park) 12, 122, 127
Royal Botanic Gardens
  (Kew) 122, **236–7** .
St James's Park 29, **80**
Syon Park 237–8
Thames Barrier Park
  261
Victoria Embankment
  Gardens 102
Victoria Tower Gardens
  77
Parliament 74–7
Parliament Hill 11, 245
Parliament Square 75
Parliament Street 73
Parthenon 136
Paternoster Square
  160–1
Pearly Kings and Queens
  11, 22
Penn, William 178
Pepys, Samuel 30, 104,
  156, 178
Peter Harrison
  Planetarium 259
*Peter Pan* statue 210,
  211
Piccadilly 113–15
Piccadilly Arcade 115
Piccadilly Circus 9,
  **89–90**
Pitt, William (the
  Younger) 169
Poet's Corner
  (Westminster Abbey) 87
Polish community 23
Pope, Alexander 156
population 313
Portcullis House 76
Portland Place 58, **129**
Portobello Road 55

postal services 313
Powell, Anthony 129
pre-Columbian artefacts 148
Pre-Raphaelites 208
HMS *President* 156
Prime Minister's Question Time 74
Primrose Hill 245
Prince Henry's Room 57
Princess Diana Memorial Fountain 211
the Proms 13, 123, 207
property market 25, 35
public holidays 313
pubs
  see also eating out
  food 50–1
  historic 12
  theatres 45
Pudding Lane 30, 172
Pugin, Augustus 32, 59, 76
Pump Room (Bath) 271
Punch & Judy 104
Purcell, Henry 173
Purcell Room 186

**Q**

Queen Anne's Gate 80
Queen Elizabeth Hall 186
Queen Victoria Memorial 82
Queen's House (Greenwich) 29, 57
Queensway 210

**R**

radio 313–14
rail travel 277, 279
  development of 32
  Docklands Light Railway 254, **278**
  Eurostar 35, 140, 277
  Underground (Tube) 276, **278**
Raleigh, Walter 78, 178
Ramsay, Gordon 47–8, 49
Ravenhill, Mark 44
Red House 262
Reformation 29
regency style 58
Regent Quarter 141
Regent Street 52, 58, **119**
Regent's Canal 11, 128, 141, **244**

Regent's Park 58, 122, 123, **127–9**
restaurants 11, **46–51**
  see also eating out
Reuters Building 155
Rhodes, Zandra 195
rhyming slang 21
Richard III, King 178
Richmond Hill 11, **238**
Richmond upon Thames 11, **238–40**, 290–1
rickshaw bicycles 103
Rigg, Diana 44
Risdill-Smith, Roger 190
The Ritz 115
Robuchon, Joël 49
Rochester 269
Rodin, Auguste 77
Rogers, Richard 59, 170
Rogers, Ruth 46
Romans **27**, 56, 146, **165**
  Roman amphitheatre 169
  Roman Baths (Bath) 270
  Temple of Mithras 56
Roosevelt, Franklin D. 118
Rossetti, Dante Gabriel 226
Rotherhithe 195
Roux, Albert and Michel 46
Royal Academy of Music 127
Royal Albert Hall 207
Royal Arsenal 260
Royal Avenue 224
Royal College of Art 207
Royal College of Music 207
Royal Courts of Justice 151
Royal Exchange **169**, 170
Royal Family 24
Royal Festival Hall 59, **186**, 187
Royal Geographical Society 207
Royal Hospital 224, **225**
Royal Mews 82
Royal Naval College 259
Royal Observatory 258–9
Royal Opera House 104
Royal Pavilion (Brighton) 270
Royal Shakespeare Company 43, 44–5, 272
Royal Society 83

Rubens, Peter Paul 72
rugby 305
Runnymede 268
Rushdie, Salman 25
Russell Square 139

**S**

Sackville-West, Vita 269
St Christopher's Place 119, 125
St James's, accommodation 285–7
St James's Palace 57, **84**
St James's Square 84
St James's Street 84
St John's Gate 164
St Katherine's Dock 31
St Martin-in-the-Fields 101–2
St Mary Overie Dock 192
St Pancras Station 35, 59, **140–1**, 279
St Paul's Cathedral 9, 30, **159–60**
  plan & highlights **176–7**
St Stephen's Hall 77
St Thomas's Hospital 184
Sargent, John Singer 227
Savile Club 116
Savile Row 115
Savoy Hotel 12, 103
Scarfe, Gerald 137
Schütte, Thomas 100
Science Museum 10, 206, **214–15**
Scott, George Gilbert 59, 73, 141, 189, 207, 208
Sea Life Aquarium 10, **185**
Selfridges 52, 53, 118, **119**, **296**
Senate House 137
sex industry 90, 92
Seymour, Jane 227
Shakespeare, William 29, 192–3
  monument 94
  open-air performances 12, 45, 123
  Stratford-upon-Avon 272
Shakespeare's Globe 11, 12, 35, 42, **190–1**
Shard of Glass 35, 58
Shaw, George Bernard 103, 119, 129, 138
Shelburne, Earl of 117
Shepherd Market 117

Sherlock Holmes Museum 127
Shillibeer, Mr 32
shoe shops 294–5
shopping 52–5, **292–7**
  Bond Street 115
  Duke of York Square 223
  Islington 243
  Knightsbridge 204–5
  museum shops 100
  Oxford Street 118–19
  Regent Street 119
  Royal Exchange 170
Sissinghurst Castle 269
skyskrapers 58, 59
slave trade 254
Sloane, Hans 222, 227
Sloane Square 222
Smirke, Robert 59
Smith, Maggie 44
Smith, Paul 53
Smith Square 78
Smithfield 163–4
smoking 314
Snowdon, Lord 128
Soane, John 141, 153, 261
Soho 90–4
  accommodation 284–5
  eating out 90, **95–7**
  nightlife 92
Soho Square 91–3
Somerset House **150**, 151
Sotheby's 115
*The Source* 161
South Audley Street 117
South Bank 35, **183–95**
  accommodation 288
  eating out 196–7
South Kensington 205–7
South London 256–63
Southbank Centre **186**, 188
Southeast London 262
Southwark **183–95**
  accommodation 288
  eating out 196–7
Southwark Cathedral 56, **192–3**
Southwark Street 193
Spacey, Kevin 44
spas 271, 305
Speaker's Corner 122, **211**
Spitalfields 54, 253
sport 305–6
Square Mile 159

Stanford's 105
Stanhope, Earl of 110
Stanstead Airport 276, 277
Staple Inn 57, 154
Stock Exchange 160–1
Stoppard, Tom 44
Strachey, Lytton 135
The Strand 102–3
Stratford-upon-Avon 272, 273, 291
street names 163
student travellers 314
swimming 12, 306
Swinburne, Algernon Charles 226
swinging sixties 34
Sydney Street 224
Syon House 237

**T**

30 St Mary Axe building 58, 59, **172**
Tate Britain 78–9
Tate Modern 9, 35, 89–90, **98–9**
Tavistock Hotel 137
tax refunds 312
taxis 22, 279
Telecom Tower 129
telephones 314
television 314
Temple Bar **154**, 159
tennis 12, 240, 305–6
Terry, Ellen 105
Thames, River
  cruises 12
  Greenwich boats 256, 260
  historic ships 10, 192, 194, 256–7
  river tours 307
  Tate boat 78, 189
Thames Barrier 260, 261
Thames Path 239
theatres **42–5**, 298–9
  Adelphi 103
  Almeida 242
  Barbican Centre 165
  Cottesloe 188
  fringe and pub 45
  London Coliseum 105
  Lyttelton 188
  National 55, 59, **188**
  Novello 45
  Old Vic 44, 188
  Olivier 188
  in the park 123

Prince Edward 91
Rose 191
Royal Court 222
Royal Opera House 105
Sadler's Wells 243
Savoy 103
The Scoop 194
seats 43
Shakespeare's Globe 11, 12, 35, 42, **190–1**
Stratford-upon-Avon 272
theatrical tours 307
tickets 13, 44
Young Vic 188
Thermae Bath Spa 271
Theroux, Paul 25
Thomas, Dylan 129
Thomas Goode & Co 117
tickets and passes
  entertainment 13
  football 243
  museums 13, 298
  transport 13, **278**
Tin Pan Alley 105
tipping 315
Tottenham Court Road 129
tour operators 315
tours, guided 306–7
Tower Bridge 9, **195**
Tower of London 9, **173**
  history 28, 56, 178
  plan and highlights **178–81**
toy shops 10, 119
Tradescant, John 183
Trafalgar Square 9, **99–101**
  eating out 106–7
  transport 276–80
  tickets and passes 13
travel agents 315
Treacy, Philip 53
Treasury 73
Trocadero Centre 89–90
the Tube 276, **278**
Tudors 28–9, 57
Turner, J.M.W. 79, 226
Turner, Kathleen 44
Tussaud, Marie 133
Twain, Mark 138
Tyburn Tree 118, 211

**U, V**

University of London 32, 135, **137–9**
Vanburgh, John 210, 268
Vaughan, Philip 187

Vauxhall Cross 79
Veeraswamy's 119
Venturi, Robert 101, 108
Victoria, accommodation 283–4
Victoria & Albert Museum 11, 206, **216–17**
Victoria Embankment 32, **102–3**
Victoria, Queen 32, 82, 83, 207, 210, 267
Victoria Station 279
Victoria Street 79
Victoria Tower 32, 76, **77**
Victorian architecture 59
villages 19, 234–41
Vinopolis, City of Wine 191–2

**W**

Wakefield Tower 179, 180
walking
  best walks 11
  tours 307
Wallace, Edgar 155
Walthamstow 247
Wanamaker, Sam 42
Wardour Street 93
Water Gate 102
Waterloo Bridge 11, 32
Waterloo Place 84
Waterloo Road 188
Waterloo Station 279
Waterloo Sunset Pavilion 187
Watts, George 167
Waugh, Evelyn 243
waxworks 132–3
Webb, Philip 262
websites 315
Wellington, Duke of 80, 204
HMS Wellington 156
Wellington Arch 11, **204**
Wellington Barracks 80
Wesley, Charles 127
Wesley, John 165
West End 89–97
West London 234–41
West Smithfield 162–3
Westminster **71–80**
  accommodation 283–4
  eating out 85
Westminster Abbey 27, 56–7, 77–8, **86–7**
Westminster Bridge 31
Westminster Cathedral 11

Westminster Hall 28, 56, **76**
Westwood, Vivienne 53, 222–3
Whistler, James 119
White Tower 28, 56, **179**
Whitechapel 253–4
Whitehall 71
Whittington, Dick 162
Wigmore Hall 125
Wilde, Oscar 91, 119, 221–2, 227
wildlife
  Camley Street nature park 141
  London Sea Life Aquarium 10, **185**
  London Zoo 10, 122, **128**
  Sea Life Centre (Brighton) 269
Wilkins, William 101, 108
William the Conqueror 28, 178
William, Prince 24
Wilton Place 221
Wimbledon 12, **240**, 290
Winchester 269
Winchester Palace 192
Windsor 267–8, 273, 291
Windsor Castle 267
Wolsey, Cardinal 29
Women's Library 253–4
Woolf, Virginia 129, 135, 136, 137
Woolwich 260
World War I 200–1
World War II 33–4, 194, 200–1, 262
Wren, Christopher 30, **57–8**
  churches 156, 161–2, 168, 173
  Greenwich 258, 259
  Hampton Court 240
  Marlborough House 83
  St Paul's 159–60, **176**

**Y, Z**

Ye Old Cheshire Cheese 12, **155**, 157
Yevele, Henry 56
youth hostels 282
Zoo, London 10, 122, **128**
Zwemmer's 105

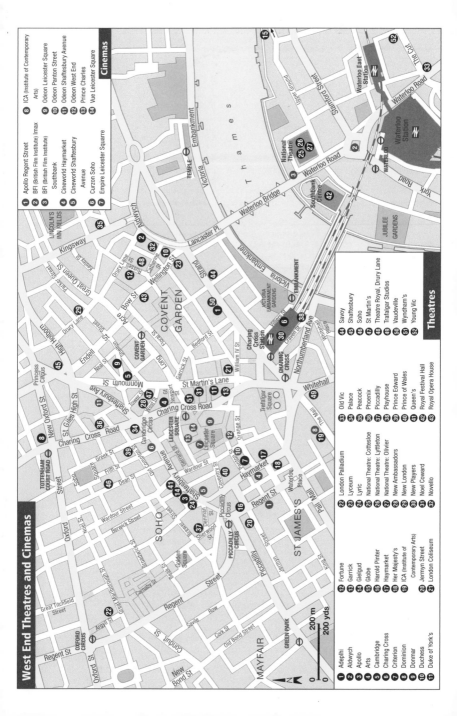

**Legend:**

- Bakerloo
- Central
- Circle
- District
- District open weekends, public holidays and some Olympia events
- Hammersmith & City
- Jubilee
- Metropolitan
- Northern
- Piccadilly
- Victoria
- Waterloo & City
- DLR
- London Overground
- Emirates Air-Line under construction
- ◯ Interchange stations
- Step-free access from street to train
- Step-free access from street to platform
- ≽ National Rail
- Riverboat services
- Tramlink
- ✈ Airport
- Emirates Air-Line

**MAYOR OF LONDON**

Website
tfl.gov.uk

24 hour travel information
0843 222 1234*